THE LATER WORDSWORTH

LONDON
Cambridge University Press
FETTER LANE

NEW YORK · TORONTO
BOMBAY · CALCUTTA · MADRAS
Macmillan

TOKYO
Maruzen Company Ltd

WILLIAM WORDSWORTH, *aged* 62

Reproduced from a drawing by H. W. PICKERSGILL, *by permission of the Master and Fellows of St John's College, Cambridge*

THE LATER WORDSWORTH

BY

EDITH C. BATHO

CAMBRIDGE
AT THE UNIVERSITY PRESS
1933

PRINTED IN GREAT BRITAIN

TO

R. W. CHAMBERS

PREFACE

RECENT biographies and studies of Wordsworth have dealt in much greater detail and with much greater sympathy with the first half of his life than with the last half, and for reasons not difficult to understand. In the story of a man's development through childhood and youth there is an appeal to more general sympathy than in that of his later years, and the stormy youth of Wordsworth offers at first sight a striking contrast to the apparent tranquillity—stagnation, some have called it—of his maturity and age. It is not unfair to point to Professor Harper's biography as indicating the relative proportions of popular interest: there, in the revised edition of 1929, 529 pages are devoted to the years between 1770 and 1815, and 83 to the years between 1815 and 1850. And a description of those later years which would be given by others besides Professor Harper is that which he chooses as the heading of his twenty-third chapter—Retreat and Surrender. By many 1815 has been taken as an approximate date "after which the decay of Wordsworth's poetic powers became obvious"; as, again, an approximate date for his "apostasy" from his earlier political and philosophical convictions. Professor Harper would himself appear to incline to that opinion, though some of the evidence which he quotes in this all too short section of his biography must by itself compel considerable modifications in it.

This study does not accept that easy and simple division of Wordsworth's life and works. It is, in particular, an attempt to discover from the available evidence—Wordsworth's own poems, prose-writings, letters, and the reports of those who came into immediate contact with him—what were his real opinions in the latter half of his life: how far they were in agreement with or in contradiction to those of the earlier half: the impression which he made upon his contemporaries: and his attitude towards them. The question has been partly discussed in Hale White's *Examination of the Charge of Apostasy against Wordsworth*, and, on the political side, in Dicey's *Statesmanship of Wordsworth*, which, however, touches only lightly on the post-Napoleonic years. To these books and to others named in the Bibliography I owe many suggestions, some of a negative kind. In spite of these obligations, however, I must take the responsibility for the opinions and conclusions which I have put forward.

I am not sure that Wordsworth himself would have approved of this book. He thought that the importance of the letters of literary men was much overrated, and he once surprised R. P. Graves by "the feeling akin to indignation which he manifested at the suggestion" that his poems should be printed in order of composition. "He said that such proceeding would indicate on the part of a poet an amount of egotism, placing interest in himself above interest in the subjects treated by him, which could not belong to a true poet caring for the elements of poetry in their right proportion, and designing to bring to bear upon the minds of his readers the best influences at his command in the way best calculated to make them effectual." Yet since some recent studies of this poet would seem to have the inevitable consequence of neutralizing any influence of his poetry, whilst a study of his relation to his background may help to bring to bear upon the minds of his readers the best influences at his command, there is reason for the completion of this book.

The chief sources have been the biographies and monographs of Bishop Christopher Wordsworth, William Knight, Professor Emile Legouis and Professor George McLean Harper; Knight's edition of the letters, whose unsatisfactory text and dating I have corrected as far as I have been able to do so; the MS. letters preserved in the British Museum and the Victoria and Albert Museum; Professor Edith Morley's edition of the correspondence of Crabb Robinson with the Wordsworth circle; Grosart's and Knight's editions of the prose works; the editions of the poetical works by Knight, Hutchinson and Mr Nowell Smith, and Professor E. de Selincourt's edition of *The Prelude*; Crabb Robinson's *Diary*, in the original manuscript; and the books named in the Bibliography. The Bibliography itself might have been considerably extended, but has been reduced to include only the books to which direct reference is made in the text. In quoting from the Crabb Robinson *Diary* or the Crabb Robinson correspondence, and even from Wordsworth's letters, I have not thought it necessary to preserve the original spelling and punctuation, where these differ widely from modern usage: in separate and complete editions there is much to be said in favour of fidelity to such details, but in a study of this kind it may merely irritate the reader.

I am deeply grateful to the Trustees of Dr Williams's Library for their courtesy in allowing me to make use of the MS. of Crabb Robinson's *Diary*. I would wish also to thank Professor de Selincourt for a correct text of some of the quotations from the letters of Wordsworth and his sister, and for the information acknowledged on pp. 39 n., 319 n. and 324; the Dean of St Asaph for reading the typescript of chapter III; and Professor R. W. Chambers for reading the whole of the typescript.

E. C. B.

University College, London
April 1933

CONTENTS

I

TWO OR THREE WITNESSES

i

THE year 1815 was from more than one point of view a decisive year in Wordsworth's life. It was the year in which, after twenty-five years of exultations and agonies, he saw tyranny, in one form at least, vanquished. We, who have lived through four years of war, and know what relief was felt, even by the insensitive, at the end—which, in spite of all subsequent disappointments, was, in the same way, at any rate not the triumph of wrong—ought to be able to enter into his feelings. For him, as for us, the moment of joyful triumph was brief; but he did not make the mistake of some of his contemporaries and some of us, who deny that there was a triumph at all.

As far as any date can be assigned to such things, the year 1815 was, too, the year when Wordsworth's poetical reputation began to grow in the eyes of the general public,[1] and as a natural consequence we have from about that time onwards more evidence of the direct personal impression which he made, and more records of his casual conversation, than for the earlier part of his life. Before that date, only those with a keen scent for the new and the good in poetry were sufficiently interested in him to wish to meet him. Two of these earlier descriptions and estimates, however, deserve to be quoted here, the first for its vividness, and the second chiefly for purposes of comparison. The one is Hazlitt's description in

[1] See Appendix A.

My First Acquaintance with Poets, referring to 1798, but possibly not written until twenty-five years later.[1]

> I think I see him now. He answered in some degree to his friend's description of him, but was more gaunt and Don Quixote-like. He was quaintly dressed (according to the *costume* of that unconstrained period) in a brown fustian jacket and striped pantaloons. There was something of a roll, a lounge in his gait, not unlike his own Peter Bell. There was a severe, worn pressure of thought about his temples, a fire in his eye (as if he saw something in objects more than the outward appearance), an intense high narrow forehead, a Roman nose, cheeks furrowed by strong purpose and feeling, and a convulsive inclination to laughter about the mouth, a good deal at variance with the solemn, stately expression of the rest of his face....He sat down and talked very naturally and freely, with a mixture of clear, gushing accents in his voice, a deep guttural intonation, and a strong tincture of the northern *burr*, like the crust on wine.

Compared with this, Crabb Robinson's account of his own first meeting with Wordsworth ten years later is commonplace, but it has the peculiar merit of giving the immediate impression, unblurred by later corrections, made by Wordsworth just after the publication of the *Poems* of 1807 and of their reviews. The two men met for the first time at Lamb's on Tuesday, March 15, 1808, and again next day at Mrs Clarkson's. Crabb Robinson, as usual, listened well and asked intelligent questions, and within a week sent a report,

[1] The essay was begun in 1817, and part of the description of Coleridge was certainly written then, but it was not finished until 1823 (cf. Howe, *Life of Hazlitt*, pp. 35 n. and 353). As the description of Wordsworth has more in common with that in *The Spirit of the Age* than with the fury of the *Lectures on the English Poets*, 1823 seems the more likely date for its composition; cf. pp. 72–6 *infra*.

marked by not uncritical enthusiasm, to his friend Thomas Robinson.

> Wordsworth is most opposite to Southey in his appearance. He is a sloven, and his manners are not prepossessing. His features are large and coarse. His voice is not attractive. His manners, though not arrogant, yet indicate a sense of his own worth. He is not attentive to others, and speaks with decision his own opinion. He does not spare those he opposes. He has no respect for great names, and avows his contempt for popular persons as well as favourite books, which must often give offence. Yet with all this, I should have a bad opinion of that person's discernment who should be long in his company without contracting an high respect, if not a love for him. Moral purity and dignity and elevation of sentiment are the characteristics of his mind and muse.
>
> As we were tête-à-tête I was gratified at being able to turn the conversation to his poetry. He expatiated with warmth on them, and spoke of them with that unaffected zeal which pleased me, though the customs of life do not authorize it.

Crabb Robinson was, on the other hand, shocked when Wordsworth said that Mrs Barbauld, whom Crabb Robinson himself admired, had a bad heart, and though he agreed with Wordsworth in despising the poetry of Rogers, he considered this "contempt of others...very censurable". Wordsworth subsequently modified his condemnation of Mrs Barbauld's heart, as well as of her poetry, and he came even to read the poems of Rogers with pleasure as he grew to love the man.

Twelve years later Crabb Robinson noted in his diary (June 21, 1820) that Wordsworth had grown "more indulgent than he used to be of the works of others, even rivals and contemporaries", and that there was "absolutely no pretence for what was always an exaggerated charge against him, that he can talk only of his own poetry, and loves only his own works". The evidence of others shows that, if there had been a change, it had come earlier. But it is possible that Wordsworth had always been, except under strong provocation, as he was in 1820, and that Crabb Robinson was unfortunate in meeting him first at a moment when he was in a mood of defiance and uncompromising dogmatism induced by the treatment of his poems in most of the reviews. R. P. Gillies in 1814 was struck by the contrary quality, his tolerance in both life and literature. Gillies was at this time a young advocate in Edinburgh, devoted to poetry, trying to write poetry himself, and eager to learn from and argue with a master in the art. He found what he wanted when Wordsworth came to Edinburgh, and their correspondence confirms his record of memories and impressions. The story of their first meeting reads as if it had been an unconscious rehearsal for Haydon's "immortal dinner". Forty years later Gillies remembered how one of the party

observing that the poet during dinner did not say much, benevolently thought that he must patronize him and draw him out, thereby assuming a lead in the conversation; and what sad blunders resulted, and how the poet himself, Mr Sharpe and the family, with whom we dined, were at length convulsed with laughter

—while only the hero-worshipping Gillies was annoyed. It would be pleasant to have Charles Kirkpatrick Sharpe's account of the evening. Gillies afterwards used to send his verses for criticism to Wordsworth, who dealt with them patiently, though confessing that he found his task difficult because of the "strong family resemblance" which each bore to the rest. He had his reward in the affection of Gillies.

Frequently in the course of these memoranda, I have been reminded of a remark made to me by another most distinguished friend, Mr Kenelm H. Digby, namely, that the most laborious and ascetic characters, those in short who are the hardest taskmasters of themselves, are invariably the most playful and unaffected in manners and the most disposed to lenity on behalf of others.... Among convivial spirits no one could be more joyous than Wordsworth;[1] no one could enter more heartily and readily into the humours of the passing hour; and among eminent authors no one could ever be found more willing than he was to make allowances for the faults of others, or to afford instruction whenever he met with a pupil whose attachment to literature was not founded on vanity or affectation.[2]

In later life Gillies abandoned the law for literature, suffered, partly but not altogether by his own fault, from perpetual financial embarrassment, and, as he tells us more than once, was deeply indebted to Wordsworth's "unalterable kindness" for help. The last of his recollections of Wordsworth,[2] indeed, is of a friend intervening in the worst of his troubles, at the end of 1848, and not spoiling the intervention by a lecture.

Some few are so very eccentric, that they do not care a rush about "respectability", nor even about the dicta of Grand-

[1] R. P. Graves, who knew Wordsworth only in his old age, thought that he "could not be said to be a genial man, though he had his genial times, but he delighted in genial men" (*Life of W. R. Hamilton*, I, 28). The statement requires some modification. Wordsworth himself recognized his dual nature (cf. 1805 *Prelude*, x, 868–71, and Professor de Selincourt's note, pp. 587–8), and so did Coleridge in that letter to Richard Sharpe (January 15, 1804) in which he at once laments Wordsworth's "occasional fits of hypochondriacal uncomfortableness" and rejoices in his being a happy man. Sara Coleridge among his intimates, agreeing with many casual acquaintances, speaks of him as being usually "cheerful and happy-minded".

[2] *Memoirs of a Literary Veteran*, II, 140–1, 138–9; III, 331.

mother Grundy! Among such extraordinary people as [were] connected with my own case, I cannot forbear noticing, with deep gratitude, the late William Wordsworth, one of the earliest, and who proved himself also among the most unalterable of my friends. I cannot forget the readiness, nay, eagerness, with which, jointly with Mr Quillinan, he came to our relief, when Christmas drew on, and our troubles increased, and I remained in prison, oppressed by the public contumely of Mr Commissioner Law's hard words, and the slander of numberless busy tongues, who volunteered their improvements thereon.

Several comments might be made on this. One is that Wordsworth's help was not given because he thought that Gillies was not responsible for any of his troubles: the Fenwick note to the sonnet which he had addressed to Gillies thirty years earlier shows that he had no illusions about him.[1] Another is that, without the light thrown on it by Gillies himself in his *Memoirs*, we should not be likely to guess from that note that Wordsworth had already helped him and would unhesitatingly answer a further call upon him, and in a way which left no feeling of discomfort in the receiver's mind. Wordsworth's carefulness of small sums, which was in part a legacy from his years of extreme poverty, was well known, and alternately amused and exasperated his friends: it was accompanied by a generosity which was not advertised, and it is only occasionally that we catch a glimpse of his charities.[2] Harriet Martineau hit on the right phrase when she wrote of his "mixture of odd economies and neighbourly generosity". As for his indifference to the standards of respectability, we shall meet that elsewhere.[3]

[1] It also implies that at the moment of dictating the note he believed Gillies to be dead.

[2] Cf. pp. 44–5, 50 *infra*. [3] Cf. pp. 69–71 *infra*.

Others besides Gillies show a Wordsworth who easily got on good terms with young men. The reason may have been that he let everyone have his say. Either he learnt patience, or the "not attentive to others" of Crabb Robinson in 1808 means that he did not pay undue deference to the opinions of others, particularly when they were the orthodox opinions of the day on poetry. Witness after witness corroborates the testimony of Mrs Alaric Watts, that

> he was a patient and courteous listener, paying the most scrupulous attention to every word, never interrupting, and with a certain fixedness of his clear grey eyes which made one feel that, whatever one's opinion might be, one must be prepared to give a substantial reason for it, and, in doing so, to discard all that might appear fanciful, and not to be readily explained.[1]

More than that, he gave young men the impression that he considered their opinions intelligent and valuable, even though they might be mistaken. John Payne Collier, writing in 1856[2] and looking back to a time thirty to forty years earlier, declared, "To this day I have a grateful recollection of the patience, I may almost say indulgence, with which this great poet listened to me, then a young man, and, I must own, not by any means an unqualified admirer of his poetry". Julian Charles Young, who met Wordsworth and Coleridge in Germany in 1828, even draws a comparison between them which is not without significance.[3]

[1] *Life of Alaric Watts*, I, 241.

[2] Preface to Coleridge's *Seven Lectures on Shakespeare and Milton*, p. liii.

[3] *Memoir of Charles Mayne Young*, I, 176–7. T. C. Grattan, a slightly older man, also met the two poets in the course of their tour, and though he admired Coleridge's conversation more and Wordsworth's less than Young did, was struck in the same way by

If Wordsworth condescended to converse with me, he spoke to me as if I were his equal in mind, and made me pleased and proud in consequence. If Coleridge held me by the button, for lack of fitter audience, he had a talent for making me feel *his* wisdom and my own stupidity; so that I was miserable and humiliated by the sense of it....

I revert with great delight to a long expedition I one day made with Wordsworth alone....Hitherto I had only seen Wordsworth in the presence of Coleridge; and had imagined him constitutionally contemplative and taciturn. Today I discovered that his reticence was self-imposed, out of consideration for the inordinate loquacity of his brother poet.

Coleridge always speechified or preached.

"His argument
Was all too heavy to admit *much talk*."

Wordsworth chatted naturally and fluently, out of the fullness of his heart, and not from a wish to display his eloquence.

Young would probably have acknowledged that he may have been prejudiced against Coleridge by the ignoring of his salutation on their first meeting, and in favour of Wordsworth by the "kindly smile and courteous recognition" of his bow which, in his own words, "promised me some compensation for the slight put upon me by his precursor". But, as far as Wordsworth is concerned, his testimony not merely corroborates that of Gillies and Payne Collier, but in its turn is

the relations between them. Wordsworth "seemed satisfied to let his friend and fellow-traveller take the lead", and Grattan also noticed in him "a total absence of affectation or egotism; not the least effort at display, or assumption of superiority". Grattan was also struck by the "real sound sense and good criticism" of his remarks on Byron, in which there was nothing "ungenerous or unfair" (*Beaten Paths*, II, 109–10, 123–8).

corroborated by that of many others.[1] Wordsworth was, in fact, and in contradiction to the general modern conception of him, on friendly terms with a good many young men of ability, who liked and respected him, but not to idolatry, and found him a candid hearer and critic of their ideas. Some of the most striking evidence of the kind of relation which subsisted between them comes from the group to which Henry Taylor belonged, and dates from about 1824 to within the last decade of Wordsworth's life. There was an inner circle of Benthamites, as they called themselves, including Hyde Villiers and Charles Villiers, Charles Austin, John Romilly, Edward Strutt and, the most famous of them all, John Stuart

[1] This is a convenient place to note a misunderstanding which must please the spirits of irony. Morley, talking to Gladstone in 1892 (*vide* his *Life of Gladstone*, Bk. x, ch. 6), told him that he had once said to Matthew Arnold that he would rather have been Wordsworth than anybody, and Arnold had replied, "Oh, no, you would not; you would wish you were dining with me at the Athenaeum. He was too much of the peasant for you". Now Gladstone had previously spoken of his own intercourse as a young man with Wordsworth, "a most agreeable man", whom he had always found "amiable, polite and sympathetic". He defended him accordingly: "No, I never felt that; I always thought him a polite and an amiable man". Gladstone's testimony to Wordsworth's politeness and amiability is interesting but not really necessary: what is amusing is what he missed or was himself too polite to point out—that Arnold was not disparaging Wordsworth, but aiming a shaft at the academic rigidity of Morley. It would seem that on the same or another occasion he used the same mischievous weapon against Herford, who proved equally impervious to it, since twice over in his last study of Wordsworth he asserted that Arnold told him at the Athenaeum that Wordsworth was a boor. Nothing can be more certain than that Wordsworth was not a boor, except that he had a good deal of the peasant in him. But that is by no means inconsistent with politeness, amiability and sympathy.

Mill—all young men of marked intellectual power and personality. Taylor himself was the connecting link, having made Wordsworth's acquaintance in 1823 through Southey, for whom his affection always remained warmer than it ever became for Wordsworth: a preference unusual enough, both then and now, to deserve noting. From 1824 onwards Taylor used to invite Wordsworth, whenever he was in London, to breakfast with the Benthamites or other friends; "and though he was old[1] and the rest so young", Taylor wrote afterwards,[2] "and he was opposed to them in politics, yet the force and brightness of his conversation, his social geniality, and the philosophic as well as imaginative largeness of his intellect, delighted them all". In 1874 Taylor was visiting the dying John Romilly: "I asked him whether he remembered a breakfast of Benthamites, I had given some forty or fifty years before, at which I had brought them acquainted with Wordsworth, and what Charles Austin had said when Wordsworth left the room; and he answered at once, 'Yes, I do. He said, "That is a MAN"'".[3]

That was the impression which remained with Taylor and Romilly when they were both old men, but that they were not mistaken then as to their feelings forty years earlier is shown by Taylor's letters. In May 1831 he wrote to tell Miss Fenwick that he had had three or four breakfasts for Wordsworth—

and he is as agreeable in society as he is admirable in his power of talking, so perfectly courteous and well-bred and

[1] He was fifty-four when the custom arose, and he was still attending these breakfasts twenty years later, when the other guests were not so young, but Taylor is referring more particularly to the years 1824–7.

[2] *Autobiography*, I, 83. [3] *Ibid.* II, 333.

simple in his manners. He met Jeffrey the other day at Sir J. Mackintosh's, and at Jeffrey's request they were introduced. Lockhart beheld the ceremony, and told me that Wordsworth played the part of a man of the world to perfection, much better than the smaller man, and did not appear to be conscious of anything having taken place between them before.

And in May 1836 Taylor told Miss Fenwick of another breakfast at which Wordsworth was brilliant, "having the advantage of Charles Austin to elicit him. A more animated and vigorous conversation than they made of it between them I have never listened to....Even Carlyle was little else than an auditor".

It was some months earlier than Wordsworth showed himself a man of the world towards Jeffrey, that that rather dissimilar man of the world, Charles Greville, met him at one of Taylor's breakfasts, on February 25, 1831, and, though not a lenient critic, was surprised into approval. Taylor had collected, he records,

the same party as when he had Southey—Mill, Elliot, Charles Villiers. Wordsworth may be bordering on sixty; hard-featured, brown, wrinkled, with prominent teeth and a few scattered grey hairs, but nevertheless not a disagreeable countenance; and very cheerful, merry, courteous, and talkative, much more so than I should have expected from the grave and didactic character of his writings. He held forth on poetry, painting, politics, and metaphysics, and with a great deal of eloquence; he is more conversable and with a greater flow of animal spirits than Southey.[1] He mentioned

[1] The comparison seems to have been unavoidable for everyone who met the two men. Thus Scott, twenty-five years earlier, to Miss Seward (April 10, 1806): "Certainly they [i.e. Southey's manners] are not always & altogether so easy & pleasing as those of Wordsworth but I think it is mere manner". The Swan of Lichfield found Scott's ranking of them so difficult to believe that, when

that he never wrote down as he composed, but composed walking, riding, or in bed, and wrote down after; that Southey always composes at his desk. He talked a great deal of Brougham, whose talents and domestic virtues he greatly admires; that he was very generous and affectionate in his disposition, full of duty and attention to his mother, and had adopted and provided for a whole family of his brother's children, and treats his wife's children as if they were his own. He insisted upon taking them both with him to the drawing-room the other day when he went in state as Chancellor. They remonstrated with him, but in vain.

The appreciation of Brougham's talents and virtues combines pleasantly with Wordsworth's hearty disapproval of almost all his activities. But Wordsworth delighted in human oddity as much as in domestic virtues, and he did not take political or religious disagreements into private life.[1]

John Stuart Mill, who was present at this breakfast, saw a good deal of Wordsworth in the following summer. He had been, as he tells us in his *Autobiography*, refreshed by Wordsworth's poetry in the spiritual dryness which was the result of his education, and he was not disillusioned by closer personal contact with the poet. He was fortunate, indeed, in visiting Rydal before the shadows fell. Dorothy Wordsworth's illness of 1829 was the first sign of her long twilight, but this was not yet realized. Wordsworth still had the full happiness of his "three wives"—an expression of Crabb Robinson's which

he repeated it with a slight difference (April 23, 1808), she asked: "Is it possible that Wordsworth can be Southey's superior in conversation? so widely as it is the *reverse* in their writings. In yours, and in Southey's all is perspicuity. In Wordsworth and still more in the Author of *Gebir* (a poem most unaccountably admired by the Bards of the Cumberland lakes) we find meaning frequently lost in a dark maze of words". This, from the Swan, is pretty good.

[1] Cf. pp. 129–30, 302 and n., *infra*.

Mary Lamb reported to them, improving it by the addition, "I long to join you and make a fourth".[1] Dorothy Wordsworth, Mary Wordsworth and Sarah Hutchinson were a harmonious trio, and Dora Wordsworth, that gay, wild, bright creature, was the apple of her father's eye. But, "There is no domestic altar in that house", Miss Fenwick wrote some years later, and Mill and others bear her out. If Sophia Scott had not read *The Lady of the Lake* because "Papa says there's nothing so bad for young people as reading bad poetry",[2] the younger William Wordsworth, at an age when he might have been expected to have heard something on the subject, did not know whether his father had ever been on Westminster Bridge.[3] Wordsworth blamed himself for the faults of his family, but he did not take any credit to himself for their virtues or impose himself upon them; they laughed at him and argued with him, even about his own poetry and his moral judgments,[4] with frank affection and respect on both sides.

It was this atmosphere of freedom which particularly delighted John Stuart Mill, the freedom from prejudice and the willingness to argue and understand the other side. In a letter written in October 1831, after his return, he described his experiences to Sterling.[5]

I was particularly struck by several things. One was, the extensive range of his thoughts and the largeness and expansiveness of his feelings. This does not appear in his writings, especially his poetry, where the contemplative part

[1] November 1816, Lucas, VI, 494.

[2] Lockhart, III, 267. [3] November 1819, Lucas, VI, 535.

[4] Cf., e.g., Dora's protest against the remarks on Crabbe in the Fenwick note on the *Extempore Effusion* (Grosart, III, 195 n.).

[5] *Letters*, ed. Elliot, I, 10–16. The letter was written from October 20 to 22. Mill was then twenty-five.

of his mind is the only part of it that appears; and one would be tempted to infer from the peculiar character of his poetry that real life and the active pursuits of men (except of farmers and other country people) did not interest him. The fact, however, is that these very subjects occupy the greater part of his thoughts, and he talks on no subject more instructively than on states of society and forms of government. Those who best know him seem to be most impressed with the catholic character of his ability. I have been told that Lockhart has said of him that he would have been an admirable country attorney. Now a man who could have been either Wordsworth or a country attorney could certainly have been anything else which circumstances had led him to desire to be. The next thing that struck me was the extreme comprehensiveness and philosophic spirit which is in him. By these expressions I mean the direct antithesis of what the Germans most expressively call onesidedness. Wordsworth seems always to know the pros and the cons of every question; and when you think he strikes the balance wrong it is only because you think he estimates erroneously some matter of fact. Hence all my differences with him, or with any other philosophic Tory, would be differences of matter-of-fact or detail, while my differences with the Radicals and Utilitarians are differences of principle; for *these* see generally only one side of the subject, and in order to convince them you must put some entirely new idea into their heads, whereas Wordsworth has all the ideas there already, and you have only to discuss with him the "how much", the more or less of weight which is to be attached to a certain cause or effect as compared with others: thus the difference with him turns upon a question of varying or fluctuating quantities, where what is *plus* in one age or country is *minus* in another, and the whole question is one of observation and testimony, and of the value of particular articles of evidence. I need hardly say to you that if one's own conclusions and his were at variance on every question which a minister or a Parliament could to-morrow be called upon to solve, his is nevertheless the mind with which one would be really in communion; our principles would be the same, and we should be like two travellers pursuing the same course on the opposite banks of a river. Then when you get Wordsworth on the subjects which are peculiarly his, such as the theory of his own art...no one can converse with him without feeling that he has advanced that great subject beyond any other man, being probably the first person who ever combined, with such eminent success in the practice of the art, such high powers of generalisation and habits of meditation on its principles. Besides all this, he seems to me the best talker I ever heard (and I have heard several first-rate ones); and there is a benignity and kindliness about his whole demeanour which confirms what his poetry would lead one to expect, along with a perfect simplicity of character which is delightful in any one, but most of all in a person of first-rate intellect. You see I am somewhat enthusiastic on the subject of Wordsworth, having found him still more admirable and delightful a person on a nearer view than I had figured to myself from his writings, which is so seldom the case that it is impossible to see it without having one's faith in man greatly increased and being made greatly happier in consequence. I also was very much pleased with Wordsworth's family—at least, the female part of it.[1] I am convinced that the proper place to see him is in his own kingdom....I was much pleased with the universality of his relish for all good poetry, however dissimilar to his own, and with the freedom and unaffected simplicity with which every person about him seemed to be in the habit of discussing and attacking any passage or poem in his own works which did not please him.[2]

[1] This does not necessarily condemn the male part: the sons were seldom at home after they grew up, John being in his parish and William presently his father's deputy in the Langdales, where he was considered the great man of the family.

[2] Cf. with the whole letter that of J. J. Tayler of July 26, 1826 (Grosart, III, 502–3), especially "He is Toryish—at least what would be considered so—in his political principles, though he dis-

Mill was writing to a sympathetic reader, whose opinion of Wordsworth was not lower than his own. Ten years later[1] Sterling declared that there were but three men in England in whom he could perceive the true elements of greatness—Wordsworth, Carlyle, and the Duke of Wellington: none of whom, it is conceivable, would have been altogether pleased to find himself in the company of the others. The Duke might have taken the conjunction with least inward protest. But it was many years before Wordsworth forgave the Duke for his share in the Convention of Cintra;[2] and though he recognized Carlyle's power, he disliked his style and detested what seemed to him the inhumanity of tone in *The French Revolution*. To a man who had lived through the Revolution, and whose own associates had been guillotined, Carlyle's grim jocularity might well seem heartless. "He says there is a want of due sympathy with mankind—scorn and irony are the feeling and tone throughout", Crabb Robinson noted in his diary (January 26, 1839). Crabb Robinson tried in vain to make him admire the book, and found himself at some disadvantage in the argument, having heard Carlyle talk about American negro slavery in a fashion which seemed to him inhumane and shocked all his anti-slavery principles. Finally Wordsworth relieved his feelings in some vigorous sonnets which, like so much of his later verse, are usually misinterpreted as a recantation of his earlier beliefs.

Carlyle, on his side, was conscious of Wordsworth's dislike—to which he believed fear was added, an odd piece of self-

claims all connection with party, and certainly argues with great fairness and temper on controverted topics....He spoke with great plainness, and yet with candour, of his contemporaries".

[1] Caroline Fox, *Memories of Old Friends*, May 20, 1841.

[2] Cf. Wordsworth to Reed, September 14, 1840.

esteem which he would have mocked in anyone else—and he had no high opinion of Wordsworth's poetic powers. Before they met he had formed a mental picture of a man to be respected for his choice of freedom with poverty, but otherwise "a rather dull, hard-tempered, unproductive and almost wearisome kind of man"; but actual contact made a considerable difference to the picture. They met at one of Taylor's breakfasts, "about 1840", Carlyle writes in the *Reminiscences*, and the exact date does not much matter. He was not moved to revise his judgment of Wordsworth as a poet, and he considered that Wordsworth thought himself the only "transcendent unlimited" poet in history and tried to diminish the stature of others; after writing which, he adds that Wordsworth "by no means said so, or hinted so, in words"—that, in fact, it was merely a vague impression of Carlyle's that he thought so. Wordsworth's talk on the technical side of poetry was beyond Carlyle's appreciation, but he could appreciate that

he talked well in his way; with veracity, easy brevity and force, as a wise tradesman would of his tools and workshop,—and as no unwise one could. His voice was good, frank and sonorous, though practically clear, distinct and forcible rather than melodious; the tone of him businesslike, sedately confident; no discourtesy, yet no anxiety about being courteous. A fine wholesome rusticity, fresh as his mountain breezes, sat well on the stalwart veteran, and on all he said and did. You would have said he was a usually taciturn man; glad to unlock himself to audience sympathetic and intelligent, when such offered itself. His face bore marks of much, not always peaceful, meditation; the look of it not bland or benevolent so much as close impregnable and hard: a man *multa tacere loquive paratus*, in a world where he had experienced no lack of contradictions as he strode along! The eyes were not very brilliant, but they had a quiet clearness; there was enough of brow and well shaped; rather too much of cheek ("horse face" I have heard satirists say); face of squarish shape and decidedly longish, as I think the head itself was (its "length" going horizontal); he was large-boned, lean, but still firm-knit tall and strong-looking when he stood, a right good old steel-grey figure, with rustic simplicity and dignity about him, and a vivacious strength looking through him which might have suited one of those old steel-grey markgrafs whom Henry the Fowler set up to ward the "marches" and do battle with the intrusive heathen in a stalwart and judicious manner.

Wordsworth showed himself willing to talk with Carlyle in a corner, when they met "in noisy extensive circles", and one of these dialogues "raised him intellectually some real degrees higher" in Carlyle's estimation. For us it has another interest as containing Wordsworth's account of the effect upon public opinion in France of the execution of Gorsas, which he himself had witnessed, if Carlyle understood his words aright.[1] To Carlyle this was merely "a true supplement" to his book, on one small point. What he found more interesting was that which followed, when they—

hastened over to England and to the noteworthy, or at least noted men of that and the subsequent time. "Noted" and

[1] That is, he was in France again in 1793–4. The evidence, apart from Carlyle's testimony, is only circumstantial, but it is strong enough for anyone who wishes to accept it as decisive to do so without the reproach of over-credulity. The main arguments are in the 1929 edition of Professor Harper's biography, pp. 150–2, in his *Did Wordsworth Defy the Guillotine?* (reprinted in *Spirit of Delight*, pp. 51–69), and in a letter by Mr James R. MacGillivray in *The Times Literary Supplement*, June 12, 1930. To these may be added the phrase of Ellis Yarnall (*Wordsworth and the Coleridges*, p. 40): "He had been much in that country at the outbreak of the Revolution and afterward during its wildest excesses". Were the September massacres or the executions during the Terror the wildest excesses of the Revolution? It is a debatable point.

named, I ought perhaps to say, rather than "noteworthy"; for in general I forget what men they were; and now remember only the excellent sagacity, distinctness and credibility of Wordsworth's little biographic portraitures of them. Never, or never but once,[1] had I seen a stronger intellect, a more luminous and veracious power of insight, directed upon such a survey of fellow-men and their contemporary journey through the world. A great deal of Wordsworth lay in the mode and tone of drawing, but you perceived it to be faithful, accurate, and altogether life-like, though Wordsworthian. One of the best remembered sketches (almost the only one now remembered at all) was that of Wilberforce, the famous Nigger-philanthropist, drawing-room Christian, and busy man and politician. In all which capacities Wordsworth's esteem of him seemed to be privately as small as my own private one, and was amusing to gather.[2] No hard word of him did he speak or hint; told in brief firm business terms, how he was born at or near the place called Wilberforce in Yorkshire ("force" signifying torrent or angry brook as in Cumberland?); where, probably, his forefathers may have been possessors, though he was poorish; how he did this and that of insignificant (to Wordsworth insignificant) nature; "and then", ended Wordsworth, "he took into the oil trade" (I suppose the Hull whaling); which lively phrase, and the incomparable historical tone it was given in—"the oil trade"—as a thing perfectly natural and proper for such a man, is almost

[1] In Carlyle's own father.

[2] This may again be a Carlylean interpretation, or it may convey the truth. Wordsworth was more intimate with Clarkson than with Wilberforce, and in the controversy which followed the publication of the *Life* of Wilberforce in 1838 he was decidedly in sympathy with the Clarksons and their champion, Crabb Robinson (*vide Crabb Robinson Correspondence, passim*). Were the rather mysterious financial losses of the end of Wilberforce's life really due to his "taking into the oil trade", i.e. investing unwisely in it, or did Carlyle confuse what Wordsworth said about that with his account of the Wilberforce forefathers, who were actually engaged in the Baltic trade?

the only point in the delineation which is now vividly present to me. I remember only the rustic picture, sketched as with a burnt stick on the board of a pair of bellows, seemed to me completely good.

Carlyle adds some notes on Wordsworth as a recognized lion in the last seven or ten years of his life: he "took his bit of lionism very quietly, with a smile sardonic rather than triumphant, and certainly got no harm by it, if he got or expected little good". There follow some waspish remarks on Mrs Wordsworth, for which both the Carlyles need forgiveness, but some amends for them in a description of a glimpse of Wordsworth at one of the lionizing dinners, "very symbolic to me of his general deportment there".

Dinner was large, luminous, sumptuous; I sat a long way from Wordsworth; dessert I think had come in, and certainly there reigned in all quarters a cackle as of Babel (only politer perhaps), which far up in Wordsworth's quarter (who was leftward on my side of the table) seemed to have taken a sententious, rather louder, logical and quasi-scientific turn, heartily unimportant to gods and men, so far as I could judge of it and of the other babble reigning. I looked upwards, leftwards, the coast being luckily for a moment clear; there, far off, beautifully screened in the shadow of his vertical green circle,[1] which was on the farther side of him, sate Wordsworth, silent, slowly but steadily gnawing some portion of what I judged to be raisins, with his eye and attention placidly fixed on these and these alone. The sight of whom, and of his rock-like indifference to the babble, quasi-scientific and other, with attention turned on the small practical alone, was comfortable and amusing to me, who felt like him but could not eat raisins.

[1] He carried a standing shade to shield his eyes from the light. Cf. chapter IV *infra*, pp. 318–31.

It is as sympathetic a portrait as could be expected from a man who cared as little for poetry as Carlyle did, and who expected a prophet to be always prophesying. It gives with not unkindly humour and genuine respect that side of Wordsworth in his hale and vigorous age which those who cared even less for poetry than Carlyle could also recognize and like. Thus it was at Bagborough in 1841, as Miss Fenwick noted with amusement[1]:

Mr Wordsworth and the Squire do very well together. The latter thinks the former a very sensible man, and the former thinks the latter a very pleasant one. The people in Somersetshire know nothing of the poet. They call him Wentworth and Wedgewood and all sorts of names. But they are kind and hospitable, and he likes to be met on the ground of his common humanity.

There Carlyle could meet him.

The younger generation who admired and sometimes laughed affectionately at Wordsworth could understand better the coexistence of prophetic and prosaic traits, and the enjoyment of the contrast is found in all the new friendships and associations of the last thirty years—with Henry Taylor and his circle of young statesmen and philosophers, with the Hamiltons, Aubrey de Vere and R. P. Graves, and even with passing visitors. One of the best instances is seldom quoted. Mrs Hemans, who was, as her letters show, a much livelier and more humorous person than her poetry would lead us to suppose, visited the Wordsworths in 1830. She must, by the way, have been almost the only person who ever found Wordsworth easier than Scott at a first meeting, but the explanation may lie in the difference between the two men in

[1] *Autobiography of Sir Henry Taylor*, I, 338–9.

their attitude to women. De Quincey was shocked because Wordsworth never thought of carrying a lady's reticule, an omission of which Scott would never have been guilty; yet Wordsworth looked upon women as giving equal companionship in all ways, and it may be doubted whether Scott always did this. Wordsworth once struck the Fletcher household by his assertion that a wife ought not to be expected to agree with her husband: if she "is always expected to conceal her difference of opinion from her husband, she ceases to be an equal"—a view with which Browning, who insisted that his wife should not obey him,[1] would have been in complete sympathy. The Fletchers and others were struck, too, by Wordsworth's distress at the "degraded view" of women which Milton expressed in "he for God only, she for God in him"—"a very low and a very false estimate of woman's condition"; and by the reasons which he gave for his respect for unmarried women.[2] There are also all the implications of the letter to his wife of July 5, 1837.[3] Mrs Hemans, who specifically mentions Wordsworth's thoughtfulness for her comfort, may also have been pleased by an unembarrassing frankness which implied neither the exaggerated homage nor the kindly condescension to which she was used in men. But her sentimentality and her sense of the ridiculous were alike startled into comment by his choice of a wedding present, which, even if we allow for suggestion from his wife, must be admitted to be unexpected.[4]

Imagine, my dear—, a bridal present made by Mr Wordsworth, to a young lady in whom he is much interested—a

[1] See her letter to her sister Henrietta, November 23 and 24, 1847.

[2] *Memoirs*, II, 440, 465; Graves, *Recollections*, pp. 311–13.

[3] See *infra*, p. 329.

[4] Chorley, II, 141–2.

poet's daughter, too! You will be thinking of a broach in the shape of a lyre, or a butterfly-shaped aigrette, or a forget-me-not ring, or some such "small gear"—nothing of the sort, but a good, handsome, substantial, useful-looking pair of scales, to hang up in her store-room! "For you must be aware, my dear Mrs Hemans", said he to me very gravely, "how necessary it is occasionally for every lady to see things weighed herself." *Poveretta me!* I looked as *good as I could,* and, happily for me, the poetic eyes are not very clear-sighted, so that I believe no suspicion derogatory to my notability of character has yet flashed upon the mighty master's mind: indeed I told him that I looked upon scales as particularly graceful things, and had great thoughts of having my picture taken with a pair in my hand.

The full flavour of the story is missed without its sequel, the Fenwick note on the *Extempore Effusion*: Mrs Hemans, with all her charm and all her gifts, did not satisfy Mrs Wordsworth's ideal of notability of character, and it was hoped that the importance attached to the pair of scales might act as a gentle monition to her. The gentleness itself of the monition carries one back twenty-five years, to Coleridge's note of the difference between Wordsworth's delicacy and Poole's bluntness in such matters.[1]

Mrs Hemans was only a passing guest, though she left pleasant memories behind her and has her place in the *Extempore Effusion*. There were other and closer ties formed in those later years, and in particular the friendship with William Rowan Hamilton was of peculiar value to Wordsworth on intellectual as well as other grounds. There were thirty-five years between them, but from the first they were on the footing of equals, and Wordsworth used to place Hamilton

[1] *Anima Poetae*, p. 70 (Coleridge to Tobin, April 10, 1804).

next to Coleridge as one of "the two most wonderful men, taking all their endowments together", that he had ever met.[1] Hamilton provides one of the rare instances of an infant prodigy who developed into a great man. One of the greatest of mathematical physicists, he was also an extraordinary linguist and had an indubitable literary gift. At three years old he could read well and was "considerably advanced in arithmetic"; at five he was able to translate and read Latin, Greek and Hebrew, and he loved to recite Dryden, Collins, Milton and Homer; by the time he was eight, he had added Italian and French to the list, and was extemporizing in Latin; before he was ten, he was studying Arabic, Sanskrit and several Indian languages; he wrote a Syriac grammar before he was twelve, and addressed the Persian Ambassador in a Persian letter at the age of fourteen. In later life, after his mathematical genius had insisted on its supremacy, he still read for pleasure in most of these languages. He had shown marked originality and power in mathematics and physics before he was twenty, and in 1827, when he was only twenty-two and still an undergraduate at Trinity College, Dublin, he was appointed Professor of Astronomy there and, in the same year, Astronomer Royal for Ireland.

It was in September 1827 that Hamilton met Wordsworth for the first time. On the following day he wrote to his sister to tell her how they had walked backwards and forwards between Ambleside and Rydal, unable to break off their conversation, "*without any companion* except the stars and our own burning thoughts and words".[2] A passage in a letter which

[1] Graves, *Life of Sir William Rowan Hamilton*, I, 269; II, 541; III, 30.

[2] *Ibid.* I, 262.

Hamilton wrote to Wordsworth shortly afterwards (December 8, 1827) helps to account for the mutual and lasting attraction.

For Science, as well as Poetry, has its own enthusiasm, and holds its own communion with the sublimity and beauty of the Universe. And in devoting myself to its pursuits I seem to myself to listen not so much to the voice of Ambition or of Patriotism, which would prompt me to labour for the reputation of myself or of my country, as to the promise of a still purer and nobler reward, in that inward and tranquil delight which cannot but attend a life occupied in the study of Truth and of Nature, and in unfolding to myself and to other men the external works of God, and the magnificent simplicity of Creation.

Graves, in his biography of Hamilton,[1] tells a story for which he does not accept full responsibility, but which, with all allowance made for exaggeration, is essentially true in its exposition of Wordsworth's proud humility before a different kind of intellectual greatness.

When Wordsworth visited Hamilton at the Observatory he took occasion to say, "I feel happy in a pleasure rarely enjoyed by me, that of being in the company of a man to whom I can look up". "If I", replied Hamilton, "am to look down on you, it is only as Lord Rosse looks down in his telescope to see the stars of heaven reflected."

Even without that story it would be clear that this new friendship, an intellectual companionship such as Wordsworth had not known for years, meant as much to the older man as to the younger. Ten days after their first meeting Wordsworth wrote to Hamilton, "Seldom have I parted—never, I was going to say—with one whom, after so short an acquaintance,

[1] *Ibid.* III, 237.

I lost sight of with more regret".[1] This, from Wordsworth, is more than mere politeness. In a later letter (July 24, 1829) he strikes out one of those flashing phrases which are too infrequent in his deliberately restrained letters, "I like to see and think of you among the stars, and between death and immortality, where three of these poems place you".

For Hamilton was also a poet, and he had sent some of his poems direct and others by his sister Eliza to Wordsworth for judgment. The verdict was, in this letter and others, that the workmanship did not come up to the conception. "You are probably aware of this", Wordsworth continues, "though perhaps not in an equal degree with myself; nor is it desirable you should, for it might tempt you to labour which would divert you from subjects of infinitely greater importance." It would be rash to conclude from this one sentence that, in Wordsworth's considered opinion, mathematics were of infinitely greater importance than poetry: he is rather informing Hamilton gently that only great labour will make him more than an amateur: he must make his choice, and the indications are, for him, towards that science in which he has already triumphantly shown his supremacy. Yet, if any poet were ever tempted to blaspheme his own art for the sake of mathematics, it might well have been Wordsworth. In 1833 he was moved by the reading of one of Hamilton's lectures to regret that he did not study mathematics in his youth. He was in fact unjust to himself, as *The Prelude* shows, to name no other evidence. A study of *The Prelude* in Professor de Selincourt's great edition will also, I think, show how his mind was quickened by his intercourse with Hamilton. For the latest, the D and E, revisions, which Professor de Selincourt proves to belong to

[1] *Life of Hamilton*, I, 268.

the years 1828–39, contain two of the noblest passages in the poem: those two passages in which Wordsworth, it is tempting to believe with Hamilton in his mind, celebrates the mathematician and, more particularly, the astronomer. The first is the best known, those great lines added to the description, in the Third Book, of Newton's statue—

> The marble index of a mind for ever
> Voyaging through strange seas of Thought, alone.

The other is the passage in the Sixth Book dealing with the delights of geometry. In the 1805 version lines 142–9 run

> With Indian awe and wonder, ignorance
> Which even was cherish'd, did I meditate
> Upon the alliance of those simple, pure
> Proportions and relations with the frame
> And Laws of Nature, how they would become
> Herein a leader to the human mind,
> And made endeavours frequent to detect
> The process by dark guesses of my own.

In the corresponding passage, lines 121–8, of the final version, the "dark guesses" are replaced by a contemplation of the infinite studies of the astronomer—

> With Indian awe and wonder, ignorance pleased
> With its own struggles, did I meditate
> On the relation these abstractions bear
> To Nature's laws, and by what process led,
> Those immaterial agents bowed their heads
> Duly to serve the mind of earth-born man;
> From star to star, from kindred sphere to sphere,
> From system on to system without end.

Wordsworth had thought to some purpose of Hamilton among

the stars. For it is worth noting that in the Fourth Book of *The Excursion* he had first written nobly of those

Ambitious Souls—
Whom Earth, at this late season, hath produced
To regulate the moving spheres, and weigh
The planets in the hollow of their hand;
And they who rather dive than soar, whose pains
Have solved the elements, or analysed
The thinking principle—

and then gone on to doubt whether

this magnificent effect of Power,
The Earth we tread, the Sky that we behold
By day, and all the pomp which night reveals
...should exist
Only to be examined, pondered, searched,
Probed, vexed, and criticised.

The doubting attitude towards these Ambitious Souls is emphasized by the Wanderer's outburst in Book VIII in praise of machines—

Yet do I exult,
Casting reserve away, exult to see
An Intellectual mastery exercised
O'er the blind Elements; a purpose given,
A perseverance fed; almost a soul
Imparted—to brute Matter.

It is not surprising that this apparent distrust of speculative science should have distressed Hamilton, who took the opportunity of Wordsworth's visit to him, during his Irish tour of 1829, to ask for an explanation. Certain passages of Eliza Hamilton's account of the visit and the conversation, written immediately afterwards, deserve quotation.[1]

Her first sight of Wordsworth was of "a tall man, with grey

[1] *Life of Hamilton*, I, 311–14.

hair, a brown coat, and nankeen trousers, on whom Smoke, our black greyhound, was jumping up in a most friendly manner, not by any means his wont with every stranger". Smoke may therefore join the terrier who used to take Wordsworth for walks, and anxiously tried to preserve his reputation for sanity (*Prelude*, Book IV), in protest against the idea of the Rydalers that he did not care for dogs. A cat will rub itself against the one person in an assembly who detests cats: a dog, less subtle or less cruel in its sense of humour, will make such advances only where it suspects a friend. And Smoke was fastidious. His health, by the way, was reported to Wordsworth thenceforward with the health of the rest of the Hamilton household.

Wordsworth was, Eliza Hamilton tells us, "in every way as complete an opposite to my preconception of him as anything could be.... He was not at all a loquacious man, nor one who seemed inclined to approach with any degree of intimacy even those of whom he knew a good deal, but at the same time, one who met every advance on the part of others with a ready and attractive affability. Other men did not seem necessary to him, or to the existence of his happiness". She was particularly pleased with the ordinariness of his ordinary conversation: "it always seemed to me quite unnatural for a poet to be very poetical in his every-day language". Presently, however, Hamilton brought up the question of the remarks about scientists in *The Excursion*. Wordsworth read the offending passage, probably that already quoted from the Fourth Book, which "contrasts the dignities of the Imagination with the presumptive littleness of certain modern Philosophers", and he then defended himself, with a beautiful mixture of warmth and temperateness, from the accusation of any want of reverence for Science, in the proper sense of the word—Science, that raised the mind to the contemplation of God in [His] works, and which was pursued with that end as its primary and great object; but as for all other science, all science which put this end out of view, all science which was a bare collection of facts for their own sake, or to be applied merely to the material uses of life, he thought it *degraded* instead of raising the species. All science which waged war with and wished to extinguish Imagination in the mind of man, and to leave it nothing of any kind but the naked knowledge of facts, was, he thought, much worse than useless; and what is disseminated in the present day under the title of "useful knowledge" being disconnected, as he thought it, with God and everything but itself, was of a dangerous and debasing tendency. For his part, rather than have his mind engrossed with *this* kind of science, to the utter exclusion of Imagination, and of every consideration but what refers to our bodily comforts, power and greatness, he would much prefer being a superstitious old woman.

My brother said of some passage that "*so far as it went*", he quite agreed with it, but "*he* would add a good deal more". "I am sure you would", said Wordsworth, with a good-humoured smile; "and if you will allow me to explain my sentiments first, I shall be glad to hear yours afterwards." He then entered very much at large on the scope of his design, repeating that Science, when legitimately pursued for the purpose of elevating the mind to God, he venerated. The only class of scientific persons against whom he had directed his battery were those whom he would compare to the pioneers of an army, who go before the hero, certainly preparing the way for him, and cutting down the obstructions that oppose his march, but who themselves have no feelings of lofty enthusiasm, or of any kind but the hope of reaping part of the plunder and sharing in the profit of success. "What", he said, "would have been the use of my praising such men as Newton? They do not need my insignificant praise, and therefore I did not allude to such sons of Science."

My brother argued that although he quite admitted that, were the faculty of Imagination to be done away with in man—*could* that be—he would be left indeed, as Wordsworth said, a most inferior being; still he thought the *Intellectual* faculties held *equal* rank at *least* with the Imaginative. But I could not help smiling at his own exemplification of the indestructibility of Imagination in any mind, but above all in those of a high order, when he told Wordsworth that *he* believed Mathematics to be a connecting link between men and beings of a higher nature; the circle and triangle he believed to have a real existence in their minds and in the nature of things, and not to be a mere creation or arbitrary symbol proceeding from human invention.

Wordsworth smiled kindly, but said *that* reminded him of the Platonic doctrine of the internal existence in the marble of those beautiful forms from which the sculptor was supposed only to withdraw the veil. William also smiled good-humouredly.

A footnote to this conversation is to be found in Wordsworth's conversation with J. P. Muirhead in 1841,[1] when he placed James Watt on a level with Newton as an example of the highest type of scientist, and spoke of his discoveries as "the most beneficial to mankind". This is not to be explained as due to politeness, Muirhead having a family connection with Watt, or to Wordsworth's memory of his own early friendship with the second James Watt: it is in entire agreement with the Wanderer's praise of machines, and not in disagreement with the conversation with Hamilton. Wordsworth could reverence either speculative or utilitarian researches, provided they did not narrow the mind of the searcher and were not, as the Wanderer expressed it, "unpropped by Virtue". He had written greatly of the Man of Science in the Preface of 1800; he had always been, and he

[1] Printed in *Blackwood's Magazine*, June 1927.

remained to the end, keenly conscious of the benefits of mechanical inventions, even while he was increasingly conscious of the industrial evils which were, if only in part, their consequence; but in the revised *Prelude* he shows himself again far more conscious of the glory of speculative science and of mathematical physics than in *The Excursion*, reverting to the position of 1800, as if inspired by intimacy with such a Man of Science as he had then described.

The friendship was kept warm and living by occasional meetings and by letters, which discuss poetry, religious and philosophical questions, politics, private affairs, sometimes gravely, sometimes lightly enough. It is pleasant, for example, to find Wordsworth parodying G. P. R. James, and describing himself (November 26, 1830) as "a solitary equestrian entering the romantic little town of Ashford-in-the-Waters, on the edge of the wilds of Derbyshire, at the close of day". Of the occasional meetings one in particular remained in Hamilton's memory. After some praise of Tennyson in a letter to Graves (July 18, 1855), Hamilton adds,

> In saying all this I feel that I only echo what Wordsworth said to me while we were boating on Windermere in 1830 (I seem to see the splash of the oar). The words I do not presume nor pretend to repeat; but the spirit certainly was, that in Alfred Tennyson, young a poet as he then was, there was a man of the highest promise.

Hamilton, it may be objected, was writing twenty-five years later, and may have mistaken the date. That is possible, but it is nevertheless certain that in November 1830, if not in July, Wordsworth was hailing the dawn of Tennyson. For on the 26th of that month, when he was staying with his brother at Trinity, he wrote to Hamilton, "We have also a respectable show of blossom in poetry, two brothers of the name of Tennyson, in particular one not a little promising". It would seem that he knew the *Poems by Two Brothers* of 1826, possibly also *Timbuctoo* of 1829 and the *Poems* of 1830; whether he inquired of his brother concerning young poets, or whether the Master told him unasked, is of little importance: the unhesitating recognition is certain and, except for one in Tennyson's immediate circle, could not have been much earlier. If FitzGerald had known of this, and of Wordsworth's repeated declarations to the same effect in the years which followed, we might never have had the nickname of Daddy Wordsworth. FitzGerald's prejudice was largely due to his dislike of Christopher Wordsworth, the Master of Trinity—the "Meeserable Sinner," as that irreverent generation called him in allusion to the Northern breadth of his vowels as he read the Litany. Tennyson shared the dislike and the prejudice, and in consequence made no attempt to meet the elder poet. It was therefore not until 1845 that they did meet, and then, as so frequently happened, the prejudice melted away in Wordsworth's presence. Aubrey de Vere, with a full sense of the humanities of the occasion, wrote to tell Miss Fenwick[1] how he had

> brought Alfred Tennyson up the hill to pay his respects to the venerable bard. Since then they met at dinner twice, and I was much pleased at finding how much the young poet had liked the old one. There was something at once amusing and touching in the account Tennyson gave me of the evening

[1] Una Taylor, *Guests and Memories*, pp. 164–5. The introduction was on May 4, as we learn from de Vere's diary for that date. Cf. also the entry for May 9 (both printed in his life by Mr Wilfrid Ward): "Alfred Tennyson came in and smoked his pipe. He told us with pleasure of his dinner with Wordsworth—was pleased as well

they passed together. He had begun by having a certain degree of prejudice against him, but he told me that as he saw the old man with his white hair sitting opposite to him, and remembered moment after moment that he was the author of the "Laodamia", "Tintern Abbey" and other poems which he had delighted in since boyhood, he could not help a strange feeling of affection for him which strengthened by degrees. He wished, he said, before bidding him adieu to express something of his veneration, but he has a great contempt for compliments; and it seems it was not until it grew quite dark, that he plucked up heart, and said something about the pleasure their meeting had given him.

Wordsworth too was pleased, both by the meeting and by Tennyson's little speech. He wrote about it to Henry Reed (July 1, 1845)—calling Tennyson "decidedly the first of our living poets", and confessing that he himself was "far from indifferent" to Tennyson's expression of gratitude to him for his writings. It was on March 6, 1842, that Aubrey de Vere had recited to him *You ask me why* and *Of old sat Freedom on the heights*: Wordsworth's comment was that they were "very solid and noble in thought", and the diction was "singularly stately".[1] In 1846 he was speaking with more emphasis to Thomas Cooper: "Mr Tennyson affords the richest promise.

as amused by Wordsworth saying to him, 'Come, brother bard, to dinner', and taking his arm; said that he was ashamed of paying Mr Wordsworth compliments, but that he had at last, in the dark, said something about the pleasure he had had from Mr Wordsworth's writings, and that the old poet had taken his hand, and replied with some expressions equally kind and complimentary. Tennyson was evidently much pleased with the old man, and glad of having learned to know him".

[1] Grosart, III, 492. De Vere was writing in 1875, but his recollection is confirmed by his diary, printed by Mr Wilfrid Ward. There the diction is called "manly".

He will do great things yet; and ought to have done greater things by this time....The perception of harmony lies in the very essence of the poet's nature; and Mr Tennyson gives magnificent proofs that he is endowed with it".

Aubrey de Vere, who had brought the two great men together, had not himself met Wordsworth until the forties, though before that time there had been links through his father, the elder Aubrey, his friend William Rowan Hamilton, and Henry Taylor, who had married his cousin, Alice Spring-Rice, herself a member of a Wordsworthian family.[1] From this group of friends and connections, from R. P. Graves, the friend and future biographer of Hamilton, and from Miss Fenwick, who was the cousin of Taylor's stepmother, we have the most intimate descriptions of Wordsworth in the last twenty years of his life.

The picture which they draw of him is by no means that of a sentimentalized Daddy Wordsworth, such as is too easily imagined from one of the Pickersgill portraits of him. It is, indeed, amusing and consoling to find one after another of Wordsworth's friends protesting against that portrait, Sara Coleridge, for example, most vehemently in a letter to Miss Fenwick (May 25, 1851)—

Pickersgill's portrait of our dear departed great poet is *insufferable*—velvet waistcoat, neat shiny boots—just the sort of dress he would not have worn if you could have hired him—and a sombre sentimentalism of countenance quite unlike his own look, which was either elevated with high gladness or deep thought, or at times simply and childishly gruff,—but

[1] Her father, Spencer Spring-Rice, anticipating the action of a later generation, had copies of *The Happy Warrior* circulated among the troops in the Crimea: it was much more likely to inspire them, he considered, than pious tracts.

never tender after that fashion, so lackadaisical and mawkishly sentimental.

These younger people, though they were not afraid of their emotions, were themselves unsentimental, witty and humorous, of strong minds and opinions which frequently differed from his, and they criticized him as frankly as they criticized themselves and each other. There is a pleasant letter from Henry Taylor to Lady Hislop (March 20, 1835), which brings out their affection, admiration and amusement at once—

> He has the simplicity and helplessness of a child in regard to the little transactions of life; and whilst he is being directed and dealt with in regard to them, he keeps tumbling out the highest and deepest thoughts that the mind of man can reach, in a stream of discourse which is so oddly broken by the little hitches and interruptions of common life that we admire and laugh at him by turns. Everything that comes into his mind comes out—weakness or strength, affections or vanities, so that, if ever an opportunity was afforded of seeing a human being through and through, we have it in the person of this "old man eloquent". He is very happy with us, and very social with everybody, and we have a variety of people to meet him every day at breakfast and dinner.

Taylor was not always so sure that he understood Wordsworth: three years later he was admitting to Miss Fenwick, "With all his simplicity and nakedness, I think him very difficult to understand". But in spite of that admission, which must be echoed by every honest observer of any other person, it is evident that Wordsworth's candour and sympathy towards the younger men and women whom he knew was repaid by candour and sympathy and a large measure of understanding. The clearest exposition of Wordsworth as they saw him, and one of the most penetrating pieces of

Wordsworthian criticism ever written, is that which R. P. Graves has left to us. Graves met Wordsworth first in 1833, and, becoming curate of Ambleside in 1835, was in close contact with him from that date onwards. The Wordsworth whom he knew and whom he described was, then, the Wordsworth of from sixty to eighty years old, as he appeared to a man whom we know from his other work to have been of singular intelligence, independence, and strength of mind and judgment.[1]

Here was no merely amiable, no merely simple, or reverential, or imaginative man, but one eminently masculine and strong: a man of strong intellect, of strong feelings, of sturdy, massive individuality. If I do not apply to him the epithet "intense", it is because I conceive it to belong more properly to a weaker type of man in a state of strain; but I never met with a mind which to me seemed to work constantly with so much vigour, or with feelings so constantly in a state of fervour: the strong intellect was, to use his own expression, "*steeped in*" the strong feeling, but the man was always master of both:[2] so broad was the basis of his mental constitution, so powerful the original will which guided and controlled his emotions. I believe the recognition of this fact of the strength of his intellectual and passionate nature to be of high importance as conducing to a right conception of his poetry. . . .

Another circumstance, which intercourse with Wordsworth was calculated to impress upon one, was his general ability. No one in the habit of conversing with him, but must have been struck with the power, the strength and effective-

[1] The passages which follow are from Graves's *Recollections*, pp. 288, 290, 296–7, 300–2.

[2] Cf. Miss Fenwick to Henry Taylor (January 4, 1839): "What strange workings are there in his great mind, and how fearfully strong are all his feelings and affections! If his intellect had been less powerful, they must have destroyed him long ago".

ness, with which he could argue upon any subject, small or great, provided it was not scientific: he could handle every side of a question, and enforce his own opinion with the energy and tenacity, but with more than the indications of conviction of a lawyer. In the same way, his faculty of observation was capable of employing itself upon objects quite different from those to which he especially consecrated it....

He seemed to regard, as I believe all great artists do, his works as something outside himself; things which he could criticise and praise, like any other person; and if he cited them oftener than the works of other poets, it was simply because the truths which they contained were to him the objects of a special love, and an absorbing interest....All the great English poets were his familiars, and received his unstinted, though discriminating, praise. And he spoke gently of even those two contemporaries, by whom he was defamed—of Byron, who was entirely out of sympathy with him—of Shelley, who had warmly appreciated him as a poet, but could not tolerate the change in his politics....He was a great deal too conscious of his own distinctive merits to be a jealous poet.

Graves noted also "another characteristic which largely enhanced one's satisfaction in intercourse with him—I mean his willingness to discuss all subjects on first principles". This was shown both in his criticism of works of art—Graves adds, "I remember well the pleasure and admiring approval with which he greeted the first publication of Mr Ruskin"—and still more in his unbigoted treatment of political and religious questions. What follows, like the second of the passages quoted above, is strikingly in accord with John Stuart Mill's letter of 1831, which Graves can scarcely have known.

His arguments had always a substantial weight, and you felt that his prophecies, issuing, as they did, from a deep knowledge of human nature, would certainly have some amount of fulfilment. He continued to the end the expression, both in conversation and in poetry, of his early love of liberty and of political action on the part of a free people; only in later years he leant more stress than he had done on the requisite qualifications for such action.

It would be interesting to know whether Wordsworth ever told Graves of his conversation with Thomas Cooper on Chartism.[1]

Graves recognized Wordsworth's passion and the strength of his feelings, but he could not, in a public lecture, illustrate them from what must, to some extent at least, have come under his notice, the relations between Dora Wordsworth and her father. How much he knew it is impossible to say, but everyone who came into contact with them seems to have known fairly completely the story of Dora's engagement and marriage. Quillinan had been friendly with the Wordsworths for years, but there were good reasons why, when he asked, some time between 1836 and 1839,[2] for Wordsworth's

[1] Cf. pp. 46–7, 197–9 *infra*.

[2] Certainly not, as Knight would have it by his dating of Wordsworth's letters on the subject (*Letters*, II, 321–3), in 1828. Professor de Selincourt points out in a private letter that "for one thing Miss Fenwick, mentioned at the end of the second letter, was not a member of the Wordsworth circle as early as 1828, for another Willy in 1828 was only 18 and would hardly at that age have been entrusted to place before Dora her father's 'judgment and feelings', for a third... the Quillinan correspondence proves that though both Dora and Quillinan had loved one another for some years, Quillinan only discovered Dora's feelings for him about 1836". Quillinan was abroad for much of 1836–7, and it seems to me possible, though it cannot be certain, that Wordsworth was not formally approached until after his return. It is odd that Crabb Robinson, though he knew all the affairs of the family, and recorded them in his diary in spite of occasional qualms of conscience at the thought that writing

consent to his marriage with Dora, Wordsworth should have been reluctant to give it. As far as Dora herself was concerned, he might have had real apprehensions on the score of health, since she had been delicate for years, with more than one threatening of what was then called a decline. He might also have objected to the difference of religion, since Quillinan was a Roman Catholic;[1] but in those days, before the promulgation of the *Ne temere* Decree, the difficulties of a mixed marriage were not so grave as they are now, and Wordsworth did not press them, though he did not ignore them. There were also serious practical difficulties, for Wordsworth's other children were not entirely independent of him, and Quillinan was not in a position to support a penniless wife. Through his first marriage, to the daughter of Sir Egerton Brydges, Quillinan had become involved in the financial operations of that astonishing person, and so in the family suits which dragged on for years and ultimately ruined nearly everyone concerned. Quillinan's honour was saved, but, as Crabb Robinson commented (Diary, March 14, 1842), "It is

might be as great a breach of confidence as speech, does not refer to this until the end of 1838 (December 16, and perhaps there is a concealed reference on December 9). He gives, however, one more definite date: on May 15, 1839, he notes that Miss Fenwick has told him "that Dora Wordsworth is to marry Quillinan with Wordsworth's forced permission, not approval". Wordsworth's letters may then be dated at the end of 1838 or early in 1839. The delay after that was apparently caused by the practical difficulties of finance; cf. pp. 41, 42–3 *infra* and Crabb Robinson's unprinted diary for December 16, 1838; May 15, June 22 and June 26, 1839; February 21 and 22, 1840; March 14 and April 19, 1842.

[1] Or, as his biographer put it, he "always spoke and wrote of himself as a Roman Catholic; and no doubt believed that he was so....He appeared practically to conform to the Church of England, while nominally he continued a Romanist" (*Memoir*, pp. xliii–xliv).

after all a melancholy mode of escaping from an imputation on one's honour by allowing that the fault must be transferred to the head". Any prudent father might well have hesitated or refused outright to consent to his daughter's marriage to a man whose prospects were so threatening. Wordsworth gave his consent, being perhaps not a prudent father, before he could know that Quillinan would be cleared in the eyes of the world, and with the knowledge that, whatever the result, he would probably have to support his daughter and her husband—no light undertaking for a man of his limited means. It was only at Quillinan's request that the allowance which he made to them was discontinued after her death, and Miss Fenwick and Crabb Robinson agreed in pointedly commending "his disinterestedness contrasted with others".[1]

Wordsworth did not take serious advantage of the excuses which lay ready for him to plead. To him they represented only secondary obstacles. He knew the truth, that he could not bring himself, without a severe struggle, to part with his daughter, and he would not lie, either to himself or to other people, about his motives. He knew what he ought to do for her happiness, and he did not want to do it, but he would not pretend that he was hesitating on purely unselfish or prudential grounds. Henry Taylor heard from Miss Fenwick of his struggles[2]—

The emotions,—I may say the throes and agonies of emotion,—he underwent, were such as an old man could not

[1] *Diary*, September 7, 1847. The reference is interesting as indicating that Miss Fenwick already knew about the Baudouin family. Crabb Robinson seems to have disliked Baudouin himself almost from the beginning: the settlement negotiations of 1834–5 convinced him that Baudouin was grasping, and the breach of contract in 1842 confirmed him in his opinion. Cf. Appendix C.

[2] *Autobiography of Sir Henry Taylor*, I, 337.

have endured without suffering in health, had he not been a very strong old man. But he was like nobody else,—old or young. He would pass the night, or most part of it, in struggles and storms, to the moment of coming down to breakfast; and then, if strangers were present, be as easy and delightful in conversation as if nothing were the matter.

When he conquered himself at last, it was no uncertain victory. On May 11, 1841, he gave Dora away in the church at Bath. "Mr Wordsworth behaves beautifully", Miss Fenwick wrote a few days before the wedding,[1] and his letters to Crabb Robinson about that time bear out the statement.

Not the least remarkable feature of the story is the close friendship and affection which persisted between the three chief actors in it throughout those years of struggle and uncertainty. By all the canons of conventional psychology, bitterness and even hatred ought to have poisoned their lives: actually Dora continued to love her father as well as her lover —this perhaps is not without parallel—and, with a more unusual generosity, Wordsworth and Quillinan to value their friendship. The story could not have worked itself out as it did if Wordsworth had been a tyrannical or even a generally unreasonable father, or Dora a crushed or undeveloped weakling; only the freedom and candour of their relations, and the strength of their feelings, made all the stages of the affair possible. Quillinan had not, it may be suspected, the passion of the other two, but he was a sensitive and high-minded man,[2] and he succeeded in maintaining his loyalty to both

[1] *Autobiography of Sir Henry Taylor*, I, 337.

[2] Perhaps a little too sensitive. In June 1839 he was hoping for the secretaryship of a new joint stock bank, and asked for Crabb Robinson's assistance in obtaining it. Crabb Robinson was willing to help, because, "If he can get this place, he may be able to marry

his friend and his love. The whole story is an instructive contrast to the almost contemporary events in Wimpole Street.

The stress of inward conflict in those years of the later thirties may be reflected in some of the descriptions of Wordsworth at that time, though the loss of his closest friends was also partly accountable for his more frequent fits of depression. John Dix saw him thus in 1836 at the first night of Talfourd's *Ion*, before the play began, but roused to enthusiastic applause by the play itself: "Indeed, he thumped with his stick most lustily, and if Talfourd saw him, he must have been not a little gratified by *such* approvals of his Tragedy".[1] Dora's marriage and his own self-conquest seem to have had an encouraging effect. To the beginning and end of 1841 belong two pleasant glimpses of him in the letters of Dr Arnold. In the first (to Rev. T. J. Ormerod, January 3) Arnold contrasts his health with the pitiable state of Southey: "Wordsworth is in body and mind still sound and vigorous; it is beautiful to see and hear him". In the second (to J. T. Coleridge, December 26) he describes Wordsworth as being "in high force". The future Dean Stanley's picture of Rogers

—and dear Dora would then be able to marry", but could do nothing. A few days later Crabb Robinson realized that his words had not been carefully enough chosen: "He is apt to take offence, and I did not recollect his sensitiveness. I wrote him a letter of apology, and I hope he will be appeased" (*Diary*, June 22 and 26, 1839). Crabb Robinson also, on one occasion, made up a one-sided disagreement between Quillinan and John Wordsworth, whose feelings were perfectly friendly (February 7, 1839); and even, after Dora's death, had to point out to Quillinan that Wordsworth's temporary reluctance to enter his house was not an insult.

[1] Dix gives a vivid picture of both moods (*Pen and Ink Sketches*, ed. 1846, pp. 202–3).

and Wordsworth, the town and the country mouse, comes halfway between these.[1]

The town-mouse a sleek, well-fed, sly, *white* mouse, and the country-mouse with its rough, weather-worn face and grey hairs; the town-mouse displaying its delicate little rolls and pyramids of glistening strawberries, the country-mouse exulting in its hollow tree, its crust of bread and liberty, and rallying its brother on his late hours and frequent dinners. There was a great complaint of the country-mouse about the dangers he ran by going in cabs;...and there was a most amusing account of their going together to Hampton Court, and how the country-mouse had fixed on the only day, and the town-mouse on the only hour, when it could not be seen, and how they were beset by fashionable acquaintances of the town-mouse, and how the country-mouse would have stayed to look at some beautiful trees in the park had not the town-mouse been engaged, of course, to a dinner in London.... And then, by a few rapid leaps, one of which was the definition of a poor man by Taylor as "a person whose conversation is tiresome", they entered on the subject of beggars, and Wordsworth gave a Wordsworthian account of how he and Talfourd had been standing under a projection in Regent Street for shelter from the rain, and Talfourd gave a shilling to a poor boy, and how the boy said nothing, but his face was lighted up with the most glorious radiance, and he ran with it to his mother, who stood at a little distance and bowed her thanks to them with the most inimitable gracefulness; and then Artevelde, the statesman overpowering the poet, exclaimed, "You have ruined that boy for life. He will now, at every shower of rain, run to the same place and look out for shillings".

Wordsworth's own treatment of beggars would hardly have satisfied the stern political economist. He seems to have

[1] *Life*, I, 298–9. Cf. also Aubrey de Vere's notes of his intercourse with Wordsworth, in those passages of his diary and letters for 1841 and 1842 which are printed by Mr Wilfrid Ward.

allowed a certain sum every day for the beggars he met,[1] and there were standing orders that every one who begged at Rydal Mount should be given bread and cheese. One morning he came in and found the cook in high indignation because a beggar had thrown the food away as soon as he reached the gate: all beggars were rogues and cheats, and she would never give anything to another. "O, don't say that, Elizabeth!" protested Wordsworth. "Go on giving, and some day the right beggar will come!"[2] Harriet Martineau would have sympathized with the cook: she complained that "one could hardly get a drop of cream with any ease of mind" for tea at the Mount, whereas milk was given to people who were quite able to pay for it themselves.

Four years later than his adventures at Hampton Court with Rogers, Wordsworth was still full of vigour and "in high force". Aubrey de Vere, writing to Henry Taylor (March 9, 1845), rejoiced in his physical and mental vigour alike: "He speaks still with as fresh an enthusiasm on all the subjects which present themselves to his moral or poetic sympathies as he would have felt when he first came to these mountains". And there was little change in the two following years. In 1846 he was visited by that interesting and attractive person Thomas Cooper, whose autobiography better deserves to be reprinted than many books which recur with wearisome repetition in the lists of cheap reprints. He was a self-educated man, a poet, and a Chartist leader who, though he had always been against the violent counsels of Feargus

[1] Cf. the evidence of Ellis Yarnall, p. 50 *infra*.

[2] I owe this story to Miss Mary Tyson of Rydal, who had it from her mother, the Agnes of the Crabb Robinson letters and diary and the transmitter of much tradition about the Wordsworths and Hartley Coleridge.

O'Connor and others, was imprisoned for two years on a charge of sedition. A little while after his release he went for a short walking-tour in the Lake Country, and when he reached Rydal decided to attempt to see Wordsworth, though he had no introduction and suspected that even if Wordsworth "should have heard that a Prison Rhyme was sent forth last year by a Chartist", that would hardly be a recommendation. He took the risk of a repulse, however, and was received in a fashion which went beyond his wildest hopes. Cooper published all that he could remember of the conversation—and he thought he could remember it all, though not in exact order—immediately after Wordsworth's death, in *Cooper's Journal*, and reprinted it verbatim in his autobiography in 1872. Dicey quoted a few sentences in *The Statesmanship of Wordsworth*,[1] but no one else, to my knowledge, has made any use of this document, which is not only interesting in itself but of real importance for the understanding of Wordsworth's later political thought. In more ways than one Cooper did not meet in his host what he had expected, and he says so frankly.

The conversation wandered naturally between politics and literature. Wordsworth knew something of Cooper's *Purgatory of Suicides*, the "Prison Rhyme" by which he hoped to gain immortality, and spoke kindly of it. Thence the transition was easy to Chartism.

"You were right", he said; "I have always said the people were right in what they asked; but you went the wrong way to get it."

I almost doubted my ears—being in the presence of the "Tory" Wordsworth. He read the inquiring expression of

[1] By an odd slip, however, he called the writer Thomas Brown.

my look in a moment,—and immediately repeated what he had said.

"You were quite right: there is nothing unreasonable in your Charter: it is the foolish attempt at physical force, for which many of you have been blamable."

After a digression on poetry, particularly on Byron and Tennyson, they came back again to politics.

"There will be great changes on the Continent", he said, "when the present King of the French dies. But *not* while he lives. The different governments will have to give constitutions to their people, for knowledge is spreading, and constitutional liberty is sure to follow."

I thought him perfectly right about Louis Philippe; and which of us would not have thought him right in 1846?...

He had the same views of the spread of freedom in England in proportion to the increase of knowledge; and descanted with animation on the growth of Mechanics' and similar institutions.

"The people are sure to have the franchise", he said, with emphasis, "as knowledge increases; but you will not get all you seek at once—and you must never seek it again by physical force", he added, turning to me with a smile: "it will only make you longer about it."

In one respect Cooper was more fortunate than almost any of the later visitors to Rydal, since he came in one of those rare intervals when Dorothy Wordsworth was capable of meeting strangers.

The poet's aged and infirm sister was being drawn about the courtyard in a wheeled chair, as we walked on the terrace. He descended with me, and introduced me to her—as a poet!—and hung over her infirmity with the kindest affection, while she talked to me.

When I hastened to depart—fearing that I had already wearied him—he walked with me to the gate, pressing my hand repeatedly, smiling upon me so benevolently, and uttering so many good wishes for my happiness and usefulness, that I felt almost unable to thank him. I left him with a more intense feeling of having been in the presence of a good and great intelligence, than I had ever felt in any other moments of my life.

Cooper's evidence, as it is among the most interesting—its credibility and importance are considered in the next chapter—is also among the latest which we have. The year 1847 was saddened by the illness and death of Dora Quillinan, which shook her father as much as the death of little Catherine thirty-five years earlier. Anyone less vigorous in mind and body must have succumbed to the violence of Wordsworth's grief. In 1848 he was still disinclined to see anyone but close friends, and rumours consequently spread that his mind was failing. In August Miss Mitford wrote to Charles Boner that even Ruskin, who had passed a fortnight at Keswick, had not seen Wordsworth, though they had often met in London: "the family did not seem to wish it, he said, and in short both he and I feared there must have been some truth in reports about the decline of intellect of the Bard of Rydal Mount". There was in fact no truth in those reports, for, though Wordsworth was beginning to show his age, he had yet, with his amazing power of recuperation, rallied from his first overwhelming grief, and was active in mind. In 1848 Crabb Robinson, for the first time for years, did not spend Christmas at Rydal, shrinking from a possible repetition of the terrible experience of the preceding Christmas Day, when Wordsworth broke down and sobbed in church. But when he felt it safe to arrive, two days later, he found both husband and wife almost cheerful, in spite of the shadow cast by the last illness of Hartley Coleridge. And in the following June Miss

Fenwick reported to Henry Taylor,[1] "I see no difference in Mrs Wordsworth; but his darker moods are more frequent, though at other times he is as strong and bright as ever.... His is a strong but not a happy old age".

He was strong enough again, indeed, to show kindness in that last summer to such visitors as John Roby, the collector of Lancashire folklore, and Ellis Yarnall, who brought an introduction from Professor Henry Reed of Philadelphia. Some of Yarnall's notes are quoted elsewhere, but a few sentences may be given here as corroborating and expanding Miss Fenwick's more intimate report.[2]

The expression of his countenance was sad, mournful I might say; he seemed one on whom sorrow pressed heavily. He gave me his hand, and welcomed me cordially, though without

[1] Taylor, *Autobiography*, II, 55.

[2] Yarnall wrote to Reed in September 1850, basing his letter on notes made immediately after his visit, which was on August 18, 1849. The letter was used in the 1851 *Memoirs* and by later biographers, and was also used by Yarnall himself when he wrote *Wordsworth and the Coleridges* (1899). I have quoted consistently from the version in this last book, except on p. 381 *infra*: it is evidently based on the same notes as the letter, and Yarnall's Preface implies that it is nearer to the original letter than the versions in the biographies: "The paper, 'A Visit to Wordsworth', was in part published by Dr Christopher Wordsworth...; passages were omitted by him because of their reference to persons then living; there is no reason now why my record should not appear as a whole". Yarnall may have varied his earlier expressions here and there, and omitted a little, but this version is everywhere more unguarded than that of the *Memoirs*, which reads as if it had undergone editorial alteration as well as omission. The oddest thing about the variants is that Knight alone should preserve the passage on Ruskin: he used a copy of the omitted passages furnished by Yarnall, and presumably Yarnall himself left this passage out by accident when he compiled his book.

smiling....I may note that Wordsworth's manner throughout was animated, and that his words were felicitous to such a degree as to enchain attention. There was sustained vigour, and a mode of expression denoting habitual thoughtfulness.... Wordsworth told me I was to say to his friends in America that he and his wife were well, that they had had a great grief of late, in the loss of their only daughter. He added, "I suppose we shall never get over it"....I could see most clearly that it was the weakness of his bodily frame which took away his power of tranquil endurance.

They went out together, and Yarnall showed Wordsworth a copy of Reed's *Selections* from his poems, which he turned over, murmuring the words now and then.

We were standing together in the road, when a man accosted us, asking charity—a beggar of the better class. Wordsworth, scarcely looking off the book, thrust his hand into his pockets, as if instinctively acknowledging the man's right to beg by this prompt action. He seemed to find nothing, however; and he said, in a sort of soliloquy, "I have given to four or five already to-day", as if to account for his being then unprovided....

The sense of Wordsworth's intellectual greatness had been with me during the whole interview. I may speak, too, of the strong perception of his moral elevation which I had at the same time. He seemed to me a man living as in the presence of God by habitual recollection. A strange feeling almost of awe had impressed me while I was thus with him.

The Robys in September found him in a livelier mood, according to a letter which Mrs Roby wrote to a friend.[1]

He chatted away on literary matters with my husband, evidently with hearty pleasure. They talked of a distinguished living writer [Macaulay?]; of his style, Mr Wordsworth remarked, that every sentence seemed finished by itself, which

[1] *Legendary and Poetical Remains of John Roby*, pp. 61–2.

was never the case with our best writers—that reviewing had an injurious effect on the style of a literary man, the reviewer has ever to be saying something that will tell, every sentence must be striking....One other remark he made must not be forgotten; speaking of a writer whom he considered not a safe guide on account of his prejudices, he said, "He is so prejudiced he does not know when he lies"....There was so much more enthusiasm about him, than from the philosophic cast of his poems I had expected....He impressed us, too, as a Christian living in obedience to, and communion with, Heaven.

He was, in this last of his eighty years, still interested in literature, and in political and religious questions, about which he was much more hopeful than he had been twenty years earlier; and his talk was still full of striking phrases. His intimates noticed the gradual shrinking of his vitality, but outsiders were still impressed, and with reason, by his energy. Thus it was that he appeared to William Johnston, Quillinan's friend, a few weeks later than the visit of the Robys.[1]

I was at Ambleside, and Mr Quillinan's guest at Loughrigg Holme for a few days, in the autumn of 1849, and I could not but observe the respectful tenderness that appeared to subsist between them [i.e. Wordsworth and Quillinan]. The last evening I was in that neighbourhood, we remained with Mr Wordsworth at Rydal Mount till ten o'clock, and when we rose to go, he proposed to accompany us a part of the way. I begged him not to expose himself to the night air, but he seemed to scorn the suggestion that any such care was necessary, and he walked with us. At the bridge which crosses the Rotha, he parted from us, and startled me by the solemnity of his farewell. "I am an old man", he said, "nearly four score, and perhaps may not live to see you again

[1] *Edward Quillinan. Poems, with a Memoir by William Johnston*, pp. xxxix–xl.

—farewell! God bless you." His figure soon disappeared in the darkness, and I saw him no more. I thought him looking well for his years, and not differing very much from what I had known him three-and-twenty years before, except that he now was apt to sit silent, which had not been his wont in former years. Mr Quillinan knew more of the sadness of his heart, but he also had hopes that "the old man eloquent" had still some years of life before him.

He had in fact six months, but there was no final yielding to the last heavy blow that had saddened him, and no pitiful decay.

ii

Knight, as he tells us in his *Life* of Wordsworth, once formed a project of collecting all the notices of him by his contemporaries, but abandoned it on realizing the amount of material available. How much excuse he had may be judged by reference to the volume published by Dr Elsie Smith in 1932, which covers only the years up to 1822, and those not with completeness. But Knight may also have shrunk from entering into a discussion of the relative value of these notices. If we consider merely those which attempt to delineate Wordsworth's character, we can make out two portraits which contradict each other in almost every feature. Of one Wordsworth we have seen something in the first part of this chapter: a man who, like Mr Bernard Shaw's Shakespeare, scorning the modest cough of the minor poet, yet did not put forward his own poetry or his own poetical views unless others showed signs of wishing to hear them; who was unusually ready to receive criticism which was honestly meant; who was remarkably kind and encouraging to younger men; whose interests were not narrow in any sense; who was admired for the fairness and openness of his mind, particularly on political and religious questions of controversy, by men who differed widely from him and among themselves. The other Wordsworth is a man who, considering himself the greatest poet of his age, was egotistic and ungenerous in his attitude to his contemporaries, dogmatic, impatient of criticism, narrow in his interests, a bigot in religion, a renegade, or at best a faintheart, in politics.

How are the contradictions to be explained? They cannot be reconciled: it is, for example, the attempt to reconcile a modified form of the "lost leader" tradition with such evidence as that of John Stuart Mill which makes the latter part of Professor Harper's biography bewildering. But there must be some explanation, and it need not be entirely dishonourable to human nature. Knight's decision seems to have been to ignore what seemed to him false representations, and to attempt to tell of Wordsworth's life with no attention to his enemies. But this method is not satisfactory: it is possible to see how the unfavourable portrait came to be drawn, and we ought, in justice to everyone concerned, not to Wordsworth alone, to consider it.

And in the first place it has not, I think, been noticed that whereas the sketches for the first portrait are spread over many years and come from a heterogeneous assemblage of people—political philosophers, poets, men of the world, men of science, intelligent women, none of them uncritical, all of marked independence of judgment—those for the second come from an almost homogeneous group of men of letters, most of whom were in close association, and that, with two or perhaps three exceptions,[1] they fall within a period of eight

[1] De Quincey and Landor, and perhaps Crabb Robinson in 1808. Cf. pp. 3–4 *supra* and pp. 89–94 *infra*.

years, from 1818 to 1825. The links which in those years connected Leigh Hunt, Keats, Haydon and Hazlitt are overlooked, and their pronouncements are regarded as being entirely independent of each other. As a fact, as we shall see, they are not. Through Leigh Hunt, again, Byron has some connection with the more closely knit group, but it will be more convenient to consider him separately, since his motives, though complicated, were not complicated by the same factor as theirs.

Byron and Wordsworth met at least once, probably, since the story comes from Lady Byron, in 1815. The record has been preserved in an unexpected place, Professor Augustus De Morgan's *Budget of Paradoxes*.[1]

Mr Crabb Robinson told me the following story more than once. He was at Charles Lamb's chambers in the Temple when Wordsworth came in, with the new *Edinburgh Review* in his hand,[2] and fume on his countenance. "These reviewers", said he, "put me out of patience! Here is a young man—they say he is a lord—who has written a volume of poetry; and these fellows, just because he is a lord, set upon him, laugh at him, and sneer at his writing. The young man will do something, if he goes on as he has begun. But these reviewers seem to think that nobody may write poetry, unless he lives in a garret." Crabb Robinson told this long after to Lady Byron, who said, "Ah! if Byron had known that, he would never have attacked Wordsworth. He went one day to meet Wordsworth at dinner; when he came home I said, 'Well, how did the young poet get on with the old one?' 'Why, to

[1] Ed. 1872, p. 435.

[2] This fixes the date, and explains why Crabb Robinson remembered the incident so vividly. The review of Byron appeared in March 1808 and Crabb Robinson first met Wordsworth at Lamb's on March 15 (cf. p. 2 *supra*). This indignant defence of Byron may have been the first words he heard Wordsworth utter.

tell you the truth', said he, 'I had but one feeling from the beginning of the visit to the end, and that was—*reverence*!'" Lady Byron told my wife that her husband had a very great respect for Wordsworth.

If this was so, Byron took an odd way of showing his respect. It would be too much to say that he is invariably disrespectful in his allusions, but the most reverential notices of Wordsworth do not go far: those, for example, in the controversy with Bowles—the citation of *The Blind Highland Boy*, the acknowledgment of Wordsworth's right to have an opinion on scenery, and the contrast drawn between Leigh Hunt's occasional vulgarity and Wordsworth's complete lack of it in spite of his treating of "low life in all its branches".[1] But some of this was written with the object of annoying Leigh Hunt. It may be doubted whether Byron's real opinion of Wordsworth as a poet ever varied much from that expressed in his letters to Leigh Hunt (October 7 and 30, 1815) on the revised *Feast of the Poets*, and the repetition of these in the letter to Moore of June 1, 1818. From the letter to Moore one significant sentence may be quoted: "Let them take Scott, Campbell, Crabbe, or you, or me, or any of the living, and throne him; but not this new Jacob Behmen, this * * * * whose pride might have kept him true, even had his principles turned as perverted as his *soi-disant* poetry".

Whose pride might have kept him true: Byron recognized in Wordsworth a pride and a spirit at least as lofty as his own. Lady Byron was probably right in her belief that Byron would not have attacked Wordsworth if he had known of Wordsworth's championship of him. But, ignorant of any personal motive for moderation, he had, apart from his misunder-

[1] *Letters and Journals*, v, 546, 588, 591.

standing of Wordsworth's political views, at least three possible motives for attack. The first was that reverence to which he confessed after their meeting. Reverence was neither a common nor a welcome feeling with him, and it would not be surprising if it were followed by a strong reaction. Next there may have been a touch of Haman's feeling towards Mordecai. "And all the king's servants, that were in the king's gate, bowed and reverenced Haman: for the king had so commanded concerning him. But Mordecai bowed not, nor did him reverence....And when Haman saw that Mordecai bowed not, nor did him reverence, then was Haman full of wrath." And, finally, no abuse that Byron published had the slightest apparent effect on Wordsworth. Southey could be goaded into public controversy, but however outrageous the accusations and insinuations in *Don Juan* might be in their attacks upon Wordsworth's political honesty and private character, they were received with a silence which must have been intensely exasperating. Wordsworth himself considered that there was a further reason for the attacks in a private letter of his own, of which Byron heard through Rogers, and in which Wordsworth had spoken of Byron's "perverted feelings".[1] Rogers was certainly culpably careless in such matters: Crabb Robinson ultimately traced back to him[2] the report, the truth of which

[1] Crabb Robinson, *Diary*, June 16, 1833; Moore, *Diary*, February 20, 1833.

[2] *Diary*, June 16, 1833, and note added in 1850; September 20 and December 13, 1836. The entry of September 20, 1836, gives a particularly good example of "Russian Scandal": "Moore also repeated to Lord Byron what Rogers told Moore Wordsworth had said of Southey's poetry". There seems also to have been some wresting of words in a letter: "It was not Rogers himself but Moore

Wordsworth indignantly denied, that Wordsworth had said he would not give five shillings for Southey's poetry—a report of which both Byron and Landor made full use. This does not necessarily mean that Rogers himself attributed the actual speech to Wordsworth; indeed, he told Crabb Robinson that Byron had misrepresented him. A polite silence—such as struck William Taylor of Norwich as remarkable when Southey's supremacy in historical prose and in poetry was asserted[1]—may easily have led to "Wordsworth obviously would not give five shillings", and that, without deliberate lying by anyone, to "Wordsworth says he would not give five shillings". Rogers, without always intending them, did almost as many injuries as kindnesses to his friends.

Imagination quails before the thought of what Byron would have said and written if he had known that Wordsworth's habitual refusal to take any notice of personal attacks was reinforced, in his case, by the belief that he was not altogether responsible for his actions. "We talked of Lord Byron",

who told Lord Byron of what Wordsworth had written about Southey which caused Lord Byron's abuse of Wordsworth". After this it is a relief to come to Southey's comment (January 16, 1837) on Landor's *Satire* (cf. pp. 91–4 *infra*): "He expressed his great regret at the publication—was sure it was founded on mistake, viz. the anecdote of what Wordsworth said of him".

[1] "He spoke of Wordsworth, praised his conversation, which he likes better than his poetry, says he is solid, dignified, simple, and eloquent. But he observed that Wordsworth seemed unwilling to render full justice to Southey. 'I told him', said William Taylor, 'I thought Southey the greatest poet and the greatest historian living, and he looked surprised.' 'No great matter of surprise', I answered, 'that Wordsworth should think himself a greater poet than Southey.' 'I never thought', replied Taylor, 'that he could presume to make any comparison.'" (Crabb Robinson, *Diary*, June 6, 1815.)

Crabb Robinson noted (May 23, 1812). "Wordsworth allowed him power, but denied his style to be English. Of his moral qualities we think the same. He adds that there is insanity in Lord Byron's family, and that he believes Lord Byron to be somewhat cracked." In writing to John Scott (April 18, 1816) when the Byron scandal was at its height and Byron's successive farewell verses to his wife were melting half England and revolting the other half, Wordsworth reverted to the same explanation. "The man is insane, and will probably end his career in a madhouse. . . . The verses on his private affairs excite in me less indignation than pity. The latter copy is the Billingsgate of Bedlam." *Don Juan* he afterwards, on general grounds of morality, characterized as "that infamous publication", which reviewers who attacked Shelley were too cowardly to condemn.[1] His letter to Rogers (January 21, 1825), written after reading Medwin's *Conversations*, is outspoken in its recognition in Byron of the coexistence of good and evil.[2]

I saw Southey the other day; he was well, and busy as usual, and as his late letter shows, not quite so charitably disposed to *Don Juan* deceased as you evidently are, if I may judge by a tribute to his memory bearing your name, which I accidentally met with in a newspaper; but *you* were the Don's particular friend. An equal indulgence, therefore, could not be expected from the laureate, who, I will not say was his particular enemy, but who had certainly no friendship for him. Medwin makes a despicable figure as the salesman of so much trash. I do not believe there is a man living, from a shoeblack at the corner of your street up to the Archbishop of Canterbury or the Lord Chancellor, of whose conversation so much worthless matter could be reported, with so little deserving

[1] *Letters*, II, 168. Knight was uncertain of the date of this letter.
[2] Cf. Appendix B.

to be remembered, as the result of an equal number of miscellaneous opportunities. Is this the fault of Lord B. or his Boswell? The truth is, I fear, that it may be pretty equally divided between them.

My amanuensis, Mrs W., says that it is not handsome in me to speak thus of your friend. No more it is, if he were your friend *mortuus*, in every sense of the word; but his spirit walks abroad, to do some good I hope, but a plaguey deal of mischief.

Byron, in spite of his recognition of Wordsworth's pride, had descended to mocking him as a needy dependent of Lord Lonsdale and Sir George Beaumont. Now the question of Wordsworth's independence in every respect is of real importance for the understanding of his relations with his literary contemporaries as well as of his political activities. Professor Harper, from whom one would not expect such an insinuation, writes in his revised *Life*,[1] "Gratitude towards the Lowther family and a sense of dependence upon persons so powerful to affect his wellbeing and that of his children... may have entered into Wordsworth's motives" in deciding him to write the pamphlets of 1818: as if Wordsworth had ever felt anything like the second emotion suggested. What surprised his contemporaries, who were prepared to find at least deference and polite yielding, was the complete absence of either in him when he was dealing with his richer friends. Thus Wilberforce recorded in his diary (June 9, 1815) that he had dined at Beaumont's to meet Wordsworth, who was "very manly, sensible, and full of knowledge, but independent almost to rudeness"—Wilberforce having obviously imagined that Beaumont stood to Wordsworth in the relation of kind and condescending patron. Thus again, Leigh Hunt recast the

[1] P. 549. Cf. pp. 157–8 and n. *infra*.

notes to *The Feast of the Poets*, and, while continuing to differ from him profoundly, went out of his way to do justice to Wordsworth's political independence,[1] the moment that he realized that Wordsworth was not a creature of Government —that is, of Lonsdale. There was between Wordsworth and his friends no relation of patron and patronized: the richer men knew how to perform, as Wordsworth knew how to accept, friendly offices, without the lowering of respect or friendship on either side. Wordsworth's letters to Lonsdale might serve as an illustration of Dr Johnson's remark about clearing one's mind of cant. "You may talk as other people do: you may say to a man, 'Sir, I am your most humble servant'. You are *not* his most humble servant....You may *talk* in this manner; it is a mode of talking in society: but don't *think* foolishly." Wordsworth may have signed himself "Your Lordship's most obedient and obliged", but neither he nor Lonsdale thought foolishly. His comment on Scott was to the point; and it should be remembered that he loved and honoured Scott. He was talking[2] of Lockhart's *Life*, which he, like everyone else, was reading or having read to him.

"Scott's sentiments (he said) sometimes shock me; and when I think of his free frank manner, of what an open creature he was, and then find that he was involved in all his load of concealment and evasion, it gives me great pain—it must do so to all his friends. The day before we parted he spoke to me much of his portion of happiness in life, which he considered great; but it appeared to me at the time that he did not truly estimate his position as a man of genius. He appeared to think that the condition of an official under Government, or

[1] Cf. Appendix A, pp. 351–6.

[2] Lady Richardson's diary, August 19, 1837; quoted in *Autobiography of Mrs Fletcher*, pp. 198–9, and in Knight's *Life*, III, 297–8.

that of a country gentleman, was a higher one than that of a man of genius." This, Wordsworth said, was the more extraordinary from Scott having been born in the rank of a gentleman, and therefore he ought more truly to have estimated the real state of the case.[1]

There was clearly not much chance of success for anyone who attempted to patronize a man who estimated so truly the real state of the case. But there are more kinds of patronage than one. This independence of Wordsworth's, in another manifestation, did him no good with Leigh Hunt.

For Leigh Hunt liked to think of himself as the discoverer and proclaimer of genius, a part which he played with credit towards Keats and Shelley and others besides, and he liked to have his good offices publicly recognized by those whom he discovered, or thought he discovered. I do not see any other explanation for his complaint in his *Autobiography*[2] against Wordsworth.

Nor do I believe, that from that day to this, he thought it becoming in him to reciprocate the least part of any benefit which a word in good season may have done for him. Lord Byron, in resentment for my having called him the "prince of the bards of his time", would not allow him to be even the "one-eyed monarch of the blind". He said he was the "blind monarch of the one-eyed".[3] I must still differ with his lordship on that point; but I must own, that, after all which I have seen and read, posterity, in my opinion, will differ not a little with one person respecting the amount of merit to be ascribed to Mr Wordsworth; though who that one person is, I shall leave the reader to discover.

[1] It is amusing to compare Scott's friendly criticism of Wordsworth as being "in society, *too much of the poet*" (Moore's *Diary*, June 10, 1828).

[2] Ed. 1850, II, 163–4; ed. 1860, pp. 247–8.

[3] See Byron to Leigh Hunt, October 7, 1815.

A graceful copy of complimentary verses, of the kind which Leigh Hunt himself bestowed upon and received from his friends: even, perhaps, a dedication: one can see what would have satisfied him. And Wordsworth, who wrote complimentary verses only when he sincerely felt complimentary, and dedicated his poems only to his closest friends, did not see what was expected of him. He had presented his works to Leigh Hunt and had called upon him, and that might have been considered sufficient acknowledgment to a man towards whom he felt no particular attraction. He did, in fact, give more, as Leigh Hunt himself knew but had, let us hope, forgotten when he wrote his *Autobiography*. There is a letter from Laman Blanchard to Hunt, preserved in Hunt's *Correspondence*,[1] which puts the matter beyond doubt.

> Among many other pleasures arising from some conversations with Mr Wordsworth when in town lately, I experienced a particular one in hearing him speak of you in a spirit the most kindly and grateful. No man has a greater *right* to speak so than he—but it is not always done; and I must confess that it did affect me much to hear from such lips an eulogism upon one to whom I am under infinite obligations for a long course of moral and literary tuition.

This was written on August 31, 1831. Wordsworth had written confidentially to Moxon on June 9, "Mr Leigh Hunt is a coxcomb, was a coxcomb, and ever will be a coxcomb"; but a coxcomb may have excellent qualities. Later in the year, the suggestion that Hunt was in need was enough to make Wordsworth overlook his coxcombry and a good deal more besides. When a subscription was raised for the publication of Hunt's collected poems, Forster reported to Bulwer Lytton that Wordsworth had "sent his illustrious name in a

[1] I, 262.

very admirable way",[1] and part of the letter in which this was done is preserved in Leigh Hunt's *Correspondence*.[2]

Mr Wordsworth, giving his name to the subscription, in a note, dated Rydal Mount, December 19th, 1831, said he was much concerned to learn that Mr Leigh Hunt was suffering from ill health and embarrassed circumstances. He regretted that he could do little more than contribute his subscription, on account of his sequestered situation. "The consideration", he observed, "of Mr Hunt being a man of genius and talents in distress, will, I trust, prevent your proposal being taken as a test of opinion, and that the benevolent purpose will be promoted by men of all parties."

Whether Wordsworth knew it or not, that ungrammatical comment hit Southey, whose rigid conscience made him refuse to give his name to the subscription.[3] Wordsworth took the sensible and charitable view that in testimonials of this sort, as in lapidary inscriptions, a man is not upon oath.

It is perhaps a digression, but if so the digression is worth making, to point out that this business of the subscription for Leigh Hunt emphasizes the improbability of Professor Harper's suggestion[4] that Wordsworth's name does not appear on the subscription list for Godwin in 1822 because he had come to disapprove of Godwin's political opinions. Wordsworth may have been unable to help at a date when his sons were at the most expensive age, or he may have helped privately as he helped Gillies: we have neither right nor reason to impute ungenerous motives to him.

Wordsworth was not without recognition of Leigh Hunt's services either to him or to literature: he repaid them in a

[1] Sadleir, *Bulwer... Edward and Rosina*, p. 293.

[2] I, 265. [3] Southey to Moxon, December 10, 1831.

[4] 1929 ed., p. 573.

practical way in 1831, by personal thanks, and by friendly utterances such as that which Laman Blanchard reported, or that other which Leigh Hunt himself records, when he took down a volume of Hunt's poems from a shelf at a bookseller's, "to show some persons how swimming ought to be described; —to wit, after the manner of the passage in Hero and Leander".[1] Leigh Hunt, in his turn, either deliberately concealed all this, or, as we may hope, forgot it. But forgetfulness of this kind is hardly innocent. The explanation may be—it is difficult to find any other—that he resented the absence of such personal intimacy with Wordsworth as he had enjoyed with Shelley and Keats, and was not happy in recollecting the part which he himself had played towards Wordsworth and Hazlitt. It was pleasanter to blame Wordsworth than himself.

A comparison of the accounts given by B. R. Haydon, Leigh Hunt and Wordsworth of the intercourse of these three during the summer of 1815 will help to make the position clear. Haydon may begin the story. He was already well acquainted with Wordsworth, whom he seems to have met for the first time at Sir George Beaumont's several years earlier, and on May 13[2] Wordsworth arrived at his house to have a cast made of his face. He endured the operation with admirable patience, and then—

came into breakfast with his usual cheerfulness and delighted us by his bursts of inspiration.[3]

[1] Leigh Hunt to De Wilde, June 6, 1859.

[2] Accepting Professor Harper's correction: Haydon wrote April 13, but Wordsworth did not arrive in London until the beginning of May. He left his card on Crabb Robinson on May 7. Haydon's next entry is for May 23.

[3] With this and what follows cf. Wilberforce's diary for May 29: "Wordsworth the poet breakfasted with us, and walked garden—and it being the first time, staid long—much pleased with him". There was little in common between Haydon and Wilberforce.

After breakfast they went to call on Leigh Hunt, and—

here again he really burst forth with burning feelings; I never heard him so eloquent before. I afterwards sauntered along with him to West-end Lane and so on to Hampstead, with great delight. Never did any man so beguile the time as Wordsworth. His purity of heart, his kindness, his soundness of principle, his information, his knowledge, and the intense and eager feelings with which he pours forth all he knows affect, interest and enchant one.

The frank, unguarded talker who delighted Haydon did not give the same pleasure to Leigh Hunt. But Leigh Hunt's mind, when he came to write down his account of the visit, many years later, was not so much at ease with regard to Wordsworth as Haydon's was.

He came to thank me for the zeal I had shown in advocating the cause of his genius. I had the pleasure of showing him his book on my shelves by the side of Milton; a sight which must have been the more agreeable, inasmuch as the visit was unexpected. He favoured me, in return, with giving his opinion of some of the poets his contemporaries, who would assuredly not have paid him a visit on the same grounds on which he was pleased to honour myself....[He] had a dignified manner, with a deep and roughish but not unpleasing voice, and an exalted mode of speaking. He had a habit of keeping his left hand in the bosom of his waistcoat, and in this attitude, except when he turned round to take one of the subjects of his criticism from the shelves (for his contemporaries were there also), he sat dealing forth his eloquent but hardly catholic judgements. In his "father's house" there were not "many mansions". He was as sceptical on the merits of all kinds of poetry but one, as Richardson was on those of the novels of Fielding.[1]

"I did not see this distinguished person again till nearly

[1] *Autobiography*, ed. 1850, II, 163–5; ed. 1860, 247–8.

thirty years afterwards", Leigh Hunt continues, not quite accurately, unless his meaning is that after the summer of 1815 he did not meet Wordsworth again for nearly thirty years. There was at least one other meeting in 1815, but this had such unpleasant associations that Leigh Hunt may have been reluctant to recall it. On Sunday, June 11, Hazlitt attacked Wordsworth violently in *The Examiner*. On the same day Wordsworth called on Leigh Hunt, and later in the week, on the 15th, he mentioned the visit to Crabb Robinson. Hunt, he said,

in a manly way asked whether Wordsworth had seen the paper of the morning; saying, if he had, he should consider his call as a higher honour. He disclaimed the article. The attack by Hazlitt was a note, in which, after honouring Milton for being a consistent patriot, he sneered at Wordsworth as the author of "paltry sonnets upon the Royal fortitude", etc., and insinuated that he had left out the "Female Vagrant", a poem describing the miseries of war sustained by the poor.

A good deal lay behind that attack, and though Hunt may not have done his duty as an editor in his hasty disclaimer, it is possible to understand that he felt himself unable to stand by his contributor. Crabb Robinson, giving us Wordsworth's explanation, says that when Hazlitt was in the Lake District in 1803 he "narrowly escaped being ducked by the populace and probably sent to prison for some gross attacks on women", the exact offence being veiled in shorthand and the decent obscurity of a learned language. The shorthand is not indecipherable, as Mr P. P. Howe supposed;[1] the Key, like the MS. of Crabb Robinson's diary, may be consulted in Dr Williams's Library; but there is no need to decipher it here. "The populace were incensed against him and pursued him",

[1] *Life of Hazlitt*, p. 80.

Crabb Robinson continues, "but he escaped to Wordsworth, who took him into his house at midnight, gave him clothes and money." Coleridge's version of the incident, contained in letters to Hugh James Rose (September 17, 1816) and Wrangham (June 5, 1817),[1] dovetails into Wordsworth's: Hazlitt had been "snatched from an infamous punishment" by Southey and himself when "men on horses" were in search of him, and Coleridge had given him all the money he had in the world and the very shoes off his feet to enable him to escape "over the mountains". This is consistent with Hazlitt's having been in need of more money and clothes when he came "over the mountains" to Wordsworth at Grasmere in the middle of the night. Coleridge would not set down Hazlitt's offence in black and white, because "the detail outraged modesty". He and Southey afterwards took the same attitude to Hazlitt as Wordsworth did, namely a "quiet withdrawing from any further connection with him (and this without any ostentation, or any mark of shyness when we accidentally met him)". Or, as Wordsworth expressed it to Crabb Robinson—

though he never refused to meet [Hazlitt] when by accident they came together,[2] [he] did not choose that with his knowledge he should be invited. In consequence Lamb never asked Hazlitt while Wordsworth was in town, which probably provoked Hazlitt, and which Lamb himself disapproved of.[3]

[1] *Unpublished Letters*, ed. E. Leslie Griggs.

[2] As, for instance, they did at Lamb's on April 19, 1808, when Wordsworth rather reluctantly read some of *The White Doe of Rylstone*.

[3] Alsop, though he was not always a trustworthy witness, can be cited for additional confirmation. He noted (I, 218) that Lamb attributed Hazlitt's secession "to pique that he had not been asked to meet Wordsworth. He had also accused Lamb of not seeing him

But Lamb, who needs very little indulgence for himself, is very indulgent towards others, and rather reproaches Wordsworth for being inveterate against Hazlitt.

It is not clear whether the last sentence is Wordsworth's comment or Crabb Robinson's: it is in keeping with the tenderness of all Wordsworth's references to Lamb,[1] but Crabb Robinson may equally well have added it.

There is no evidence that Wordsworth gave Lamb, earlier than 1814, detailed reasons for not wishing to meet Hazlitt, and Lamb's letter of December 28, 1814, implies that he had not done so. Nor have I found evidence that Wordsworth ever told the full story to anyone but Lamb and, in this moment of confidence, Crabb Robinson. And finally, I can discover no evidence that Wordsworth was, as Mr Howe suggests, "smarting under the sense that Hazlitt was no fit person to review his *Excursion*", or that it was Hazlitt's review which was the cause of Wordsworth's request to Lamb that he and Hazlitt should not be asked to meet each other.[2] His visit to Leigh Hunt certainly indicates no displeasure at the review; Dorothy Wordsworth, writing to Mrs Clarkson (October 9, 1814), expressed some disappointment that Hazlitt had, as she thought, shown less discernment than might have been expected of him, but that is a very different matter. Wordsworth's letter to Lamb, to which Lamb's of December 28 is a reply, appears to be lost, or, more probably, was destroyed: the expressions in Lamb's letter make it doubtful whether

when with Wordsworth in Holborn. Lamb was most pleased with Wordsworth's attentions, saying, 'He gave me more than half the time he was in London, when he is supposed to be with the Lowthers'". This seems to have been in 1820.

[1] Cf., e.g., *Lines written after the Death of Charles Lamb*, ll. 32–7.

[2] *Life of Hazlitt*, pp. 79, 188–9.

Wordsworth did more than give historical reasons why Hazlitt's favourable review of *The Excursion* had made no difference to his reluctance to meet Hazlitt.

Mr Howe does his best to defend Hazlitt and to discredit Wordsworth's testimony: Coleridge's letters, which have been quoted above, were not published when the *Life of Hazlitt* was written, and Mr Howe was rightly distrustful of what appeared to be mere gossip of the Gillmans.[1] It may still be argued that what Coleridge, who was not invariably accurate in his statements, wrote in 1816 and 1817, with reference to events of 1803 which he thought explained Hazlitt's hostility to him, should be taken with caution, and there is some point in the argument. But what Coleridge wrote to Rose and Wrangham, what we can infer from Lamb's letter that Wordsworth wrote in the lost letter to Lamb, and what Wordsworth said to Crabb Robinson, are in too close agreement to be ignored or easily set aside. That Southey, writing to Richard Duppa six weeks after Hazlitt's departure, does not mention the incident, but calls him a man of genius, proves nothing either way. It is impossible, as Mr Howe sees, to imitate the amiable habit of Jane Bennet, and seek to clear one party without involving the other. We have to believe either that Hazlitt was in fact guilty of discreditable behaviour at Keswick, or that Wordsworth and Coleridge were deliberately exaggerating an unfortunate but harmless love affair. It is not without significance that Hazlitt did not seek any explanation from them, and it is difficult not to conclude that he did not need one: he realized why they were avoiding his company.

Not the weakest argument in favour of this view of the

1 *Ibid.* pp. 80–1.

quarrel, if it can be called a quarrel, is Wordsworth's tolerance. He had grown up in a robust peasant society, and he was not easily shocked. His sympathy for those for whom the flesh was too strong has scandalized many worthy persons: it comes out in his defence of Burns, which goes very near antinomianism; again in *The Waggoner*—Burns himself, as Hale White remarked, could not have loved Benjamin more than Wordsworth did; in a slightly different form, as an enjoyment of lawlessness, in his praise of Rob Roy; and in "that delicacy towards aberrations from the strict path" which Lamb noted in *The Farmer of Tilsbury Vale*, and in *The Two Thieves*.[1] And this sympathy did not weaken with age: it caused, for example, real distress and perplexity to Harriet Martineau, who might note with approval that "in regard to politics...and even to religion, he grew more and more liberal in his latter years",[2] but did not approve of the same liberality in other manifestations. As she indignantly protested—[3]

> I, deaf, can hardly conceive how he, with eyes and ears and a heart which leads him to converse with the poor in his incessant walks, can be so unaware of their social state. I dare say you need not be told how sensual vice abounds in rural districts. Here, it is flagrant beyond any thing I ever could have looked for, and here, while every justice of the peace is filled with disgust and every clergyman with almost despair at the drunkenness, quarrels and extreme licentiousness with women—here is dear good old Wordsworth for ever talking of rural innocence and deprecating any intercourse with towns lest the purity of his neighbours should be corrupted.

[1] Lucas, VI, 461.

[2] *Autobiography*, II, 240.

[3] To Elizabeth Barrett, February 8, 1846; copied by Crabb Robinson, and printed in *Crabb Robinson Correspondence*, II, 620–2.

He little knows what elevation, self-denial and refinement accrue in towns from the superior cultivation of the people.

Wordsworth probably knew considerably more than Miss Martineau about the elevation, refinement and the cultivation of the people in the great manufacturing towns of Lancashire and Yorkshire, as well as the conditions of the Lake District. Like many people of advanced views, she was fundamentally respectable: he, like other prophets, knew that "sensual vice" is not the most soul-destroying.

But this was not a matter of "sensual vice" and passion: it was an offence against ordinary decency. Wordsworth helped Hazlitt out of the district, and quietly dropped any intimacy with him. Trouble was bound to follow when Hazlitt realized that he was being avoided, not by Wordsworth only, but by Southey and Coleridge as well, and the realization would seem to have come when Wordsworth called, to return his thanks for *The Examiner's* review of *The Excursion*, not upon the reviewer, but upon the editor of *The Examiner*. Hazlitt's attacks upon all three date from that moment.

Coleridge escaped at first, until the publication of *Christabel* gave Hazlitt his chance. But Southey and Wordsworth could be attacked at once, and the first blows fell in that article on the revival of *Comus* which appeared in *The Examiner* for June 11, 1815, and for which Leigh Hunt apologized to Wordsworth. Milton, says Hazlitt, "did not retract his defence of the people of England; he did not say that his sonnets to Vane or Cromwell were meant ironically; he was not appointed Poet Laureat to a Court which he had reviled and insulted". So far Southey is the victim, but here Wordsworth joins him. "He accepted neither place nor pension; nor did he write paltry sonnets upon the 'Royal fortitude' of the

House of Stuart, by which, however, they really lost something." And then comes the footnote, that his readers may be in no doubt of his meaning—

In the last edition of the Works of a modern Poet there is a Sonnet to the King, complimenting him on "his royal fortitude", and (somewhat prematurely) on the triumphs resulting from it. The story of the *Female Vagrant*, which very beautifully and affectingly describes the miseries brought on the lower classes by war, in bearing which the said "royal fortitude" is so nobly exercised, is very properly struck out of the collection.

This is unjust,[1] but comparatively mild. In the lectures on the English poets, delivered early in 1818 and published in the same year, Hazlitt let himself go, not so much against Southey and Coleridge as against Wordsworth. His greater fury against Wordsworth is not difficult to understand: Southey came seldom to London, Coleridge went little into society, but Wordsworth came to London more often and stayed longer than is usually recognized, and he did not lead a secluded life when he was there. It is evidence of Wordsworth's tact that Hazlitt was so long in realizing that his company was not desired; but once the fact was realized, every sight of Wordsworth in the street, every accidental encounter in a friend's house, must have been maddening, the more so since Wordsworth gave no excuse on such occasions for a personal outburst. It is not in the least surprising, and only interesting as indicating Wordsworth's indifference to attack, that Lamb should write to him (February 18, 1818), "W. H. goes on lecturing against W. W. and making copious use of quotations from said W. W. to give zest to said lectures". W. W. was an obsession with W. H.: he

[1] Cf. pp. 122–3, 131–3 *infra*.

interrupted the argument, without being named, for a paragraph in the lecture on Shakespeare and Milton: his defence of Burns was misrepresented in the lecture on Burns and the Old English Ballads:[1] and he had to withstand Hazlitt's full and direct onslaught in the lecture on the living poets. The earlier part of the passage contains praise so high that the attack, when it comes, is all the more deadly.

Mr Wordsworth is at the head of that which has been denominated the Lake school of poetry....A thorough adept in this school of poetry and philanthropy is jealous of all excellence but his own. He does not even like to share his reputation with his subject; for he would have it all proceed from his own power and originality of mind. Such a one is slow to admire any thing that is admirable; feels no interest in what is most interesting to others, no grandeur in any thing grand, no beauty in anything beautiful. He tolerates only what he himself creates; he sympathizes only with what can enter into no competition with him, with "the bare trees and mountains bare, and grass in the green field". He sees nothing but himself and the universe. He hates all greatness and all pretensions to it, whether well or ill-founded. His egotism is in some respects a madness; for he scorns even the admiration of himself, thinking it a presumption in any one to suppose that he has taste or sense enough to understand him.[2]

[1] Wordsworth had written, for example, "It is probable that he would have proved a still greater poet if, by strength of reason, he could have controlled the propensities which his sensibility engendered; but he would have been a poet of a different class; and... had that desirable restraint been early established, many peculiar beauties which enrich his verses could never have existed". Hazlitt translates, "Burns would have written differently, and almost as well as *he* does". This is the mildest instance of Hazlitt's misrepresentation of Wordsworth's argument.

[2] In other words, "He did not thank me for my review of *The Excursion*".

He hates all science and all art; he hates chemistry, he hates conchology; he hates Voltaire; he hates Sir Isaac Newton; he hates wisdom; he hates wit; he hates metaphysics, which he says are unintelligible, and yet he would be thought to understand them; he hates prose; he hates all poetry but his own; he hates the dialogues in Shakespeare; he hates music, dancing, and painting; he hates Rubens, he hates Rembrandt; he hates Raphael, he hates Titian; he hates Vandyke; he hates the antique; he hates the Apollo Belvidere; he hates the Venus of Medicis. This is the reason that so few people take an interest in his writings, because he takes an interest in nothing that others do!

This, as Wordsworth remarked to Wrangham on another occasion, is very fair for pointing a sentence, but it is not the truth.[1] It would be easy to take it clause by clause, and show how in each Hazlitt has either set down the exact contrary to the truth, or twisted a half-truth into a falsehood. It would be easy, but it is not necessary: Hazlitt himself, in *The Spirit of the Age*, has saved us even that trouble.

His standard of poetry is high and severe, almost to exclusiveness. He admits of nothing below, scarcely of any thing above himself. . . . Milton is his great idol, and he sometimes dares to compare himself with him. His Sonnets, indeed, have something of the same high-raised tone and prophetic spirit. Chaucer is another prime favourite of his, and he has been at the pains to modernize some of the Canterbury Tales. Those persons who look upon Mr Wordsworth as a merely puerile writer, must be rather at a loss to account for his strong predilection for such geniuses as Dante and Michael Angelo. We do not think our author has any very cordial sympathy with Shakespear. How should he? Shakespear was the least of an egotist of any body in the world. He does not much relish the variety and scope of dramatic com-

[1] Wordsworth to Wrangham, December 3, 1808.

position. "He hates those interlocutions between Lucius and Caius." Yet Mr Wordsworth himself wrote a tragedy when he was young....Our critic has a great dislike to Gray, and a fondness for Thomson and Collins. It is mortifying to hear him speak of Pope and Dryden, whom, because they have been supposed to have all the possible excellences of poetry, he will allow to have none.[1] Nothing, however, can be fairer, or more amusing, than the way in which he sometimes exposes the unmeaning verbiage of modern poetry....Mr Wordsworth is, we must say, a perfect Drawcansir as to prose writers. He complains of the dry reasoners and matter-of-fact people for their want of *passion*; and he is jealous of the rhetorical declaimers and rhapsodists as touching on the province of poetry. He condemns all French writers (as well of poetry as prose) in the lump. His list in this way is indeed small. He approves of Walton's Angler, Paley, and some other writers of an inoffensive modesty of pretension. He also likes books of voyages and travels, and Robinson Crusoe. In art, he greatly esteems Bewick's woodcuts, and Waterloo's sylvan etchings. But he sometimes takes a higher tone, and gives his mind fair play. We have known him enlarge with a noble intelligence and enthusiasm on Nicholas Poussin's fine landscape-compositions, pointing out the unity of design that pervades them, the superintending mind, the imaginative principle that brings all to bear on the same end; and declaring he would not give a rush for any landscape that did not express the time of day, the climate, the period of the world it was meant to illustrate, or had not this character of *wholeness* in it. His eye also does justice to Rembrandt's fine and masterly effects. In the way in which that artist works some-

[1] For Wordsworth's real opinion of Pope and Dryden, *vide* the marginal note on the MS. of Barron Field's *Memoir* (quoted by Knight, *Letters*, III, 122), which refers directly to Hazlitt's statement; the letters to Scott of January 18 and August 4, 1808; the 1815 *Preface*—whose praise of Pope's art is not outdone even by Miss Edith Sitwell; the letter to Dyce of January 12, 1829; and cf. p. 376 *infra*.

thing out of nothing, and transforms the stump of a tree, a common figure into an *ideal* object, by the gorgeous light and shade thrown upon it, he perceives an analogy to his own mode of investing the minute details of nature with an atmosphere of sentiment; and in pronouncing Rembrandt to be a man of genius, feels that he strengthens his own claim to the title. It has been said of Mr Wordsworth, that "he hates conchology, that he hates the Venus of Medicis". But these, we hope, are mere epigrams and *jeux-d'esprit*, as far from truth as they are free from malice; a sort of running satire or critical clenches—

> "Where one for sense and one for rhyme
> Is quite sufficient at one time."

A reader who found no malice in the first passage would find no grudging in the second, and one would like Hazlitt better if he had either maintained the heat of his fury or apologized frankly. Yet, in his own distorted fashion, he did try to apologize, and the inferences need only to be drawn: a man who admires Dante, Milton, Chaucer, Thomson, Collins, Isaac Walton and Defoe in literature, Michael Angelo, Nicholas Poussin and Rembrandt in art, cannot fairly be accused of narrowness of appreciation; and if he is supposed to admire the great because he feels his kinship with them, there seems a certain want of logic in suggesting that he likes smaller writers because they cannot be his rivals. Hazlitt, in fact, cannot have it both ways. And, as usually happens, the half-hearted retractation has not effected its purpose: Hazlitt's denunciation of a bloodless, rigid, narrow, egotistic Wordsworth is still quoted as an authority for further denunciation.

For support of Hazlitt's statements we are sometimes referred to Keats and Haydon.[1] But the time when Hazlitt's

[1] Less frequently to Landor and De Quincey, who are more generally recognized as questionable witnesses. Cf. pp. 89–94 *infra*.

hatred for Wordsworth reached its fullest expression coincides exactly with the time of Keats's personal intercourse with Wordsworth and the time when Keats's admiration for Hazlitt was at its height, though he had ceased to admire Leigh Hunt.[1] It coincides also with the period of Haydon's closest intimacy with Leigh Hunt. The letters of Keats and the journal of Haydon were written in good faith, but they are too often read without consideration of the influences which may have affected them, without reflection that they may need revision or expansion, and without attention to evidence which sometimes flatly contradicts the impression which they give.

No one would deny, for example, that Wordsworth had a high opinion of his own powers. It is sometimes forgotten that Keats also had a high opinion of his own powers, and that in the Leigh Hunt circle he had grown accustomed to the full recognition of them. It is frequently forgotten that Keats was young enough to be Wordsworth's son, and that Wordsworth would naturally look upon him at first as a very young man who had already written some good poetry. It is very doubtful whether he had read the *Poems* of 1817 before they met: when he, as we are told, characterized the *Hymn to Pan* as "a very pretty piece of paganism"—which it is—it is exceedingly doubtful whether he had heard any more of *Endymion.* When Keats accuses Wordsworth of egotism, we listen without much question, and it does not occur to us that

[1] Cf., e.g., his letter to George and Georgiana Keats of February 14–March 13, 1819, in which he sets forth the grounds on which he deserves charity, among them that "he doth not admire Sheil's play, Leigh Hunt, Tom Moore, Bob Southey, and Mr Rogers; and does admire Wm. Hazlitt; moreoverer, for as more as he liketh half of Wordsworth, and none of Crabbe", etc., etc. As early as 1817 he had realized Leigh Hunt's "self-delusions".

Keats was not altogether free from egotism in taking offence at that criticism, and that on the only occasion when we have any detailed record of their conversation in a mixed company, it was Keats, and not Wordsworth, who remembered his own poetry.[1]

For direct evidence of Wordsworth's egotism and impatience of criticism, we are sometimes referred to Keats's letter to his brothers (February 21, 1818), in which he writes, "I am sorry that Wordsworth has left a bad impression wherever he visited in town by his egotism, Vanity, and bigotry"; and that to Haydon (April 8): "I am afraid Wordsworth went rather huff'd out of Town—I am sorry for it—he cannot expect his fireside Divan to be infallible—he cannot expect but that every man of worth is as proud as himself". As to the first assertion, it is enough to note that Wordsworth's circle was considerably larger than that of Keats. The second is at least partly explained by the fact that when Wordsworth left London, early in 1818, Hazlitt was making his attacks on him in the lectures on the English poets. A young man, a fervent admirer of Hazlitt, might well suppose that Wordsworth would be "huff'd": actually he took no more notice of them than of the attacks by Byron and Shelley. And just as in later years, as R. P. Graves observed, he never spoke otherwise than kindly of Byron and Shelley, so, after Hazlitt's

[1] Cf. p. 82 *infra*. It is only fair to Keats to point out that one of his phrases, "the Wordsworthian or egotistical Sublime" (to Woodhouse, October 27, 1818), is often applied in a sense in which he never intended it. He is distinguishing the two classes of poets, those who are always themselves, and those who have something of the nature of the chameleon. Wordsworth made the same distinction (*Memoirs*, II, 437), and would have acknowledged his own description; cf. pp. 374–5 *infra*.

death, he made no reference to his attacks, but wrote to his son (May 23, 1834) a friendly letter which dealt only with their acquaintance before 1803.

The most curious and definite evidence of the weight which Hazlitt's judgment carried, even with those who did not altogether like him, is to be found in B. R. Haydon's *Journals* and *Autobiography*. Their intercourse began in 1812, but ended not without anger a little while before Hazlitt's death in 1830. In 1818, however, there was no suggestion of estrangement.

Now in 1815, as we have seen, Haydon found Wordsworth the most delightful of companions,[1] and was almost inclined, in his enthusiasm, to worship him as a purified being. In December 1817 we have still the same Wordsworth, taking his full share in the joys and difficulties of what Haydon thenceforward called "the immortal dinner". His account of it was written up for the *Autobiography* in 1841, and may contain a little reminiscent exaggeration, but if not every glorious detail is true to fact, it yet has the accent of truth, and it can to some extent be checked by Keats's letter to his brothers of January 5, 1818. The date of the dinner was Sunday, December 28, and the guests originally invited were Keats, Lamb, Landseer, Monkhouse and Wordsworth.

> Wordsworth was in fine cue, and we had a glorious set-to—on Homer, Shakespeare, Milton and Virgil. Lamb got exceedingly merry and exquisitely witty; and his fun in the midst of Wordsworth's solemn intonations of oratory was like the sarcasm and wit of the fool in the intervals of Lear's passion. He made a speech and voted me absent, and made them drink my health. "Now", said Lamb, "you old lake poet, you rascally poet, why do you call Voltaire dull?" We

[1] Cf. pp. 64–5 *supra*.

all defended Wordsworth, and affirmed there was a state of mind when Voltaire would be dull. "Well," said Lamb, "here's Voltaire—the Messiah of the French nation, and a very proper one too."

He then, in a strain of humour beyond description, abused me for putting Newton's head into my picture; "a fellow", said he, "who believed nothing unless it was as clear as the three sides of a triangle". And then he and Keats agreed he had destroyed all the poetry of the rainbow by reducing it to the prismatic colours. It was impossible to resist him, and we all drank "Newton's health, and confusion to mathematics". It was delightful to see the good humour of Wordsworth in giving in to all our frolics without affectation and laughing as heartily as the best of us.

By this time other friends joined, amongst them poor Ritchie who was going to penetrate by Fezzan to Timbuctoo. I introduced him to all as "a gentleman going to Africa". Lamb seemed to take no notice; but all of a sudden he roared out: "Which is the gentleman we are going to lose?" We then drank the victim's health, in which Ritchie joined.

In the morning of this delightful day, a gentleman, a perfect stranger, had called on me. He said he knew my friends, had an enthusiasm for Wordsworth, and begged I would procure him the happiness of an introduction. He told me he was a comptroller of stamps, and often had correspondence with the poet. I thought it a liberty; but still, as he seemed a gentleman, I told him he might come.

When we retired to tea we found the comptroller. In introducing him to Wordsworth I forgot to say who he was. After a little time the comptroller looked down, looked up and said to Wordsworth: "Don't you think, sir, Milton was a great genius?" Keats looked at me, Wordsworth looked at the comptroller. Lamb who was dozing by the fire turned round and said: "Pray, sir, did you say Milton was a great genius?" "No, sir; I asked Mr Wordsworth if he were not." "Oh," said Lamb, "then you are a silly fellow." "Charles! my dear Charles!" said Wordsworth; but Lamb, perfectly innocent of the confusion he had created, was off again by the fire.

After an awful pause the comptroller said: "Don't you think Newton a great genius?" I could not stand it any longer. Keats put his head into my books. Ritchie squeezed in a laugh. Wordsworth seemed asking himself: "Who is this?" Lamb got up, and taking a candle, said: "Sir, will you allow me to look at your phrenological development?"[1] He then turned his back on the poor man, and at every question of the comptroller he chaunted:

> "Diddle diddle dumpling, my son John
> Went to bed with his breeches on".

The man in office, finding Wordsworth did not know who he was, said in a spasmodic and half-chuckling anticipation of assured victory: "I have had the honour of some correspondence with you, Mr Wordsworth". "With me, sir?" said Wordsworth, "not that I remember." "Don't you, sir? I am a comptroller of stamps." There was a dead silence, the comptroller evidently thinking that was enough. While we were waiting for Wordsworth's reply, Lamb sung out:

> "Hey diddle diddle,
> The cat and the fiddle".

"My dear Charles!" said Wordsworth.

"Diddle diddle dumpling, my son John", chaunted Lamb, and then rising, exclaimed: "Do let me have another look at that gentleman's organs". Keats and I hurried Lamb into the painting-room, shut the door and gave way to inextinguishable laughter. Monkhouse followed, and tried to get Lamb away. We went back, but the comptroller was irreconcilable. We soothed and smiled and asked him to supper. He stayed though his dignity was sorely affected. However, being a

[1] Keats preserves Lamb's accents: "Lamb got tipsey and blew up Kingston—proceeding so far as to take the Candle across the Room hold it to his face and show us wh-a-at-sort-fello-he-waas".

good-natured man, we parted all in good humour, and no ill effects followed.[1]

All the while, until Monkhouse succeeded, we could hear Lamb struggling in the painting-room and calling at intervals: "Who is that fellow? Allow me to see his organs once more".

It was indeed an immortal evening. Wordsworth's fine intonation as he quoted Milton and Virgil, Keats' eager inspired look, Lamb's quaint sparkle of lambent humour, so speeded the stream of conversation, that in my life I never passed a more delightful time. All our fun was within bounds. Not a word passed that an apostle might not have listened to. It was a night worthy of the Elizabethan age, and my solemn Jerusalem flashing up by the flame of the fire, with Christ hanging over us like a vision, all made up a picture which will long glow upon

"that inward eye
Which is the bliss of solitude".

Keats made Ritchie promise he would carry his *Endymion* to the great desert of Sahara and fling it in the midst.

Poor Ritchie went to Africa, and died, as Lamb foresaw, in 1819. Keats died in 1821, at Rome. C. Lamb is gone, joking to the last. Monkhouse is dead, and Wordsworth and I are the only two now living (1841) of that glorious party.

A fortnight later Haydon was writing to Keats of Wordsworth, "I reverence him and love him devotedly".[2] But the next references to Wordsworth in the printed *Journals* are in

[1] Wordsworth carried matters so far as to dine with the offender and victim on the following Saturday, an act of courtesy of which Keats makes not very gracious fun (January 5 and April 8, 1818). But Keats's letter of January 5 does not support Dilke's account of his first call on Wordsworth—which suggests extraordinary egotism on Keats's part. Why should Wordsworth insult his host by arriving late, because Keats called on him just before dinner? Dilke is probably mistaken: at least we may hope so.

[2] *Letters of Keats*, I, 84 n.

an entirely different tone. The good-humoured, unaffected figure, willing to laugh at himself as well as other people, who can be matched from other witnesses, turns into something like the figure painted by Hazlitt, remains thus for about ten years, and then, with equal rapidity, turns back into the first figure.

Thus in 1821 we have a comparison between Wordsworth and Scott, decidedly to the disadvantage of Wordsworth, and in 1824 a series of really obscure and puzzling entries. On March 3 Wordsworth called on Haydon, and they had a friendly discussion on art. A few weeks later[1] Haydon records some notes of Moore's conversation, remarking parenthetically that Moore never talked of his own works, "from intense consciousness that everyone else did, while Wordsworth is always talking of his own productions from apprehension that they are not enough matter of conversation". From this he comes to two anecdotes about Wordsworth, of which one is Moore's and the other his own. Moore's may be relegated to a footnote: it was hearsay even to him, and possibly to his informant, and what the soldier said is not evidence.[2] Haydon's story is at least first-hand.

[1] On March 23, 1824. The month is supplied by inference from Moore's diary, Moore not having been in London on April 23. He dined at the Davys' on March 22, and Haydon may be included in his "etc."

[2] Moore tells the story in his diary for October 27, 1820, having heard it from Lady Davy, who may have been present herself or may have heard it from her husband. The story is intended to illustrate Wordsworth's high opinion of himself, and tells how he leaned forward at dinner and said to Davy, nothing having led up to the question, "Do you know the reason why I published the *White Doe* in quarto?" "No, what was it?" "To show the world my own opinion of it." Moore does not explain the bearing of this. Byron and Scott published their verse romances in quarto, and Words-

Once as I was walking with Wordsworth in Pall Mall we ran into Christie's, where there was a very good copy of the Transfiguration, which he abused through thick and thin. In the corner stood the group of Cupid and Psyche kissing. After looking some time he turned round to me with an expression I shall never forget, and said, "The Dev-ils!"

There are two possible interpretations of this story. One is that Wordsworth was not in the mood to look at works of art—was, perhaps, in a difficult mood altogether. It is not clear whether he abused the copy or the original of the *Transfiguration*, but we may perhaps see here the germ of Hazlitt's "He hates Raphael". The other possible interpretation is that he was making fun of Haydon, and Haydon misunderstood him. And there are at least two impossible interpretations, that he hated art and hated or was afraid of passionate love. Both can be proved impossible not merely from his own writings but from the evidence, not always approving evidence, of others—of, for example, Haydon himself in other places, of Hazlitt in *The Spirit of the Age*, of Miss Martineau. The story cannot be safely used in proof either of Wordsworth's sense of fun or of his rigidity.[1] All that we can

worth, as his correspondence shows, was deliberately challenging comparison with them, writing a romance in which the adventures were of the spirit.

[1] Yet Mr Aldous Huxley makes much of his argument in *Wordsworth in the Tropics* hang on this ambiguous anecdote, which, it may be noted, has in his memory lost its first half and burgeoned luxuriously in its second half. He has a real philosophical quarrel with Wordsworth—put crudely, if Wordsworth's interpretation of life is sound, Mr Huxley is unnecessarily miserable—and it is a pity that he should weaken his case by careless statement. The dangers of the significant anecdote could hardly be more clearly illustrated.

be sure of is that for some reason Haydon was annoyed with Wordsworth.

After 1824 there seems to have been a gap in their intercourse, though Wordsworth was in London more than once. But in 1831 we find Haydon as admiring and affectionate as he had been in 1815 or 1817. On April 12, he notes, "Wordsworth called after an absence of several years. I was glad to see him. He spoke of my Napoleon with his usual straightforward intensity of diction. We shook hands heartily. He spoke of Napoleon so highly that I wrote and asked him to give me a sonnet. If he would or could, he'd make the fortune of the picture".

Wordsworth did not fail him: the sonnet arrived on June 12, with an accompanying letter which must have given equal pleasure.

> You know how much I admired your picture both for the execution and the conception. The latter is first-rate, and I could dwell upon it for a long time in prose, without disparagement to the former, which I admired also, having to it no objection but the regimentals. They are too spruce, and remind one of the parade, which the wearer seems to have just left.... You are at liberty to print the sonnet with my name, when and where you think proper. If it does you the least service the end for which it is written will be answered.

There are no indications here that Wordsworth had changed since 1815, when he had also sent a letter with a sonnet: the letters are equally frank, and the later differs from the earlier only in its greater cordiality and its greater eagerness to help a friend less fortunate than he deserved to be.[1]

It cannot be safely argued that Wordsworth went through a period of arrogance between 1817 and 1830, afterwards

[1] Cf. also Wordsworth to Haydon, September 4, 1840.

returning to an earlier, simpler and more generous temper: the evidence of the Benthamites and Charles Greville is clear against that explanation.[1] But it is significant that Haydon's unfavourable notices of Wordsworth date from 1821 and 1824; that Hazlitt's *Lectures on the English Poets* belong to 1818, and *The Spirit of the Age* to 1825; and that from 1831 the Wordsworth who meets us in Haydon's journal is again the Wordsworth of the 1815 entries and of the immortal dinner. It is not necessary to quote all Haydon's references, but two successive entries from 1842 may be given for their connection with what has gone before.

[June] 14th. Out on business. Saw dear Wordsworth, who promised to sit at three. Wordsworth sat and looked venerable, but I was tired with the heat and very heavy, and he had an inflamed lid and could only sit in one light, a light I detest, for it hurts my eyes. I made a successful sketch. He comes again to-morrow.

We talked of our merry dinner with C. Lamb and John Keats. He then fell asleep, and so did I nearly, it was so hot; but I suppose we are getting dozy.

16th. Wordsworth breakfasted early with me, and we had a good sitting. He was remarkably well, and in better spirits, and we had a good set-to.

I had told him Canova said of Fuseli, "*Ve ne sono in gli arti due cose, il fuoco e la fiamma*". "He forgot the third," said Wordsworth, "and that is *il fumo*, of which Fuseli had plenty."

His knowledge of art is extraordinary. He detects errors in hands like a connoisseur or artist. We spent a very pleasant morning. We talked again of our old friends, and to ascertain his real height I measured him, and found him, to my wonder, eight heads high, or 5 ft. 9⅞ in., and of very fine, heroic proportions. He made me write them down, in order, he said, to show Mrs Wordsworth my opinion of his proportions.

[1] Cf. pp. 9–15 *supra*.

The time came and he went, wishing me prosperity, and blessing me with all his honest heart.

Perhaps I may never see him again. God bless him!

They did in fact meet again, when Wordsworth came to London in 1845 to pay his only visit to Court. Leigh Hunt also met him, after thirty years, and records the meeting with as much real discernment as might be expected.

I should venture to say, his manner was greatly superior to what it was in the former instance; indeed, quite natural and noble, with a cheerful air of animal as well as spiritual confidence; a gallant bearing, curiously reminding me of the Duke of Wellington, as I saw him walking some eighteen years ago by a lady's side, with no unbecoming oblivion of his time of life.

Leigh Hunt tried to draw him out by remarking on the diabolical feeling attributed to the angels in *Paradise Lost*, Book III, ll. 516–25.

Mr Wordsworth pondered, and said nothing. I thought to myself, what pity for the poor devil would not good uncle Toby have expressed! Into what indignation would not Burns have exploded! What knowledge of themselves would not have been forced upon those same coxcombical and malignant angels by Fielding or Shakespeare!

It may fairly be asserted that no one but Leigh Hunt has ever imagined the possibility of Wordsworth's expressing himself like my Uncle Toby. Yet there is no lasting malice in any of his jaunty criticisms, merely an incapacity to recognize a larger and simpler nature than his own.

I have suggested that this group was strongly affected by the attitude taken up by Hazlitt towards Wordsworth; that Leigh Hunt, in particular, did not easily get over the trouble of 1815, and that Keats and Haydon were influenced by others of their circle. But there is a further explanation, which relates to others besides this group, of the accusations of egotism and vanity or arrogance brought against Wordsworth. He was the only poet of his generation to whom poetry was the serious business of his life, and who made no attempt to disguise the fact. Haydon, when he was left to himself, before the Hazlitt trouble and after 1830, saw in Wordsworth an artist who was as naturally, simply and absorbingly interested in the problems of his art as Haydon was in his own problems, and who was, outside those problems, equally natural and simple. Keats, if he had been a little older and freer from the excusable egotism of youth, would have realized that what, following his friends, he condemned as egotism and vanity in Wordsworth, was the same thing as he knew in himself as the sense of power and the dedication to his art. R. P. Graves, years later, though not an artist himself, saw in Wordsworth the impersonal attitude of the artist towards his work, but the poets and critics of the first three decades of the century took much longer to see it. They could understand Scott, the lawyer and country gentleman, and Byron and Moore, and Rogers, whose poetry was kept in the background or allowed to be seen only as an additional ornament, but a poet who was a poet before he was anything else was new to their experience. He did not conceal his opinion that his poetry was worth reading, he was ready to talk shop without apology in literary circles, he supposed that people who expressed an interest in his poetry or in poetry generally were really interested: he must, therefore, be vain, egotistic, conceited, arrogant—the adjectives vary with the writer's feeling for the meaning of words. Crabb Robinson thought that Wordsworth grew milder between 1808 and 1820, and it is probable that he did in fact mellow; but in estimating the value of such comparisons as Leigh Hunt's between 1815 and 1845 we ought not to overlook the probability that the writer had gradually and insensibly come to realize that Wordsworth talking about poetry, even his own poetry, was not to be judged by the same standard as would be applied to Moore or Rogers, if either of them had fallen into such an indiscretion. The busy, chattering literary cliques of the early century judged him as if he had been one of themselves; outsiders, like the witnesses who have been cited in the earlier part of this chapter, or a serious though not a great artist like Haydon, as long as he was looking at Wordsworth with his own eyes, were simpler and truer in their vision and understanding.

There remain two accusers who should receive some attention—De Quincey and Landor.

De Quincey's anecdotal writings are not malicious, though there are a good many touches of felinity. There must always have been a certain incompatibility of temper between De Quincey and Wordsworth, as between De Quincey and Southey, and Crabb Robinson may have been right in his belief that De Quincey was finally turned against Wordsworth by the failure of "the ladies of Wordsworth's house" to pay a ceremonial call on Mrs De Quincey after her marriage.[1] Presumably he blamed Wordsworth for this. It seems a small cause of offence, but he may have been sensitive on the point. His irresponsibility, inaccuracy and indiscretion, amounting sometimes to bad taste, have always been

[1] Cf. the relevant passage from Crabb Robinson's *Reminiscences*, printed by Professor Edith Morley (*Blake, Coleridge, Wordsworth, Lamb*, p. 58).

recognized—how could he, who prided himself upon the delicacy of his feelings, have referred as he did to Dorothy Wordsworth's decline?—but he is almost always amusing, and, better than anyone else, he gives us glimpses of that side of Wordsworth's character which W. P. Ker used to call his lawlessness. The horrific tale of the leaves cut with a buttery knife may be an artistic exaggeration, but it expresses the truth, not about Wordsworth's habitual treatment of books, but about his natural impatience. Was it the control of that impatience, as of other elements in his nature, which acted ultimately as an intolerable though unconscious reproach to the want of self-control and the instability of others besides De Quincey—of John Wilson in particular—so that in self-defence they tried to find in Wordsworth sins to which they did not themselves incline?

Southey read De Quincey's papers as they appeared, and was made very angry by them. Wordsworth, more wisely, refused to read them. Crabb Robinson read between indignation and amusement, and could not refrain presently from telling Wordsworth one thing which De Quincey had said:[1]

> "that Mrs Wordsworth is a better wife than you deserve". "Did he say that?" Wordsworth exclaimed in a tone of unusual vehemence, "Did he say that? That is *so* true that I can forgive him almost anything else he says".

There is comedy of more than one kind here, especially when we remember what De Quincey said of Wordsworth's unchivalrous attitude to his wife and to women in general. Miss Fenwick, who was a good judge of manners, characterized his words on that point as "the falsest thing that could be said".[2]

[1] *Blake, Coleridge, Wordsworth, Lamb*, p. 59.
[2] To Henry Taylor, August 18, 1838.

With Landor, however, we come near to tragedy. His two attacks on Wordsworth, the *Satire against Satirists* of 1836 and the *Imaginary Conversation between Southey and Porson* of 1842, contain nothing essentially new, except a charge of plagiarism from Landor himself: for the rest there are the familiar allegations of arrogance and contempt for the work of others. In the *Satire* Landor expressed particular indignation that Wordsworth "had said he would not give five shillings" for Southey's poetry, and declared that he himself was a witness that at the first night of Talfourd's *Ion* Wordsworth was the only person present who did not applaud. But, as we have already seen, John Dix saw Wordsworth thumping lustily with his stick,[1] and Miss Mitford in contemporary letters refers as an eye-witness to Wordsworth's evident pleasure at his friend's success.[2] Crabb Robinson, in the second of the two tactful letters[3] by which he induced Landor to withdraw the *Satire* after publication, suggested that as Landor was sitting at the back of the box, he could not have seen very well what was happening—as likely an explanation as any. But why, then, did he make the accusation? Was he, in Wordsworth's own phrase, so prejudiced that he did not know he was lying? And if so, how did he acquire his prejudice? For he and Wordsworth had been on friendly epistolary terms for years, and had liked each other when they met face to face. "To my great surprise and pleasure", Wordsworth wrote to Crabb Robinson (July 21, 1832), "Landor appeared at Moresby near Whitehaven (having come by steam from Liverpool), when I was on a visit there to

[1] Cf. p. 43 *supra*.

[2] Cf. her letter to Harness, October 19, 1835, and those to her father, May 1836.

[3] *Crabb Robinson Correspondence*, I, 326–33.

my son. I followed him to Wastdale, where I spent a day in the same house with him. We went on through Borrowdale to Mr Southey's. He appears to be a most warm-hearted man, his conversation very animated, and he has the heartiest and happiest laugh I ever heard from a man of his years." The Boythornic laugh had been noted in an earlier letter to William Rowan Hamilton, written on June 25, a week after the meeting—"His conversation is lively and original, his learning great, though he will not allow it, and his laugh the heartiest I have heard for a long time". Landor would not have made so happy an impression on Wordsworth if Wordsworth had not made a happy impression on him. And there was no sign of any diminution in Landor's friendliness, as there was certainly none in Wordsworth's, until, with no warning, the *Satire* was published.

For some time later Wordsworth remained ignorant both of the change in Landor's feelings and of the resultant *Satire*. On March 22 in the following year, when he and Crabb Robinson were on their way to Italy, he spoke of the attack with dignity and moderation.[1]

It may not be unworthy to mention that Wordsworth heard only of Landor's *Satire* from Quillinan in Portugal. He said he regretted Quillinan's indiscretion, and he felt much obliged to all his London friends for their never mentioning the circumstance to him. He never saw nor means to see the *Satire*, so that it will fall ineffectual if it were intended to wound. He had heard that the pamphlet imputed to him a depreciation of Southey's genius; but as he felt a warm affection for Southey and an admiration of his genius, he never could have said that he would not give 5/- for all Southey had ever written. He had in consequence written a few lines to

[1] Crabb Robinson, *Diary*, March 22, 1837.

Southey.[1] Notwithstanding his sense of the extreme injustice of Landor towards him, he willingly acknowledged his sense of Landor's genius. As to the image of the sea-shell,[2] he acknowledged no obligation to *Gebir* for it. From his childhood the shell was familiar to him, and the children of his native place always spoke of the humming sound as indicating the sea, and its greater or less loudness had a reference to the state of the sea at the time. The circumstance, however, gave him little annoyance: the malignancy of one person was balanced by the kindness shown by so many friends in their silence.

There the matter might have ended, especially as Landor withdrew the *Satire*, but after the publication of the *Imaginary Conversation* in 1842 it was not surprising that Wordsworth should feel more strongly. Quillinan had retorted effectively in *Blackwood's* (April 1843), and Wordsworth wrote on the subject to Hamilton.[3]

The attack upon W. S. L. to which you allude was written by my son-in-law; but without any sanction from me, much less encouragement; in fact I knew nothing about it, or the preceding article of Landor that had called it forth, till after Mr Quillinan's had appeared. He knew very well that I should have disapproved of his condescending to notice anything that a man so deplorably tormented by ungovernable passion as that unhappy creature might eject. His character may be given in two or three words; a madman, a bad man, yet a man of genius, as many a madman is.

The phrase "bad man" is justifiable if, like Wordsworth, we look on this second attack as a deliberate repetition of what Landor had already acknowledged by his withdrawal of them to be baseless accusations, and a deliberate attempt to make

[1] See Knight, *Letters*, III, 128–9. [2] *The Excursion*, IV, 1132–40.
[3] *Life of Hamilton*, II, 410.

mischief between two men who respected and liked one another. Yet, after all, Southey was not likely to take Landor's words too seriously: he had told Crabb Robinson after the publication of the *Satire* that "Landor was always doing things he was sorry for afterwards—that people thought him crazy, or he would have been killed before now";[1] and at another time he[2] spoke of Landor as having "deep thoughts, a clear intellect, with an insane temper". The most probable explanation of the whole unhappy business is that a sudden gust of that insane temper which spoilt so much in Landor's life, spoilt his relations with Wordsworth and shook them with Southey, whom he had persuaded himself he was championing.

iii

Landor's detailed allegations fall to the ground, but it is only fair to him and other accusers, as well as to Wordsworth, to consider whether there was a real justification for the belief, which, for that matter, is still held, that Wordsworth undervalued or was jealous of the work of his contemporaries, or, alternatively, that he cared for no poetry but his own. It is true that, after reading much of the criticism and literary gossip of his day, one begins to suspect that charges of jealousy, envy and conceit were thrown about recklessly in literary circles, almost as part of the convention of literary life, and were taken far less seriously by their authors and hearers than by us. Miss Mitford, for example, a really amiable person, becomes ridiculous in her description of the effect of success on Talfourd: he looked down on everyone

[1] Crabb Robinson, *Diary*, January 16, 1837.

[2] Una Taylor, *Guests and Memories*, p. 47; cf. *Correspondence of Sir Henry Taylor*, p. 294.

else, and was furiously jealous, she declares, of herself and of Wordsworth. Her first impressions of Wordsworth himself were that he was "delightfully mild and placid, and most kind" to her, "an adorable old man", a "kind, simple, gracious man", but when she discovered that he had not trumpeted her praise wherever he went, she decided that he was "fair and false" and full of conceit.[1] That something also should be allowed for the touchiness of the literary mind is shown strikingly by James Montgomery. He is best remembered now for his hymns, but he was the author also of some good and many less good lyrics of a more secular cast, and it was possible for reviewers to name him and Wordsworth in the same breath. He will not stand that comparison, but he was not a poetaster. One of his poems, *A Field Flower*, deserves Wordsworth's reference to it in the note on the first *Daisy* poem in the *Poems* of 1807.

> This Poem and two others to the same Flower...were written in the year 1802; which is mentioned, because in some of the ideas, though not in [the] manner in which those ideas are connected, and likewise even in some of the expressions, they bear a striking resemblance to a Poem (lately published) of Mr Montgomery, entitled, a Field Flower. This being said, Mr Montgomery will not think any apology due to him; I cannot however help addressing him in the words of the Father of English Poets.
>
> "Though it happe me to rehersin—
> That ye han in your freshe songis saied,
> Forberith me, and beth not ill apaied,
> Sith that ye se I doe it in the honour
> Of Love, and eke in service of the Flour."

[1] Cf. her letters to her father written in May 1836 and to Miss Jephson, June 19, 1836, with that to Charles Boner, November 20, 1854.

This, to an unbiased reader, seems a pleasant and even graceful compliment to a fellow-poet. But even saintly minds are sometimes unexpectedly irritable, and Montgomery showed in a letter to Daniel Parken that he was irritated.[1]

> To *you* I need not add that his frigid mention of my name in his first note has not influenced me to speak more favourably of him than I otherwise should have done. It is a proud and almost contemptuous notice which he has taken of me and my "Daisy" (I won't change *mine* for his *three daisies*), and was more calculated to mortify and provoke a jealous temper than to soothe and disarm one who had the power and the opportunity to humble a rival in the eye of the public. No! I am persuaded, in my own mind, that I have done him justice to the best of my knowledge.

Montgomery reviewed the *Poems* for the *Eclectic Review*, and he deserves some credit for suppressing his private grief, as his article shows he did.[2] But if he could so mistake a piece of courtesy, and so expect to be placated, it is not surprising that men of less integrity and generosity of spirit should fall far below him.

Yet it may be argued that there must have been some foundation, stronger than has hitherto appeared, for the accusation made—though also, as we have seen, contra-

[1] Holland and Everett's *Life*, II, 184.

[2] Cf. pp. 345–6 *infra*. According to Grosart (III, 505), Montgomery afterwards changed his opinion about the *Daisy* note. "Nothing gratified this 'sweet Singer' so much as these words of Wordsworth. He used to point them out to visitors if the conversation turned, or was directed, to Wordsworth." "Or was directed" is pleasant. It is fair to Montgomery to add that he was probably not in the least influenced by the change in Wordsworth's reputation. The two men were introduced by Crabb Robinson (May 13, 1812) and liked each other.

dicted—in Wordsworth's lifetime and repeated to the present day. Did Wordsworth undervalue his contemporaries?

There is, I think, a certain amount of unrealized confusion of terms. When a reviewer of the first fifteen years of the nineteenth century spoke of Wordsworth's contemporaries, he had not the same people in mind as we have. He meant those acknowledged and respected masters of the art of poetry, Rogers, Campbell, Scott, Southey and Moore, possibly Crabbe, and a little later Byron, with others who are now entirely forgotten. He might, with some hesitation, add Coleridge; he would not think of Blake, and he would naturally not mention Keats or Shelley, of whom we sometimes forget that they were of the younger generation. On the other hand, in any estimation of Wordsworth's poetic rank we ourselves should remember out of the reviewer's list only Coleridge, Scott and Byron, and perhaps Crabbe: the rest would not enter into our consideration. The difference of values is brought out by the comparison of a passage from Byron, whose judgment agreed on the whole with that of his age, with one from Crabb Robinson, whose judgment agrees with ours. The first has already been quoted: it occurs in that letter to Moore in which Byron protests against Leigh Hunt's estimate of Wordsworth: "Let them take Scott, Campbell, Crabbe, or you, or me, or any of the living, and throne him; but not this new Jacob Behmen". The other shows Crabb Robinson realizing the eccentricity of his own ranking of the poets: of the dinner at Monkhouse's on April 4, 1823, he notes in his diary: "Our party consisted of Wordsworth, Coleridge, Lamb, Moore and Rogers, five poets of very unequal worth and most disproportionate popularity, whom the public would arrange probably in the very inverse order, except that it would place Moore above Rogers".

Now it was in the first fifteen years of the century that the opinion became fixed that Wordsworth undervalued his contemporaries, and the exact meaning of that was that he refused to admit that Rogers, Moore and Campbell were his equals, far less, as most people thought, his superiors: a refusal with which we should entirely concur. He may, in conversation with Hazlitt in 1803 or with Crabb Robinson in 1808, have used rather stronger language about them than he would have permitted himself in later life, but if we realize the height of the claims which he was expected to acknowledge, we may be willing to make some allowance for that. And are the verse romances of Scott and Byron really to be put above those poems which Wordsworth would have put above them—not only his own work, but the poems of Coleridge and Blake? If he had been asked a few years later who, of the men of his own generation, would survive with him, he would have replied, Coleridge unquestionably, both in his own work—though Wordsworth never rightly appreciated *The Ancient Mariner*—and through his "seminal mind"; Scott, for his novels rather than his verse romances, which Wordsworth considered good enough of their kind but unworthy of the great powers with which he credited Scott; Lamb—"Charles Lamb's verses are always delightful, like everything he writes, for he both feels and thinks"; Landor; Southey, like Scott, for his prose rather than his poetry; Byron, if the force of his genius could ultimately outweigh his faults of temper and diction. Of his older contemporaries he would add Burns, who was in fact a closer contemporary than Byron, and with him Blake, whom he considered to have "the elements of poetry a thousand times more than either Byron or Scott". And again we should concur with him.

Of the younger men he would be slower to speak, partly because in the last thirty years of his life he was increasingly dependent on the eyes and memory of others for his knowledge of them, and partly, especially in his last years, for reasons which, hinted at in several places, are most clearly expressed in a letter to Aubrey de Vere (November 16, 1842).[1]

In respect to your father's poems, your own, and all other new productions in verse, whether of my friends or of strangers, I ought frankly to avow that the time is past with me for bestowing that sympathy to which they are entitled. For many reasons connected with advanced life, I read but little of new works either in prose or verse. Rogers says of me, partly in joke and partly in earnest, as he says of himself and others as frankly, and has avowed in one of his letters written when he was an old man, "I read no poetry now but my own". In respect to myself, my good old friend ought to have added that if I do read my own, it is mainly, if not entirely, to make it better. But certain it is that old men's literary pleasures lie chiefly among the books they were familiar with in their youth; and this is still more pointedly true of men who have practised composition themselves. They have fixed notions of style and versification, and their thoughts have moved on in a settled train so long that novelty in each or all of these, so far from being a recommendation is distasteful to them, even though, if hard put to it, they might be brought to confess that the novelty was all improvement.... I have many times, when called upon to give an opinion on works sent, felt obliged to recommend younger critics as more to be relied upon, and that for the reason I have mentioned. It is in vain to regret these changes which Time brings with it; one might as well sigh over one's grey hairs.

[1] *Recollections of Aubrey de Vere*, pp. 127–8.

Such clear-sighted recognition of the natural contraction of the power of enjoying the new, and admission of its probable merit, suggests that Wordsworth was not as incapable of appreciating it as he, and still more as others, would make him appear. And in fact his judgments, unmethodical and infrequent as they are, are usually not far removed from the judgment of posterity.[1] His letter to Crabb Robinson of March 1821 does not, in spite of Professor Harper's interpretation, bear any reference to Keats and Shelley, but refers simply to that swarm of imitators of Byron, imitators of Scott, imitators of Moore, imitators even, though it may seem impossible, of Campbell and Rogers, whose works disfigure the magazines and publishers' lists of the period: poets far weaker than Barry Cornwall, whose tragedy *Mirandola* Wordsworth has just been discussing with friendly lenience:[2] "frog-poets (the Croakers), mice-poets (the Nibblers), a class *rhyming* to mice that shall be nameless, and fly-poets. (Gray in his dignified way calls flies the 'Insect Youth', a term wonderfully applicable upon this occasion!) But let us desist, or we shall be accused of envying the rising generation", Wordsworth adds prophetically. When he spoke of Shelley and Keats, it was in a different tone, as of writers of the immortal race who could endure criticism. In 1826, J. J. Tayler records,[3] "he told us he thought the greatest of modern geniuses, had he given his powers a proper direction, and one decidedly superior to Byron, was Shelley, a young man, author of *Queen Mab*, who died lately at Rome". He repeated the praise with a slight variation in the following year: "Shelley is one of the best *artists* of us all: I mean in

[1] Cf. Appendix B.

[2] See p. 371 *infra*.

[3] Grosart, III, 503.

workmanship of style";[1] and he told Gladstone in 1836 that he "thought Shelley had the greatest native powers in poetry of all the men of this age".[2] It seems to have been Wordsworth's insistence that Shelley was a better poet than Byron which encouraged Crabb Robinson to try him again after having been put off *Prometheus Unbound* by the *Quarterly Review*.[3] At the same time he considered it regrettable that Shelley had, like Hartley Coleridge, so defective an historical sense that he lost his temper at the mere mention of kings and priests, without reflecting that they would not have endured so long if there had not been some value in them: "I object to the perpetual ill-humour with things around them", he told Caroline Fox in 1842, "and ill-humour is no spiritual condition which can turn to poetry".[4] One general comment on Keats and Shelley, preserved by Sara Coleridge, has a dangerous truth in it: that they "would ever be favourites with the young, but would not satisfy men of all ages". The danger for both Keats and Tennyson, he told Quillinan, was over-

[1] *Memoirs*, II, 474.

[2] *Diary*, June 8, 1836; printed in Morley's *Life*.

[3] "I began Shelley's Prometheus, which I could not get on with. I was quickened in my purpose of throwing it aside by the Quarterly Review, which exposes the want of meaning in his poems with considerable effect. It is good to be now and then withheld from reading bad books" (December 28, 1821). "Began this evening to look into Shelley's poems.... I think him worth studying and understanding if possible. I recollect Wordsworth places him above Lord Byron" (December 20, 1827).

[4] Cf. also a remark of 1833, recorded by Aubrey de Vere (in a letter of December 12, 1882, printed by Mr Wilfrid Ward); when Miss de Vere "referred to some high traits of character indicated by Shelley's poetry, Wordsworth answered: 'Doubtless he was a man with beautiful dispositions; but dispositions are one thing and character is another'".

lusciousness, but we have seen how early and constant he was in his praise of Tennyson, and there was a deep compliment in the pleasure which R. P. Graves notes he felt at having anticipated in one of his sonnets, *Praised be the art*, with only a slight difference, the thought of the *Ode on a Grecian Urn*: "not that he suggested any borrowing of the idea on the part of Keats".[1]

What he valued in poetry, to the end, was vigour and feeling, the qualities which he missed in the poets whom the early reviewers told him to admire. "Your Poem is vigorous, and that is enough for me.... You feel strongly; trust to those feelings, and your poem will take its shape and proportions as a tree does from the vital principle that actuates it", he wrote, with perhaps too generous commendation, to Heraud (November 23, 1830). His complaint against Elizabeth Barrett Browning was that she lacked vigour. He thanked Kenyon (February 26, 1839) for sending her poems, remarking that she appeared to be "a very interesting person, both for genius and attainments", but he would not write to her personal friend what he had said in conversation to Crabb Robinson and Miss Fenwick. "He spoke of poetry on occasion of Miss Barrett", Crabb Robinson records (January 3, 1839). "'Her poems are too ideal for me—I want flesh and blood—even coarse nature and truth, where there is a want of refinement and beauty, is better than the other extreme. At the head of this *natural* and sensual school is Chaucer, the greatest poet of his class. Next comes Burns. Crabbe too has great truth, but he is too far removed from beauty and refinement.' I told him that in this he unconsciously sympathises with Goethe", Crabb Robinson concludes, rejoicing in his hit.

[1] *Recollections*, p. 302.

It was one of his griefs that Wordsworth refused to admire Goethe whole-heartedly. One would have expected a liking for Robert Browning to be a consequence of that liking for flesh and blood, but actually there is scarcely a reference to him; it is pleasant, however, to find Wordsworth in 1846 wishing happiness to that "very able man" and his wife, "not doubting that they will speak more intelligibly to each other than (notwithstanding their abilities) they have yet done to the public".[1]

The liking for vigour and feeling explains his attitude to the poets who wrote to him for advice. The greater poets do not usually seek advice from their elders: they know what they are trying to do, and they occasionally accept criticism from their contemporaries. Those who wrote to Wordsworth were for the most part minor poets, but if they showed any gleam of the qualities he valued he took endless pains with them, even as he expected them to take pains in their turn. Turgidity and bombast in a young poet might not be bad signs: he himself and Coleridge had shown them both. And thus we have the spectacle of Mr Robert Montgomery, bleeding from the onslaughts of the reviewers led by Macaulay, appealing to Wordsworth for sympathy, and receiving a guarded but kindly reply (February 1835) whose ambiguity does not seem to have struck him.

> Do not, my dear sir, be anxious about any individual's opinion concerning your writings, however highly you may think of his genius, or rate his judgement. Be a severe critic to yourself, and, depend upon it, no person's decision upon the merit of your works will bear comparison in point of value with your own....Add to this reflection another, which I press upon you—as it has supported me through life—viz.

[1] To Moxon, October 12, 1846.

that Posterity will settle all accounts justly; that works which deserve to last will last; and, if undeserving this fate, the sooner they perish the better.

If we translate "undervalued the poetry of his contemporaries" by "refused to admit that mediocre verse was great poetry, and judged great poetry by the highest standards", we shall be near the truth. If we add that Wordsworth did not consider that his own poetry was invariably good, we shall be nearer still to it. "The stupidity of Mr Gifford and the impertinence of Mr Jeffrey" might convince Wordsworth that the opinions of certain reviewers were of little or no importance, but he was willing not merely to listen to but to act on fair criticism. He would adopt almost any change suggested by Coleridge or Lamb, not always to the improvement of the poem concerned, and with Barron Field and even less well-equipped critics he reasoned on equal terms. Very few poets can ever have been so devastating in comment on their own work as Wordsworth was on that Skylark poem which begins *Up with me!*[1]

I like, however, the beginning of it so well, that for the sake of that I tacked to it the respectably tame conclusion. I have no objection, as you have been pleased with it, to restore the whole piece. Could you improve it a little?

He was right: the conclusion was respectably tame; and since Barron Field, though ready with criticism, shrank from emendation, and inspiration did not here revisit Wordsworth, respectably tame it remains.

On the other hand, when Wordsworth had written well, he saw no reason why he should not say so, with that imper-

[1] To Barron Field, October 24, 1828.

sonality of the artist which R. P. Graves noted and which Mrs Alaric Watts also noted.[1]

Of his own poems he expressed himself with a confidence not unlikely to be misunderstood by strangers, whom he might not have had the opportunity of impressing (as a very short conversation would ensure his doing) with the entire singleness and sincerity of his nature. He asked me what I thought the finest elegiac composition in the language; and, when I diffidently suggested *Lycidas*, he replied, "You are not far wrong. It may, I think, be affirmed that Milton's *Lycidas* and my *Laodamia* are twin Immortals". I admired *Laodamia*, and was quite willing that so it should be.

Or we may cite his criticism to Aubrey de Vere of the sonnets of Sir Aubrey de Vere.[2]

I was much pleased by finding that Wordsworth, a poet hard to please, thought very highly of my father's "Sonnets", stating that he believed they were the best of the age. He added soon afterwards, "I need not remind you, Mr de Vere, that in making such a remark one does not mean to institute anything in the way of comparison between oneself and another writer".

Sir Aubrey's sonnets were good, but Wordsworth's were at least as good: Wordsworth knew it, and he preferred truth to a false politeness. The younger de Vere had enough humour and humanity, and was a good enough poet himself, to value a direct simplicity and sincerity which might easily have given offence or been misunderstood.

How far Wordsworth's character and utterances were misunderstood by some of his contemporaries, and how far deliberately misrepresented, is a matter for debate, but that

[1] *Life of Alaric Watts*, I, 240.
[2] *Recollections*, p. 130.

there was much conscious misrepresentation is indubitable. Wordsworth inspired a good deal of positive dislike, as well as ardent friendship and admiration, and there were sometimes fundamental differences of temperament which were bound to lead to that kind of prejudice which chooses the more unfavourable, if also the less likely, of two interpretations. Some instances have already been given, but one more may be cited. There is a story, which may be apocryphal, that Milton's watch was passed round an assembly, whereupon Wordsworth passed his own watch round after it; and the inference we are supposed to draw is one of petty vanity and conceit. But when Wordsworth wished to even himself with Milton, he did so without subterfuge: *Lycidas* and *Laodamia* were twin immortals. It would be a perfectly natural thing for a man interested, as he was, in machines and mechanical contrivances to offer his own watch for comparison, either as an old-fashioned one not unlike Milton's, or to indicate particular differences in shape or construction. Authentic or not, the story is typical of a certain kind of Wordsworthian gossip.

iv

A recent interpretation of Wordsworth ought to be considered, if only as an example of theorizing in opposition to the facts. According to this, Wordsworth, having loved Annette Vallon, deserted her, became respectable and ashamed of his early passion, concealed the whole business, and in consequence suffered from various complexes, with disastrous results to his moral nature, his political and religious opinions, and his poetical powers. We are not concerned for the moment with his political and religious opinions or his poetical powers:

all that matters is that the interpretation is based on a complete mis-statement or misunderstanding of the premises. Wordsworth did not desert Annette Vallon: he did not marry her, but that is a very different thing. It may even be doubted whether the first step of withdrawal was on his side, as is commonly, on very insufficient grounds, assumed. The discussions have been conducted by men who, whether out of chivalry or out of the bland conviction that the woman in such cases is always passive and always anxious for matrimony, have overlooked any indications that Annette Vallon does not fit into their pattern. We cannot be sure even that, if she had wished to marry her young lover—four years her junior, it must be remembered—in 1792 or 1802,[1] she could not have done it; a ceremony in 1792 might not have been strictly legal, but she could have held him by it. From 1792 onwards she had her daughter and her Royalist intrigues: if she married him, she would no longer have complete control of her daughter's education, and she would receive no sympathy with her endeavours in the Bourbon cause; she would have to live in England, she, a middle-class Frenchwoman who, by the time marriage was, as far as we can tell, possible, was over thirty. If she did not marry him, she was sure of his financial help, she retained her personal liberty and her daughter, whom she could educate in sound Royalist principles, and she might, if she wished, make a suitable and sensible marriage in France. Of course she wrote in the early days, asking Wordsworth to return and marry her: it was the proper thing to say; but in

[1] In the years between 1792 and 1802 it would have been much more difficult for Wordsworth to reach her and marry her than it would now be for an Englishman to reach and marry a girl, suspected of counter-revolutionary activities, who lived in a town remote from the recognized tourist routes of Russia.

the only letters of hers which we know she is already more interested in Caroline than in Caroline's father, and it is more than probable that her passion cooled before his. Yet their passion had not been ignoble, though it had been evanescent, and the best proof of the sanity and normality of both lies in their subsequent relations and intercourse, which were accepted easily not only by Mrs Wordsworth, whose acceptance might be explained as due to her generosity, but also by Mrs Wordsworth's family. Crabbe might have written on their story a more cheerful *Natural Death of Love*.

Further, Wordsworth helped Annette financially from the first, as Professor Harper has shown, and testified his sense of responsibility towards his daughter Caroline not merely by repeatedly acknowledging his paternity and by standing godfather to her eldest child, but by visiting her whenever he was in Paris—in 1837 Crabb Robinson's diary shows him to have spent almost his whole time with her and her children—and by making an annual allowance to her after her marriage until 1835, when it was replaced by a settlement.[1] Her projected visit to him in England in 1814 could not have been carried through with any concealment of her relation to him. Everyone who had any right to know the story knew it, and a good many who had very little right. That Wordsworth's sons do not appear to have known it at the time of his death is probably explicable as due to oversight, to his belief that they knew at least the bare facts. These ignorances, sometimes almost incredible, do arise in families.

But, it is argued, Wordsworth concealed the facts from the public in *The Prelude*, and thereby falsified the story of his life. That there was any real falsification may be seriously

[1] Cf. Appendix C.

questioned. An old lady of ripe experience and unimpeachable morality, after hearing the story of Wordsworth and Annette, remarked scornfully, "All that fuss about a young man's fancy!" When all is said, and when all allowances are made for the fact that the young man, being a man who took all emotions hard, took hard what might have been a very unimportant affair to many, it was a young man's fancy; and Wordsworth himself came to see that it was of far less significance in his spiritual development than the sisterly love of Dorothy, or the friendship of Beaupuy and Coleridge, or the later love—which was also the earlier friendship and possibly even the love—of Mary Hutchinson. Even at its strongest, it had to fight a rival passion at least equally strong and of more enduring quality, the passion of sympathy for what he saw as the ideals of the French Revolution. In 1849 he wondered audibly, in the presence of Ellis Yarnall,[1] that he could have stayed so long in Orleans when such great things were afoot in Paris: the words were not hypocritical, nor did they imply forgetfulness of the past, but they are a startling indication of the relative importance of the passions of his youth. The one was a consuming interest to the end of his life: the other a flame, not false but not enduring, which flared up and was gone—of which, indeed, but for the birth of Caroline, we might have known nothing. That brought to her father responsibilities which he neither shirked nor misused, and from the dead passion itself came an unusual legacy from a young man's fancy, a refraining from condemnation and even

[1] *Wordsworth and the Coleridges*, p. 40. It should be added that, after a little more talk, Wordsworth said, "I should like to spend another month in France before I close my eyes". Some of the month would almost certainly have been spent with the Baudouins, in spite of Baudouin's behaviour in 1842. Cf. again Appendix C.

a pitying reverence for women who were deserted by the men who had betrayed them: he had neither betrayed nor deserted Annette, but he had ceased to love her, and that cessation of love is painful to a generous mind. It may also have been one of the factors which decided him against taking orders.[1] And because of his acceptance of his responsibilities he was even poorer than he would otherwise have been; but that is a merely external consideration.

There were other reasons too why Wordsworth should not have told the full story of his French love in *The Prelude*, and Professor de Selincourt has set them out—delicacy towards Annette and his wife, the intimacy between him and Coleridge which made the telling unnecessary. We might also note that on one occasion Wordsworth did openly and plainly express his relation to Caroline. If no one took literally the words "dear child" of the sonnet *It is a beauteous evening*, he is scarcely to be blamed. Do his judges seriously think that he ought to have added a note, "The reference is to my illegitimate daughter"?

Nor can he be blamed for the concealment, or rather the bare hinting at the story, in his nephew's biography, and the nephew himself is not altogether fairly blamed. Wordsworth had wished that the facts of his life should be told only so far as they explained his poetry, and it is obvious that there might be two opinions on the necessity of doing more than refer briefly to the French episode during the lifetime of his widow. Christopher Wordsworth, though he "did not consider it necessary, in the discharge of his duty as a biographer, to make any mention of the French entanglement of 1791–2", was willing to tell the whole story rather than have an ex-

[1] Cf. pp. 258–61 *infra*.

aggerated version put out, as the Baudouins were, perhaps unjustly, suspected of intending to do. His views were explained by Cookson, Wordsworth's executor, in a letter to Crabb Robinson:[1] with a better sense of proportion than some later writers, he would have pointed out "the age of the actor, influence under which he was placed, state of society in France at the time, subsequent visit of his sister and himself to the parties (in 1802) and knowledge of the main fact by his sister and intended wife". The Baudouins did not in fact publish the story, and Christopher Wordsworth accordingly did not consider that he need do so. But he was, as A. C. Benson protested,[2] "not in the least a cautious conventional ecclesiastic....He was orthodox, in a way, but I don't expect that his thoughts ever dwelt very much on respectability". A man of strict veracity, he would not pretend that his uncle had lived a blameless youth, even though he would not narrate the details. A few extracts from Crabb Robinson's diary for March 1851 will illustrate the sequel.

Tuesday 18th....[John] Wordsworth shewed me the proof sheets of the Life, in which I was sorry to see a canting commonplace remark on the perils to which Wordsworth was exposed in his youth at Paris, which might make one utterly ignorant of Wordsworth's personal character imagine he had been guilty of some immorality! I wrote a short letter on this to Quillinan....

Friday 21st....Then I called on Moxon about the Life. In the first proof, which I supposed to be the revise, John Wordsworth shewed a passage of which I have spoken in the last page. Quillinan sent my letter to the Doctor [i.e. the biographer]—he and Miss Fenwick and Mrs Wordsworth all

[1] August 31, 1850 (*Crabb Robinson Correspondence*, II, 756–7).

[2] In the letter which Professor H. W. Garrod quotes in the Preface to the second edition of his *Wordsworth*.

agreeing with me; but Moxon is sure that the objectionable passage has been expunged, and at all events it will be if Mrs Wordsworth requires it, and I wrote a letter to Quillinan to say as much....
25th Tuesday....From Moxon I learned what provoked me, that the injudicious paragraph about Wordsworth's residence in France is retained, which I thought had been omitted, and I wrote to Quillinan in consequence....
Thursday 27th....A call from John Wordsworth just after a letter from Quillinan. Quillinan would submit to the Doctor's insertion of the offensive paragraph, but I advise him and his mother to prohibit it absolutely. Moxon will do what they wish....
Wed. [Apr.] 2nd....I had a call from Quillinan, quite unexpected. I am sorry to find that Dr Wordsworth has not yielded to remonstrances....

And there the offensive paragraph remained, to be entirely neglected by its readers.[1]

Wordsworth's condition in France was a very critical one: he was an orphan, young, inexperienced, impetuous, enthusiastic, with no friendly voice to guide him, in a foreign country, and that country in a state of revolution; and this revolution, it must be remembered, had not only taken up arms against the monarchy and other ancient institutions, but had declared war against Christianity. The most licentious theories were propounded; all restraints were broken; libertinism was law. He was encompassed with strong temptations; and although it is not the design of the present work to chronicle the events of his life except so far as they illustrate his writings, yet I could not pass over this period of it without noticing the dangers which surround those who in an ardent emotion of enthusiasm put themselves in a position of peril, without due consideration of the circumstances which ought to regulate their practice.

[1] *Memoirs*, I, 74–5.

There is a touch of the pulpit about the end of this, but it does not deserve Crabb Robinson's condemnation of it as canting. It shows both sanity and charity, and it is hard that the unfortunate author should be accused by his own generation of injudicious insinuations and by ours of Victorian prudery and concealment.

Wordsworth cannot, in his relations with Annette Vallon and with their daughter and grandchildren, be fairly accused of hardening in his emotional or moral nature. Nor can he in his other personal relations. De Quincey thought his grief for little Thomas and Catherine, several years after their death, painful and even blameworthy in its freshness: De Quincey himself, though even foolishly fond of Catherine while she was alive, had scarcely felt her death, and her father's easily quickened sorrow and open expression of it embarrassed him. Dora's death would have killed Wordsworth if he had been less physically strong, and the breakdown of his self-control distressed Crabb Robinson almost as much as the earlier outburst had embarrassed De Quincey. It was perhaps one of the bonds between Scott and Wordsworth that each was a man of strong passions and almost equally strong self-restraint which so rarely gave way that many, even of those who knew them well, did not guess what forces lay behind it. "Few know *how* Wordsworth loves his friends", said Rogers, and even Lamb warned Crabb Robinson in 1812 that the reconciliation which he was trying to bring about between Coleridge and Wordsworth would probably fail because "Wordsworth was cold". In fact Crabb Robinson found his difficulties not with Wordsworth, who was eager to go to the extremest verge of truth and friendship to put things right, but with Coleridge, who dissolved into tears over his own hurt feelings.[1] Yet Coleridge must have known in his heart, as everyone else realized who knew the persons concerned, that Wordsworth could not have used the language of which he complained, that he himself was wronging Wordsworth by making himself believe it, yielding to his own sick mind and desire to be a martyr. When all was patched up as well as it could be patched, Coleridge expressed his gratitude to Crabb Robinson in fitting terms: Wordsworth said less, but asked to be introduced to Crabb Robinson's friends at Robinson's own discretion, an evidence of trust from which most of us would shrink.

It is an ungracious business to revive these old sorrows, but we shall be guilty of injustice to Wordsworth if we accept without corroboration Coleridge's cries of anguish as decisive proof that Wordsworth had treated him badly or unkindly, still more if we go along with Mr Herbert Read and argue that Wordsworth was growing cold and, in particular, was growing cold towards Coleridge. Not the least important evidence is given by Alsop, who, having heard Coleridge's story first and been definitely prejudiced against Wordsworth by it, subsequently admitted his own injustice. When he met Wordsworth, he tells us (I, 222–3), "taken altogether, he impressed me very favourably, and I regret deeply that I did not avail myself of subsequent opportunities not seldom proffered by Lamb and Coleridge, of meeting him

[1] See the full account of the negotiations in *Blake, Coleridge, Wordsworth, Lamb* (Professor Morley); and also the correspondence between Crabb Robinson and Mrs Clarkson (*Blake, Coleridge, Wordsworth, Lamb*, pp. 156–8; *Crabb Robinson Correspondence*, I, 70–7); she, loving Coleridge, was exasperated to fury by his behaviour in the business and in the renewed estrangement of 1812–13.

frequently. But I then laboured under the impression that he had not acted kindly to that dear and loved being, whom I loved living and honour dead". It was not easy for Alsop to reconcile his loyalty to the dead with justice to the living, but he did his best: he had "laboured under an impression", and he tacitly admits that it was false.

One other point may fairly be made. Dykes Campbell, in his *Life of Coleridge* (p. 195), wrote that the bond between Coleridge and Wordsworth "was broken in an unguarded moment; soon after it was mended, Wordsworth, under stress of sorrow, seems to have been driven to break it afresh". In a copy of the *Life* preserved in the British Museum, Hale White has underlined the last three words and written in the margin, "How?" How indeed? Coleridge, on hearing of the death of little Thomas Wordsworth, wrote to Wordsworth a letter which seems to have been as much about his own hopeless love for Sarah Hutchinson as about his friend's bereavement. He then took offence because Wordsworth did not answer it immediately. Now in the first place, the letter, if it was of that kind, must have been an extraordinarily difficult one to answer; in the second, a mourner might well be allowed a few weeks' grace in replying to any letter; and in the third, Mrs Clarkson's letter to Crabb Robinson of March 10, 1813, shows that Wordsworth had in fact replied with reasonable quickness, and that he and his sister had since written several letters—which, like his first, were unanswered by Coleridge—begging him to go to them as soon as he could do so without neglecting his own interests. If any other men but Coleridge, for whom no one can help making allowances, and Wordsworth, for whom allowances are seldom made, had been concerned, there would have been no question where the unkindness and injustice lay. As Mrs Clarkson wrote with some bitterness, "Whom the Lord loveth he chasteneth, and Coleridge, if he love anybody but himself, he shows it by tormenting them....He does not, I know, give pain for the sake of giving pain. But who does, except the Archfiend?"

A letter written late in 1817 may be quoted as giving some indication of Wordsworth's tenderness and admiration for Coleridge at that date.[1] Coleridge was preparing a set of lectures, and thought that the newspapers and other critics were not likely to be fair to him. He himself wrote to various friends, and Wordsworth's letter to the young Payne Collier explains itself.[2]

> Coleridge, to whom all but certain reviewers wish well, intends to try the effect of another course of Lectures in London on Poetry generally, and on Shakespeare's Poetry particularly. He gained some money and reputation by his last effort of the kind, which was, indeed, to him no effort, since his thoughts as well as his words flow spontaneously. He talks as a bird sings, as if he could not help it: it is his nature. He is now far from well in body or spirits: the former is suffering from various causes, and the latter from depression. No man ever deserved to have fewer enemies, yet, as he thinks and says, no man has more, or more virulent. You have long been among his friends; and as far as you can go, you will no doubt prove it on this as on other occasions. We are all anxious on his account. He means to call upon you himself, or write from Highgate, where he now is.

We ought always to reckon, and we frequently forget to do so, with Wordsworth's comparative inarticulateness about his deepest feelings and affections. Even Coleridge, though he

[1] See also pp. 7–8 *supra*, 367–71 *infra*.

[2] Preface to Coleridge's *Seven Lectures on Shakespeare and Milton*, pp. lv–lvi.

knew that "Wordsworth's words always mean the whole of their possible meaning",[1] sometimes forgot it, and it is not surprising that others should not even perceive it. In an age of flamboyance and facile emotion he was not flamboyant, and his reticence, like his independence of literary coteries, told against him.

V

When all this is considered, it would appear that the picture of Wordsworth in his later years which was set out in the first part of this chapter is nearest to the truth: that he was a man of strong passions and feelings, strong and vigorous intellect, clear and independent thought and judgment in life, letters and politics, in the last as in the first half of his life. He mellowed, as good men of strong character do: the second member of Sterling's great trio, the Duke of Wellington, is a striking contemporary example; but he did not weaken, nor did he become rigid in mind and thought. We cannot fairly say that he hardened in the second decade of the century; the evidence of John Stuart Mill would prove that he had not hardened by the fourth, of Carlyle, not an altogether friendly witness, by the end of the fifth, and of R. P. Graves by the end of his life. And these witnesses do not stand alone.

But if this is the true picture of Wordsworth, how are we to account for those developments in his political and religious thought which distress nearly all those who have written about him, particularly of late years? It might be enough to say that he, if any man, had a right to his opinions and beliefs, even if those of his later life were in contradiction to those of his youth. In fact, much of the criticism of

[1] To Southey, August 14, 1803.

Wordsworth's later years rests on political and religious prejudice—"Can a free spirit vote Tory and hold family prayers?"—and even more admits without examination statements which need careful investigation. Wordsworth had a right to change his political opinions, and, since he did not ossify at twenty-five, he did change some of them; but it does not follow that he adopted others in flat contradiction to those of his youth. And he did not do so: his political development was consistent, not a bold advance followed by retrogression, but the development of a statesman who kept to the end much of the faith and ardour of his youth.

II

POLITICS

i

WHEN Christopher Wordsworth's biography of his uncle first appeared, a reviewer in the *Gentleman's Magazine* (August 1851) expressed serious doubts whether Wordsworth's political "revolution in sentiment" had been as complete as it was represented to be by the biographer. The doubts were not echoed by many at that time, nor for many years afterwards: there was little questioning of the view taken by Byron and Shelley that Wordsworth was an apostate from the glorious cause of liberty, more or less excuse being made for him according to the discernment or charity of the critic. They were revived by Hale White in his *Examination of the Charge of Apostasy against Wordsworth* (1898) and by Dicey in his *Statesmanship of Wordsworth* (1917); but the first of these books has received little attention, and the second does little more than indicate some of the reasons for the doubts. More recent writers are still obviously unhappy about Wordsworth's later political views. To some extent their unhappiness may be attributed to their acceptance of one of the two favourite theories of the present day about the right and just political attitude of poets: that they should be good democrats, or that they should be rebels. The one of these is a descendant of the conventional Liberalism which coloured much of the literary criticism of the last century and, for that matter, is not yet dead: an extension of the political franchise is good, and the abolition of religious disqualifications is good: since, therefore, Wordsworth disapproved of the Reform Act of 1832 and of Roman Catholic Emancipation and of certain concessions to Nonconformists, he had abandoned the cause of liberty and democracy. The other theory, that a great poet should be a rebel against the political and also, preferably, the moral order of the world, seems to be due to a corrupt following of Blake. It is amusing to consider for a moment how the great English poets stand the tests of democracy and rebellion: they have been haters of oppression, but seldom rebels in the complete Byronic sense, and few of them reach a satisfactory standard of democracy. Chaucer loved his pilgrims impartially, but it would not have occurred to him that the Sumnour or the Manciple had an equal right to rule with the Knight. Spenser's hatred of oppression was combined with so strong a love of order that he even lays himself open, as in Book v of *The Faerie Queene*, to the charge of siding with the oppressor. Shakespeare loved his muddle-headed citizens and countrymen, but he did not consider them capable of ruling themselves, much less of ruling him; and as a rebel he is by no means satisfactory. Milton, who is held up as the arch-rebel, was an intellectual aristocrat with a clear mental distinction between License and Liberty and a scorn for the common people which he put even into the mouth of Christ. Two of Wordsworth's contemporaries, Byron and Shelley, may fairly be called rebels, but Byron was certainly no democrat: a typical aristocratic republican, he scarcely paid even lip-service to the ideals of fraternity and equality which we sometimes attribute to him. "What is (*in fact*) democracy?" he enquired of himself; "an Aristocracy of Blackguards".[1] Shelley believed passionately in fraternity and equality, but he would have found it difficult to answer the

[1] See the passage in *Letters and Journals*, v, 405–6.

challenge implied in Milton's "License they mean when they cry Liberty". How are the wicked to be prevented from reimposing their domination over the good and virtuous? Even Shelley himself, as in *The Revolt of Islam* and in the last chorus of *Hellas*, sometimes doubted.

It was this problem which Wordsworth faced, and his answer was neither in the scornful paternalism of Spenser nor in the aristocratic disdain of Milton or Byron, nor again in the precipitate hopefulness of Shelley. The "raskall rout", the people "of whom to be dispraised were no small praise", were not in his view unteachable or incapable of ultimate self-government. He would have been not a noble idealist but a dreamer unable or afraid to face realities if, after his observation of the development of the French Revolution, he had persisted in the belief of his enthusiastic youth, that freedom was a gift easily given and received without danger, and that it would by its own virtue immediately or after a brief period of disorder make the sovereign people capable of ruling itself wisely and temperately and incorruptly. There are the wicked to consider: there are, moreover, the fools who are sometimes more dangerous than the wicked. Wordsworth ended by keeping the Miltonic distinction between License and Liberty, and keeping also his faith in the teachableness of the English people. His poems on National Independence and Liberty and his poems on Liberty and Order are one indivisible series and might almost exchange names. But he did disapprove of the Reform Bill and of other enlightened legislation.

No responsible writer would now bring against Wordsworth the charge of apostasy from the ideals of his youth, but more than one responsible writer has brought against him a

charge of premature ageing, of ossification and timidity, leading to a withdrawal into a comfortable conservatism. But the evidence of younger men who did not expect to receive understanding and sympathy from one so much older than they and so different, they had supposed, in his outlook on life, is, as we have seen, clean against the theory of ossification; and up to his last years we find him, in writing and in speech, bolder than many of those who regretted his Toryism. If we accept the theory, what is to be done with the testimony of the Benthamites and John Stuart Mill, which dates from the time when Wordsworth's feeling against the Reform Bill agitation was at its height? Still more, what is to be done with the *Postscript* of 1835, weakened though it was at the entreaty of that firm Liberal, Crabb Robinson, and with the conversation with Thomas Cooper ten years later? What becomes of the fiery passages in *The Excursion* and in the latest version of *The Prelude*? Wordsworth may have changed his mind on certain points, but, as Hale White justly argued, he would not have sanctioned, by continuing to reprint, poems which he had come to think definitely wrong or mistaken in their opinions.

And, indeed, too much has been inferred, and even false conclusions drawn, from his alterations in his earlier poems. It was perhaps excusable in Hazlitt to suggest that he omitted *The Female Vagrant* from the *Poems* of 1815 because he no longer looked with such horror upon the evils of war. The inclusion of the poem in its longer form, *Guilt and Sorrow*, in later editions disproved that jibe, but it has been suggested by sober critics that the cutting down of the stanzas describing the eviction indicates a change in Wordsworth's attitude to landlords. Yet the departure from the "old hereditary nook" is still, in the revised version, due to "cruel wrong"—that is, obviously, to an oppressive landlord, since no one else would be in a position to commit that particular cruel wrong; all that Wordsworth has done is to cut out details which interrupt the main theme of the poem. The man who in the same year, 1836, disturbed the legal mind of J. T. Coleridge by the delight with which he trespassed on land which he considered to have been unrighteously enclosed, and the vehemence with which he defended his action, had not changed his opinions about the oppressions of landlords.[1] So again, in revision he actually strengthened the end of the *Descriptive Sketches*, which has in spite of that been adduced to prove a change from the revolutionary to the conservative. It is true that as late as 1820 the original ll. 780–7 survived with only verbal changes, still containing an unclouded anticipation of the new earth—

> Nature, as in her prime, her virgin reign
> Begins, and Love and Truth compose her train;
> While with a pulseless hand, and stedfast gaze,
> Unbreathing Justice her still beam surveys;

whereas in 1836 Wordsworth substituted for them a passage which recognizes that the new earth has not, in fact, come to maturity. But even here it is a wresting of his sense to suggest that he has lost his hopes of that new earth: on the contrary, though experience has taught him that men will not achieve their earthly paradise until they strive for it in the right way and with the right aims, he is not despairing:

> All cannot be—

[1] Grosart, III, 425 n. The story which Knight tells in the Preface to his *Life* may refer to another occasion or may be an exaggeration of this.

which does not mean that nothing at all can be—

> All cannot be: the promise is too fair
> For creatures doomed to breathe terrestrial air:
> Yet not for this will sober reason frown
> Upon that promise, nor the hope disown;
> She knows that only from high aims ensue
> Rich guerdons, and to them alone are due.

Something will be achieved, though not all that is hoped for. This is not despair, and the passage which follows shows even more clearly how Wordsworth's thought had developed and deepened rather than changed. In the 1793 edition ll. 792–809 read:

> Oh give, great God, to Freedom's waves to ride
> Sublime o'er Conquest, Avarice, and Pride,
> To break, the vales where Death with Famine scow'rs,
> And dark Oppression builds her thick-ribb'd tow'rs;
> Where Machination her fell soul resigns,
> Fled panting to the centre of her mines;
> Where Persecution decks with ghastly smiles
> Her bed, his mountains mad Ambition piles;
> Where Discord stalks dilating, every hour,
> And crouching fearful at the feet of Pow'r,
> Like Lightnings eager for th' almighty word,
> Look up for sign of havoc, Fire, and Sword;
> —Give them, beneath their breast while Gladness springs,
> To brood the nations o'er with Nile-like wings;
> And grant that every sceptred child of clay,
> Who cries, presumptuous, "here their tides shall stay",
> Swept in their anger from th' affrighted shore,
> With all his creatures sink—to rise no more.

In the last revision of 1836, which improves on that of 1820, the bombast has been removed and the grammar simplified, with the result that the lines (now 652–64) are considerably more effective in their anticipation of the irresistible advance of Freedom:

> Great God! by whom the strifes of men are weighed
> In an impartial balance, give thine aid
> To the just cause; and, oh! do thou preside
> Over the mighty stream now spreading wide:
> So shall its waters, from the heavens supplied
> In copious showers, from earth by wholesome springs,
> Brood o'er the long-parched lands with Nile-like wings!
> And grant that every sceptred child of clay
> Who cries presumptuous, "Here the flood shall stay",
> May in its progress see thy guiding hand,
> And cease the acknowledged purpose to withstand;
> Or, swept in anger from the insulted shore,
> Sink with his servile bands, to rise no more!

There is, it will be noted, one significant change: in 1793 Wordsworth anticipated no alternative to the violent destruction of the tyrants, whereas in 1836 he had some hope of their conversion. But that he should in 1836—the version of 1820 agrees with that of 1793—appeal to God to make it clear to the presumptuous child of clay that those who oppose "the just cause" are opposing the will of God, is scarcely evidence that he had lost faith in that just cause or in its ultimate triumph.

Yet this thought, the hope that the world may be set free without bloodshed or violence, though it is not in this particular poem obvious until 1836, had not occurred then to Wordsworth for the first time. Within a year of publishing the first version of the *Descriptive Sketches*, in the early summer of 1794, Wordsworth was expressing to his friend

Mathews his horror of that revolutionary violence which he had certainly not condemned twelve months before.

> I conceive that a more excellent system of civil policy might be established amongst us; yet, in my ardour to attain the goal, I do not forget the nature of the ground where the race is to be run. The destruction of those Institutions which I condemn appears to me to be hastening on too rapidly. I recoil from the bare idea of a Revolution; yet, if our conduct with reference both to foreign and domestic policy continues such as it has been for the last two years, how is that dreadful event to be averted? Aware of the difficulty of this, it seems to me that a writer who has the welfare of mankind at heart should call forth his best exertions to convince the people that they can only be preserved from a convulsion by economy in the administration of the public purse, and a gradual and constant reform of those abuses which, if left to themselves, may grow to such a height as to render even a Revolution desirable.... After this need I add that I am a determined enemy to every species of violence?... I deplore the miserable situation of the French; and think we can only be guarded from the same scourge by the undaunted efforts of good men in propagating with unremitting activity those doctrines, which long and severe meditation has taught them are essential to the welfare of mankind.... When I observe the people should be enlightened upon the subject of politics, I severely condemn all inflammatory addresses to the passions of men, even when it is intended to direct those passions to a good purpose.

Many years later Wordsworth wrote to his brother Christopher (April 1, 1832), "I have witnessed one revolution in a foreign country, and I have not courage to think of facing another in my own". This is sometimes quoted as evidence of political timidity, merely because the Reform Act did not actually lead to a revolution: but it is no stronger than the words of this letter of 1794, when, also, serious popular discontent did not lead to a revolution. "I recoil from the bare idea of a Revolution. . . . Need I add that I am a determined enemy to every species of violence? . . . I severely condemn all inflammatory addresses to the passions of men." It is the same man speaking from experience, whether that be recent or vividly remembered after forty years.

The whole of this letter of 1794 should make those pause who think of the twenty-four-year-old Wordsworth as being filled with reckless Revolutionary ardour. And even two years earlier he had shown more steadiness and coolness of judgment than most of his critics would allow him at that time.

> The approaching summer will undoubtedly decide the fate of France. It is almost evident that the patriot army, however numerous, will be unable to withstand the superior discipline of their enemies. But suppose that the German army is at the gates of Paris, what will be the consequence? It will be impossible to make any material alteration in the Constitution, impossible to reinstate the clergy in their antient guilty splendour, impossible to give an existence to the *noblesse* similar to that it before enjoyed, impossible to add much to the authority of the King.[1]

The Revolution had happened, and its effects could not be undone. There could never be more than a temporary and unreal return in France to the old conditions, and, though Wordsworth does not press the argument so far, the rest of Europe could not remain unaffected by the changes in France. Wordsworth's distress at the part taken by England in the earlier Revolutionary wars was not complicated by any fear of the return of the old tyrannies. Feeding on a day of vengeance yet to come, he was confident that the old oppressions could not revive: tyranny must find other forms, and

[1] To Mathews, May 17, 1792.

some of those forms he recognized earlier than most of his liberty-loving contemporaries. He had a suspicion of them even at twenty-three, and expressed it in a passage of the letter to the Bishop of Llandaff which Dicey rightly stresses:[1] it must be admitted, "from the abuse of the executive power in States, that there is not a single European nation but what affords a melancholy proof that if, at this moment, the original authority of the people should be restored, all that could be expected from such restoration would in the beginning be but a change of tyranny". At that time he was almost willing to take a risk whose existence an orthodox Girondin would not have confessed; as time passed he became less and less willing to expose his own country to anguish which might be prevented by the methods of patience. He emerged from the long agony of the later Revolution, the Revolutionary Wars and the Napoleonic Wars with a clear perception that men could not be freed at a stroke without preparation, and that too great haste in bestowing a nominal freedom upon the unready and uneducated would lead to one form or another of despotism. Whether in English politics he carried his reasoned dislike for hasty and ill-considered reform too far, in practice if not in logic, is a question which will presently be discussed. It is easy, but not safe, to answer it at once with an affirmative—to quote words of Crabb Robinson which have too often been quoted, and think that the matter is summed up by them, to say that Wordsworth "lost his love of liberty, not his humanity but his confidence in mankind".[2] But in the first place we have no right to accept any evidence, even from

[1] *Statesmanship of Wordsworth*, pp. 66–7.

[2] *Diary*, recording a letter which he had just written to Mrs Fletcher, June 24, 1844.

the trustworthy Crabb Robinson, without examination, and in the second this hasty generalization is contradicted by Crabb Robinson himself in other places. Wordsworth's principles and conclusions led to actions which could be, and were, gravely misapprehended or misrepresented by his contemporaries, even by those who knew him well; with a hundred years of history between him and us, and with some events of the later years illuminating his utterances, we are in a better position to understand him and to do him justice.

One point ought to be made before we go further, and that is that, if we leave Wordsworth's own writings out of account, we see him, especially in his later years, almost entirely through the eyes of declared Liberals. It would almost seem that he preferred as friends and intimates those who did not altogether agree with him in their political and religious views. Crabb Robinson suggested to himself, as an explanation,[1] that Wordsworth was tolerant of religious and political differences where he found agreement on poetical matters, but in fact he was tolerant of poetical differences too, and was prepared to argue about them all. It is probable that, as Aubrey de Vere thought,[2] he sometimes argued for amusement, and among his most constant companions and correspondents he found few who were not willing to argue with

[1] *Diary*, May 13, 1836.

[2] Cf. his story of Wordsworth's attempt to draw him into a comparison between the English and the Swiss mountains. "Travellers often make their boast of Swiss mountains, on the ground of their being two or three times as high as the English; but I reply that the clouds gather so low on them that half of them remain commonly out of sight." De Vere refused to be drawn, and, finding that he was not to be indulged with opposition, Wordsworth uttered his last word—"But I must admit, *you know that they are there*" (*Recollections*, p. 125).

him. The usual picture of a circle of admirers at Rydal echoing everything Wordsworth said is very far from the truth. His family did not always agree with him; the Arnolds were Liberals, so were the Fletchers, so were the Clarksons and Crabb Robinson, and none of these held his religious views. "Our intercourse with the Wordsworths was one of the brightest spots of all", Dr Arnold wrote to J. T. Coleridge (April 5, 1832); "nothing could exceed their friendliness—and my almost daily walks with him were things not to be forgotten. Once, and once only, we had a good fight about the Reform Bill during a walk up Greenhead Ghyll to see 'the unfinished sheepfold' recorded in 'Michael'. But I am sure that our political disagreement did not at all interfere with our enjoyment of each other's society: for I think that in the great principles of things we agreed very entirely—and only differed as to the τὰ καθ' ἕκαστα." Crabb Robinson wrote to Thomas Robinson (January 7, 1836) in the same strain, noting how he and Wordsworth "manage to differ without acrimony". According to Aubrey de Vere,[1] Arnold and Wordsworth had to exclude politics from their subjects of conversation, but if he was correct in this statement it can be true only of the last years of Arnold's life, and is likely to have been due to his sensitiveness as much as to Wordsworth's, if not more. Arnold's letters do not give any great impression of understanding the other point of view, and his language about Tories and Newmanites is at least as strong as Wordsworth's about Whigs and Dissenters.

De Vere, that shrewd observer, suggested also the existence in Wordsworth of a desire to defend what had become the weaker side.[2]

[1] *Recollections*, p. 126. [2] Grosart, III, 490.

To the end his sympathies were ever with the cottage hearth far more than with the palace. If he became a strong supporter of what has been called "the hierarchy of society", it was chiefly because he believed the principle of "equality" to be fatal to the well-being and the true dignity of the poor. Moreover, in siding politically with the Crown and the coronets, he considered himself to be siding with the weaker party in our democratic days.

His support of the Crown, however, was remarkably unsentimental: he had not Oastler's zeal for "Throne and Altar", even though in Book VI of *The Excursion* the Crown and Throne are symbols of freedom; and, at least until long after the accession of Queen Victoria, he had no particular reverence for the wearers of the crown. He did not share Scott's romantic devotion to the monarchy and its representative. Professor Harper argues that from Dorothy Wordsworth's approval of Southey's *Vision of Judgment* "we may fairly conclude that her brother tolerated that piece of sycophancy".[1] But, leaving Southey's "sycophancy" out of the question, toleration is far too warm a description of Wordsworth's amused verdict on the *Vision of Judgment*:[2]

> He is about to publish a Poem, occasioned by the death of his late Majesty, which will bring a nest of hornets about his ears; and will satisfy no party. It is written in English Hexameter verse, and in some passages with great spirit. But what do you think; in enumerating the glorified spirits of the reign of George III admitted along with their earthly sovereign into the New Jerusalem, neither Dr Johnson nor Mr Pitt are to be found. Woe to the Laureat for this treasonable judgement! will be the cry of the Tories.

[1] 1929 ed., p. 572.
[2] To Crabb Robinson, January 23, 1821.

In a letter of condolence to Lord Lonsdale, who had had a personal affection for the old King, Wordsworth had indeed suggested consolation "in the reflection that George the Third will be ranked by posterity among the best and wisest kings that ever sat upon the throne of England". Posterity has not yet raised him as high as this, though he stands considerably higher than he did at the beginning of this century. But as far as Wordsworth is concerned, it would be fairer to draw our conclusions as to his feelings, not from this isolated condolence given with generous exaggeration four days after the old King's death[1]—and in the immediate, though undeclared, contemplation of his successor—nor from such insufficient evidence as Dorothy Wordsworth's approval of the *Vision of Judgment*, but from his own deliberate utterances in his two sonnets on George III. The first is that sonnet on the royal fortitude at which Hazlitt sneered when it was first published in the volume of 1815. The sheer inhumanity of Reformers and Liberals to the old man who, with all his mistakes, was much better as both man and king than they admitted, is a saddening thing: even Shelley was not exempt from it: Byron, with his half-contemptuous mercy at the end of his *Vision of Judgment*, shows, not for the only time, a generosity in which most of his friends were lacking.[2] It was not to Wordsworth's discredit that, in the moment of victory, he should have had a thought for the old man, "lamentably wrapped in twofold night", whose stubborn courage, for good as well as evil, was a matter of sober fact. As for the sonnet on his death, it is all that a poem written on

[1] George III died on January 29, and the letter was written on February 2, 1820.

[2] Cf. also Byron to John Murray, February 21, 1820.

that occasion ought to have been: there is the sense, known again to Englishmen in 1901, that an epoch is ended, and for the dead man himself there is awed pity. Southey would have done well to show equal restraint.

Ward of the Law!—dread Shadow of a King!
  Whose realm had dwindled to one stately room;
  Whose universe was gloom immersed in gloom,
Darkness as thick as life o'er life could fling,
Save haply for some feeble glimmering
  Of Faith and Hope—if thou, by nature's doom,
  Gently hast sunk into the quiet tomb,
Why should we bend in grief, to sorrow cling,
When thankfulness were best?—Fresh-flowing tears,
  Or, where tears flow not, sigh succeeding sigh,
  Yield to such after-thought the sole reply
Which justly it can claim. The Nation hears
In this deep knell, silent for threescore years,
  An unexampled voice of awful memory!

As for George IV, he certainly did not awaken in Wordsworth the chivalrous loyalty which he inspired in Scott, and William IV was "our poor Jack Tar of a King" (to Henry Taylor, April 25, 1834)—a disrespectful allusion not to be accounted for merely by William's relations with the Whig ministry. To the end Wordsworth seems to have felt little but an abstract recognition of the convenience of the monarchy, though two of his letters to Reed (November 18, 1844, and July 1, 1845) may suggest the dawn of a warmer feeling. But he was never a Royalist, and it was not to the Crown so much as to other elements that he looked for the strengthening of the bonds which ought to unite the nation. And that union, whether for action towards foreign nations or for reform at home, was in his thought the one thing necessary.

ii

The development of Wordsworth's views on a right and wise foreign policy, up to 1815, was fully discussed by A. V. Dicey in *The Statesmanship of Wordsworth*, and there is no need to recapitulate the discussion here. Wordsworth's position was clear and intelligible: a nation has the right to choose its own government, but it has no right to force its ideas of government on other nations, even though these ideas may be better than those which are held by the other nations. Therefore he sympathized intensely with France in the early Revolutionary wars and, as he afterwards explained in a letter to his friend Losh (December 4, 1821), "abandoned France, and her rulers, when *they* abandoned the struggle for liberty, gave themselves up to tyranny, and endeavoured to enslave the world".[1] He was, as Dicey showed, sometimes mistaken in detail: thus, for example, the facts of the French invasion of Switzerland were not entirely as he believed them to be, and it is extremely doubtful whether he represented, as he supposed, the general feeling of Englishmen towards the war in its early stages. But Wordsworth's retort on those who accused him of inconsistency and desertion remains true, and is valid for other

[1] Cf. also the second *Address* of 1818: "Numbers, I am aware, do not cease vehemently to maintain, that the late war was neither just nor necessary; that the ostensible and real causes of it were widely different; that it was not begun, and persisted in, for the purpose of withstanding foreign aggression, and in defence of social order: but from unprincipled ambition in the Powers of Europe, eager to seize that opportunity of augmenting their territories at the expense of distracted and enfeebled France.—Events ever-to-be-lamented do, I grant, give too much colour to those affirmations....But the military successes of the French...in course of time placed the policy and justice of the war upon a new footing".

matters besides this: "If I were addressing those who have dealt so liberally with the words 'renegade', 'apostate', etc., I should retort the charge upon them, and say, *You* have been deluded by *places* and *persons*, while I have stuck to principles". After the war he still stuck to principles, and to the same principles: there might be, and ought to be, sympathy for the Liberal or Nationalist party in other countries, but sympathy gave no title to interfere in the domestic concerns of those countries.

Wordsworth's comparative silence on continental politics after Waterloo might easily be, and was, misjudged, and Crabb Robinson protested against it in a letter to Dorothy Wordsworth (February 20, 1826).

I assure you it gives me real pain when I think that some future commentator may possibly hereafter write—"This great poet survived to the fifth decennary of the Nineteenth Century, but he appears to have died in the year 1814, as far as life consisted in an active sympathy with the temporary welfare of his fellow creatures. He had written heroically and divinely against the tyranny of Napoleon, but was quite indifferent to all the successive tyrannies which disgraced the succeeding times. The Spaniards, the moment they were under the yoke of the most odious and contemptible tyrant that ever breathed, ceased to be objects of interest. The Germans who emancipated themselves were most ungratefully neglected by their sovereigns and the poet. The Greeks began a war as holy as that of the Spaniards. He was silent. He had early manifested a feeling for the negroes, and the poet did honour to his friend Clarkson. That source of sympathetic tears was dried up. A new field of enterprise was opened in America. The poet's eye was not a prophetic one. There is proof that he was alive about 1823–4, when the new churches were built in London, but otherwise he took no care about any of the events of the day. He had indeed the wisdom and dignity not to expose himself to the imputations, exaggerated by party feeling, but not unfounded, which were heaped upon the Laureate".

...Nothing, as you know, equals the love and admiration I bear to your brother's poetical character. And I am not unfrequently mortified, when I am unable to repel the bitter and scornful attacks which low-minded adversaries make against him. I am, however, more pained when I hear the lamentations of some of the most excellent persons I know, that occasion should be given to the railings of the baser sort. In favour of my affectionate attachment to your brother's fame, do forgive this digression. And, as I said above, keep it to yourself.

It might have been supposed that Crabb Robinson had made himself clear here, that he knew Wordsworth to be not indifferent to the tyrannies of the times, that he is not reproaching him with actual want of sympathy with noble causes, but pointing out the danger to his reputation of not expressing it publicly in verse. Yet the letter has been used to support that very accusation of coldness, indifference, and hardening.

Wordsworth accidentally read the criticism of his silence, which had not been intended to reach him, and was not offended. He might have replied that his earlier sonnets supplied sentiments for anyone who wanted them, but he merely observed with good humour, "Your supposed Biography entertained me much. I could give you the other side"; and left it at that. He may have had in mind that grave sonnet, written shortly after Waterloo but not published until 1827, when events had turned it from a warning into a condemnation no less decided for preserving the form of an admonition.

Emperors and Kings, how oft have temples rung
With impious thanksgiving, the Almighty's scorn!

. . . .

Now, from Heaven-sanctioned victory, Peace is sprung;
In this firm hour Salvation lifts her horn.
Glory to arms! But, conscious that the nerve
Of popular reason, long mistrusted, freed
Your thrones, ye Powers, from duty fear to swerve!
Be just, be grateful; nor, the oppressor's creed
Reviving, heavier chastisement deserve
Than ever forced unpitied hearts to bleed.

Yet, though he rebuked the Emperors and Kings, Wordsworth did not join Byron and Shelley in seeing Europe falling back under their oppression into a worse slavery than before. He did not like the Holy Alliance, but he looked on it as a transitory thing. Once or twice, indeed, we find him anticipating a possible clash between it and England. Thus Crabb Robinson noted in 1824 (*Diary*, April 22) that Wordsworth disapproved of the conduct of Canning, who, "to gain the Whigs and popularity", had used unnecessarily rash and insulting language against the Holy Alliance: "a war will certainly take place in a few years...and the absolute sovereigns will make a further attack on representative governments. In such a state of things Canning is not the man who will be competent to the great task of defending this country! These were Wordsworth's chief declarations—I was less inclined to doubt the facts than to be surprised at the feeling with which they were contemplated". There may be undue and, for Wordsworth, unusual apprehension of the powers of tyranny here, but there is certainly not tolerance of them. His usual view, however, was that, bad as the Alliance was, time would attend to it, and worse had been escaped; and his criticism of some of those who took a different view does not lack point and vigour. Thus, he wrote in the first *Address* of 1818:

Peace has indeed come; but do they who deprecated the continuance of the war, and clamoured for its close, on any terms, rejoice heartily in a triumph by which their prophecies were belied? Did they lend their voices to swell the hymn of transport, that resounded through our Land, when the arch-enemy was overthrown? Are they pleased that inheritances have been restored, and that legitimate governments have been re-established, on the Continent? And do they grieve when those re-established governments act unworthily of the favour which Providence has shown them? Do not too many rather secretly congratulate themselves on every proof of imbecility or misconduct there exhibited; and endeavour that attention shall be exclusively fixed on those melancholy facts, as if they were the only fruits of a triumph, to which we Britons owe, that we are a fearless, undishonoured, and rapidly improving people, and the nations of the Continent owe their very existence as self-governed communities?

And he returned to the charge in the second *Address*:

Thousands are so framed, that they are but languidly conscious of their love of an object, unless while they feel themselves in an active state of aversion to something which they can regard as its opposite.... Through this infirmity, many were betrayed into taking part with the Men whom they had heretofore despised or condemned; and assisted them in reviling their own Government for suffering, among the States of the Continent, institutions to remain which the respective nations (surely the best, if not the only judges in the case) were unwilling to part with, and for having permitted things to be done, either just and proper in themselves, or if indeed abuses, abuses of that kind which Great Britain had neither right to oppose, nor power to prevent. Not a Frenchman is in arms in Spain! But (alas for the credit of the English Cabinet!) Ferdinand, though a lawful, appears to be a sorry King; and the Inquisition, though venerated by the People of Spain as a holy tribunal, which has spread a protecting shade over their religion for hundreds of years, is, among Protestants, an abomination! Is that, however, a reason why we should not rejoice that Spain is restored to the rank of an Independent nation; and that her resources do not continue at the disposal of a foreign Tyrant, for the annoyance of Great Britain? Prussia no longer receives decrees from the Tuilleries; but nothing, we are told, is gained by this deliverance; because the Sovereign of that Country has not participated, as far as became him, a popular effervescence; and has withheld from his subjects certain privileges which they have proved themselves, to all but heated judgments, not yet qualified to receive.

There is no friendliness here for that sorry King, Ferdinand of Spain, nor for the King of Prussia, who, even if his subjects have been asking more than they are yet qualified to receive, is slack and sluggish. And when a thoroughly bad government was overthrown by its own subjects, Wordsworth was as delighted as any man was who called himself a Liberal, and who was continually demanding British intervention on behalf of oppressed minorities or majorities. The French Revolution of 1830 rejoiced him, though he did not, as many people did, expect that it would have no dangerous or unpleasant consequences. Thus in two letters[1] to George Huntly Gordon he shows satisfaction and a reasoned apprehension, both of which were justified by events.

I cannot but deeply regret that the late King of France and his ministers should have been so infatuated. Their stupidity,

1 *Letters*, II, 424, 442; uncertain dates in 1830 or 1831.

not to say their crimes, has given an impulse to the revolutionary and democratic spirit throughout Europe which is premature, and from which much immediate evil may be apprehended, whatever things may settle into at last. Whereas, had the government conformed to the increasing knowledge of the people, and not surrendered itself to the counsels of the priests and the bigoted royalists, things might have been kept in an even course to the mutual improvement and benefit of both governed and governors.

And again,

One is glad to see tyranny baffled and foolishness put to shame; but the French King, and his ministers, will be unfairly judged by all those who take not into consideration the difficulties of their position. It is not to be doubted that there has long existed a determination, and that plans have been laid, to destroy the government which the French received, as they felt, at the hands of the allies, and their pride could not bear. Moreover, the constitution, had it been their own choice, would by this time have lost favour in the eyes of the French, as not sufficiently democratic for the high notion *that* people entertain of their fitness to govern themselves; but, for my own part, I'd rather fill the office of a parish beadle than sit on the throne where the Duke of Orleans has suffered himself to be placed.

In 1846 Wordsworth thought that the Orleanist monarchy would last the lifetime of Louis Philippe, but not longer;[1] there he was out, but the next twenty years of French history would have confirmed him in his theory that too rapid democratization leads to the return of a despotism.

Crabb Robinson did not include in his list Italy, which was ultimately the only oppressed country for which Wordsworth's deep sympathy was fully expressed in verse, and this

[1] Cf. p. 47 *supra*.

at a date when sympathy for Italy was not fashionable among the English poets or even among English Liberals.[1] This fact may, indeed, explain Crabb Robinson's omission: he had all the sympathies and beliefs of an orthodox Liberal, and it is amusing to note his alternate understanding and complete misunderstanding of Wordsworth, who, to his bewilderment, shared some of his enthusiasms, went beyond him in some points—notably in the sentiments expressed in the *Postscript* of 1835—and yet showed regrettable Tory tendencies. But though Crabb Robinson had so little feeling for Italy that he left her out, he would probably not have gone so far as that other stout and orthodox Liberal Dr Arnold. One sentence in a letter from Arnold to Cornish (August 24, 1830) is almost incredible in its preferences. "I was delighted also with Venice; most of all delighted to see the secret prisons of the old aristocracy converted into lumber rooms, and to see German soldiers exercising authority in that place, which was once the very focus of the moral degradation of the Italian race, the seat of falsehood and ignorance and cruelty." That there could be any moral degradation, falsehood, ignorance or cruelty in Austrian domination does not seem to have occurred to Arnold in his admiration of order. Wordsworth, who had lamented the extinction of the Venetian Republic, was not consoled by the sight of German soldiers, and was convinced, as few foreigners and not too many Italians were then convinced, of the possibility of a revival of Italian independence and unity.

Fair Land! Thee all men greet with joy; how few,
Whose souls take pride in freedom, virtue, fame,
Part from thee without pity dyed in shame:
I could not—while from Venice we withdrew,

[1] Cf. Dicey, pp. 82, 115.

Led on till an Alpine strait confined our view
Within its depths, and to the shore we came
Of Lago Morto, dreary sight and name,
Which o'er sad thoughts a sadder colouring threw.
Italia! on the surface of thy spirit,
(Too aptly emblemed by that torpid lake)
Shall a few partial breezes only creep?—
Be its depths quickened; what thou dost inherit
Of the world's hopes, dare to fulfil; awake,
Mother of Heroes, from thy death-like sleep!

As indignation mastered grief, my tongue
Spake bitter words—

he continues, and the indignation and grief, mingled with faith in the soul of Italy and hope when all hope might have seemed vain, sound clearly in two sonnets dealing with an earlier part of his journey of 1837—*At Rome*, and *From the Alban Hills, looking towards Rome.* What intercourse had Wordsworth had with the men of the Risorgimento? These lines do not read as if they were the result of hearsay alone.

They—who have heard some learned Patriot treat
Of freedom, with mind grasping the whole theme
From ancient Rome, downwards through that bright dream
Of Commonwealths, each city a starlike seat
Of rival glory; they—fallen Italy—
Nor must, nor will, nor can, despair of Thee!

The second is even more definite.

Forgive, illustrious Country! these deep sighs,
Heaved less for thy bright plains and hills bestrown
With monuments decayed or overthrown,
For all that tottering stands or prostrate lies,
Than for like scenes in moral vision shown,
Ruin perceived for keener sympathies;

> Faith crushed, yet proud of weeds, her gaudy crown;
> Virtues laid low, and mouldering energies.
> Yet why prolong this mournful strain?—Fallen Power,
> Thy fortunes, twice exalted, might provoke
> Verse to glad notes prophetic of the hour
> When thou, uprisen, shalt break thy double yoke,
> And enter, with prompt aid from the Most High,
> On the third stage of thy great destiny.

There is no coldness nor lack of faith or vision or love of liberty in these poems. The *Memorials of a Tour in Italy* are too frequently neglected: Professor Harper, for instance, gives them a brief mention, with no consideration of their political importance, in his longer biography, and in the shorter does not even refer to them. But to ignore or misunderstand them is as dangerous as to ignore or misunderstand the *Postscript* of 1835, that revolutionary document which will be discussed in its place. The Fenwick note to the *Sonnets after leaving Italy* shows that his interest and sympathy were still alive—

> I had proof in several instances that the Carbonari, if I may still call them so, and their favourers, are opening their eyes to the necessity of patience, and are intent upon spreading knowledge actively, but quietly as they can. May they have resolution to continue in this course, for it is the only one by which they can truly benefit their country.

This was dictated in 1843 or later, some years after Mary Fletcher had recorded that on Italian politics he was "all we can desire". And she continued,[1]

> Wordsworth spoke with strong and deep feeling of the present state of Italy, and the crushing despotism of Austria, supported, as it is in secret, by Russia and Prussia. . . . I

[1] *Autobiography of Mrs Fletcher*, pp. 212–13. The date is August 1839.

cannot think that Milton himself could have talked more loftily against despotism, or more excellently on truth and justice.

In expressing so much more strongly, in public and in private, his indignation at the position of Italy than his disapproval of the governments of Spain, Austria or Prussia—though, as we have noticed, he was not altogether silent on them—Wordsworth was perfectly consistent. Part of Italy, if not all, was suffering under a foreign, not a native, tyranny. He held, in Dicey's words,[1] "the strong, probably the too vehement, belief in the certainty that a nation, so long as it was not ruled by foreigners, would in the end by its own natural vigour rid itself of every kind of bad government"; and therefore Spain and Austria and Prussia would ultimately find their salvation. At the same time, he was not in favour of an immediate armed uprising in Italy, partly because the lovers of freedom were so ill-organized that their struggles would only make matters worse, and partly because of his growing preference for peaceful methods.

It would be untrue and absurd to suggest that Wordsworth, as he grew older, became a pacifist in the usual sense of the term; but it is possible to observe him becoming more and more uncertain of the good of employing violence even in the righteous cause of freedom. Good might come out of violence in the end, but violence was the last, most desperate, weapon to be used. This is the meaning of the much misunderstood lines of the 1815 *Ode*—

> Thy most dreaded instrument,
> In working out a pure intent,
> Is Man—arrayed for mutual slaughter,
> —Yea, Carnage is thy daughter!

[1] Cf. the whole passage in Dicey, pp. 110–11.

When Wordsworth modified the lines in 1845, it was for the sake of avoiding offence, not because he thought them false in themselves, and indeed it was the expression, not the sense, which he modified—

> But Man is Thy most awful instrument,
> In working out a pure intent;

the context shows that the working out is not peaceful. The thought had already been expressed more soberly in an essay contributed to *The Friend* in 1809.[1]

> Happy moment it was for England when her Chaucer, who has rightly been called the morning star of her literature, appeared above the horizon; when her Wicliffe, like the sun, shot orient beams through the night of Romish superstition! Yet may the darkness and the desolating hurricane which immediately followed in the wars of York and Lancaster, be deemed in their turn a blessing, with which the Land has been visited.... The hundred years that followed the usurpation of Henry IV, were a hurling back of the mind of the country, a dilapidation, an extinction; yet institutions, laws, customs, and habits, were then broken down, which would not have been so readily, nor perhaps so thoroughly destroyed by the gradual influence of increasing knowledge; and under the oppression of which, if they had continued to exist, the virtue and intellectual prowess of the succeeding century could not have appeared at all, much less could they have displayed themselves with that eager haste, and with those beneficent triumphs, which will to the end of time be looked back upon with admiration and gratitude.

With the candour which John Stuart Mill and other political opponents recognized in him, Wordsworth acknowledged the force of the argument when it was turned against him.

[1] Knight, *Prose Works*, I, 91–2.

Thus Orville Dewey, an American visitor, tells us how in 1833, in argument with Wordsworth, he himself was maintaining that

> in the civilized world, the course of opinion was irresistibly setting towards universal education and popular forms of government; and nothing was to be done but to direct, modify, and control the tendency. [Wordsworth] fully admitted this; said that, in other centuries, some glorious results might be brought out—

but he did not enjoy the immediate prospect.[1] No more in 1809 and 1815 than in 1833 did Wordsworth consider war and turmoil as to be desired, and as he grew older he grew firmer in his trust in "the gradual influence of increasing knowledge" and the justice of the cause, whether the cause were the struggle with Napoleon, the freeing of Italy, or the spread of political freedom in England itself. What he experienced was not a failure of courage but an increase of faith, combined with a clearer comprehension of the dangers of internecine strife.

Three instances, at ten-year intervals, will show his almost religious belief in the triumph of the just cause. The first, of 1827, is a passage from a letter to Southey, whose *Peninsular War* he had been reading.

> I did not notice a single sentiment or opinion that I could have wished away but one—where you support the notion that if the Duke of Wellington had not lived and commanded, Bonaparte must have continued the master of Europe. I do not object to this from any dislike I have to the Duke, but from a conviction—I trust, a philosophic one—that Providence would not allow the upsetting of so diabolical a system as Bonaparte's to depend upon the existence of any individual.

[1] Orville Dewey, *The Old World and the New*, p. 93.

The next is comprised in the three sonnets which consider the Italian situation in 1837, *At Bologna, in remembrance of the late insurrections.*

Ah why deceive ourselves! by no mere fit
Of sudden passion roused shall men attain
True freedom where for ages they have lain
Bound in a dark abominable pit,
With life's best sinews more and more unknit.
Here, there, a banded few who loathe the chain
May rise to break it: effort worse than vain
For thee, O great Italian nation, split
Into those jarring fractions.—Let thy scope
Be one fixed mind for all; thy rights approve
To thy own conscience gradually renewed;
Learn to make Time the father of wise Hope;
Then trust thy cause to the arm of Fortitude,
The light of Knowledge, and the warmth of Love.

That this is a reasoned policy, springing from faith in the cause and consciousness of the slow processes of life and growth in a nation, not a calling of mean things by noble names, appears in the answer to impatient objectors.

Hard task! exclaim the undisciplined, to lean
On Patience coupled with such slow endeavour,
That long-lived servitude must last for ever.
Perish the grovelling few, who, prest between
Wrongs and the terror of redress, would wean
Millions from glorious aims. Our chains to sever
Let us break forth in tempest now or never!—
What, is there then no space for golden mean
And gradual progress?—Twilight leads to day,
And, even within the burning zones of earth,
The hastiest sunrise yields a temperate ray;
The softest breeze to fairest flowers gives birth:
Think not that Prudence dwells in dark abodes,
She scans the future with the eye of gods.

As leaves are to the tree whereon they grow
  And wither, every human generation
  Is to the Being of a mighty nation,
Locked in our world's embrace through weal and woe;
Thought that should teach the zealot to forego
  Rash schemes, to abjure all selfish agitation,
  And seek through noiseless pains and moderation
The unblemished good they only can bestow.
Alas! with most, who weigh futurity
  Against time present, passion holds the scales:
  Hence equal ignorance of both prevails,
And nations sink; or, struggling to be free,
  Are doomed to flounder on, like wounded whales
Tossed on the bosom of a stormy sea.

Ten years later still the thought of the three sonnets was summed up in the advice given to Thomas Cooper. "I have always said the people were right in what they asked;[1] but you went the wrong way to get it....The people are sure to have the franchise, as knowledge increases; but you will not get all you seek at once—and you must never seek it again by physical force: it will only make you longer about it."

Wordsworth may be accused with some justice of having developed too mystical a faith in the ultimate triumph on earth of the doctrines which he had upheld in his youth, but he cannot fairly be accused, as he was accused by uncomprehending Liberal friends and enemies in his lifetime, of having "lost faith in humanity". He refused to subscribe to the sentimental creed which takes no account of the actual state of humanity; he refused to believe against all his experience that "the people", as long as they remained untrained and unthinking, were fit to rule themselves; but he was convinced

[1] Cf. pp. 197–9 *infra* for the extent of Wordsworth's approval of the Chartist demands.

that they were capable of being trained; and his fears were, not that anarchy or tyranny would ultimately triumph, but that impatience on the part of the lovers of freedom would delay the triumph of freedom longer than need be.

iii

Wordsworth's unwillingness to make premature extensions of nominal freedom is seen at its strongest with regard to Ireland. In effect he took up the Tory attitude, but, as in other matters in which he was apparently to be ranked among Tories, his companions might reasonably look upon him with grave distrust. He might seem to come to some of their conclusions, but he based them on different premises, and it was quite possible that he would go on to other conclusions of which they would not approve.

As far as Ireland was concerned, he set out with what looks at first sight like a healthy Tory and Protestant prejudice against the influence of the Roman Catholic priests. It was in fact not pure prejudice: it was based on his own observations in youth in France and Italy, and was combined with a sympathy, and even a respect, by no means common, especially in his time, for the faith of individual Roman Catholics.[1] There was no real bigotry in the man who took the trouble, when he was in Rome in 1837, to procure rosaries blessed by the Pope for his daughter and, perhaps, his granddaughter. He did not, however, believe, as a result of his experience, that, in his own words (to Wrangham, April 1809), "their profession of faith is in itself as good as ours, as consistent with Civil Liberty". The behaviour of the restored "legitimate"

[1] Cf. the next chapter, pp. 254–6, 292–8.

governments in Southern Europe after Waterloo was not such as to change Wordsworth's opinion of the incompatibility of civil liberty with strong Roman Catholic clerical influence. From this it was easy to take a step further and conclude that concessions to Roman Catholics might reasonably be considered as endangering civil, possibly also religious, liberty in Ireland, where they were much in the majority. That they had any right to concessions, merely because they were the majority in Ireland, Wordsworth would not admit, partly because he did not believe that the majority was always to have its will, partly because he refused to reckon Ireland apart from Great Britain. For him, as for almost all Englishmen, the problem was how to pacify and govern a division of the United Kingdom which was always seething with disaffection in one form or another. Repeal of the Union might be urged by O'Connell, but it was many years before the English Parliament was prepared to consider that possibility seriously. Agrarian reform, Catholic Emancipation, partial or total disendowment of the Irish Church, disestablishment of the Irish Church—concessions of various sorts were suggested and disapproved in varying degrees according to the real or imagined liberality of opinion in their advocates, but always with the confidence that this or that reform would remove discontent, and make all difficulties disappear.

It is clear from his earliest to his latest utterances that Wordsworth had no such easy confidence. One concession must lead to another, and if men were not prepared to make the last, they must not make the first. "Be not startled", he wrote to Losh (December 4, 1821), "when I say that I am averse to further concessions to the Roman Catholics. My reasons are, that such concessions will not produce harmony among the Roman Catholics themselves; that those among them who are most clamorous for the measure care little about it but as a step, first, to the overthrow of the Protestant establishment in Ireland, as introductory to a separation of the two countries—their ultimate aim." It would be interesting to hear his comments on the last eighty years of Irish history.

There is no need to multiply quotations: the long letter of 1829 to Bishop Blomfield[1] covers the whole question of Catholic Emancipation as Wordsworth saw it, with the probable consequences to Ireland, the Irish Church, the Union, and civil and religious liberty. It is, however, to be remarked that his visit to Ireland in that year had shown him things to which some observers were blind. He was struck to the heart by the miserable poverty and ignorance which he saw, and, unlike Southey, who thought that the extension of the Poor Laws to Ireland would mend matters, he saw no immediate remedy. "The subject of the Poor Laws was never out of my sight whilst I was in Ireland", he wrote to George Huntly Gordon (December 1, 1829); "it seems to me next to impossible to introduce a general system of such laws, principally for two reasons: the vast numbers that would have equal claims for relief, and the non-existence of a class capable of looking with effect to their administration." In the letter to Bishop Blomfield he broke out strongly and indignantly on the causes and dangers of this wretchedness.

And now these swarms of degraded people, which could not have existed but through the neglect and misdirected power of the sister island, are by a withdrawing of that power to have their own way, and to be allowed to dictate to us.

[1] Grosart, I, 261–70; Knight, *Prose Works*; not given in full by Knight in the *Letters*.

A population, vicious in character as unnatural in immediate origin (for it has been called into birth by short-sighted landlords, set upon adding to the number of votes at their command, and by priests who for lucre's sake favour the increase of marriages), is held forth as constituting a claim to political power strong in proportion to its numbers, though in a sane view that claim is in an inverse ratio to them.

Southey would have joined in that recognition of English sin, but it would not have been welcomed by many of those who agreed with Wordsworth in opposing concessions to Ireland, nor would his attitude towards Roman Catholicism on its devotional side have been approved by many who agreed with him in opposing Catholic Emancipation. In Ireland, as elsewhere, he was not the usual type of English Protestant critic. Few of his contemporaries would either have felt or expressed the sympathy which, writing to his brother Christopher (September 5, 1829), he shows for the poor woman who brought her child for healing to St Kevin's pool.

It would have affected you very much to see this poor confiding creature, and to hear the manner in which she expressed her faith in the goodness of God and St Kevin. What would one not give to see among Protestants such devout reliance on the mercy of their Creator, so much resignation, so much piety, so much simplicity and singleness of mind, purged of the accompanying superstitions!

Yet the very simplicity and singleness of mind which Wordsworth reverenced in this example would make the uneducated Irish more likely to be the prey of unprincipled leaders, and nominal concessions to them, in those present circumstances, were likely only, he considered, to increase their misery and, by the strengthening of Irish influence at Westminster, to bring disaster to England.

iv

Wordsworth's views on political conditions in England itself were those of an idealist with a strong sense of reality and of history. He believed that men were capable of living together in happiness, as far as happiness can be secured by externals, and with freedom to develop their own natures. This, it may be objected, is the belief of all idealists, and does not allow for the practical difficulties. But Wordsworth was not blind to the difficulties. If he had contented himself with continuing to express a lofty desire for universal freedom and brotherhood, and a vehement hatred of the tyranny of governments, particularly monarchical and ecclesiastical governments, he would have preserved with no trouble a reputation for advanced and liberal thought. But he concerned himself with the state of England as it was in consequence of centuries of slow growth, with the problem of bringing about reforms that, in an imperfect world of imperfect men ruled by passion more than by reason, would not do more harm than good, with the problem of uniting liberty and stability at a time when both were threatened by social changes, by a long war and a peace which did not bring all the relief that was hoped from it. The conclusions which he reached are not satisfactory either to the conventional reactionary or to the conventional revolutionary either of his own day or of to-day. The reactionary would find him the more disturbing, if he understood him, all the more because of what would at first seem to be an agreement on some of the questions which are usually—and again conventionally—regarded as providing a test of liberality of thought and opinion.

In matters of internal politics Wordsworth acted on two

constant principles. One was that of the necessity of managing political reforms so that they did not bring about anarchy, reaction and the repetition of the struggle for liberty: something has already been written on this point, and more remains to be written. The other, the more fundamental—it might indeed be argued that the first springs from it—was that of the necessity of unity within the country. On one side this principle combined with early loyalties and an innate and increasing love of old and familiar things to produce what his distressed Liberal friends called Toryism and his enemies apostasy: on the other it combined with indignant compassion and the sense of the nobility of man to produce what was so far in advance of most contemporary radicalism as not to be recognized for the dangerous stuff it was. The first has been over-emphasized and the second almost entirely ignored; but both, however many contributory streams ran into them, spring from this one principle, the conviction that a house divided against itself cannot stand. That conviction was one of the reasons for Wordsworth's dislike of the Whigs: during the war they had not, as a party, worked to present a united front to the enemy, and he was in consequence inclined to distrust all their later policy as intended for their private or party advantage rather than for the good of the country. But he was not much better pleased with the Tories, whom he regarded as also inclined to act on momentary and personal expediency rather than on principle. He was to the end a severe judge of Pitt, though he was amused by the unrelenting disapproval which led Southey to imply doubts of Pitt's ultimate salvation.[1] "For my own part," he wrote to Sir George Beaumont on hearing of Pitt's death (February 11,

[1] Cf. p. 131 *supra*.

1806), "as probably you know, I have never been able to regard his political life with complacency. I believe him, however, to have been as disinterested a man, and as true a lover of his country, as it was possible for so ambitious a man to be. His first wish (though probably unknown to himself) was that his country should prosper under his administration; his next that it should prosper. Could the order of these wishes have been reversed, Mr Pitt would have avoided many of the grievous mistakes into which, I think, he fell." With this it is interesting to compare Haydon's record in his journal for May 23, 1815, which points towards a famous passage in *The Prelude*.

Breakfasted with Wordsworth, and spent a delightful two hours. Speaking of Burke, Fox, and Pitt, he said: "You always went from Burke with your mind filled; from Fox with your feelings excited; and from Pitt with wonder at his having had the power to make the worse appear the better reason". "Pitt", he said, "preferred power to principle."

Fox had attracted him at first by his generosity of spirit, but did not satisfy him. Crabb Robinson noted (June 6, 1812), a few years earlier than Haydon made his note, that Wordsworth had been speaking freely on the character of Fox, "to whom he denied the higher qualities of the mind, philosophy and religion; and with reason denied his assertion of human rights in matters of religion to be a proof of religion".

The three passages taken together explain why the name of Fox did not appear in the earlier versions of *The Prelude* in the passage referred to above, and why it was omitted from the latest version. We have in the first versions of Book VII the description of the orator, the spinner of words—in brief,

Pitt.[1] He has the advantage of a name which "from Childhood we had heard Familiarly"; he is

> no trifler, no short-flighted Wit,
> No stammerer of a minute, painfully
> Deliver'd. No! the Orator hath yoked
> The Hours, like young Aurora, to his Car....
> ... Like a Hero in Romance
> He winds away his never-ending horn,
> Words follow words, sense seems to follow sense;
> What memory and what logic! till the Strain
> Transcendent, superhuman as it is,
> Grows tedious even in a young Man's ear.[2]

In the earlier versions Wordsworth's scorn for Pitt is not balanced by admiration for anyone else; nothing of this sort appears until after the C version, until, that is to say, about 1820.[3] Then was added the passage on Burke, including a few lines on Fox—

> Who sits
> Listening beside thee—no—no longer near
> Yet still in heart thy friend. Illustrious Fox
> Thy grateful pupil. In the power of words
> Thundering and lightning when his turn shall come
> A British Pericles.

[1] M. Legouis was misled by the Shakespearian allusion into supposing that the scene is the House of Lords. But (*a*) the context shows that it is the House of Commons, (*b*) Pitt's inexhaustible flow of oratory was well known, (*c*) "one among the prime" and the name known familiarly from childhood point definitely to the Prime Minister and the great Pitt name. Cf. also the Fenwick note to *Monument of Mrs. Howard*: "I had so often seen Mr Pitt upon his own ground at Cambridge and upon the floor of the House of Commons."

[2] 1805 version; in the latest *seemed* replaced *is* in the penultimate line: Wordsworth would leave no doubt of his estimate of Pitt.

[3] Cf. de Selincourt, pp. xviii–xix, 246, 547.

The emphasis here, as in the conversation with Haydon in 1815, is on the power which Fox possessed of exciting the emotions. But Fox was not in agreement with Burke, though "still in heart" his friend, and on second thoughts Wordsworth cut the lines out, in 1828 or later.[1] There is no question of his abandoning generous early enthusiasms: the lines were not inserted until late, and held their place for only a few years; he had, in *Loud is the vale*, celebrated the greatness of Fox, and in its later version he strengthened his expression of admiration;[2] but Fox exercised on him neither the repellent effect of Pitt nor the permanent influence of Burke. He went from Burke with his mind filled, even in the early days when he differed from him in opinion;[3] and he did well to acknowledge that influence. In his maturity and later life the sense of the nation as a unity, an organic whole, and the historical sense which prefers development and growth to violent change, owe something of their strength to Burke. The debt is often, though not always, recognized by those who write on Wordsworth.

The enemies of national unity are many, and there is a passage in the second of the *Addresses* of 1818 where Wordsworth attacks them in an unexpected fashion. Of all election addresses these are surely the most outspoken in their criticism of the government whose candidates they are supposed to be supporting. Professor Harper, it may fairly be said, has misunderstood the real significance of Wordsworth's

[1] *Ibid.* p. 547.

[2] The original *But when the Mighty pass away* became in 1837 *But when the great and good depart.*

[3] As Dicey pointed out, the influence of Burke is clear in the letter to the Bishop of Llandaff (*Statesmanship*, pp. 46, 52–3 n., 59–70).

part in that election. The *Addresses* are not, to begin with, simply a repetition of the usual arguments for "the machine": his view of this, as of other political events in Wordsworth's life, is not uncoloured by modern American conditions.[1] There was a good deal of pure local feeling in Wordsworth's objection to Brougham's candidature: Brougham—who had already given evidence of his fatal cleverness—was, in all but birth, an outsider, a "foreigner" sent into the country to contest the seat because there was not enough Whig opinion in Westmorland to supply a local man. Crabb Robinson, reading the pamphlets in 1839 in cold blood, recognized this: they "are a very spirited and able vindication of the voting for the two Lowthers, against the Radical parvenu—and have in them very little that I now dissent from" (*Diary*, February 1, 1839). And Crabb Robinson was no Tory.

Apart from the personal objection to Brougham, Wordsworth had general objections to the Whigs. They had not behaved well during the war, particularly during the later

[1] A protest may also be entered against the implications of his sentence on Wordsworth's nomination to the Commission of Peace: "As a seal and sign of social rank, and in recognition of his services to the Tory party, Wordsworth was appointed Justice of the Peace" (p. 556, ed. of 1929). The proposal was of course made to Wordsworth with a certain amount of snobbery: the friend of Lonsdale and brother of Dr Wordsworth must be a suitable person for a J.P., in spite of his habit of "booing about the country"—to use the expressive description by one of his neighbours of his trick of reciting poetry during his walks. Wordsworth might have refused the nomination: he accepted it, after hesitation, from the motives which still affect Englishmen in his position: it was an uncongenial public duty, but not to be shirked. Early nineteenth-century benches of magistrates were not made up exclusively of stiff-necked Tories who spent their time sending poachers and political agitators to prison and transportation for life.

stages of it; they had conducted themselves "more like allies to a military despot, who was attempting to enslave the world, and to whom their own country was an object of paramount hatred, than like honest Englishmen, who had breathed the air of liberty from their cradles", and they must accordingly "reconcile themselves as well as they can to dislike and disesteem, the unavoidable results of behaviour so unnatural". It was true, as he had written to John Scott two years earlier (April 18, 1816), that if the Whig Opposition were in power, reliance might be placed "on the salutary restraint which a change of situation would impose upon their opinions, and in the favourable alteration which would be wrought in their passions by the kindly moulding of new circumstances". But he preferred to help to keep the Whigs out, rather than to trust to that moderating effect of power which has been noted, with relief or indignation, in governments of a later day. The best way to keep the Whigs out was to help the Tories to get in; but disapproval of the Whigs did not for him connote approval of the Tories, who were only comparatively, not positively, deserving. It was not, as a hasty or superficial reading of the first sentences in the passage which follows might suggest, that they were not Tory enough for him. His charges go deeper than that.

But there are points of domestic policy in which his Majesty's Ministers, not appearing in counterview with their Opponents, are seen less to their honour. Speaking as an Individual, and knowing that here I differ from many Freeholders with whom it is an honour to co-operate in the present struggle, I must express my disapprobation of the patronage afforded by several persons in power, to a Society by which is virtually propagated the notion that Priesthood, and of course our own inestimable Church Establishment, is superfluous. I condemn their sanction (and this attaches to the whole body) of the malevolent and senseless abuse heaped upon the Clergy in the matter of Tythes, through the medium of papers circulated by the Agricultural Board. I deprecate the course which some of them take in the Catholic Question, as unconstitutional; and deplore the want of discernment evinced by men who persuade themselves that the discontents prevalent in Ireland will be either removed or abated by such concession. With these errors and weaknesses the Members of the Administration (as appears to me) may be justly reproached; and a still heavier charge will lie against them, if the correction of the Poor Laws be longer deferred. May they exhibit, in treating this momentous subject, a tenderness of undeceived humanity on the one side, and a sternness of enlightened state-policy on the other! Thus, and thus only, can be checked immediately, and in due course of time perhaps removed, an evil by which one claim and title is set in array against another, in a manner, and to an extent, that threatens utter subversion to the ancient frame of society.

This is the heaviest burthen that now lies upon England!—Here is a necessity for reform which, as it cannot prosper unless it begin from the Government and the upper ranks in society, has no attraction for demagogues and mob-exciting patriots. They understand their game; and, as if the people could in no way be so effectually benefited as by rendering their Government suspected, they declaim against taxes; and, by their clamours for reduction of public expenditure, drown the counter-suggestions from the "still small voice" of moderation appealing to circumstances.

The faults of the Tory government are failure to uphold the Established Church and encouragement of her adversaries, and, far worse, neglect of the sufferings of the poor, whose cause is not a subject of popular clamour, but whose severance from the rich is the greatest of the national dangers. All are to Wordsworth branches of the same offence, acts or refusals to act which threaten the unity of the country.

Wordsworth's spiritual beliefs will be considered in the next chapter: they are not deeply concerned in this matter, though his personal allegiance to the Church of England strengthened his feelings with regard to ecclesiastical politics. But his argument in this *Address* and elsewhere is not primarily religious, and it may even seem in some respects wanting in religious confidence. It was his firm conviction that a close alliance between the State and religion was advantageous to both. Many would agree with him here. He went further, arguing that, to be effective, this alliance could exist between only one form of religion and the State. Here, too, many, especially in his own time, and not only of his own communion, would agree with him. But it did not follow for others, as it did for him, that anything which tended to weaken the temporal power of the Church of England, or to introduce other spiritual authorities, was an attack upon the whole life of the country, upon the unity which it should be the part of every Englishman to maintain. Hence his opposition to Catholic Emancipation on the one hand, and to concessions to the Nonconformists on the other. Both kinds of relief tended to introduce a confusion of authorities and interests, both in Parliament and in the nation at large. "With the Methodists on one side, and the Catholics on the other, what is to become of the poor Church and people of England, to both of which I am most tenderly attached?" he wrote once to Wrangham (April 1809). His view of the consequences of Catholic Emancipation has already been considered.[1] From the Nonconformists he had no apprehensions as regarded

[1] Cf. pp. 149–52 *supra*.

civil and religious liberty, but he disliked the thought of the presence of Nonconformists, as of Roman Catholics, in large numbers in the House of Commons, because they would attack the Church and because they would add to the disunity of Parliament, and for the same reasons he opposed the abolition of University tests.

> For myself I would oppose tooth and nail the petition from Cambridge in behalf of the Dissenters, because it is hypocritical and, if granted, will inevitably lead to a demand for Degrees, which will give Votes, open to them the emoluments and offices of the University, and make them a part of the governing Body. An event which for innumerable reasons, and not the least for its tendency to overthrow the Established Church, I earnestly deprecate.

Thus he wrote to Crabb Robinson (April 3, 1834), and a few more of the "innumerable reasons" were given to his nephew Christopher some weeks later (May 15, 1834), but the thought behind them all is that of unity.

> I regard the prayer of the petitioners to whom you are opposed as formidable still more from the effect which, if granted, it will ultimately have upon the Church, and through that medium upon the Monarchy and upon social order, than for its immediate tendency to introduce discord in the Universities.

The varying opinions of its members seemed to him one of the greatest objections to the young University of London.[1]

[1] The other was the absence of religious teaching at University College. How, he demanded, was a regular and liberal course of education to be supplied if Christianity was to be excluded? "Plague upon such liberality!" (To Crabb Robinson, February 1838.) Dr Arnold, who was seldom in theological harmony with Wordsworth, agreed with him here, and resigned from the Senate on the question of requiring some religious knowledge from all students.

"Your University and College are humbugs", he wrote to Crabb Robinson (March 26, 1838); "all these attempts to make men co-operate whose opinions are, or, were they conscientious men, ought to be, so widely different, are founded on false views of human Nature." The early history of University College, especially the Martineau affair of 1866 which caused the resignation of Augustus De Morgan, shows that there was more truth in Wordsworth's objections than it is pleasant for the zealots of co-operation to admit. His thought is clear: it was possible to be on terms of the closest personal friendship with those from whom one differed profoundly in political and religious views, as he himself proved, but to attempt to work together with them in the very matters where the differences were deepest could lead only to hypocrisy or disaster. And to introduce fresh discordant elements into deliberative assemblies and governing bodies, which even without them were scarcely harmonious, was sheer madness. Though, like most Anglicans, he had an eye for the faults of his Church, the Church of England seemed to him a beneficent and a unifying influence in the country, and to give power to her enemies to attack her was to be untrue to the interests of the whole nation.

Worse than the disunity caused by diversity of religious and political opinions in the governing classes was, Wordsworth continued to assert, the disunity caused by diversity of interest between governors and governed, between rich and poor.[1] It is the gravest of his accusations against the Ministry

[1] And, in a smaller sphere, between servants and masters. The Wordsworth servants looked on the family as theirs. Cf. for the reason of this relation the conversation of December 21, 1841, recorded by Lady Richardson (Grosart, III, 438): "He talked with

in 1818 that they are ignoring the necessity for Poor Law reform. This, social reform generally, and Parliamentary reform are all connected in Wordsworth's mind. A survey almost strictly chronological will bring out the connection of the subjects and the essential consistency of his thought: from time to time his opinion of the expediency of details varies, and at one period he seems to be denouncing what both before and after he acknowledges to be the ideal, but he ends with a corrected version of his first ideas. "I should think that I had lived to little purpose", he wrote honestly and wisely to Losh (December 4, 1821), "if my notions on the subject of government had undergone no modification. My youth must, in that case, have been without enthusiasm, and my manhood endued with small capability of profiting by reflection". Yet it is to neglect half the evidence to assert that there was any fundamental change in his principles of action. Unfortunately, half the evidence usually is neglected.

The letter addressed, though not sent, to the Bishop of Llandaff in 1793 expresses in the strongest terms Wordsworth's early ideas for the regeneration of society. It is the work of a young man of generous enthusiasms and little experience, who believes that a few changes in the external arrangements of society will, men being naturally reasonable, lead to complete happiness. Universal and equal suffrage,

great animation of the separation of feeling between the rich and poor in this country;...the line of demarcation not being so clearly laid down...by the law...people fancy they must make it for themselves....He spoke of his own desire to carry out the feeling of brotherhood with regard to servants....He doubted whether he might not have had better servants on a different system; but he thought it right to endeavour to inspire your domestics with a feeling of common interest".

recourse to a referendum before laws are finally passed, Parliaments of short duration, the prohibition of re-election after a certain period of service—these would prove to be remedies for almost all the evils of society; "as laws, being but the expression of the general will, would be enacted only from an almost universal conviction of their utility, any resistance to such laws, any desire of eluding them, must proceed from a few refractory individuals". There is much immaturity of thought here, but much also which Wordsworth retained to the end of his life. Universal and equal suffrage, for example, he looked upon in later years as an unmitigated evil if it were granted hastily to those who were not ready to receive it, but it still remained for him the ultimate goal.[1]

A remarkable feature in this letter, however, is that it already contains those points which were to modify all Wordsworth's easy theorizing. "Your Lordship will scarcely question that much of human misery, that the great evils which desolate States, proceed from the governors having an interest distinct from that of the governed. It should seem a natural deduction, that whatever has a tendency to identify the two must also in the same degree promote the general welfare." Much of human misery—not all. And, Wordsworth was presently to consider, was there only one way of destroying the evil of "the governors having an interest distinct from that of the governed"? Was even the best way to make the governed also the governors immediately, or might not something, less spectacular but possibly more effective, be done by rousing the consciences of the governors and leaving no grounds for the mistrust of the governed—by creating a real unity of spirit between the unlike, rather than

[1] Cf. pp. 197–9 *infra*.

by attempting to set up and maintain an artificial political equality? Even in 1793, in a passage which has been already quoted,[1] Wordsworth admitted that he was "well aware, from the abuse of the executive power in States, that there is not a single European nation but what affords a melancholy proof that if, at this moment, the original authority of the people should be restored, all that could be expected from such restoration would in the beginning be but a change of tyranny". In 1793, unorthodox Republican though he was in admitting the evil, Wordsworth was prepared to accept such a change of tyranny, trusting that "having dried up the source from which flows the corruption of the public opinion...the stream will go on gradually refining itself". The events of the next few years were to make him look less complacently upon the process.

In little more than a year, indeed, Wordsworth was beginning to see certain advantages even in the "present Constitution". Horne Tooke was acquitted on the charge of high treason on November 22, 1794—as he would certainly not have been if the conditions had been reversed and he had been tried in France—and a few weeks later Wordsworth wrote to his friend Mathews in comment on the result of the trial.

I rejoice with you on the acquittal of the prisoner, and on the same grounds....The late occurrences in every point of view are interesting to humanity. They will abate the insolence and presumption of the aristocracy, by shewing it that neither the violence nor the art of power can crush even an unfriended individual, though engaged in the propagation of doctrines confessedly unpalatable to privilege; and they will force upon the most prejudiced this conclusion that there is

[1] Cf. p. 128 *supra*.

some reason in the language of reformers. Furthermore, they will convince bigoted enemies to our present Constitution that it contains parts upon which too high a value cannot be set. To every class of men occupied in the correction of abuses it must be an animating reflection that their exertions, so long as they are temperate, will be countenanced and protected by the good sense of the country.

These are not the words of a man bent upon immediate and complete revolution. They were written in the first days of 1795: how far are they in thought from the second *Address* of 1818?

Government and civil Society are things of infinite complexity, and rash Politicians are the worst enemies of mankind; because it is mainly through them that rational liberty has made so little progress in the world. You have heard of a Profession to which the luxury of modern times has given birth, that of Landscape-Gardeners, or Improvers of Pleasure-grounds. A competent Practitioner in this elegant art begins by considering every object, that he finds in the place where he is called to exercise his skill, as having a right to remain, till the contrary be proved. If it be a deformity he asks whether a slight alteration may not convert it into a beauty; and he destroys nothing till he has convinced himself by reflection that no alteration, no diminution or addition, can make it ornamental. Modern Reformers reverse this judicious maxim. If a thing is before them, so far from deeming that it has on that account a claim to continue and be deliberately dealt with, its existence with them is a sufficient warrant for its destruction.

It is not enough to answer simply that Wordsworth was in 1818 supporting the Lowther candidates, and that he had therefore accepted the Tory view of politics—that his plea for gradual reform was in effect a plea to let things remain as they were. As we have seen, he took the opportunity to speak severely of the Tory government. But though he could not altogether approve of the Tories, they were at least better than the Whigs: they had at least taken the right attitude towards Napoleon, and if a Tory government were sufficiently egged on by its supporters, it might carry through reforms of social miseries and even of Parliamentary representation at a pace which would not endanger the stability of society.

V

It seems to be the question of Parliamentary representation which convinces many of Wordsworth's critics that he had become a thorough Tory. When he wrote the letter to the Bishop of Llandaff, he advocated universal and equal suffrage: "if there is a single man in Great Britain who has no suffrage in the election of a representative, the will of the society of which he is a member is not generally expressed; he is a Helot in that society". And there was to be no delay in granting the suffrage. In 1809 he wrote to Daniel Stuart (March 31):

Books will do nothing of themselves nor institutions without books. Two things are absolutely wanted in this country—a thorough reform in Parliament and a new course of education; which must be preceded by some genuine philosophical writings from some quarter or other, to teach the principles upon which that education should be grounded. We have in our language better books than exist in any other and in our land better institutions, but the one nobody reads, and the others are fallen into disorder and decay.

Parliamentary reform and education were already closely connected in his mind. Two months later, on May 25, he wrote again to Stuart, and more fully, on the first of them.

If we, who wish for a temperate reform, are utterly to reject all assistance from all those who do not think exactly as we do, how is it to be attained? For my part, I see no party or set of men with whom in regard to this measure I could act with entire approbation of their views; but I should be glad to receive assistance from any. If I have a hill to climb, and cannot do it without a walking stick, better have a dirty one than none at all. I do not think the reform will ever be effected, unless the people take it up, and if the people do stir, it can only be by public meetings, and it is natural that in meetings of this kind the most violent men should be most applauded; but I do not see that it necessarily follows that their words will be realised in action. The misfortune of this question of reform is that the one party sees nothing in it but dangers, and the other nothing but hopes and promises. For my part, I think the dangers and difficulties great, but not insurmountable. Whereas if there be not a reform, the destruction of the liberties of the country is inevitable.

By 1812 the question of Parliamentary reform was more obviously complicated by the growing popular discontent, which was due partly to the dragging out of the war and partly to the consciousness of bad industrial conditions. Southey anticipated the breaking out of a class war,[1] and Wordsworth agreed with him on the danger. On May 31, 1812, Crabb Robinson recorded that—

Wordsworth spoke with great feeling of the present state of the country. He considers the combinations among journeymen and even the Benefit Societies and all associations of men, apparently for the best purposes, as very alarming: he contemplates a renovation of all the horrors of a war between the poor and the rich, a conflict of property with no property.... And Wordsworth contemplated the manufacturing system as a most menacing evil.

[1] Cf. his letter to Sir George Beaumont, May 29, 1812.

And the man who had as early as 1794 condemned "all inflammatory addresses to the passions of men" was not likely to approve of the violent language of many reformers, social and political. He had hoped in 1809 that their words would not be realized in action, but he presently saw signs that that hope might be vain. Crabb Robinson gives us a definite illustration of this point. After the reconciliation between Coleridge and Wordsworth brought about by that able negotiator, Wordsworth, "without saying a complimentary thing to me", Crabb Robinson reported to Thomas Robinson (May 20, 1812), "has done what really flattered me, has offered to go and visit any one of my friends to whom I wish to introduce him". Crabb Robinson accordingly took him to see Mrs Charles Aikin, who came up to Wordsworth's idea of "a Woman whose countenance and manner are what a Woman's ought to be". James Montgomery also delighted him. But, as Crabb Robinson wrote in his diary (May 13, 1812),

A political dispute rather disturbed us for a time. Wordsworth, speaking of the late assassination [of Perceval], and of Sir Francis Burdett's speech ten days ago, when he spoke of the soldiers as murdering the people, said that probably the murderer heard that speech, and [that this], operating on his mind in its diseased and inflamed state, *might be the determining motive* to his act. This was taken up as a reflection on Sir Francis Burdett and resented warmly by young Roscoe, who in a rude offensive manner immediately contradicted Wordsworth bluntly. Yates did the same. (Indeed, I believe, except myself, Wordsworth had everybody against him.) Wordsworth, in the further explanation of his assertion, observed that men who are about to do a horrid act are anxious to conceal from themselves the motive, and wish to dress it out with a shew of virtuous feeling; that therefore, though revenge might be the first stimulating motive, it might be confirmed and determined by such a suggestion. In this sense, and in reference to the possibility of such a connection of ideas, I supported Wordsworth, but the conversation took a bad turn from the remark. Roscoe said Sir Francis Burdett's was a constitutional speech, and asked what the people were to do who were starving. "Not murder people", said Wordsworth, "unless they mean to eat their hearts."

A Johnsonian retort which seems to have silenced the opponent, "a very shallow fellow", as Wordsworth afterwards called him.

That kind of irresponsible talk among comfortable people was bound to anger a man who knew by experience what it might lead to. There were too many materials for a revolution in England in those last years of the war for him to be able to listen with patience to rhetorical questions whose implications had not been considered. When peace came, the situation did not improve: to the troubles with which we are familiar after a war were added those of popular discontent beyond anything we have experienced—riots and arson and sedition which went beyond the mouthings of young Roscoe. The Peterloo Massacre was a deplorable business, but we are unjust to the government of that day if we remember it and forget the Cato Street Conspiracy and other things of the same sort. We are apt to look at the politics of the second decade of the nineteenth century with the eyes of Shelley, who could see in the government only shameful tyrants, not a set of fairly honest, though not very brilliant, men who were doing their best in desperate circumstances. His sonnet on England in 1819 is taken as expressing the views of all thoughtful and liberal Englishmen: we forget that if there had not been a general feeling that some measures of restraint were necessary, it would either have been impossible to carry the Six Acts of that year through Parliament, or they would have provoked the revolution which they were designed to prevent. General moderate opinion is expressed, as so often, by Crabb Robinson (*Diary*, December 9, 1819).

There are a few seditious spirits in the country who would raise a rebellion if they could, but they cannot; and there are some among the ministers perhaps who would not scruple to give the Crown powers fatal to the liberties of the people. But neither the courts of law nor the people, who as jurymen concur in the administration of the law, would assist in a project destructive of liberty, nor would the ministry themselves dare make a violent attempt. At the same time, the laws are objectionable.

Crabb Robinson described himself in 1833 as a cheerful alarmist, and Wordsworth and Southey as alarmists of a more gloomy outlook. The three men differed over details, sometimes very widely: Southey, for instance, had thought in 1812 that there ought to be a strong censorship of the press; Wordsworth was at that date against it, but a few years later thought that some kind of curb might be necessary;[1] Crabb Robinson was, with some qualms, for complete freedom. But Wordsworth, far more than Southey, distrusted the putting of large powers in the hands of the government, and wrote to that effect to Daniel Stuart (June 22, 1817): of Southey he wrote—"In his vivid perception of the danger to be apprehended from the disaffected urging on the rabble, and the consequent necessity of Government being empowered to keep them down, he does not seem sufficiently jealous of the

[1] Wordsworth to Lonsdale, February 9, 1814; *Blake, Coleridge, Wordsworth, Lamb*, p. 67; Crabb Robinson, *Diary*, September 9, 1816.

power whose protection we all feel to be necessary"; and he quoted a maxim from memory from his own tract on the Convention of Cintra:

> "There is, in fact, an unconquerable tendency in all power, save that of knowledge, acting by and through knowledge, to *injure the mind* of him by whom that power is exercised." I pressed this upon Southey's consideration with a wish that his excellent letter to Mr W. Smith, in which he proposed to state his opinions and to recommend measures, might contain some wholesome advice to Ministers grounded upon this law of our infirm nature.

Where Wordsworth differed from Southey less than from most of his contemporaries was in taking a wide and comprehensive view of the circumstances of the time: details such as seditious publications and sporadic rioting were merely symptoms of a deep-seated disease of the commonwealth. All the troubles, it seemed to him, sprang from the increasing disunity of classes, and could only be remedied by forging new links to take the place of the old which had been destroyed. Hence his hope, in an earlier letter (to Lonsdale, February 9, 1814) which shocks Professor Harper, that the yeomanry then being raised might prove to be such a link.

> Everyone knows of what importance the equestrian order was in preserving tranquillity and a balance and gradation of power in ancient Rome; the like may take place among ourselves through the medium of an armed yeomanry; and surely a preservative of this kind is largely called for by the tendencies of things at present.... If the whole island was covered with a force of this kind, the Press properly curbed, the Poor Laws gradually reformed, provision made for new Churches to keep pace with the population (an indispensable measure), if these things were done and other improvements carried forward as

they have been, order may yet be preserved among us, and the people remain free and happy.

The yeomanry are not to be used, it is to be observed, as a permanently repressive force, but simply at the moment as a kind of police against the forces of anarchy, which were in fact, not merely in his imagination, threatening the liberty as well as the happiness of the people; and ultimately they were to be the nucleus of a class which should unite the classes on either side of them. For the government which used, and indeed misused, the force which had been raised, Wordsworth had less than liking. He did not, as he told Crabb Robinson (August 2, 1816), respect the personal character of the members of the Ministry, with the exception of Lord Hawksbury, and we have seen how, even in the act of writing pamphlets in support of Tory candidates in 1818, he could not help belabouring the Tory government. His fullest expression of opinion on this question of unity in these years—the question on which he thought the government chiefly to blame—is in two letters written to Daniel Stuart in 1817. In the first, of April 7, he tells Stuart that he does not anticipate a revolution, but at the same time he is not happy about public feeling:

The spirit among the labouring classes (with the exception of the populace of Carlisle) is incomparably better than it was in 1794 and 5. The agricultural population of Cumberland and Westmoreland is at present sound; but I would not engage that it will continue so, in case rebellion should get the upper hand in other parts of the Island. A Revolution will, I think, be staved off for the present; nor do I even apprehend that the disposition to rebellion may not without difficulty be suppressed notwithstanding the embarrassments and heavy distresses of the times. Nevertheless I am, like you, an alarmist, and for this reason, I see clearly that the principal ties which kept the different classes of society in a vital and harmonious dependence upon each other have, within these thirty years, either been greatly impaired or wholly dissolved. Everything has been put up to market, and sold for the highest price it would buy. Farmers used formerly to be attached to their landlords, and labourers to the farmers who employed them. All that kind of feeling is vanished. In like manner, the connexion between the trading and landed interests of country towns undergoes no modification whatsoever from personal feeling, whereas within my memory it was almost wholly governed by it....All this moral cement is dissolved; habits and prejudices are broken and rooted up, nothing being substituted in their place but a quickened self-interest, with more extensive views and wider dependencies, but more lax in proportion as they are wider. The ministry will do well if they keep things quiet for the present, but if our present constitution in church and State is to last, it must rest as heretofore upon a moral basis. And they who govern the country must be something superior to mere financiers and political economists.

In the second, of June 22, from which some sentences have already been quoted, he returns to the same problem of growing disunity:

If I had access to a Cabinet Minister, I would put these questions. Do you think that the fear of the law, and mere selfish or personal calculations as to profit and loss, in matters of property or condition, are sufficient to keep a numerous people in due subordination?—"No."—What loss has the Country sustained, within these last twenty or thirty years, of those habits, sentiments, and dispositions, which lend a collateral support, in the way of buttresses, of equal importance for the preservation of the edifice with the foundation itself? If the old props have been shaken or destroyed, have adequate new ones been substituted?

There is something familiar in these laments over a vanished community of feeling between classes; it may have been neither so recent nor so permanent as Wordsworth supposed, but it was none the less an evil, even in the mildest form which he mentions, that of the breach of steady relations between tradesmen and those who had been their regular customers. In its more serious forms it was, as he saw, a menace to the unity of the State, and one of which the popular advocates of economy and reform took little notice. Their attention was fixed on the wrongs of the unfranchized: most of them were blind to the possibilities of class warfare, and to those who saw them class warfare did not seem a great evil. Naturally, therefore, seeing that Wordsworth was not definitely with them, and on some points was definitely against them, those who called themselves reformers put him down as an obscurantist Tory.

It was in the belief that some such complete change had taken place in Wordsworth's political opinions that his friend Losh wrote to him on October 7, 1821.[1]

> They tell me you have changed your opinions upon many subjects respecting which we used to think alike; but I am persuaded we shall neither of us change those great principles which ought to guide us in our conduct, and lead us to do all the good we can to others. And I am much mistaken if we should not find many things to talk about without disturbing ourselves with political or party disputes.

Wordsworth had taken no notice of attacks by Shelley, Byron, Hazlitt, and a tribe of lesser men, but when an old friend wrote with this affectionate and charitable recognition of his sincerity, the case was altered. He replied, on December 4,

[1] *Memoirs*, II, 22–3.

with equal frankness in a letter from which certain passages have already been quoted.[1]

> Your letter ought to have been much earlier acknowledged, and would have been so, had I not been sure you would ascribe my silence to its true cause, viz. procrastination, and not to indifference to your kind attention. There was another feeling which both urged and indisposed me to write to you,—I mean the allusion which, in so friendly a manner, you make to a supposed change in my political opinions. To the scribblers in pamphlets and periodical publications who have heaped so much obloquy upon myself and my friends Coleridge and Southey, I have not condescended to reply, nor ever shall; but to you, my candid and enlightened friend, I will say a few words on this subject, which, if we have the good fortune to meet again, as I hope we may, will probably be further dwelt upon.

Then follows his defence of the right and natural change from youth to maturity, and his assertion that in foreign politics his accusers have been deluded by places and persons while he has stuck to principles.

> I disapproved of the war against France at its commencement, thinking—which was perhaps an error[2]—that it might have been avoided; but after Buonaparte had violated the independence of Switzerland, my heart turned against him, and against the nation that could submit to be the instrument of such an outrage. Here it was that I parted, in feeling, from the Whigs, and to a certain degree united with their adversaries, who were free from the delusion (such I must ever regard it) of Mr Fox and his party, that a safe and honourable peace was practicable with the French nation, and that an ambitious conqueror like Buonaparte could be softened down into a commercial rival.

[1] Cf. pp. 134–5, 150–1, 164 *supra*. [2] Cf. p. 134 n. *supra*.

This is enough for foreign politics, as influencing my attachments.

There are three great domestic questions, viz. the liberty of the press, Parliamentary reform, and Roman Catholic concession, which, if I briefly advert to, no more need be said at present.

A free discussion of public measures through the press I deem the *only* safeguard of liberty; without it I have neither confidence in kings, parliaments, judges, or divines. They have all in their turn betrayed their country. But the press, so potent for good, is scarcely less so for evil; and unfortunately they who are misled and abused by its means are the persons whom it can least benefit. It is the fatal characteristic of their disease to reject all remedies coming from the quarter that has caused or aggravated the malady. I am *therefore* for vigorous restrictions; but there is scarcely any abuse that I would not endure rather than sacrifice—or even endanger—this freedom.

When I was young—giving myself credit for qualities which I did not possess, and measuring mankind by that standard—I thought it derogatory to human nature to set up property in preference to person, as a title for legislative power. That notion has vanished. I now perceive many advantages in our present complex system of representation, which formerly eluded my observation. This has tempered my ardour for reform; but if any plan could be contrived for throwing the representation fairly into the hands of the property of the country, and not leaving it so much in the hands of the large proprietors as it is now, it should have my best support; though even in that event there would be a sacrifice of personal rights, independent of property, that are now frequently exercised for the benefit of the community.

Then follows the passage already quoted on concessions to Roman Catholics, and one on "the Church establishment", which Wordsworth views as "not only a fundamental part of our Constitution, but one of the greatest upholders and propagators of civilisation in our own country, and, lastly, the most effectual and main support of religious toleration";

I cannot but look with jealousy upon measures which must reduce her relative influence, unless they be accompanied with arrangements, more adequate than any yet adopted, for the preservation and increase of that influence, to keep pace with the other powers in the community.

Clearly, in both of these passages, Wordsworth comes as near as no matter to the theory that "interests" rather than individuals should be represented; it is usually considered a Tory doctrine, but it is not necessarily combined with other Tory doctrines. It is consistent, for example, with a belief in universal suffrage, though not with one in equal suffrage. Moreover, Wordsworth is not opposed to Parliamentary reform; but a reform which would have satisfied him would not have been one which satisfied the Whig "large proprietors" any more than it would have pleased most Tories; it would have been one which gave a predominating influence to those classes which seemed to him to contribute most to the best life of the country. But all schemes of reform which were proposed gave in effect a predominating influence to the manufacturing "interest", and though there were many bad landlords, there were, in Wordsworth's eyes, few good manufacturers. It is important to realize that, as he saw it, nothing but evil could be expected from any change in Parliamentary representation which shifted the balance of political power to any marked extent, more particularly if a heavy advantage were suddenly given to men who were unaccustomed to any reckonings but those of financial profit and loss.

It was probably in 1831[1] that Wordsworth wrote to Lord Lonsdale:

I do confidently affirm that there are materials for constructing a party which, if the bill be not passed, might save the country. I have numerous acquaintances among men who have all their lives been more or less of Reformers, but not one, unfastened by party engagements, who does not strongly condemn this bill.

There were in fact many men, far more definite in their Toryism than he, who in the late 1820's were adopting electoral reform as a weapon against the great Whig families and high finance, with the aim of creating an alliance between the Tory aristocracy and gentry and "the people". Wordsworth would, however, hardly have approved of this, which savoured too much of intestine division. Most interesting of his letters of the years which immediately preceded the Reform Act is another to Lord Lonsdale, probably again of 1831.[2]

The scheme of regulating representation by arbitrary lines of property or numbers is impracticable; such distinctions will melt away before the inflamed passions of the people. No

[1] The letter is undated: Knight (*Letters*, II, 315) puts it, for no ascertainable reason, under 1827, but Reform was not a question of that year. 1822, when Lord John Russell made his first serious proposals, is too early a date: Wordsworth is clearly referring to a Bill which had some chance of passing. The first form of the Bill which became the Act of 1832 was brought forward on March 1, 1831.

[2] Knight again (II, 316–7) dates this letter in 1827; but references (not quoted above) to an "altered bill" and a proposed £10 franchise leave very little doubt that it was written after April 18, 1831, when a modified version of the Bill first proposed on March 1 was introduced. There is an interesting allusion in the passage quoted which may help to confirm a date considerably later than

government will prove sufficiently strong to maintain them, till the novelty which excites a thirst for further change shall be worn off, and the new constituency have a chance of acquiring by experience the habits of a temperate use of their powers.... Then will follow frequent Parliaments—triennial perhaps at first—which will convert the representatives into mere slavish delegates, as they now are in America, under the dictation of ignorant and selfish numbers, misled by unprincipled journalists, who, as in France, will—no few of them—find their way into the House of Commons, and so the last traces of a deliberative assembly will vanish. But enough of this melancholy topic.

There is a startling note of fulfilled prophecy here in the apprehension that M.P.s will be in danger of becoming mere delegates, as in the anticipation that unprincipled journalists may exercise undue influence. One possibility, it must be admitted, did not occur to Wordsworth: that journalists might find their way into the House of Lords. And even though we may consider some of his fears, if not excessive, at least not justified by later events, there is an uncomfortable amount of truth in many of his predictions of disaster, and he was undoubtedly right, as against most of those who supported the Reform Bill, in his insistence that a purely arbitrary

1827: the reference to the influence of journalists in the French Parliament. "Journalism" was a new word in 1830, borrowed from France, and "journalist", though not new, had acquired a new shade of meaning, because of the part played by journalists in the July Revolution (cf. Halévy, III, 16 n., and O.E.D.). Knight's misdating of letters, sometimes by a good many years, has misled some of the commentators on Wordsworth's later political views. Another example will be found on p. 219 n. *infra*. In the instances here, it must make a considerable difference to our opinion of Wordsworth, whether he was writing in 1831 on actual proposals or in 1827 on evils that might never be proposed.

franchise based on an artificial property qualification could never be a final settlement, and that the business of reform was sure to go further than some of its supporters wished. As he wrote to J. K. Miller (December 17, 1831):

In the present stage of our affairs, the class that does the most harm consists of well-intentioned men, who, being ignorant of human nature, think that they may help the thorough-paced reformers and revolutionists to a certain point, then stop, and that the machine will stop with them. After all, the question is, fundamentally, one of piety and morals; of piety, as disposing men who are anxious for social improvement to wait patiently for God's good time; and of morals, as guarding them from doing evil that good may come, or thinking that any ends can be so good as to justify wrong means for attaining them. In fact, means, in the concerns of this life, are infinitely more important than ends, which are to be valued mainly according to the qualities and virtues requisite for their attainment; and the best test of an end being good is the purity of the means, which by the laws of God and our nature, must be employed in order to secure it. Even the interests of eternity become distorted the moment they are looked at through the medium of impure means.

On this argument, the means employed to carry the Reform Bill were of a nature to make the end itself very questionable. And indeed the Bill itself, in its successive refashionings, seemed to him so definitely bad that in revulsion he found in the Constitution in its actual condition virtues which he had not seen before.

The Constitution of England, which seems about to be destroyed, offers to my mind the sublimest contemplation which the history of society and governments have ever presented to it; and for this cause especially, that its principles have the character of preconceived ideas, archetypes of the pure intellect, while they are in fact the results of a humble-minded experience.

This sentence (from a letter to W. R. Hamilton, November 22, 1831), though it is usually quoted by his biographers as a typical utterance, is not in fact typical—it is exceptional. His constant mind is shown by the earlier citations here and by others of later date, of which this extract from a letter to Lord Lonsdale (February 24, 1832) is really typical.

Could a conservative Ministry be established, the certain ruin that will follow on the passing of this bill might be avoided. Thousands of respectable people have supported both bills, not as approving of a measure of this character and extent, but from fear that otherwise no reform at all would take place. Such men would be ready to support more moderate plans if they found the executive in hands that could be relied upon. Too true it is, no doubt, as Lord H[olland] has observed, that opinions as to the extent and nature of advisable reform differ so widely as to throw great difficulties in the way of a new bill. But these, in my humble opinion, might be got over.

But the Duke of Wellington did not succeed in 1832 in forming his government, and the Bill which Wordsworth disliked was passed. Some of the poems of 1833 express his apprehensions of coming trouble, but it is characteristic of him that he includes one which looks beyond a stormy immediate future to better times—he could never despair ultimately of England. As it was when he wrote the great sonnet *When I have borne in memory*, so it was twenty-five years later.

Despond who will—*I* heard a voice exclaim,
"Though fierce the assault, and shatter'd the defence,
It cannot be that Britain's social frame,
The glorious work of time and providence,

> Before a flying season's rash pretence
> Should fall; that She, whose virtue put to shame,
> When Europe prostrate lay, the Conqueror's aim,
> Should perish, self-subverted. Black and dense
> The cloud is; but brings *that* a day of doom
> To Liberty? Her sun is up the while,
> That orb whose beams round Saxon Alfred shone:
> Then laugh, ye innocent Vales! ye Streams, sweep on,
> Nor let one billow of our heaven-blest Isle
> Toss in the fanning wind a humbler plume".

These lines are some months later than the letter to Crabb Robinson (February 5, 1833) in which Wordsworth protested against being supposed to be an anti-Reformer, and explained his objections to the Bill which had become an Act.

You mistake in supposing me an Anti-Reformer—*that* I never was—but an Anti-Bill man, heart and soul. It is a fixed judgement of my mind, that an unbridled Democracy is the worst of all Tyrannies. Our Constitution had provided a check for the Democracy in the regal prerogative, influence and power, and in the House of Lords acting directly through its own Body and indirectly by the influence of individual Peers over a certain portion of the House of Commons—the old system provided in practice a check, both without and *within*. The extinction of the nomination-boroughs has nearly destroyed the internal check. The House of Lords, as a body, have been trampled upon by the way in which the Bill has been carried, and they are brought to that point that the Peers will prove useless as an external check, while the regal power and influence has become, or soon will, mere shadows—

> "She opened, but to shut
> Excelled her power",

as your friends, the Bill-men of all denominations, have found or soon will find.

And, as he wrote to Lady Frederick Bentinck,[1] "I cannot see how the government is to be carried on, but by such sacrifices to the democracy as will, sooner or later, upset everything. Whoever governs, it will be by outbidding for popular favour those who went before them".

Wordsworth's doubts have been shared by many who would not have considered their political opinions the same as his. Even Crabb Robinson, though he usually put a brave face on politics in writing to Wordsworth, was much less certain in addressing other friends. His two letters from Italy to the Pattissons, of June and September 1831,[2] show his uneasiness.

> I was always a moderate Reformer; and, now that success seems at hand, I think more of the dangers than the promises...
>
> Now that the mob are become Reformers, I am alarmed. Indeed, I have for years perceived this truth, that it seems to be the great problem of all institutions to put shackles as well on the people as on the Government....And my fear is, that under the proposed new House of Commons, there will be no check on popular passions.

This was before the Act was passed: it is perhaps more remarkable that in the hundred years since then there have been echoes of Wordsworth's objections from political thinkers who have never, and rightly never, been accused of reactionary tendencies. What he disliked in particular was the sudden shifting of the balance of power to one class, and the artificial uniformity of the franchise. Now it was exactly the consequences of these changes, and the changes themselves,

[1] Undated, but written before the passing of the Corporation Act, i.e. not later than 1835. Knight puts it in 1832, probably too early.

[2] Sadler, II, 508–9.

which Walter Bagehot condemned in his essay on *Lord Althorp and the Reform Act of 1832.*[1]

The "Reform Bill"...abolished a multitude of nomination boroughs, gave members to large towns and cities, and changed the franchise, so that in all boroughs, at any rate, the middle classes obtained predominant power. And no one can deny that the good so done was immense; indeed, no one does now deny it, for the generation of Tories that did so has passed away....But these benefits were purchased at a price of the first magnitude, though, from the nature of it, its payment was long deferred. The reformers of 1832 dealt with the evils of their time, as they would have said, in an English way, and without much thinking of anything else. And exactly in that English way, as they had under their hands a most curious political machine which had grown without design, and which produced many very valuable, though not very visible effects, they, without thought, injured and destroyed some of the best parts of it.

First, the old system of representation, as we have seen, was based on a variety of franchises. But in order to augment the influence of the middle class, the reformers of 1832 destroyed that variety; they introduced into every borough the £10 household franchise, and with a slight exception, which we need not take account of, made that franchise the only one in all boroughs. They raised the standard in the boroughs in which it was lower than £10, and lowered it in those where it was higher; and in this way they changed the cardinal principle of the system which they found established for uniformity as the rule instead of variety.

And this worked well enough at first, for there was not for some years after 1832 much wish for any more change in our constituencies. But in our own time we have seen the harm of it. If you establish any uniform franchise in a country, then it at once becomes a question, What sort of franchise is it to

[1] *Biographical Studies*, 1881, pp. 308–17.

be? Those under it will say that they are most unjustly excluded; they will deny that there is any real difference between themselves and those above; they will show without difficulty that some whom the chosen line leaves out, are even better than those whom it takes in. And they will raise the cry so familiar in our ears—the cry of class legislation. . . . The case is the stronger because one of the most ancient functions of Parliament, and especially the Commons House of Parliament, is the reformation of grievances. This suited very well with the old system of variety; in that miscellaneous collection of constituencies every class was sure to have some members who represented it. There were then working-class constituencies sending members to speak for them. . . . And in cases of popular excitement, especially of erroneous excitement, this plan insured that it should have adequate expression and so soon made it calm. But the legislation of 1832 destroyed these working-men's constituencies; "they put the country", as it was said afterwards, "under ten-pounders only". And in consequence there are in our boroughs now nothing but working-class constituencies; there are no longer any ten-pound householders at all. There is throughout our boroughs a uniform sort of franchise, and that the worst sort—a franchise which gives the predominance to the most ignorant and the least competent, if they choose to use it. The middle classes have as little power as they had before 1832, and the only difference is, that before 1832 they were ruled by those who were richer than themselves, and now they are ruled by those who are poorer.

No doubt there is still an inequality in the franchise between counties and boroughs—the sole remnant of the variety of our ancient system. But that inequality is much more difficult to defend now when it stands alone, than it was in old times when it was one of many. . . . In a few years probably there will be but one sort of franchise throughout all England, and the characteristic work of 1832 will be completely undone; the middle classes, whose intelligence Macaulay praised, and to whom he helped to give so much power, will have had all that power taken away from them.

No doubt, too, there is still a real inequality of influence, though there is a legal equality of franchise. The difference of size between different boroughs gives more power to those in the small boroughs than to those in the large. . . . But here, again, the vicious precedent of establishing uniformity set in 1832 is becoming excessively dangerous. Being so much used to it people expect to see it everywhere. There is much risk that before long there may be only one sort of vote and only one size of constituency all over England, and then the reign of monotony will be complete.

And, secondly, the reformers of 1832 committed an almost worse error in destroying one kind of select constituency without creating an intellectual equivalent. We are not used now-a-days to think of nomination boroughs as select constituencies, but such, in truth, they were. . . . They were an organ for what may be called specialized political thought, for trained intelligence busy with public affairs. Not only did they bring into parliament men of genius and ability, but they kept together a higher political world capable of appreciating that genius and ability when young, and of learning from it when old. . . . The effect of all this was to raise the intellectual tone of Parliament. . . . Intellectual deference used to be paid to members of Parliament, but now, at least in London, where the species is known, the remains of that deference are rare.

The other side of the same phenomenon is the increased power of the provinces, and especially of the constituencies. Any gust of popular excitement runs through them instantly, grows greater and greater as it goes, till it gains such huge influence that for a moment the central educated world is powerless. No doubt, if only time can be gained, the excitement passes away; something new succeeds, and the ordinary authority of trained and practised intelligence revives. But if an election were now to happen at an instant of popular fury, that fury would have little or nothing to withstand it. And, even in ordinary times, the power of the constituencies is too great. They are fast reducing the members, especially the weaker sort of them, to delegates. There is already, in many places, a committee which often telegraphs to London, hoping that their member will vote this way or that, and the member is unwilling not to do so, because at the next election, if offended, the committee may, perchance, turn the scale against him. And this dependence weakens the intellectual influence of Parliament, and of that higher kind of mind of which Parliament ought to be the organ.

We must remember that if now we feel these evils we must expect ere long to feel them much more. The Reform Act of 1867 followed in the main the precedent of 1832; and year by year we shall feel its consequences more and more. The two precedents which have been set will of necessity, in the English world, which is so much guided by precedent, determine the character of future Reform Acts. And if they do, the supremacy of the central group of trained and educated men which our old system of parliamentary choice created, will be completely destroyed, for it is already half gone.

This was written in 1877. It has been quoted at some length, because it shows on the one hand that "one of the shrewdest and most separate of the politicians of this generation", as R. H. Hutton called him, saw in process of fulfilment that political development which Wordsworth had foreseen nearly fifty years earlier, and saw that it came from those very mistakes in the Reform Act which Wordsworth pointed out; and because it shows on the other hand that Bagehot in his turn foresaw those further developments which are alarming many in these days who are, no more than he, reactionaries. There are no longer any inequalities in the franchise; those, comparatively unimportant as they are, which remain in the size of constituencies cause distress to the theorists, and will therefore probably not long survive; the only remaining select constituencies, the universities, have already received one severe attack. The resultant monotony is not a thing to be viewed with complacency. In the course of a debate on the abortive Representation of the People Bill of 1931, on May 20 of that year, Miss Eleanor Rathbone, an independent member with no party ties, spoke against the proposed abolition of university representation, using, in the main, arguments which agree with Bagehot's. Her speech was remarkable, not merely for its own sake, but for the respectful comment which it received from critics of all parties. We can hardly assert with truth that politics in the last thirty years have been free from those evils which Bagehot foresaw, the stampeding of an unwieldy, imperfectly educated electorate, the pressure of constituencies—and of other bodies—upon Members of Parliament, converting them, in Wordsworth's phrase, into "mere slavish delegates"; and those other evils which Wordsworth described more vigorously than Bagehot, who scarcely noticed them, if at all—the mass bribery of the electorate, not by one party only, and the misleading of the electorate by "unprincipled journalists". Is Wordsworth to be condemned as a reactionary because he was a prophet? He is perhaps rather to be reckoned in the company of Jeremiah and Micaiah the son of Imlah, whose prophecies, it is usually forgotten, came true. The consequences which Wordsworth saw to the Reform Act did not follow as quickly as he expected, and because of that very delay were not as fatal as he feared they might be, but we are not yet clear of the dangers which he foresaw. And there was more excuse for his apprehensions of immediate revolution than is commonly realized now. The Reform Act of 1832 was not followed by a violent revolution, and we therefore suppose that it could not have been. But the Bristol Riots, which are still faintly remembered, were only the most alarming of a series of disturbances all over the country; the July Revolution had stirred up all the revolutionary elements in England; the government did, as Wordsworth insisted, show want of courage in yielding to the threat of force; there was plenty of inflammable stuff about if there had been such leaders ready in England as there had been in France. There were not such leaders ready; but there had been no sign of them in France when the first revolution began. They were thrown up there: they might have been thrown up in England. Moreover, the English mob of 1832 was unlike the English crowd of 1932. Even now an English crowd can show the corporate cruelty of any crowd, though it seldom does; it is usually, as we like to think it always is, a good-humoured body. But the mob of 1832 had most things in common with the mob of the Gordon Riots of fifty years before, an event which was well within the memory of Wordsworth's generation. The sense and courage which George III displayed on that occasion was one of the reasons for the respect which, in spite of the Whig wits and the younger poets, his people preserved for him to the end of his life; and the insensate brutality of the mob was impressed upon them by frequent outbreaks, not only up to the Reform Act, but well into the Victorian Age. Wordsworth's dread of mob rule was due not to timidity, nor to a mistaken analogy drawn between English and French conditions, but to experience and knowledge of recent English history.

Besides, he did not see in political changes of the kind which the Reform Act introduced any real remedy for social evils which arose from human sin and folly. Some years later he wrote to Crabb Robinson (April 10, 1839) with reference to an article which had appeared in the *Westminster Review* "on the duty and Policy of redressing the grievances of the working Classes. I cannot see how any good purpose can be answered by such writing—which *indirectly* holds out Universal Suffrage for the redress of grievances, most of which, from the nature of things, can never be eradicated". He was not referring to attacks upon the factory system, whose adversaries he supported with lively sympathy, or to anything else of that sort: what he was condemning was that easy optimism which is sure that, if the political system is changed, every desirable reform will inevitably follow. As he had told Orville Dewey in 1833,[1] "the world is running mad with the notion that all its evils are to be relieved by political changes, political remedies, political nostrums—whereas the great evils, sin, bondage, misery, lie deep in the heart, and nothing but virtue and religion can remove them". There might be certain alleviations, social reforms of the kind which had his heart, but even these would be swept away if a weak government led to anarchy and that, as he had seen it do in France, to tyranny. His disapproval of the Reform Act was due to his conviction that it was a hasty and ill-considered attempt to deal with problems which needed careful and gradual solution: it promised far more than it could perform, and its inadequacy must soon become evident and lead to further demands; it had been passed, if not by actual violence, yet by the threat of violence, and was therefore a direct encouragement to the threat or employment of greater violence to extort greater concessions. The fullest extent of his apprehensions is seen in a letter to Moxon of January 1835:

[1] Orville Dewey, *The Old World and the New*, p. 92.

Soon, alas! it is likely to be found that power will pass from the audacious and wicked to the more audacious and wicked, and so to the still more and more, till military despotism comes in as a quietus. And then, after a time, the struggle for liberty will recommence; and you, young as you are, should your life be prolonged to the seventy years of the psalmist, will not live to see her cause crowned with success.

It is easy for us to say that he was unnecessarily alarmist, that no such bloody revolution or even such confusion as he anticipated did in fact break out, that the experience of France was not repeated in England; but a careful reading of his words may leave us a little less complacent, and a little less sure that he can be accused with justice of retreating from the ideals of his youth. He shocked Orville Dewey and others in his own lifetime, and has shocked many ingenuous democrats since, by his refusal to admit that the mass of the people were in 1832 or would be for many years sufficiently educated in politics to be able to govern themselves. But was he, after all, mistaken? And even if he were, does it follow that he had, to use that hasty expression of Crabb Robinson's which has already been quoted,[1] "lost his love of liberty, not his humanity but his confidence in mankind"? We cannot fairly maintain that view, with the sonnet of 1833 before us, and his conviction, repeatedly expressed then and later, that, if liberty were destroyed for a time, the struggle for liberty would begin again—even that, ultimately, the disorder which he would have averted might lead to good. It may be objected that the sonnet was written in 1833 and that the interview with Dewey belongs to the same period, that the letter to Moxon was written in 1835, and that Crabb Robinson's

[1] See p. 128 *supra*.

complaint, made in 1844, shows a later development. But in fact it is not easy to find an anticipation of serious trouble later than that letter to Moxon: Crabb Robinson would seem to have been led by that customary vehemence of expression, which more than once involved Wordsworth in difficulties or misunderstanding, into forgetting the other side of his thought, the confidence in England, if not in other countries, the certainty that the love of liberty was indestructible among her sons. It is remarkable that after 1835 this confidence finds frequent expression, whereas the converse doubts are scarcely mentioned. One interesting piece of evidence is to be found in the diary of Gladstone, who at that date (June 8, 1836) was still the hope of the stern and unbending Tories, and was shocked by Wordsworth's views on the extension of the franchise—

> He described to me his views; that the Reform Act had, as it were, brought out too prominently a particular muscle of the national frame: the strength of the towns; that the cure was to be found in a large further enfranchisement, I fancy, of the country chiefly; that you would then extend the base of your pyramid and so give it strength. He wished the old institutions of the country preserved, and thought this the way to preserve them. He thought the political franchise upon the whole a good to the mass—regard being had to the state of human nature; against me—

Gladstone firmly concludes.[1] It was long before he was converted to any extension in the franchise, and then hardly because he shared Wordsworth's faith in the virtue of a wide and equally extended franchise.

Whether Wordsworth's renewed confidence is to be accounted for by the movement of public opinion against the

[1] *Diary*, quoted in Morley's *Life*.

Reform Parliament which became obvious about 1835, whether, again, it was encouraged by the continental tour of 1837, which may have brought home to him the comparatively stable condition of England, must remain uncertain. "He is in good spirits about politics", Aubrey de Vere wrote to his sister on June 25, 1841, "—he says he does not wish to be called either Conservative or Reformer, but an 'improver'". When the Whig Ministry fell in that year, he was "not triumphant at Tory success", Crabb Robinson noted (July 10, 1841), but he may well have considered that a Tory government was a sign that the country was prepared to sit down and digest some measures of change before proceeding to others. He was neither a Peelite nor a Protectionist, however, and his indifference to party politics in 1845–6 struck Crabb Robinson as remarkable and as due to an expectation of "no good from the success of anyone".[1] It is equally likely to have been due to that distrust of successive governments which is noticeable from beginning to end of his life: one after another, they neglected what they ought to have done, particularly in social reform, they were blind to the signs of the times, and their chief concern seemed to be the retention of power for the benefit of their members.[2] His

[1] *Diary*, December 23, 1845.

[2] 1806: "I think William seems to consider it as almost indifferent what Administration we have, that there is no true honour or ability amongst them" (Dorothy Wordsworth to Mrs Clarkson, March 2). 1816: "For the personal character of the present ministry...I cannot say to you that I entertain any high respect" (Wordsworth to Crabb Robinson, August 2). For his views on the ministry generally in 1818, cf. pp. 157–61 *supra*. 1834: "The dissolution of the Melbourne Ministry was by me received rather with fear than pleasure. You have known from the first my opinion of the reform bill—to speak of it in the mildest

faith in governments did not increase with age, but his faith in his fellows, though it was sometimes staggered, was never destroyed.

In the last years of his life, indeed, he is more easily recognizable than ten or twenty years earlier as the man who

terms, it was an unwise measure carried by unworthy means" (Wordsworth to Crabb Robinson, November 24). 1835: "As Wordsworth says, 'We can hardly be said to have a government, when the men at the helm must shift their course every instant at the will of a public body over whom they have an uncertain influence'" (Crabb Robinson, *Diary*, March 12). 1838: "I learn from a pretty good quarter that the Tories are building high hopes upon the humiliation of the present Ministry. I wish I could share them, but I see no prospect of forming a Government at present in which any one party in the State can take a lead without compromises and inconsistencies which are likely to make common honesty a thing no longer to be looked for in public men" (Wordsworth to Crabb Robinson, February). 1846: "Harriet Martineau as well as H. C. R. is a sort of Peelite, but the Wordsworths are utterly against him.... He is a protectionist, but much more zealously of the Church than of the Land" (Crabb Robinson to Thomas Robinson, January 2). "I am indignant with our Ministers, especially Sir James Graham, who told us the other day in his place in Parliament that we are, and of course ought to be, more and more a manufacturing people—in other words, the white negroes of all the world. If these opinions mean anything, it is this, that with the British agriculture should henceforth be considered as holding a subordinate place to manufacture and commerce, and the one be encouraged by government at the expense of the other if necessary. My own opinions on this matter were given to the world more than thirty years ago, and I have since found no reason for changing them, and therefore I cannot but hold in detestation this doctrine of our present Government" (Wordsworth to Crabb Robinson, May 20). It may also be noted that though, in later versions of *The Prelude*, he toned down the accusations of knavery against the government in the nineties, he emphasized their timidity and folly. Cf. de Selincourt, pp. 398–9, 583.

in the nineties had declared that if there was a single man in Great Britain who had no suffrage in the election of a representative, the will of the nation was not generally expressed. He did again, it is clear, look forward to a time when education and general enlightenment had done their work. His words to Thomas Cooper may be quoted again—

> He had the same views of the spread of freedom in England in proportion to the increase of knowledge; and descanted with animation on the growth of Mechanics' and similar institutions.
>
> "The people are sure to have the franchise", he said, with emphasis, "as knowledge increases; but you will not get all you seek at once—and you must never seek it again by physical force", he added, turning to me with a smile: "it will only make you longer about it."

He even went so far as to declare, "I have always said the people were right in what they asked; but you went the wrong way to get it....There is nothing unreasonable in your Charter: it is the foolish attempt at physical force, for which many of you have been blamable".

Now it may be argued that a loose phrase of Wordsworth's had developed in Cooper's mind, and that is probably true of certain passages in the report. When Wordsworth is said to have "descanted with animation on the growth of Mechanics' and similar institutions", we may fairly suspect either that Cooper translated a general approval of such institutions into a particular approval of Mechanics' Institutes, of which Wordsworth, regarding their type of education as incomplete and even dangerous in its concentration on facts, definitely disapproved; or that he forgot the modifying phrases. And again as to the report of his approval of Chartism we may suspect that the approval was of the Charter generally rather than of all its details. To take one point of which we can be certain, he disliked intensely the proposal of secret ballot, which he regarded as both cowardly and likely to lead to fraud—a view of it which the remarkable results of elections in some countries, where the number of votes cast has been known to exceed the number of the electors, goes some way to justify. The objection to the secret ballot, it may be noted, is not necessarily a proof of reactionary political views, though it is frequently urged against Wordsworth as if it settled the question.

The conclusion of this is that it is probable that Cooper misunderstood or misrepresented Wordsworth in some details, but there are strong reasons to believe that in essentials he gave a true report. In the first place, Wordsworth's opinions were not in the least those which Cooper had expected to find in him, and his words, being thus unexpected, are most likely to have struck Cooper so forcibly that he recollected them with as much accuracy as can be assumed of any man. He may have omitted some qualifications: he is not likely to have turned a negative into an affirmative. And in the second place, if his witness is disallowed by an undue scepticism, there cannot be the same objection to Wordsworth's own letters; and one written to Reed on November 10, 1843, nearly three years earlier than this interview with Cooper, confirms Cooper's impression exactly. Wordsworth was distressed and indignant at the failure of the State of Pennsylvania to meet its financial obligations at that time, and his chief reason was not even his pity for small investors, but a sense that a political ideal was being betrayed:

I mourn even still more for the disgrace brought upon, and the discouragement given to, the self-government of nations by the spread of the suffrage among the people. For I will not conceal from you that, as far as the people are capable of governing themselves, I am a Democrat.

It was more unusual in 1843 to avow oneself a democrat, even with a qualification, than in 1832. In 1832 it meant that one was a supporter of the Reform Bill, a popular measure; in 1843 it might imply sympathy with the Chartists, of whom even those of Liberal opinions disapproved and were a little afraid.[1] Thus Caroline Fox, the Liberalism of whose family was beyond any question, recorded in her diary on April 3, 1839:

We were pleased to hear of the exile of the Chartists from Devizes by the public spirit of its inhabitants. Talked about their principles and the infidelity they have been preaching everywhere, our mines included. Sir Charles Lemon said they have been declaring that the difference between the rich and poor abundantly proved the non-existence of a God.

Caroline Fox's horror was typical of the feeling of a large section of Liberal opinion—not of all: Dr Arnold may be taken as an example of the opposite kind[2]—and of the possessing classes generally towards a movement which was almost confined to the lowest and most miserable of workers.[3] It was not Wordsworth's, as Cooper discovered, and as Crabb Robinson, after a false start, and with a slight shock at first, also discovered. In June 1839 Crabb Robinson was procuring

[1] "In 1846 [Democracy] meant something sinister" (Hill, *Toryism and the People*, p. 90, and cf. pp. 91–2, 199).

[2] Cf. Stanley's *Life*, especially for the years 1839–40. It was one of the matters of agreement between Arnold and Wordsworth.

[3] Cf. Halévy, III, 305 *sqq*.

a copy of Capel Lofft's *Ernest* for Wordsworth, who wanted to read it, though his friend doubted whether the small print would allow it and whether he would tolerate the book's "ultra-radicalism or Chartism".[1] There is no evidence that Wordsworth failed to tolerate it, if he was physically able to read it; his powers of toleration were always considerably larger than his Liberal friends, judging him by their own ideas of orthodoxy, found it easy to believe. But in the dangerous year of 1848 Crabb Robinson recollected hearing him say, "half in joke, half in earnest, 'I have no respect whatever for Whigs, but I have a great deal of the Chartist in me'"; and realized the truth of the remark.[2] It is only surprising that he, who had acted as amanuensis for the *Postscript* of 1835, had not realized it earlier. Or it would be surprising, if later critics had not been equally slow to realize the implications and assertions not merely of the *Postscript* but of other writings of Wordsworth's later life.

vi

In one of the most striking passages of *The Prelude* Wordsworth tells how, walking with Beaupuy, he met

> a hunger-bitten girl,
> Who crept along fitting her languid gait
> Unto a heifer's motion, by a cord
> Tied to her arm, and picking thus from the lane
> Its sustenance, while the girl with pallid hands
> Was busy knitting in a heartless mood
> Of solitude, and at the sight my friend
> In agitation said, "'Tis against *that*
> That we are fighting".

[1] *Diary*, June 11 and 15, 1839.
[2] To Mary Wordsworth, March 7, 1848.

He had encountered a form of poverty different from any which he had known in his boyhood in the North, though he was afterwards to meet something more like it in Southern England. When he referred to "humble and rustic life" and the strength and virtues which it fostered, he was thinking of the life he had known as a boy, but his later experience prevented him from being blind to the evil sides of country life. And if the life of the agricultural labourer was hard, what of the town worker? Wordsworth's prose writings and poems alike are full of the pain of the world, the problems of making life better for the classes which did the heaviest and least enjoyable work and received the least reward. One of the earlier documents in this matter is his letter to Fox of January 14, 1801, of which certain points deserve emphasis. It is, as always, the growth of conditions which destroy the unity of the family and the unity of the country, as well as the personal self-respect which is one of the elements of both, that Wordsworth sees and shudders at.

> Recently, by the spreading of manufactures through every part of the country, by the heavy taxes upon postage, by workhouses, houses of industry, and the invention of soup-shops, etc., superadded to the increasing disproportion between the price of labour and that of the necessaries of life, the bonds of domestic feeling among the poor, as far as the influence of these things has extended, have been weakened, and in innumerable instances entirely destroyed.

When this letter was written, distress among the poor was very great, and conditions did not improve, except temporarily, in the years which followed. In *The Excursion* Wordsworth expressed vigorously, if not always in his highest strain of poetry, his indignation at the misery of town-worker and agricultural labourer alike, with the impartial fury of a man who had no axe of party or class to grind. The Wanderer opens the attack with his description of the ceaseless labour of factories and its effect upon the workers, especially upon children, and upon home life (VIII, 174–85, 297–334). The Solitary retorts that tramps and the most miserable beggars are to be found in the country districts, and that the staring ploughboy is hardly a proof of the beneficent influences of nature (395–432). The Wanderer, though pleased by this generous heat, is for the moment prevented from replying by the Pastor, but they fall to it again presently. The Wanderer admits the wrongs of the country boy (IX, 156–64), but argues that his wrongs are recognized by everyone, whereas the evils of industrial life are worse and more dangerous because they are cloaked by the names of civilization and progress (182–98)—

No one takes delight
In this oppression; none are proud of it;
It bears no sounding name, nor ever bore;
A standing grievance, an indigenous vice
Of every country under heaven. My thoughts
Were turned to evils that are new and chosen,
A bondage lurking under shape of good,—
Arts, in themselves beneficent and kind,
But all too fondly followed and too far;—
To victims, which the merciful can see
Nor think that they are victims—turned to wrongs,
By women, who have children of their own,
Beheld without compassion, yea, with praise!
I spake of mischief by the wise diffused
With gladness, thinking that the more it spreads
The healthier, the securer, we become;
Delusion which a moment may destroy!

Crabb Robinson, as so often, supplies independent illustration of Wordsworth's charge. Thus he notes (May 18, 1823) a meeting with a friend, Thomas Stansfeld, who was a factory owner:

> I was glad to see him, for he is a most excellent man—yet we got into an argument on factories and the employment of children in them which somewhat ruffled me. I should have been disgusted at the arguments used by Stansfeld had they been used by any other man, but in him they proceeded from a most pure and benevolent mind. Yet even from such a man it was painful to hear of the use of keeping children of 10 years of age employed 11 or 12 hours at work, and some being at work all night, others all day!!! For though *he* has a plan of putting part of their wages into a saving bank, this will scarcely become a general practice. All Manufacturers will have their motives of interest, few his of benevolence.

Stansfeld was honest and benevolent in intention, and so were many other factory owners, whose opposition to the Factory Acts was not always based on self-interest, and whose relations with their workpeople were often friendly or paternal.[1] But whatever the intention, the practice was often deplorable; there was usually a strong element of self-interest behind the practice; there was, as Wordsworth complained, the misuse of the names of civilization and progress, and there was sometimes a misuse of the appeal to education and culture. Wordsworth's retort to that hypocrisy is found in his much misunderstood railway sonnets and letters of 1844.

Wordsworth himself was amused by contemporary perversions of his protest against the proposed railway through

[1] Cf. Hill, *Toryism and the People*, pp. 178–80; or, for a more intimate study, Mrs Gaskell's *North and South*.

the Lake District,[1] but it is scarcely amusing that they should be repeated a hundred years later. He was, to begin with, on firmer ground than many critics of railways and of machinery in general. He did not consider machinery to be in itself a curse: he looked on James Watt as one of the greatest benefactors of the human race, because his discovery of the steam engine had relieved men of so much drudgery; he spoke, in the passage from *The Excursion* just quoted, of "arts, in themselves beneficent and kind"; and the sight of a great machine working like a living thing inspired him by its proof of the power of the human mind which had created it:

Yet do I exult,
Casting reserve away, exult to see
An intellectual mastery exercised
O'er the blind elements; a purpose given,
A perseverance fed; almost a soul
Imparted—to brute matter. I rejoice,
Measuring the force of those gigantic powers
That, by the thinking mind, have been compelled
To serve the will of feeble-bodied Man.
For with the sense of admiration blends
The animating hope that time may come
When, strengthened, yet not dazzled, by the might
Of this dominion over nature gained,
Men of all lands shall exercise the same
In due proportion to their country's need.[2]

It was not the use of machines, but the exploiting of human beings as if they too were machines, that infuriated him. In the same way, he did not condemn railways in themselves. They made travel easier, even if they made impossible such thrills of discovery as were the result of the long waits

[1] Cf. Knight's *Life*, III, 451–2.
[2] *The Excursion*, VIII, 199–213.

between stages—such a thrill, for example, as he himself had once experienced at St Albans, when he had wandered into the little church of St Michael and, all unprepared, had been confronted by the figure of Bacon, seated as in life. Like other consequences of the discoveries of James Watt, railways are evidence of the creative power of the human mind, and in the 1833 sonnet on *Steamboats, Viaducts and Railways* Wordsworth even goes so far as to argue that, though they may not be in one sense beautiful, yet

Nature doth embrace
Her lawful offspring in Man's art.

And he startled Gladstone by defending the form of the steamboat as "rather poetical than otherwise to the eye".[1]

His objection to the proposed extension of the railway "from Kendal to Low Wood, near the head of Windermere", with the possibility that it might be afterwards carried on to Grasmere, was neither reactionary nor selfish. He did not object to the fixing of the terminus at the Bowness end of Windermere, where it still is. His objections were the reasonable ones that access to the Lakes was already easy, and that to carry the railway further would spoil the very seclusion which is one of the charms of the Lake District—the arguments which would be put forward now by members of the Council for the Preservation of Rural England, which is not generally considered to be an obscurantist body. In the second letter, however, Wordsworth develops an argument which would not now, owing to changed conditions, be used in exactly the same form. The supporters of the scheme had argued that visits to the scenery of the Lakes would have

[1] *Diary*, June 8, 1836; quoted in Morley's *Life*.

educational value for the inhabitants of the great manufacturing towns of Lancashire; to which Wordsworth had replied that it took time to learn to appreciate scenery. Visitors to the British Museum and National Gallery were then brought up as witnesses against him:

"There", they add, "thanks to the easy entrance now granted, numbers are seen, indicating by their dress and appearance their humble condition, who, when admitted for the first time, stare vacantly around them, so that one is inclined to ask what brought them hither. But an impression is made, something gained which may induce them to repeat the visit until light breaks in upon them, and they take an intelligent interest in what they behold." Persons who talk thus forget that, to produce such an improvement, frequent access, at small cost of time and labour, is indispensable. Manchester lies, perhaps, within eight hours' railway distance of London: but surely no one would advise that Manchester operatives should contract a habit of running to and fro between that town and London, for the sake of forming an intimacy with the British Museum and National Gallery? ...Nor would it fare better with them in respect of trips to the lake district....

I should not have detained the reader so long upon this point, had I not heard (glad tidings for the directors and traffickers in shares!) that among the affluent and benevolent manufacturers of Yorkshire and Lancashire are some who already entertain the thought of sending, at their own expense, large bodies of their workmen, by railway, to the banks of Windermere. Surely these gentlemen will think a little more before they put such a scheme into practice. The rich man cannot benefit the poor, nor the superior the inferior, by anything that degrades him. Packing off men after this fashion, for holiday entertainment, is, in fact, treating them like children. They go at the will of their master, and must return at the same, or they will be dealt with as transgressors.

A poor man, speaking of his son, whose time of service in the army was expired, once said to me, (the reader will be startled by the expression, and I, indeed, was greatly shocked by it), "I am glad he has done with that *mean* way of life". But I soon gathered what was at the bottom of the feeling. The father overlooked all the glory that attaches to the character of the British soldier, in the consciousness that his son's will must have been in so great a degree subject to that of others.... This extreme instance has been adduced to show how deeply seated in the minds of Englishmen is their sense of personal independence. Master-manufacturers ought never to lose sight of this truth. Let them consent to a Ten Hours' Bill, with little, or, if possible, no diminution of wages, and the necessaries of life being more easily procured, the mind will develop itself accordingly, and each individual would be more at liberty to make, at his own cost, excursions in any direction which might be most inviting to him. There would then be no need for their masters sending them in droves scores of miles from their homes and families to the borders of Windermere, or anywhere else.

Not many champions of humanity—or even of the Ten Hours' Bill—would have seen their chance here, in what might have been regarded simply as an aesthetic question, to strike a blow for human dignity and independence against mock philanthropy and the fussy desire to improve the poor, or struck it with such shrewd vigour and scornful glee as Wordsworth did.

These railway letters touch only one side of the industrial problem, and go out of their way to touch it. Others are considered, with more obvious relevance, in the Fenwick notes, dictated at about the same time, to some of the poems, and in the slightly earlier *Postscript* to the edition of 1835, which Professor Harper strangely describes as discussing "the Poor Laws, the condition of workmen in factories, and the question of Church disestablishment, all from the conservative point of view"—that is, as far as we can judge from Professor Harper's use of terms, from the point of view of a man opposed to all measures of reform. If a less honest scholar than Professor Harper were concerned, one might question whether he had read the *Postscript* at all: it discusses various proposals for internal Church Reform, and it must be admitted that Wordsworth finds some excuse for pluralities, but only by a scarcely legitimate interpretation does it even touch disestablishment—Wordsworth was dealing only with contemporary attacks upon ecclesiastical revenues, and did not insist that they would inevitably be carried to their logical conclusion of disestablishment and disendowment; and the discussion of "the Poor Laws and the condition of workmen in factories" would at any time be startling reading for the kind of man whom, it would seem, Professor Harper would call "a conservative". With Professor Harper the misleading description must be due, like his description of the 1818 *Addresses*, to a genuine misunderstanding, but it is even more difficult to explain. For how far does he think that such a man would go in agreement with Wordsworth's definite statements that a man, if he is unable to obtain work or high enough wages to support him properly, has the right to some assistance from the State: that it is not degrading to him to accept such help, but, on the contrary, it should add to his sense of human dignity to realize that, unimportant though he may seem, his life is yet of value: that it may even be suggested that he has a right to take what is denied him, provided he can do so without injuring anyone else: and that, if the State does not help a man who is in real need of help, it has no right to his allegiance?

If self-preservation be the first law of our nature, would not every one in a state of nature be morally justified in taking to himself that which is indispensable to such preservation, where, by so doing, he would not rob another of that which might be equally indispensable to *his* preservation? And if the value of life be regarded in a right point of view, may it not be questioned whether this right of preserving life, at any expense short of endangering the life of another, does not survive man's entering into the social state; whether this right can be surrendered or forfeited, except when it opposes the divine law, upon any supposition of a social compact, or of any convention for the protection of mere rights of property?

But, if it be not safe to touch the abstract question of man's right in a social state to help himself even in the last extremity, may we not still contend for the duty of a Christian government, standing *in loco parentis* towards all its subjects, to make such effectual provision, that no one shall be in danger of perishing either through the neglect or harshness of its legislation? Or, waiving this, is it not indisputable that the claim of the state to the allegiance, involves the protection, of the subject? And, as all rights in one party impose a correlative duty upon another, it follows that the right of the state to require the services of its members, even to the jeoparding of their lives in the common defence, establishes a right in the people (not to be gainsaid by utilitarians and economists) to public support when, from any cause, they may be unable to support themselves....

In the *Paradise Lost*, Milton represents Adam, after the Fall, as exclaiming in the anguish of his soul—

> Did I request Thee, Maker, from my clay
> To mould me man; did I solicit Thee
> From darkness to promote me?
> ...My will
> Concurred not to my being.

Under how many various pressures of misery have men been

driven thus, in a strain touching upon impiety, to expostulate with the Creator!...But as long as, in our legislation, due weight shall be given to this principle, no man will be forced to bewail the gift of life in hopeless want of the necessaries of life.

A more discerning critic than Professor Harper was that Lord Somerville who in 1805 told Southey that, however he and Wordsworth might have got into good company, he might depend upon it they were still Jacobins at heart.[1] Hale White saw the same thing.[2]

If Wordsworth had been in the House of Commons he would have been considered dangerous, for it is a recurrence to first principles which has produced every great revolution, whether in religion, morals, politics, or art....It would not have excused him in the eyes of a Tory whip that he voted for a Lowther against a Brougham if he could quote that tremendous passage from Milton just cited, and assert that the State could not lawfully ask for obedience from those whom it would not feed when they were starving. The whip would have known that no dependence could be placed upon such a man, either on a second reading, or in Committee.

And the results of a personal experiment bear out Lord Somerville and Hale White. A few years ago an extract from this part of the *Postscript* was set for précis in an examination, the source not being given. The candidates, though they were not asked to do so, chose to name a speaker. About half of them began, "The Labour speaker, defending the dole, said...", most of the others began, "The Labour Candidate said...", and one, showing real intelligence, began, "Mr A. J. Cook said...".

[1] Southey, *Life and Correspondence*, II, 343, and Knight's errata to vol. I of *Life* of Wordsworth.

[2] *Examination*, p. 19.

Wordsworth's principles may have led him into bad political economy, but they were principles of humanity, and he himself would have accepted almost as a compliment the accusation of bad political economy. If he was mistaken, it was in the direction of humanity—in the same direction as a generous-minded Labour leader. Whether in fact he would have approved of the remedies approved by the late Mr A. J. Cook for the evils of society may be doubted, since in this same *Postscript* he made it clear that he disliked Trade Unions, as tending to make their members slaves to their leaders. He preferred to urge justice from masters to men, co-operation, and particularly the formation of co-operative societies. In fact, apart from names, he was upholding the ideals of his youth, Liberty and Fraternity, and even Equality, since that is endangered by class warfare more than by any other foe. It cannot be doubted that he was a very queer Tory in his own age, and he would not be approved by all who call themselves Tories to-day, though the Tory party has moved on. His views were too strong for that excellent Liberal Crabb Robinson, who, acting as amanuensis, helped him to correct the MS. of the poems and the *Postscript* before printing, and wrote that his own moderating interference "was not always in vain". "Wordsworth", he added, however, "will aggravate antipathies by his polemical notes".[1] It would be interesting to know how far his interference went. In one passage at least it is perhaps not fanciful to hear Wordsworth replying to an obvious practical objection raised by his amanuensis.

Such is the view of the case that would first present itself to a reflective mind; and it is in vain to show, by appeals to

[1] *Diary*, March 22 and 23, 1835.

experience, in contrast with this view, that provisions founded upon the principle have promoted profaneness of life, and dispositions the reverse of philanthropic, by spreading idleness, selfishness, and rapacity:

—all the evils, in fact, which we associate with Speenhamland, and which the New Poor Law was designed to cure—

for these evils have arisen, not as an inevitable consequence of the principle, but for want of judgment in framing laws based upon it; and, above all, from faults in the mode of administering the law. The mischief that has grown to such a height from granting relief in cases where proper vigilance would have shown that it was not required, or in bestowing it in undue measure, will be urged by no truly enlightened statesman, as a sufficient reason for banishing the principle itself from legislation.

Yet all this can be, and is, passed over or misrepresented by nearly everyone who writes on Wordsworth's political views. He disapproved of Trade Unions: therefore he was a reactionary. His reason for disapproving of Trade Unions and his alternative remedies are not taken into consideration. Can it be said with truth that Trade Unions, with all the good that they have done, have never justified his suspicions; or that the best and wisest of Trade Unionists and their leaders and of factory owners are not inclined to place much more reliance now upon the remedies which Wordsworth advocated —education, co-operation, the encouragement of a feeling of corporate responsibility—than upon the methods of strife which he hated?

Education came first in his list of requirements; the Wanderer urges the necessity of elementary education, provided by the State, in the Ninth Book of *The Excursion* (ll. 293 *sqq.*), and when Wordsworth dictated the Fenwick notes in 1843 he did not retract the arguments of thirty years before.

> Reviewing at this late period, 1843, what I put into the mouths of my interlocutors a few years after the commencement of the century, I grieve that so little progress has been made in diminishing the evils deplored, or promoting the benefits of education which the 'Wanderer' anticipates. The results of Lord Ashley's labours to defer the time when children might legally be allowed to work in factories, and his endeavours to limit still further the hours of permitted labour, have fallen far short of his own humane wishes, and of those of every benevolent and right-minded man who has carefully attended to this subject; and in the present session of Parliament (1843) Sir James Graham's attempt to establish a course of religious education among the children employed in factories has been abandoned, in consequence of what might easily have been foreseen, the vehement and turbulent opposition of the Dissenters; so that for many years to come it may be thought expedient to leave the religious instruction of children entirely in the hands of the several denominations of Christians in the Island, each body to work according to its own means and in its own way.

He returned to the dangerous ignorance of the working classes in a letter to Crabb Robinson (December 8, 1844):

> We are all much concerned for the distracted state of the Church, and for the privations of so many among the labouring poor. As to the former, it may in time work to some good, for the latter I cannot foresee any material benefit. They multiply in all directions, the standard of civilisation being so low among them, evil proceeding from ignorance for which the upper classes have not virtue enough to prepare a remedy or material palliation.

Education could provide some palliation, but it could not do everything, and Wordsworth's views on education did not agree with those of most educational reformers of his day. Now and then he found a kindred spirit, as in his intercourse with Hugh Seymour Tremenheere, of which Harriet Martineau preserves a pleasant story. Tremenheere came to Ambleside in the autumn of 1845, and she arranged an interview with Wordsworth, from which Tremenheere returned in high satisfaction. He had enjoyed the conversation, and even hoped for a sonnet—presumably on education—from Wordsworth. "Mr Wordsworth", he observed, "discoursed to me about Education, trying to impress upon me whatever I have most insisted on in my Reports for seven years past: but I do not expect him to read Reports, and I was very happy to hear what he had to say." Next time she met Wordsworth, he said, "I have to thank you for procuring for me a call from that intelligent gentleman, Mr Tremenheere. I was glad to have some conversation with him. To be sure, he was bent on enlightening me on principles of popular education which have been published in my poems these forty years: but that is of little consequence. I am very happy to have seen him". This tolerance of mutual instruction in their own doctrines is highly creditable to both.

On the positive side Wordsworth went further than many of his philanthropic contemporaries, by pointing out that it was not only "the poor" who needed educating. "My dear Wrangham", he wrote on June 5, 1808, "begin your education at the top of society; let the head go in the right course, and the tail will follow." Twenty-three years later he was writing to Montagu to the same effect:

We are on fire with zeal to educate the poor, which would be all very well if that zeal did not blind us to what we stand still more in need of, an improved education of the middle and upper classes; which ought to begin in our great Public Schools, thence ascend to the Universities (from which the first suggestion should come), and descend to the very nursery.

Though, as these letters indicate, he could look forward to the reform of all national education, more frequently he had in view the actual conditions of his own time. Through his brother and nephews, through such friends and acquaintances as Dr Arnold and Hugh James Rose, he was in touch with the questions of the Universities and Public Schools; there was also the pressing problem of how to begin to educate a population with a very high proportion of illiterates. The process, as Wordsworth rightly pointed out, could not be carried through quickly, and the country might pay heavily for mistakes. "It is hard", he wrote to Rose in 1828,

> it is hard to look upon the condition in which so many of our fellow-creatures are born, but they are not to be raised from it by partial and temporary expedients: it is not enough to rush headlong into any new scheme that may be proposed.... We must bear the sight of this, and endure its pressure till we have by reflection discovered the cause, and not till then can we hope even to palliate the evil. It is a thousand to one but that the means resorted to will aggravate it.

Education, to be effective, must be a slow and natural development of the powers of the individual mind. As a first step, "it is undoubtedly to be desired that every one should be able to read, and perhaps (for that is far from being equally apparent) to write"; and with all his insistence on a religious basis to education, Wordsworth would not have united with many pious persons to consider religious literature as the only suitable literature for the poor, any more than for the rich.

He had made that clear in a letter to Wrangham many years earlier—in 1808—but there is no reason to suppose that he ever changed his mind; all great poets, as he told Landor (January 21, 1824), were in one sense powerful Religionists, and he enjoyed such less obviously religious books as *Robinson Crusoe* too much to wish to deprive his poorer neighbours of them. The emphasis in the earlier letter to Wrangham is laid on the necessity for the general cultivation of the mind and the moral and spiritual powers, as distinct from the accumulation of facts and "useful knowledge",[1] and it agrees thus with a much later letter to the elder Christopher Wordsworth (April 27, 1830):

> The more I reflect upon the subject, the more I am convinced that positive instruction, even of a religious character, is much overrated. The education of man, and above all of a Christian, is the education of *duty*, which is most forcibly taught by the business and concerns of life; of which, even for children—especially the children of the poor—book-learning is but a small part. There is an officious disposition on the part of the upper and middle classes to precipitate the tendency of the people towards intellectual culture in a manner subversive of their own happiness, and dangerous to the peace of society. It is mournful to observe of how little avail are lessons of piety taught at school, if household attentions and obligations be neglected in consequence of the time taken up in school tuition; and if the head be stuffed with vanity, from the gentlemanliness of the employment of reading.

That is to say, the cultivation of intellectual snobbery and conceit are not education, and they may lead to untold harm. Compared with some other European countries and with certain parts of the British Empire, England itself has suffered

[1] Cf. pp. 289–90 *infra*.

little from these consequences of an unwise plan of education, but it would be absurd to say that it has not suffered, or that serious damage, not only to individual minds but to the State which has been responsible for their training, has not been done in the last hundred years by exactly that limited conception of the task which Wordsworth condemned.

In other respects Wordsworth would probably find more agreement now, after a century of experiment, than among the educational theorists and practitioners of his own time: in his insistence[1] on the dangers of cramming, of expecting too much from school teaching, and of the want of co-operation between the influences of home and school. He is scarcely obscurantist even in his complaint that there is "too much indiscriminate gratuitous education in this country": we all know that it is true, though we do not see how to remedy that particular evil without the risk of depriving those of education who could profit by it. And though a smile may be provoked by the wording of his inquiry whether it can, "in a *general* view, be good that an infant should learn much which its *parents do not know*?", it is only fair to remember, first, that Wordsworth himself recognized that this objection would not be valid after the next generation, and, secondly, that the children of entirely or almost entirely illiterate parents do in fact sometimes despise their parents—hardly a satisfactory state of affairs. It is frequently argued that the moral confusion of many young Americans is due to the association by the first literate generation of fixed standards of morality with the illiteracy and ignorance of their parents.

[1] The points in this passage come from the letters on Education addressed to Hugh James Rose; cf. the whole of Appendix IV in Knight's *Life*.

This may be questioned, but the difficulty certainly exists; a striking instance of the strength which it has, even with generous minds, may be seen in that remarkable book, Mr George Thomas's *A Tenement in Soho.*

Wordsworth's ideal of education was the free development of the whole being, without forcing, interference, or a too patronizing attitude towards "the poor", who are, Wordsworth repeats more than once, not the only people who need to be educated. His views differed fundamentally from those of the founders of Mechanics' Institutes and other places of instruction, but they were neither narrower nor lower, and they stand the test of experience considerably better.

vii

Wordsworth's support of the Ten Hours' Bill and other schemes for the reform of factory life was akin to his interest in and his independent view of other questions of humanitarianism.

In Crabb Robinson's letter of 1821 negro slavery was mentioned as one of the iniquities on which Wordsworth had not recently spoken out. It was not, however, a matter on which he grew colder or less decided with advancing years. Mary Howitt, in the summer of 1845, gives a lively account, directly derived from her husband, of a battle at Rydal Mount.[1]

Dear Mrs Wordsworth sat mending her shoe, while the room was full of strangers, who had called to honour the poet. There was, among others, an American general there, an advocate of slavery, with whom William and Mr Wordsworth had a great argument. All the day afterwards Words-

[1] *Autobiography*, II, p. 32.

worth kept rejoicing that they had defeated the general. "To think of the man", said he, "coming, of all things, to this house with a defence of slavery! But he got nothing by it. Mr Howitt and I gave it to him pretty well."

One of Wordsworth's letters to Reed of the same year expresses his readiness to do what he can to help the cause of abolition in the United States, although he was conscious, as many abolitionists were not, of the practical difficulties, particularly if it were immediate and if the owners were not compensated. His doubts on that subject are shown in a letter to Benjamin Dockray of a dozen years earlier[1] on the question, at that time being decided, of emancipation in the West Indies. He considered that a slave-owner, "taking a right view of the case", ought to be prepared to make financial sacrifices, and that on the other hand a slave might be found willing "to make a recompense for the sacrifice should

[1] Knight dates this letter in 1840, but complete abolition in the West Indies had been carried in 1833. Knight's dating was based on the assumption that Dockray's *Egeria*, the receipt of which Wordsworth acknowledges, was published in 1840. But though the third part of *Egeria* was published in 1840 or later, the first two parts, though they are usually bound up with it, have a different title-page, without the author's name and with a different publisher's imprint; and they may have been issued separately at any date subsequent to June 21, 1832, which is the date on the last page of the second part. Wordsworth's letter is dated April 25, and the year should be 1833: the assignment to a later date makes nonsense not merely of the letter itself but of Dockray's "most valuable paper on Colonial Slavery", which it discusses. I have not seen this paper, but there are some remarks in an earlier paper of Dockray's (*Remarks on Catholic Emancipation*, printed in the *Lancaster Gazette* in November 1828 and reprinted with additions as a pamphlet in 1829) which show that he felt strongly and in harmony with Wordsworth on slavery; see pp. 24–5 in that paper.

the master, from the state of his affairs, feel himself justified in accepting a recompense". But it seemed clear to him that nothing could justify "the *third* party, the people of England, who through their legislature have sanctioned and even encouraged slavery", in abolishing it with no compensation to the owner: he had a healthy dislike of the high moral attitude taken up by some abolitionists. Characteristically, he went on to consider the nature of slavery.

> They who are most active in promoting entire and immediate Abolition do not seem sufficiently to have considered that slavery is not in itself, at all times, and under all circumstances, to be deplored. In many states of society it has been a check upon worse evils; so much inhumanity has prevailed among men, that the best way of protecting the weak from the powerful has often been found in what seems at first sight a monstrous arrangement—viz. in one man having a property in many of his fellows....No man can deplore more than I do a state of slavery in itself. I do not only deplore, but I *abhor* it, if it could be got rid of without the introduction of something worse, which I much fear would not be the case with respect to the West Indies, if the question be dealt with in the way many excellent men are so eagerly set upon.

This is not a matter, as Dr Cobban strangely asserts,[1] of "exerting his public influence in defence of such institutions as...slavery, and the legal immunity of cruelty to animals". Wordsworth is writing a private letter in which he makes it repeatedly clear that he abhors slavery, but points out the indubitable facts that "in many states of society it has been a check upon worse evils", that certain unwise abolitionists are almost inciting the West Indian negroes to attack their

[1] *Edmund Burke and the Revolt against the Eighteenth Century*, p. 150.

former masters, and that the English people, having formerly "sanctioned and even encouraged slavery", have no right now to try to get out of the business cheaply. The last phrase of Dr Cobban's sentence turns a negative into a positive. It is based on a passage in the same letter which was omitted above because, as Wordsworth himself admits, it is merely an illustration, and it interrupts the argument with one which an enemy might use and which has actually been used to twist the general sense of the letter. For this and other reasons it ought to be considered separately.

Some time ago many persons were anxious to have a Bill brought into Parliament to protect inferior animals from the cruelty of their masters. It has always appeared to me that such a law would not have the effect intended, but would increase the evil. The best surety for an uneducated man behaving with care and kindness to his beast lies in the sense of the uncontrolled property which he possesses in him. Hence a livelier interest, and a more efficient responsibility to his own conscience, than could exist were he made accountable for his conduct to law. I mention this simply by way of illustration, for no man can deplore more than I do a state of slavery in itself.

This reasoning, carried to its logical conclusion, would have prevented Wordsworth from taking the warm and energetic interest which he did take both in the fight against slavery and in the fight against the abuses of the industrial system. It may be partly connected with the persistent memory of that poor man whose grief for the last of the flock made so deep an impression on him forty years earlier. But what is most remarkable is that Wordsworth, in spite of experience, found it almost impossible to believe that a man may be guilty of the baseness of cruelty to any living being, man or beast, out of that very "sense of the uncontrolled property which he possesses in him". And yet, unpractical as this part of the letter is, especially when compared with the rest, it brings out one of his profoundest convictions, that reforms, like liberty, must begin in the hearts of men: the best way to put an end to cruelty is to convert the cruel.

On one form of man's inhumanity to man, the penal system, Wordsworth's later utterances have given great offence for the usual reason: humanitarians have noted that he opposed the complete abolition of the penalty of death, and that has been enough for them, without investigation of his arguments. In the *Sonnets upon the Punishment of Death*, written in 1839, when its abolition for certain offences had in effect led to the consideration of its entire abolition, Wordsworth thinks aloud, as in so many of his poems. His conclusions are not, except in one respect, inconsistent with his earlier thought, and they are not unmerciful, though their view of mercy is not that held by those of their critics who look upon death as necessarily unmerciful. In his letter to the Bishop of Llandaff he had defended the right of the State to use violence in order to establish peace and right government:

> [Liberty] deplores such stern necessity, but the safety of the people, her supreme law, is her consolation.... Political virtues are developed at the expense of moral ones; and the sweet emotions of compassion, evidently dangerous when traitors are to be punished, are too often altogether smothered.

That argument is repeated in the *Sonnets*, particularly the eighth, but some of the other arguments are of more interest. The victims of the criminal after all deserve as much compassion as the criminal (III); death is not the greatest of evils (IV, IX–XII), or even the least merciful of punishments:

imprisonment for life is far more hopeless and cruel, and transportation for life—which in the Godwinian days of *The Convict* Wordsworth had favoured—tempting to a relapse, whereas the certainty and approach of death may lead to the criminal's repentance:

> Ah, think how one compelled for life to abide
> Locked in a dungeon needs must eat the heart
> Out of his own humanity, and part
> With every hope that mutual cares provide;
> And, should a less unnatural doom confide
> In life-long exile on a savage coast,
> Soon the relapsing penitent may boast
> Of yet more heinous guilt, with fiercer pride.
> Hence thoughtful Mercy, Mercy sage and pure,
> Sanctions the forfeiture that Law demands,
> Leaving the final issue in *His* hands
> Whose goodness knows no change, whose love is sure,
> Who sees, foresees; who cannot judge amiss,
> And wafts at will the contrite soul to bliss.

To a modern reader there is something familiar in this chain of argument, and reflection will show that the resemblance is to the final stages of that debate of the Pope with himself which ends in the condemnation of Guido Franceschini.

> My last act, as my first,
> I owe the scene, and Him who armed me thus
> With Paul's sword as with Peter's key. I smite
> With my whole strength once more, then end my part,
> Ending, so far as man may, this offence.
> And when I raise my arm, what plucks my sleeve?
> Who stops me in the righteous function,—foe
> Or friend? O, still as ever, friends are they
> Who in the interest of outraged truth
> Deprecate such rough handling of a lie!

The facts being proved and incontestable,
What is the last word I must listen to?
Is it "Spare yet a term this barren stock,
We pray thee dig about and dung and dress
Till he repent and bring forth fruit even yet"?
Is it "So poor and swift a punishment
Shall throw him out of life with all that sin?
Let mercy rather pile up pain on pain
Till the flesh expiate what the soul pays else"?
Nowise! Remonstrance on all sides begins
Instruct me, there's a new tribunal now
Higher than God's—the educated man's!...

The educated man used a different plea in the Rome of the seventeenth century from those of English humanitarians in the nineteenth century, but the Pope's reply was Wordsworth's:

For the main criminal I have no hope
Except in such a suddenness of fate.
I stood at Naples once, a night so dark
I could have scarce conjectured there was earth
Anywhere, sky or sea or world at all:
But the night's black was burst through by a blaze—
Thunder struck blow on blow, earth groaned and bore,
Through her whole length of mountain visible:
There lay the city thick and plain with spires,
And, like a ghost disshrouded, white the sea.
So may the truth be flashed out by one blow,
And Guido see, one instant, and be saved.
Else I avert my face, nor follow him
Into that sad obscure sequestered state
Where God unmakes but to remake the soul
He else made first in vain; which must not be.

The Pope, like Wordsworth, was a merciful man, but he might not have shared Wordsworth's hope that the "awful rod" might at last drop from Law's firm hand "for lack of use". There might be grave doubts, Wordsworth thought, of the validity of the statistics quoted by opponents of capital punishment with the object of proving that it was no longer necessary. Thus he inquired of Henry Taylor (November 3, 1841):

May it not be mainly, not that there is less occasion for them, but that notions of a feeble and narrow humanity, and a spurious Christianity, have spread so as to prevent prosecutions, or have influenced judges in their charges (for instance, Judge M. in more than one) and juries in their verdicts?

But, in spite of these doubts, in the last decade of his life Wordsworth had not lost faith in the possibility of a golden world.

viii

It is clear that in his later years Wordsworth had not lost in any true sense of the word his enthusiasm for liberty and humanity, though he was, not unnaturally, more conscious of the dangers which beset them than in his youth. It is equally clear that his mind had not closed or become rigid: all the Liberals and Radicals of his own day who talked with him bear independent witness to his candour and readiness to consider the arguments and point of view of the other side—Mill and the Benthamites, J. J. Tayler, Crabb Robinson, have been quoted, and others might have been added to the list; it is chiefly the illiberal dogmatism of later writers, their insistence on shibboleths and ignoring, if not ignorance, of historical circumstances, which have fixed upon him the reputation of a narrowing and stiffening reactionary, a High Church Tory of the dullest kind. Wordsworth was slow, and rightly slow, to accept the label of Tory: as he wrote to Landor (January 21, 1824) with complete accuracy:

My politics used always to impel me more or less to look out for cooperation with a view to embody them in action; of this interest I feel myself utterly deprived, and the subject, as matter of reflection, languishes accordingly. Cool heads no doubt there are in the country, but moderation naturally keeps out of sight, and wanting associates I am less of an Englishman than I once was or could wish to be.—Show me that you excuse this egotism, if you can excuse it, by turning into the same path, when I have the pleasure again to hear from you.

His early and persistent dislike and distrust of the Whigs carried him, during the Reform years, further into the Tory camp than he would otherwise have gone, and writers with "the Whig view of history" have never forgiven him; but his letters and the 1835 *Postscript* show how little party politics really entered into his calculations. It was still co-operation which he desired—co-operation between the actual classes of men, not between the fictitious political parties. In his old age he called himself a Conservative, but a more correct label for him would be that which has been applied to others—that of a Revolutionary Tory. Too much stress has usually been laid on his Toryism, except in his early days, when it is overlooked, and too little on the revolutionary elements in that Toryism. Moreover, few of his critics have realized the close connection between certain kinds of Toryism and more than one kind of Radicalism, particularly in the later years of Wordsworth's life. A study of Mr Richard Hill's brilliant essay, *Toryism and the People, 1832–1846*, will help to show Wordsworth's position, and also that he was in many respects nearer to the revolutionaries than to the Tories. He had most in common with such a Tory as Richard Oastler.

> A correspondent in a local newspaper suggested that "the direct and visible object of the inventor and mover of the Factory Bill was to run his bill against Parliamentary reform, slave emancipation", and the like. "I'll be bound for it", retorted Oastler, springing at the neck of this intruder, "he is a genuine Liberal of the Nineteenth Century—a man who *professes* to feel for sufferings he never witnessed, a trumpet-tongued declaimer against abuses by which he has never profited."...Excited mobs of hungry working men would gather round [Oastler] in Huddersfield or Leeds, and he would appear among them dishevelled and waving a silk hat battered by Whig opponents. "This is Whig liberty, my friends!" he would cry; "Look also at my coat—rent from bottom to top by Whig patriots", and, after a speech of fierce eloquence, he would assure them that their wrongs would be avenged, that God had not gone to sleep.[1]

Wordsworth would have applauded another outburst of Oastler's against a critic of Factory Reform—

> I have dwelt in the midst of the ravages of the Factory system, I have witnessed its destruction of the human frame, its dreadful havoc on the moral faculties, its smothering and withering of all domestic ties, its ruinous effect on the religious principles both of its victims and of its priests.[2]

Like Oastler, too, he had sympathies with the Chartists: "I have no respect whatever for Whigs, but I have a great deal of the Chartist in me". Professor Harper—is it impertinent to doubt whether he would have been much of a Chartist in 1848?—thinks that Wordsworth might have made his sympathy more obvious; the 1835 *Postscript* was there for anyone

[1] Hill, *Toryism and the People*, pp. 24–5.
[2] Quoted from Hill, *op. cit.* p. 24.

to read, and it left no doubt where Wordsworth's sympathies lay in the matters chiefly in debate. There was an actual alliance between Tories and Chartists in certain places and at certain times, notably in 1841 at Manchester, where they united in an invitation to John Walter to stand as their candidate, in their common hatred for the Whigs. It was the same at Leicester, where John Mason, as Cooper tells us, inveighed against "the authors of the accursed Poor Law", who had let "the people" down over the Reform Act. "Municipal Reform has been for their benefit—not for yours. All other reforms the Whigs boast to have effected have been for the benefit of the middle classes—not for yours", John Mason told them,[1] and the indictment was just. It is true that, as Thomas Cooper warned Walter when he was returned for Nottingham, a good many Chartists meant to use the Tories to cut the throats of the Whigs, and then themselves to cut the throats of the Tories;[2] but the alliance was based on something deeper than political expediency. Tories and Chartists—or those who were called by those names—alike hated the smug complacency of progressive Radicals and political economists. "Political economy was anathema to the working classes", writes Mr Hill,[3] and he gives satisfactory reasons for their detestation of it.[4] In his denunciations of the political eco-

[1] Cooper, pp. 136–7, 148–9.

[2] *Ibid.* p. 149.

[3] *Op. cit.* p. 121.

[4] "When they were told by the unanimous voice of orthodox Political Economists that their own economic condition was governed by the laws of Competition and that industrial distress was capable of explanation in terms of the law of supply and demand, they came to regard Political Economy, not as an explanation of their evil case, but as an excuse for keeping them down....Political Economy looked dangerously like a trumped-up, *ex post facto* justification of a policy of wage-cutting and labour sweating" (*op. cit.* pp. 152–3).

nomists, in the *Postscript* and elsewhere, Wordsworth was in complete accord with Parson Lot's denunciation of those men who[1]

arrogantly talk of Political Economy as a science, so completely perfected, so universal and all-important, that common humanity and morality, reason and religion, must be pooh-poohed down, if they seem to interfere with its infallible conclusions;

and his views on the principles which should lie behind the Poor Law bring him into unexpected partnership with Cobbett, who[2]—

with only a few months of life still remaining in front of him, fought the Bill with heart and soul. The House, he said, was about to do a terrible thing. They were about to dissolve the bonds of society; they were going to break faith with the working man....It was said in Scripture...and Cobbett resorted to the Bible as the poor man's last defence.

He was in agreement with Cobbett and other Radicals again in his protest against over-centralization in government, and against the perpetual citing of foreign examples. Thus Cobbett broke out against the arguments of the authors of the Local Courts Bill[3]—

I wish these fellows would cease to refer us to the "Continent" for examples for us to imitate. There is something suspicious in the very circumstance, that the scheme seems to come from the hellish governments of Germany. But, as the "all-jaw and no-judgment" *feelosofers* must send us *abroad* for an example, *why not send us to the United States of America*, where our own common law was, and is, in existence?

[1] Quoted from Hill, *op. cit.* p. 154.
[2] Hill, *op. cit.* p. 189. The dots do not indicate omissions.
[3] *Political Register*, July 13, 1833.

And Wordsworth wrote, with the same impatient English feeling, to Crabb Robinson (July 7, 1839):

In the proceedings of Government at this time what I detest most is the practice of metropolitan organisation. Upon this subject D'Israeli spoke in Parliament like a philosopher. Relieve the *people* of the burden of their duties, and you will soon make them indifferent about their rights. There is no more certain way of preparing a people for slavery than the practice of central organisation, which our philosophists with Lord Brougham at their head are so bent upon importing from the Continent—I should have thought that in matters of government we Englishmen had more to teach those nations than to learn from them.

Cobbett and Wordsworth differed on many subjects, but in their detestation of those whom the one called *feelosofers* and the other *philosophists* they were united.

This agreement was not purely accidental: as Mr Hill has shown, there were strong Tory elements among those who called themselves Radicals, and it is a commonplace that a large proportion of those who carried through the Factory Acts, from Lord Shaftesbury downwards, were Tories. It is often difficult to decide whether a man is a Tory Revolutionary or a Revolutionary Tory. It does not matter greatly in which category we set Wordsworth, but it is of real importance that we should neglect neither the Tory nor the Revolutionary in him. He himself once criticized Canning for "losing sight of things in names" (to G. H. Gordon, February 26, 1829), and in his letter to Losh he insisted that he had been faithful to principles while his critics had been led away by names. Both criticism and claim are fair and defensible, but Wordsworth's indifference to nomenclature where realities were concerned has perhaps been partly responsible for the wrong valuation of his political opinions in later as in earlier life. In 1792 he was not a thorough-going revolutionary, in 1842 he was not a Tory of the type which now vexes Mr Baldwin: he was, to echo Hale White, that most dangerous kind of revolutionary who goes back to first principles. It is amusing, if hardly profitable, to speculate on his party allegiance to-day. His horror of class warfare would keep him out of the ranks of the Communists, but a good case might be made out for several other possibilities. Yet however good the case, it would be necessary to remember that Wordsworth would always persist in thinking for himself. He was not a Tory simply because he was inclined to think of "interests" rather than numbers as the proper basis of Parliamentary representation, nor was he a Socialist simply because he urged the duty of the State to come to the support of the individual. But he was definitely not a nineteenth-century Liberal, and most of his critics, being more or less of that orthodoxy, have found it easier to lament a retrogression in his opinions and find plausible explanations of it, than to consider the evidence against their theories. As Hale White wrote:

The explanation of the vulgar mistake with regard to Wordsworth I believe mainly to be that more than most men he has suffered from cursory inspection. A large part of what he wrote is not externally attractive, and is little read. Nevertheless, he is a man of such mark that all cultivated men and women feel that they must have something to say about him, and so they take up "Lucy Gray" and "1815" and pass on, summing him up in a phrase, "inspired poet, dullest of renegades". The antithesis does not exist, and could not have existed; but it saves them much trouble, not only in criticism and conversation, but in their own thinking....Another reason why the renegade half of the antithesis is popular is that people are disappointed that Wordsworth did not develop after the ordinary fashion. If he had become a poet of revolt and despair, he would have been more acceptable to most of those persons who make poems, review them, or read them.

"The antithesis does not exist, and could not have existed": the words deserve emphasis. A man does not abandon all the faith and hope and charity of his youth, grow cold and hard and timid; and at the same time retain his interest in social reform, his passionate personal affections, his enjoyment of the society of young men of parts; nor are such young men found in their turn enjoying the humanity, wideness of vision and frankness of discussion of an elder man who, differing profoundly from them in his conclusions, does not in fact possess those qualities of fairness which they declare he does possess. Wordsworth did not desert the ideals of his youth: what happened was rather that he was seldom deceived by Diabolonians who took fair-sounding names and tried to pass themselves off as lawful inhabitants of Mansoul. If he sometimes suspected innocent Mansoulians of being Diabolonians in disguise, he was but human. But in fact the last hundred years have justified his doubts to a far greater extent than it is pleasant or flattering to ourselves to acknowledge. He saw the dangers of the times and the future with a mournful clearness which was unwelcome to the cheerful complacency of the nineteenth century, but no man less despaired of the end. At the present time many people regard Liberty and Equality, in the older senses of the words, as dreams, and hardly desirable dreams, and have transformed Fraternity into racialism, nationalism or class loyalty. It is not surprising that men holding these views should quarrel with Wordsworth's, but it is surprising that men with Wordsworth's own ideals should fail to see the encouragement which is to be found in his later as in his earlier writings. He was to the end passionate against injustice and wrong, but he saw that the roots of them went deeper than he had realized in the years of the French Revolution, and that the remedies must be more profound. It was neither strange nor a sign of retrogression that he came to trust in the slow and patient processes of divine action and in those gradual changes in human institutions which imitate them, rather than in the hasty measures which promise well and lead to confusion. "All change is perillous and all chaunce unsound", Spenser had written: it was characteristic of Wordsworth's thought that when he borrowed the phrase he altered it significantly—"Perilous is sweeping change, all chance unsound".[1] His political development was a consistent development, not a swing to the left followed by a swing to the right; and we shall see that his religious development was equally consistent.

[1] *Faerie Queene*, v, 2, 322; *Sonnets dedicated to Liberty and Order*, iv (written in 1838).

III

RELIGION

i

MOST of those who have written on Wordsworth's religious and philosophical opinions have been either Anglicans, to whom the connection or sometimes the derivation has been so obvious as scarcely to need comment, or unassociated with any ecclesiastical organization of formulated creeds, and therefore unaware of the connection. Or, where their creed is formulated, it differs in so many important respects from the Anglican that there is plenty of room for misunderstanding. A Roman Catholic would probably make very few mistakes: anyone brought up in a Calvinistic tradition, however much weakened, would mistake Wordsworth's meaning as often as the Calvinistic Evangelicals of his own time mistook it. Probably the best person to write on his development would be someone who, brought up in another form of Christianity or outside organized Christianity, had become an Anglican and was therefore conscious, as most Anglicans are not, of the points of difference. An Anglican bred may observe only the more startling oversights and misapprehensions of some of the critics, but has at least been warned by their example against taking too much for granted.

Two points must strike the reader of even the best recent criticism of Wordsworth: the first, an implication that he had no religious ideas, properly so called, or philosophical ideas, merely a welter of vague impressions and half-recognized beliefs, until his intercourse with Coleridge tidied his mind:

the other, a suggestion that he abandoned his "early pantheism" and "naturalism" for a regrettable "later orthodoxy". On the other hand the theologians, who ought, one would suppose, to be consulted on the matter, seem to be very little troubled by "early pantheism", and Dean Inge, who, if any man, knows what pantheism is, distinguishes clearly and carefully[1] between pantheism and the doctrine to be found in any of Wordsworth's poems. Dr Elias Munk,[2] approaching the question from a different angle, comes to exactly the same conclusion: Wordsworth was a panentheist[3] all his life, but not, except by a loose application of the term, a pantheist. And there is nothing mutually contradictory between panentheism and Christian orthodoxy: they are, in fact, in complete agreement. Dr Munk has indicated the weakness of much Wordsworthian criticism in a single question:

Hat man Recht getan, wenn man nach gelegentlichen Aussprüchen von Coleridge den jungen Wordsworth als "semi-atheist", sein späteres Gebaren mit dem Schlagwort "I and my brother the Dean" kennzeichnete, und damit der Totalität seines religiösen Lebens gerecht zu werden glaubte?

The easy contrast is too frequently made; like most easy contrasts it does not present the truth, and it would scarcely be made if as much attention were paid to Wordsworth's religious background in childhood and youth as to casual remarks in Coleridge's letters. Nor should Coleridge's

[1] In *Christian Mysticism*, in *Personal Idealism*, in *English Mystics*, and in *The Platonic Tradition in English Religious Thought*.

[2] *William Wordsworth: Ein Beitrag zur Erforschung seiner religiösen Entwicklung*.

[3] "Panentheism or panpsychism, a belief that all things are in different degrees animated and sacred" (Inge, *Platonic Tradition in English Religious Thought*, p. 80). Cf. also pp. 244–9 *infra*.

religious presuppositions be ignored. But the study of the currents in the English religious world of 1770–1850 is not always considered necessary for students of Wordsworth, and if we consider them at all we often take with us too many of our own presuppositions.

In what follows I would not be taken as undervaluing the work of such scholars as Professor Arthur Beatty or Professor Melvin Rader. The point that I would wish to make is this, that Wordsworth's philosophical thought, particularly in its later developments, has always troubled those who insist on regarding it apart from his theology. It cannot be accounted for purely on philosophical grounds, on his reading of the philosophers and on those conversations with Coleridge which may have saved him some reading. There were actually in his early training exactly those elements of pantheism and transcendentalism which are frequently ascribed to the influence of Coleridge, who did not have them to the same degree in his early training. They were part of Coleridge's mature intellectual equipment: they were among the earliest ideas with which Wordsworth became acquainted. Coleridge's metaphysical conversation at the most gave him intellectual confirmation of what he knew already, partly from education and partly from personal experience. And it may even be suggested that Coleridge, with his quickness and interest in ideas, any kind of ideas,[1] took something from Wordsworth. Wordsworth's acknowledgment of his intellectual debt to Coleridge, and Coleridge's assertion of it, may, it is possible, mislead us into thinking the profit entirely

[1] There is a significant admission in one of Coleridge's letters to Estlin (May 14, 1798): "Though Christianity is my passion, it is too much my intellectual passion".

on one side. But this is by the way. The main truth is that there were elements in Wordsworth's early training which must be reckoned with as entering into all his mature thought, and which are usually entirely overlooked.

ii

Wordsworth was baptized in the Church of England, and the evidence of his own words and of those of his contemporaries shows that he was brought up in a definite school of it—so far as it is accurate to speak of definite schools of thought in a body where the gradations of opinion have always been so subtle as not easily to be understood by those who are not members of it. In Wordsworth's time the gradations were perhaps fewer and in some ways more marked. There had been in the Church of England something, though on a much smaller scale, comparable to that eighteenth-century cleavage among Nonconformists which had left a relatively small remnant faithful to the Calvinistic theology of their forefathers: the majority of the old Nonconformist stock either tended to Unitarianism—in all its many gradations from something hardly distinguishable from Trinitarianism, to ethical teaching with the slightest Christian flavour—or were increasingly affected by the second wave of the religious revival which, beginning with the Wesleys and Whitefield, was now spreading from the lower to the upper classes of society, and, though sometimes Calvinistic, was more often anti-Calvinistic in its theology. There was, that is to say, among the older Nonconformist bodies a turning away from the old paths, frequently due to a moral revolt against Calvinism, in the direction either of what may be called for convenience Unitarianism, or of a more emotional religion.[1] The Church was not affected in quite the same way, but there was a small section in it which at least tended to semi-Socinianism, the old Low Church and High Church parties were still recognizable, and an increasingly large number of all parties were being affected by Evangelicalism. The opponents of Evangelicalism were, both within and without the Church, those who disliked what in the mid-eighteenth century had been called "enthusiasm" but what was now called "fanaticism"—that is, the Unitarians, the diminishing older school of Nonconformists, and the torpidly respectable

[1] The first chapter of the *Life* of F. D. Maurice may be consulted for a description of what is there called "the passage of the Old Puritans into the Modern Unitarians" and the consequent cleavages within families. Cf. Wilberforce's report (Diary, *Life*, III, 24) of a visit from a well-known minister, Mr Hughes of Battersea. "He confessed, not one in twenty of Doddridge's pupils but who turned either Socinian or tending that way; (he himself strictly orthodox); and he said that all the old Presbyterian places of worship were become Socinian congregations." This was an exaggeration, but it was the Presbyterians who, for definite historical reasons, were particularly affected, the Independents to some extent: otherwise these were rigid in the tradition. A typical case is that of Crabb Robinson, an Independent who revolted on moral grounds from the Calvinism in which he had been brought up, and ultimately found his home in the Unitarian Association. He once described himself at a German inn, which insisted on knowing his religion, as a Muggletonian, on which Mrs Wordsworth commented, "You might have signed it Muddletonian". "The dear good woman fancies nothing to be *clear* but the 39 Articles—or rather the liturgy—God bless her", Crabb Robinson charitably remarked to his friend Thomas Robinson (January 17, 1847). A study of the relevant passages in his diary is of great historical and psychological interest, and induces both sympathy for him and a suspicion that Mrs Wordsworth was as shrewd as usual.

and slovenly Low Church.[1] Nineteenth-century developments have led us nowadays, often with imperfect accuracy, to identify the Low Churchman and the Evangelical, but it is more than inaccurate to make the identification for a hundred to a hundred and fifty years ago. The religious revival of the mid-eighteenth century had been led by High Churchmen, and High Churchmen fifty to a hundred years later, though they might distrust the increasingly close alliance between Methodism and Dissent, had much in common with Evangelicalism when that was not allied—and within the Church it was, in spite of some notable exceptions, usually not allied—with Calvinism.

It is the High Church of which we ought chiefly to think in connection with Wordsworth. We are apt to look upon it as being in the latter half of the eighteenth century not merely high but dry. To a certain extent this is true; yet there were such laymen as that John Russell who painted Wilberforce's portrait as a boy, "a religious man, very high church indeed",[2] and there were such pious households as those from which

[1] Cf. Balleine, *History of the Evangelical Party*, 2nd ed., pp. 137–40 and 144. Balleine notes particularly (p. 144) that the chief opposition to the Oxford Movement in its early stages came not from Evangelicals but from Low Churchmen: "they hated Popery even more than prayer-meetings, and they turned aside from persecuting 'the nasty and numerous vermin of Methodism' to exterminate 'the pragmatical, perpendicular, Puseyite prigs'. The language is that of Sydney Smith, their chief spokesman in the Press".

[2] Russell was that interesting character, a High Church Methodist, like Wesley himself. He was "converted September 30, 1764, aetat. 19, at about half an hour after seven in the evening", by Madan, whose theology the convert, as often happens, did not adopt in every point. Cf. *John Russell, R.A.* (George C. Williamson), esp. pp. 9, 25, 44.

Keble and Pusey sprang. A fair specimen of the average conscientious High Church parish priest is the Rev. William Cole, as we know him from his diaries. All the materials for the Tractarian Revival are there: the strong historical sense, passing into antiquarianism, the sense of duty towards the spiritual needs of his parishioners, the sense of the Church, the sacramental sense leading to a strong sympathy with Roman Catholicism on the sides of religious devotion and ceremonial. Cole was one of many who transmitted the Anglican tradition, which, like the general Catholic tradition at its best, is marked by liberty of intellectual speculation and a large measure of Platonism in its thought[1]—the tradition of Hooker and Andrewes, of Herbert and Vaughan and Thomas Traherne, of Laud, that much misunderstood man who has scarcely yet in popular opinion recovered from Macaulay's ignorant attack, and Jeremy Taylor, of Ken and William Law. At the end of the century the stream of tradition was little more than a trickle: but the channels were still there, and they were not altogether dried up.

Now it was in this tradition that Wordsworth was brought up, and to ignore it in a consideration of his thought is as if one ignored orthodox theology in a consideration of the thought of *Piers Plowman* and concentrated on the Peasants' Revolt and the doctrines of the Lollards. The comparison does injustice to some of the Evangelical leaders, but it will serve. It is clear from everything he wrote that, bred an Anglican, he was not bred either a Low Churchman or an Evangelical.

[1] "Even to this day, I doubt whether any one can be an orthodox theologian without being a Platonist. Our creeds are the formulae of victorious Platonism" (Inge, *Personal Idealism and Mysticism*, p. 67). Cf. pp. 290–2 *infra*.

It is equally clear that he had the same roots as his brother Christopher and his episcopal nephews and great-nephew—Charles of St Andrews, Christopher of Lincoln, John of Salisbury: all High Churchmen with the characteristic regret for the destruction at the Reformation of so much that was noble, the characteristic wish to revive it, the characteristic respect for the religious devotion of Roman Catholics, and the characteristic dislike for the Roman Church.[1] He shows the same distinguishing marks, not because, as is sometimes said, in later life he conformed to their beliefs, but because, it must be repeated, he had the same roots. And these roots go down, not merely to a conception of the Church which, by its insistence upon the importance of the community as well as of the individual, affected his political thought, but to an interpretation of Christian doctrine which, though frequently ignored by his critics, cannot be neglected without the risk of misunderstanding his intellectual and moral as well as his spiritual development.

One of Wordsworth's episcopal nephews, Charles of St Andrews, wrote a book on Shakespeare's knowledge of the Bible, in the course of which he referred[2] with justifiable severity to those Shakespearian commentators who timidly

[1] Cf. Professor Clement Webb's description of the Tractarian Movement as one "the essence of which consisted in a revival of attention to certain elements in the Anglican tradition, in virtue of which it was distinguished from the general tradition of Protestantism and approximated to the Catholic tradition, while at the same time claiming to retain others, in virtue of which the Church of England could not throw in its lot with the Roman Church as actually existing" (*Religious Thought in the Oxford Movement*, p. 29).

[2] *Shakespeare and the Bible*, pp. 305–6: "The truth is, I fear, that whatever else our poet's critics have been strong in, they have, for the most part, not been strong in knowledge of the Scriptures".

suggest an original in one of the Synoptic Gospels for a phrase which might come from any of them or from elsewhere in the New Testament: they forget that, even if the Scriptures are not familiar to them, Shakespeare must have heard them read so frequently in church that his phraseology and his thought alike became soaked in them. To Wordsworth also the Bible was more familiar than any other book, and next to it came the Prayer Book and the works of the great Anglican divines which were commonly used for purposes of devotion. He was brought up on the Church Catechism, and if, as has been declared, no one who has learnt the Shorter Catechism of the Church of Scotland can ever escape from it, the same is true of the Church Catechism. The phrases of "The Desire" may prove elusive, but the rest sticks. And there is something Wordsworthian in its very beginning, with its revelation of the mysteries that lie hidden in the apparently ordinary; it is less magnificent than the opening of the Shorter Catechism, but its educational method might be put higher.

Q. What is your Name?
A. William.
Q. Who gave you this Name?
A. My Godfathers and Godmother in my Baptism; wherein I was made a member of Christ, the child of God, and an inheritor of the kingdom of heaven.

Beyond this Wordsworth learnt that a sacrament has two parts, an outward visible sign and an inward spiritual grace: with other things which need not concern us here.

The effect upon Wordsworth, not of the Church Catechism alone, but of the whole Prayer Book and all his Anglican training, is usually overlooked, and sometimes with consequences of serious misunderstanding. One example, not serious but of importance in its way, may be adduced from Hale White's *Examination*: why, Hale White wondered, should Wordsworth in the *Ecclesiastical Sonnets*, after a series of sonnets celebrating the liturgy, write one on Mutability? "Is mutability, then, so characteristic of things ecclesiastical that when the thoughts are turned to them it naturally presents itself?" Hale White was not a Churchman, or he would have known that the answer was "Yes". There are at least three places in the Prayer Book which consider that precise point of the mutability of rites and ceremonies: the *Preface*, that other or second preface *Of Ceremonies, why some be abolished and some retained*, and the XXXIVth Article, *Of the Traditions of the Church*. It will suffice to quote part of the last.

> It is not necessary that Traditions and Ceremonies be in all places one, or utterly like; for at all times they have been divers, and may be changed according to the diversities of countries, times, and men's manners, so that nothing be ordained against God's Word....
>
> Every particular or national Church hath authority to ordain, change, and abolish, ceremonies or rites of the Church ordained only by man's authority, so that all things be done to edifying.

Wordsworth did not need to look this up: the whole question of the value, meaning and position of ceremonies in religion was a part of the furnishing of his mind as an ordinary instructed Anglican, and he therefore summed it up naturally and without effort in one of the most magnificent of his sonnets, which, as is the habit of great poetry, goes far beyond the local and temporary matters from which it sets out, the rush-bearing at Grasmere and the survival of Christmas decorations from so many vanished "graceful rites and usages"—

> From low to high doth dissolution climb,
> And sink from high to low, along a scale
> Of awful notes, whose concord shall not fail;
> A musical but melancholy chime,
> Which they can hear who meddle not with crime,
> Nor avarice, nor over-anxious care.
> Truth fails not; but her outward forms that bear
> The longest date do melt like frosty rime,
> That in the morning whitened hill and plain
> And is no more; drop like the tower sublime
> Of yesterday, which royally did wear
> His crown of weeds, but could not even sustain
> Some casual shout that broke the silent air,
> Or the unimaginable touch of Time.

A more serious example may suggest that even a smattering of Anglican divinity might save a good deal of ink-spilling over Wordsworth. Illustrations might be made from many books, but it will suffice to quote from one of the most popular Anglican books of devotion well into the nineteenth century, and one still not disused—Jeremy Taylor's *Holy Living*. This is how Taylor begins his instruction on the practice of the Presence of God.

> That God is present in all places, that He sees every action, hears all discourses, and understands every thought, is no strange thing to a Christian ear....God is wholly in every place; included in no place; not bound with cords except those of love; not divided into parts; not changeable into several shapes; filling heaven and earth with His present power and with His never absent nature; and we can no more be removed from the presence of God than from our own being....

God is present by His essence, which, because it is boundless or infinite, cannot be contained within the limits of any place; and because He is of an essential purity and spiritual nature, He cannot be undervalued by being supposed present in the places of unnatural uncleanness: because as the sun, reflecting upon the mud of strands and shores, is unpolluted in its beams, so is God not dishonoured when we suppose Him in every one of His creatures, and in every part of every one of them; and is still as unmixed with any unhandsome adherence, as is the soul in the bowels of the body.

God is everywhere present by His power. He rolls the orbs of heaven with His hand....

We should be on safer ground than in most parallel-hunting if we saw a direct relation between this and *Tintern Abbey*:

> A presence that disturbs me with the joy
> Of elevated thoughts; a sense sublime
> Of something far more deeply interfused,
> Whose dwelling is the light of setting suns,
> And the round ocean, and the living air,
> And the blue sky, and in the mind of man:
> A motion and a spirit, that impels
> All thinking things, all objects of all thought,
> And rolls through all things.

There is no need to emphasize the unusual *rolls*: the syntactical use of the verb is different, though Wordsworth's use might be due to unconscious reminiscence. In a much later poem, *In the Woods of Rydal*, he has it in exactly Taylor's sense, possibly with conscious reminiscence:

> And rolls the planets through the blue profound.

Jeremy Taylor was one of his favourite authors, and we cannot exclude the possibility of reminiscence in either poem. But it is not essential to the argument. Taylor is merely expressing one of the ordinary tenets of Christianity, and it may be accidental that his phraseology bears a resemblance to Wordsworth's. The important thing is that Wordsworth's thought, expressed most clearly here, can be called pantheistic only by a loose application of the term. It might perhaps be interpreted as akin to that Christian adaptation of the doctrine of the "soul of the world" which is found, for example, in Henry More, and which may seem to be indicated in Wordsworth's phrase about the "souls of lonely places". But it does not seem to be identical with it: it implies one divine spirit of life. The doctrine, that is to say, is panentheistic, or, if we use the theological terms which are in fact more appropriate, that doctrine of the divine immanence which he recognized from his personal experience of contact with the divine through nature, and from the sacramental teaching of his childhood and youth. Professor Rader combines Hazlitt's interpretation of the *Tintern Abbey* lines—as an expression of Wordsworth's necessitarianism—with the influence of Spinoza.[1] If Wordsworth's lines are necessitarian and Spinozistic, so are Jeremy Taylor's words, an anachronistic though not exactly absurd conclusion. Both Wordsworth and Jeremy Taylor are in entire harmony with that passage of St Athanasius which Dean Inge quotes as being "not far from Wordsworth's own theological attitude":[2]

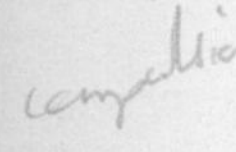

The all-powerful, all-perfect, and all-holy Word of the Father, descending upon all things, and everywhere extending His own energy, and bringing to light all things, whether visible or invisible, knits and welds them into His own being,

[1] *Presiding Ideas in Wordsworth's Poetry*, p. 169.

[2] *Studies of English Mystics*, p. 206; the passage from St Athanasius is quoted again in *The Platonic Tradition in English Religious Thought*, p. 81.

leaving nothing destitute of His operation. And a certain marvellous and Divine harmony is thus veritably brought to pass by Him.

Like Jeremy Taylor, like St Athanasius, Wordsworth knew perfectly well the difference between Spinozism and the Christian doctrine that God at once reveals Himself through and is present in nature, and is more than nature. It is this, not any "return to orthodoxy" from earlier convictions, which underlies Wordsworth's protest against the accusation of Spinozism, which had been brought against him by a friend of Mrs Clarkson.

She talks of my being a worshipper of Nature. A passionate expression, uttered incautiously in the poem upon the Wye, has led her into this mistake; she, reading in cold-heartedness, and substituting the letter for the spirit. Unless I am greatly mistaken, there is nothing of this kind in *The Excursion*. There is indeed a passage towards the end of the fourth book, where the Wanderer introduces the simile of the Boy and the Shell, that has something ordinarily (but absurdly) called *Spinozistic*. But the intelligent reader will easily see the *dramatic* propriety of the passage. . . . She condemns me for not distinguishing between Nature as the work of God, and God himself. But where does she find this doctrine inculcated? Whence does she gather that the author of *The Excursion* looks upon Nature and God as the same? He does not indeed consider the Supreme Being as bearing the same relation to the Universe, as a watchmaker bears to a watch. In fact, there is nothing in the course of the religious education adopted in this country, and in the use made by us of the Holy Scriptures, that appears to me so injurious as perpetually talking about *making by God*.[1]

Wordsworth's dislike of Paleyism, which comes out so clearly here, might lead him sometimes to indiscretion of

[1] Written in 1814 or 1815. Cf. pp. 269–70 *infra*.

statement, but we have no right to disallow his explanations in the interests of our own theories of his development. It is sometimes argued either that he mistook his own philosophical opinions or that he was trying to recant, but a consideration of his religious background and training makes both suggestions unnecessary. Again, Professor Rader argues:[1]

The latter part of the letter...proves that his position corresponded with Spinoza in an important respect: the philosopher also inveighed against the idea of "making by God", and sought to prove that "God is the indwelling and not the transient cause of all things". (*Ethic*, pt. I, prop. xviii.)

By the same argument we might prove that Spinoza was a Christian. For this is not simply Spinozism: it is Catholic Christianity, in its essence the doctrine of the Incarnation and the foundation of the whole sacramental view of the world.[2]

[1] *Op. cit.* p. 203.

[2] Cf. Dr F. L. Cross: "The essence of the religion of the Incarnation is the doctrine that God can be discovered in and through nature.... Yet, it may be objected, does not such a doctrine land us in pure pantheism? If God is really present everywhere in nature, are we not back again at the standpoint of Spinoza, *deus sive natura*? At this point we have to face the most serious challenge which can be urged against the principle of the Incarnation....Briefly, the reply which I give to the challenge just mentioned—and it is a reply which has been deeply incorporated into the Christian tradition—is to be found in a doctrine with which some modern thinkers have made us familiar under the name of "degrees of truth and reality". It amounts to this, that, though God reveals himself through nature, yet God is himself more than nature. Though there is some essential likeness between God and nature, yet God transcends nature" ("Anglo-Catholicism and the Incarnation", *Hibbert Journal*, April 1932).

Wordsworth did not need the intervention of Coleridge to introduce the idea to him.

iii

Two of Wordsworth's memories of his mother, who died when he was eight, were connected with church-going. One was of her decking him with a nosegay when he went, according to custom, to be catechized in church—a custom, by the way, not entirely in agreement with the modern belief in the clerical slackness of the eighteenth century. It was not peculiar to Cockermouth, or even to the north of England: the Rev. William Cole, for example, used to catechize the Bletchley children in church every Sunday in Lent. The other childish reminiscence was of her robust retort, that he deserved to be disappointed if he went to church for gain, when he complained that he had not received the penny to which he had believed himself entitled for going to church to see a woman do penance in a white sheet. That piece of tradition would not have been observed at Bletchley: as Mr Cole remarked (January 16, 1766), "As the Discipline of our Church, thro' the Practices of the Dissenters, is now so relaxed as to come to nothing, there is no Parleying with your Parishioners on any Point of Doctrine or Discipline: for if you are rigid, they will either abstain from all Ordinances, or go over to the Dissenters". There was perhaps less competition from the Practices of the Dissenters at Cockermouth and in those other parts of England where the custom of doing penance in a white sheet survived well into the nineteenth century; and the custom of the Scottish Church, not many miles away, would support it. The matter, as it regards Wordsworth, is of importance only as indicating how the older customs were living influences for him in his boyhood—another, which he mentions in the sonnet on *Decay of Piety* and the Fenwick note to it, was the attendance at church on Wednesdays and Fridays and holy days, at least of the older generation. It also, perhaps, indicates how the obligation of disinterested church-going, of church-going as a duty to be fulfilled apart from any obvious profit or enjoyment, was inculcated in him. The full effect of the lesson was not to be seen for a good many years, but it is another of the things in the background which should not be forgotten. Dr Munk's suggestion that Wordsworth had been "fromm aber nicht kirchlich erzogen" is hardly supported by this evidence, scanty though it is.[1] On the other hand he is obviously right in his contention that Wordsworth's dissatisfaction with the religious life, or rather want of life, which he found when he went up to Cambridge, was not a dissatisfaction with Christianity: "denn schon damals hatte Wordsworth für die christliche Lehre Verständnis".[2] Wordsworth has told us in *The Prelude* (III, 407–25) of his dislike, which on later reflection included disapproval, of compulsory attendance at dull and perfunctory recitals of the offices in the college chapel. Bishop Christopher Wordsworth, while quoting the condemnation, tried to minimize its force,[3] but Wordsworth did

[1] In the same way it seems to me that the Rev. Stephen Liberty, in his *Religion in Wordsworth*, has overlooked the evidence for the religious practices of the country people, and made too much of Wordsworth's early loss of his parents. The Jesuits would not, unless they are misrepresented, have been dissatisfied if they had had him for a year less than his mother had him, and his father lived six years longer. And Christopher Wordsworth had exactly the same background as his elder brother.

[2] Munk, *op. cit.* p. 40.

[3] *Memoirs*, I, 47–8; II, 265–6.

not himself minimize it. He suggested that the services might be reformed, but he went no further.

It is remarkable, however, and indeed to be emphasized, that he did not find religious nourishment in the same quarter as many of his contemporaries did. In the years when he was at Cambridge, the Evangelical movement was already strong and growing stronger. Charles Simeon had been appointed to Holy Trinity in 1783, and his church was always crowded with undergraduates, while Isaac Milner was appointed President of Queens' in 1788 and immediately began to make the college "a sort of School of the Prophets, the stronghold of Evangelicalism in Cambridge".[1] But Wordsworth was not affected by these stirrings of new religious life. It is possible that his immunity from the enthusiasm which infected so many others was partly due to the overmastering strength of his political interests at that time, but on the other hand his brother Christopher, who had not the same political interests, also remained outside the Evangelical circle. He may have gone to hear Simeon as an undergraduate, and he certainly went in 1800, after his ordination,[2] but he was not influenced in a "party" direction by what he heard. An explanation which is at least probable is that the political preoccupations of one brother and the scholarly interests of the other were reinforced by their common religious tradition against one which, if not in Simeon himself, yet in some of his fellows was in some ways less liberal and less profound. Whatever the explanation, the fact remains that Wordsworth never learnt the Evangelical vocabulary, and since religious critics of his

[1] Balleine, *op. cit.* pp. 86–8.

[2] Canon C. Wordsworth, *Social Life in English Universities*, p. 599.

poetry were, for thirty years or more, of Evangelical opinions, whether within or without the Church of England, and accustomed to that vocabulary, they missed the familiar phrases and the recognized trains of thought, and complained of his want of true evangelical piety and his tendency towards a "natural" religion. *The Excursion* gave real pain to pious souls of this kind, as we shall see.

It was natural that Wordsworth's guardians should wish him to take orders. His own early inclination towards the law may have been little more than the result of admiration for his father, though the odd episode of the forged documents many years later showed him displaying detective ability as well as legal skill in marshalling an argument.[1] In his old age he once said that he "shrank from the law" and "always fancied that he had talents for command; and he at one time thought of a military life, but then he was without connections".[2] Neither the law nor the army was a practical choice for him: lack of money and influence by themselves would have been sufficient obstacles, even without the physical disability from which he suffered, the violent headaches which prostrated him at more or less frequent intervals for years before the eye trouble, of which they were a symptom, declared itself.[3] There was, on the other hand, clerical influence in his mother's family, and he was evidently, though not satisfactory in all respects—and though he had, by his devotion to Italian rather than to mathematics, lost his chance of a fellowship and its openings towards promotion—a young man of serious and religious temper: a presentation to a living would probably be

[1] Southey, *Life and Correspondence*, VI, 297–300.
[2] Lady Richardson, November 8, 1845 (Grosart, III, 451–2).
[3] Cf. pp. 318–35 *infra*.

found for him without any difficulty. Some later words, in the *Postscript* of 1835, give Wordsworth's own comment on that kind of situation.

> In a country so rich and luxurious as England, the character of its clergy must unavoidably sink, and their influence be everywhere impaired, if individuals from the upper ranks, and men of leading talents, are to have no inducements to enter into that body but such as are purely spiritual. And this "tinge of secularity" is no reproach to the clergy, nor does it imply a deficiency of spiritual endowments. Parents and guardians, looking forward to sources of honourable maintenance for their children and wards, often direct their thoughts early towards the church, being determined partly by outward circumstances, and partly by indications of seriousness, or intellectual fitness. It is natural that a boy or youth, with such a prospect before him, should turn his attention to those studies, and be led into those habits of reflection, which will in some degree tend to prepare him for the duties he is hereafter to undertake. As he draws nearer to the time when he will be called to these duties, he is both led and compelled to examine the Scriptures. He becomes more and more sensible of their truth. Devotion grows in him; and what might begin in temporal considerations, will end (as in a majority of instances we trust it does) in a spiritual-mindedness not unworthy of that Gospel, the lessons of which he is to teach, and the faith of which he is to inculcate.

Those sentences bear the mark of direct observation, whether in his own family or outside we need not inquire, and it is probable that Wordsworth's development would have followed the same course if things had fallen out a little differently—if, for example, his guardians had not agreed that a good knowledge of French would be useful to him. There can be no doubt of his seriousness, intellectual fitness, or religious impulses: they can be seen even in the scanty contemporary evidence, as distinct from the later evidence of *The Prelude*. "Among the more awful scenes of the Alps", he wrote to Dorothy in the long letter of September 1790, "I had not a thought of man, or a single created being; my whole soul was turned to Him who produced the terrible majesty before me." The *Descriptive Sketches* in their first version show, besides that general sense of religion connected, as Dr Munk points out, with the sense of the numinous and of the past—always unusually strong in Wordsworth—religious sympathies of a more definite kind: horror at the sacrilege which had molested the Grande Chartreuse—

> The cloister startles at the gleam of arms,
> And Blasphemy the shuddering fane alarms....
> The cross with hideous laughter Demons mock,
> By angels planted on the aereal rock—

and respect for the prayers of the peasants at mountain shrines—

> Oh give not me that eye of hard disdain
> That views undimm'd Einsiedeln's wretched fane...
> While loud and dull ascends the weeping cry,
> Surely in other thoughts contempt may die.
> If the sad grave of human ignorance bear
> One flower of hope—Oh pass and leave it there....
> Yes I will see you when ye first behold
> Those turrets tipp'd by hope with morning gold,
> And watch, while on your brows the cross ye make,
> Round your pale eyes a wintry lustre wake.
> —Without one hope her written griefs to blot,
> Save in the land where all things are forgot,
> My heart, alive to transports long unknown,
> Half wishes your delusion were its own.

The exaggerated gloom here is not wholly insincere, but it

is not to be taken too seriously.[1] The last few lines do not necessarily, as Professor Garrod suggests, express a general religious scepticism: the tone of other passages, for example that quoted above on the Grande Chartreuse, is against that theory; nor are they to be put down, as Dr Munk would have it, to the want of affection which he thinks Wordsworth displays for ecclesiastical forms in his remarks on "chapels" in *The Prelude*. The young Wordsworth knew that the proper thing for an enlightened thinker was to feel contempt for Popish superstition and ignorance, and he found it impossible to do so in the face of so much human suffering and devotion. He had not attained to the deep and gentle sympathy which he expressed in later versions of the passage, or in the letter to his brother on the poor woman at the pool of St Kevin;[2] but he could not be a scorner. His instinct, when he found men on their knees, was to kneel with them.

It is, further, remarkable that there was in him, both in 1789 and later, no anti-clericalism, none of that hatred of official or unofficial Christianity which accompanied the French Revolution as it accompanied the Russian Revolution. In the letter to the Bishop of Llandaff he has nothing to say against the French clergy of the lower ranks; indeed, he is glad to think that they have profited from the redistribution of clerical property. He retained that good opinion of them sixty years later, telling Ellis Yarnall that "he had known many of the abbés and other ecclesiastics, and thought highly of them as a class: they were earnest, faithful men: being unmarried, he must say they were the better able to fulfil their sacred duties; they were married to their flocks. In the towns

[1] Cf. Legouis, *Early Life*, pp. 153–60.

[2] Cf. p. 152 *supra*.

there seemed, he admitted, very little religion; but in the country there had always been a great deal".[1]

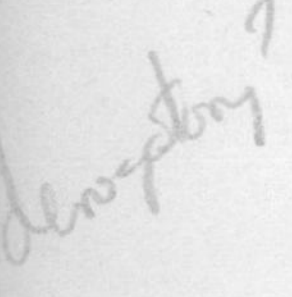

At the same time, Wordsworth clearly felt no sense of vocation to the clerical life, and no great eagerness to enter upon it. "I cannot deny", he wrote to Mathews (September 23, 1791), "that were I so situated, as to be without relations, to whom I were accountable for my actions, I should perhaps prefer your idea"—of throwing everything up—"to your present situation, or to vegetating on a paltry curacy." How far his sense of frustrated ambition and capacity for leadership, of "talents for command", was responsible for his unwillingness to settle down, it is impossible to say; he had practical ability, and he had to face in more forms than one the temptation of the thinker to use his powers for obvious personal advantage. The situation looked simpler to his relations: as Dorothy Wordsworth put it,[2] "he must, when he is three-and-twenty, either go into Orders or take pupils". Wordsworth was not at that date or later convinced of the alternatives. A curacy at Harwich, with the promise of succeeding to the living, was offered to him, but the fact that he was, when he took his degree, two full years below the canonical age for ordination prevented its immediate acceptance. The interval was to be spent not in idleness but in the acquirement of languages, French in particular, which, Dorothy explained to Jane Pollard (December 7, 1790), would "qualify him for the office of travelling companion to some young gentleman". His uncle William also suggested

[1] *Wordsworth and the Coleridges*, p. 40.

[2] To Jane Pollard, March 30, 1790. She dated it April 30, but her statement that "he will be twenty in April" shows that this was a slip.

that Oriental languages might be useful, and the younger William, who for all his wilfulness was usually reasonable, consented to study them when he should return from the Continent. "But what must I do amongst that immense wilderness?" he inquired ruefully of Mathews (November 23, 1791). He may have thought the chances of a travelling tutorship as remote as those of a reputation for Oriental scholarship; at any rate he wrote to Mathews in a decided tone from Blois on May 17, 1792:

It is at present my intention to take orders, in the approaching winter or spring. My uncle the clergyman will furnish me with a title. Had it been in my power, I certainly should have wished to defer the moment. But though I may not be resident in London, I need not therefore be prevented from engaging in any literary plan, which may have the appearance of producing a decent harvest....I shall return to England in the autumn or the beginning of winter....We might then more advantageously than by letter consult upon some literary scheme, a project which I have much at heart.

There are two things to be noted about this letter. One is the cool and businesslike tone, the view of the taking of orders as a preliminary to engaging in a literary plan, which may be compared with that of the letter written to Wrangham on March 7, 1796:

I sincerely congratulate you on your late induction, as it must set you entirely above the necessity of engaging in any employment unsuited to your taste and pleasures.

The young man who wrote those letters might have developed into a hard-working priest, as his friend did, but he shows little sign of it here. The other point to be noted is that Wordsworth was writing seven months before the birth of his daughter Caroline.

Most of the discussion, prolonged and weary though it has been, of the relations between Wordsworth and Annette Vallon has ignored the practical effect of Caroline's birth upon his proposed career. If he married Annette, a Frenchwoman, a Roman Catholic, who had already borne him a child, there would be no chance of promotion in the Church for him; he would be fortunate if the influence of his uncles obtained a paltry curacy. Annette's social position, besides, would not be enviable. And it was more than doubtful whether a young man who had made such an unsuitable marriage would be selected for either a travelling or a stationary tutorship. In the light of his correspondence of 1791–3, it seems to me very questionable whether, as Professor Garrod and others have suggested, Wordsworth's affair with Annette was a matter of inverted principle, a deliberate flouting of the convention of marriage. He was not at this time affected by Godwinian or other advanced views of social relationships; moral fashions in France were lax among many who were horrified by revolutionary morality; Annette's surviving double letter to him and Dorothy, with its suggestion of his return to marry her, even if not entirely sincere implies her belief that he intended a marriage, however long delayed, between them. He was a hot-blooded young man—as his sister remarked, "excuse might have been found in his natural disposition"[1]—attracted by a woman who herself was evidently not cold, who was by several years his senior, and who possessed for him, as he did for her, the glamour of strangeness. The most likely explanation is that the two were carried away by the impulse of the moment. If they had any other motive, it may have been the certainty that Annette's family would never consent

[1] To Jane Pollard, June 11, 1793.

to a marriage, unless indeed they were shocked into it. But even an illegitimate child may have seemed to the realistic good sense of a French bourgeois, Royalist and Catholic family a less embarrassing addition to it than a penniless young Englishman of heretical religious and political opinions. Annette's chances of marriage were not spoilt by her adventure, and her family could save her from the consequences of her folly by withholding consent to this most undesirable alliance.

Further, it should be remembered that Wordsworth had grown up in a peasant society where a woman was not thought much the worse of for having had a child before marriage, provided marriage followed. M. Legouis was startled by that passage in *The Prelude*[1] in which Wordsworth expresses gratitude for the rough school life which taught him

> to endure and note
> What was not understood though known to be;
> Among the mysteries of love and hate,
> Honour and shame, looking to right and left,
> Uncheck'd by innocence too delicate
> And moral notions too intolerant,
> Sympathies too contracted;

and he rightly connected it not merely with that general tenderness towards sinners which shocked Miss Martineau, but with this specific incident in his life. Wordsworth's elderly and more sophisticated uncles would take another view of his actions. And if Wordsworth were unable to marry Annette—and each year as it passed increased both the outward and the inward obstacles—his own view would change. If he could neither get to France nor get Annette and her

[1] XIII, 313–25 (1805); XIV, 329–41 (1850).

child to England for a marriage, and if his own passion and his desire for marriage had faded, what was he to do?

This train of thought, it seems to me, combined with his natural restlessness, accounts for the two explanations which he himself gave of his ultimate abstention from taking orders. On February 16, 1793, four months after Caroline's birth, Dorothy Wordsworth wrote to Jane Pollard, "I look forward to receiving you in my little parsonage"—the parsonage at Harwich or in some other place where she would keep house for her brother until he married. A year later Wordsworth wrote to Mathews (February 17, 1794), "All professions I think are attended with great inconveniences, but that of the priesthood with the most.... What is to become of me I know not. I cannot bow down my mind to take orders". But it was not until Raisley Calvert's legacy fell to him, a year later again, that he definitely abandoned the idea. Here, then, is one explanation: he found it hard to reconcile himself to the necessary restrictions on his freedom, as he wrote to Mathews at the time, but he admitted to Sir George Beaumont ten years later (February 20, 1805) that he would have been forced into accepting them, had not Calvert left him that legacy. But there is another explanation, given in conversation in 1812—"he declared himself not virtuous enough for a clergyman".[1] He repeated this many years later to the Fletcher family: "He did not feel himself good enough for the Church, he felt that his mind was not properly disciplined for that holy office, and that the struggle between his conscience and his impulses would have made life a torture".[2] A young man who found himself unable and increasingly reluctant to

[1] Crabb Robinson, *Diary*, May 31, 1812.

[2] November 8, 1845, Lady Richardson's diary (Grosart, III, 451).

marry a woman who, in his view at least, had Annette Vallon's claim on him, might well consider that he was falling below a clerical standard. Wordsworth's morality in these matters was a compound of the direct peasant view and of a decency and common sense which are not confined to any particular class, and it cannot be explained by any modern view which either minimizes his action or gives him the sense of guilt which would be felt by the weak young man in a certain type of Victorian novel. He was not the victim of a complex, but he felt, with some justice, that he was not good enough for the Church.

iv

We have grown so much accustomed to the declarations of men that they are leaving or have left the Church, not because they are not good enough for it but because it is not good enough for them—because they have doubts of the authority of the Bible or the Creeds or the validity of Anglican orders or some other point which seems essential to them—that we are inclined to take such motives for granted where they do not exist. This caution has special bearing on Wordsworth's history. There is no evidence that he had chafed consciously against anything but what may be called the physical ties of the parson, the inability to satisfy his wandering, even gipsy, instincts; no evidence that, like his friend Mathews, he would ever have abandoned the intention, though the unenthusiastic intention, of years, on grounds of intellectual religious disbelief. Yet the mere abandonment may have made him realize that he had to some extent drifted in thought from the faith in which he had been educated, and may therefore have been in part responsible for the state of dejection which overwhelmed him in the year which followed. But, again, there is no evidence that, like Coleridge, he left the Church of his baptism and returned: and here comes in something which affects our whole understanding of Wordsworth's attitude towards the Church.

There are two types of Christians, who may, for this purpose and without prejudice, be called Catholic and Protestant, though they do not necessarily belong by profession to the religious bodies which these titles suggest. The Protestant, when he finds himself in disagreement with the body to which he has hitherto belonged, protests and leaves it: religion is for him an entirely personal thing. The Catholic may also, though he does not always, protest: he may reason with his fellows, he may reluctantly conclude that they are not at present to be persuaded and so keep his private opinions to himself, he may even be induced to remain where he is by spiritual humility, a sense that he is but one and fallible, that the consensus of opinion may be right as against him, and that even if it is wrong on some points the Church of his allegiance holds more of the truth than he will find elsewhere, and that the loss of community and communion is greater than can be compensated for by yielding to what is as likely to be intellectual arrogance as honesty. The Protestant has no such doubts of himself, and is inclined to look upon the Catholic of this type as at the best weakly surrendering his sacred private convictions to an imagined ideal of fellowship, and at the worst intellectually dishonest or cowardly. It is perfectly true that Bishop Blougram is a degenerate specimen of the type, but in all his special pleading Blougram makes some valid points, and he does, after all, represent only the degenerate form of a type which at its other extreme is neither dishonest nor cowardly.

This sort of loyal independence, if not confined to those who would call themselves, though perhaps not each other, Catholics, is most common among them, because they have been educated in the belief of the importance of the society and of its claim upon the individual, who is only one member of it. The frequency of its appearance and of its recognition even by ecclesiastical authorities, who might be expected to be unfavourable to it, is shown by such figures, by no means uncommon, as those very different men, Lord Acton and Baron Friedrich von Hügel, in the Roman Church, and in the Anglican Church by that tolerated variety of opinion which makes those who prefer more sharply defined limits call it the City of Confusion. But it should be noted that it is scarcely possible to anyone brought up in a religious school which lays disproportionate stress on the emotional response of the believer. Bunyan drew the moral of the sad fate of Ignorance, whose heart told him, quite mistakenly, that he was saved; but the Evangelicals of the late eighteenth and the nineteenth centuries, whether they inclined towards Bunyan's Calvinism or towards an Arminianism which he condemned, were uneasy about the salvation of anyone whose heart did not tell him emphatically that he was saved. Their insistence on the necessity of emotional certainty, while it sometimes led to great personal holiness, also led to exaggerated individualism, and sometimes to morbid despair or a reaction to infidelity when the emotional response weakened or failed. And on those who never felt the strong emotional conviction which they were assured was required of them, the effect was sometimes the encouragement of antagonism not to Evangelicalism alone, but to Christianity, of which they knew only this limited and particular orthodoxy.

But if Evangelicalism did not make enough allowance for the varieties of religious experience, or for the recurrence of periods of spiritual aridity or intellectual disquiet after that "conversion" of which they recognized only one kind, the same mistake was not made by all sections of the Church of England. The High Church might at that time, with more or less justice, be accused of dryness and formality, but that very insistence on external forms and obligations would have the effect of impressing upon a man brought up in it the possible existence of truths which were not at every moment emotionally felt or believed, or received with complete and overpowering intellectual conviction. Even a strong intellectual disagreement, or an emotional desolation, would not make such a man feel that he must exclude himself from the Church; and the Church would not exclude him.[1]

The past tense has been used here, but the present tense might have been used equally well. For the nobler kind of Evangelicalism is fortunately not dead, and has lost some of its dangerous exaggerations; but the less noble kind is also not dead, and it is the form of religion most familiar to the majority of those who have recently written on Wordsworth, particularly in America. The assumptions which underlie their attempts to trace his religious development puzzle an English reader at first, especially if that reader happens to be

[1] Crabb Robinson (*Diary*, December 20, 1835) was distressed by Alsop's quotation, from hearsay, of words attributed to Wordsworth in reply to the inquiry whether he was really a Christian: "When I am a good man, then I am a Christian". The words are not sufficiently authenticated, but if we choose to accept them we ought not with Crabb Robinson to consider them equivocal: we should do better to look upon them as expressing Wordsworth's recognition of his own varying emotional states.

an Anglican; until it is realized that he is looked upon with the eyes of men who have revolted from the narrow Fundamentalism of the most influential and numerous bodies of American Protestants, and suppose all orthodoxy to be the same, narrow and intolerant of any deviation from a creed which it is difficult for a man with any respect for modern knowledge to accept. Most of the Englishmen who call themselves Fundamentalists would be looked upon with grave suspicion by those who take the same title in America. But Wordsworth had little in common with an easily recognizable American type, the man who, brought up in this narrow orthodoxy, breaks away from it either to a liberalism which may become so vague as ultimately to contain the smallest possible modicum of religious aspiration, or to a definite dislike of religious creeds. A return to the limited orthodoxy of his boyhood might in such a man imply intellectual suicide, and when some of Wordsworth's American critics talk of his return to orthodoxy and lament over it, it is this process which they believe him to have gone through. But there was no breaking away to liberalism and subsequent recantation in him: there was a religious development parallel to, supporting and supported by his mental and moral development, interrupted like that by a brief though severe attack of Godwinism, and resumed in the same way after the interruption. All this is not intended to deny that Wordsworth went through a period during which he probably abandoned spiritual as well as moral problems in despair: but it is asserted without any hesitation that the "orthodoxy" of his later years was a natural growth from the orthodoxy of his youth, and that neither depended on a rigid interpretation and acceptance of a small and limiting set of theological propositions. The two sides of Wordsworth which Coleridge once described as "I and my brother the Dean" were not mutually contradictory, and they were in him from the beginning.

We ought not to lay stress upon Coleridge's casual utterances on Wordsworth's religious views until we have examined them more carefully than is usually done. What religious training had Coleridge had, and what were his own opinions? At first blush his training would seem to have been the same as Wordsworth's: a family tradition more obviously clerical than Wordsworth's, a school which was also a definitely Anglican foundation, and Cambridge. But in fact the likenesses are only superficial. Coleridge went so early to Christ's Hospital that family influence counted for very little, and the religious atmosphere of his school was far enough removed from that connection with real life which Wordsworth's more healthy and normal upbringing impressed upon him. The "infidelity" for which, "wisely, as I think—soundly, as I know", Boyer flogged Coleridge when he was about thirteen, was due to the vanity of a clever boy rebelling against authority.[1] The Unitarianism which he adopted at Cambridge was in part, as he afterwards declared, a consequence of his "strong sense of the repugnancy of the doctrine of vicarious atonement to the moral being",[2] but in part also, it may seem, due to the same revolt against authority. Priestley represented Unitarianism, and he also represented civil and religious liberty. Coleridge's Unitarianism was always a brand of his own, between 1795 and 1800 he was gradually abandoning it in consequence of his growing transcendentalism, and it is not always easy at any

[1] *Table Talk*, May 27, 1830.
[2] *Ibid*. June 23, 1834.

specific date to decide exactly what Coleridge believed, and exactly what the standard was by which he was measuring Wordsworth. When he wrote to Thelwall (May 13, 1796) that Wordsworth was, "at least, a semi-atheist", what did he mean? The term itself, though taken seriously and solemnly repeated by later biographers, is almost meaningless, reminiscent of the phrase of that housekeeper at the *Spectator* offices who delighted Meredith Townsend by describing herself as "a moderate atheist".[1] Can it be stretched into meaning more than that Wordsworth had intellectual or moral difficulties in believing what actually were, what were commonly taken to be, or what seemed to Coleridge to be, fundamental points of the Christian creed? If that is the meaning, Wordsworth remained a semi-atheist to the end of his life. But that the standard is one set up by Coleridge himself, and by Coleridge only at that stage of his development, is suggested by two later letters. The first was written from Racedown in June 1797 to Estlin; "This is a lovely country", Coleridge tells him, "and Wordsworth is a great man. He admires your sermon against Payne much more than your last; I suppose because he is more inclined to Christianity than to Theism, simply considered". In the other, of May 1798, also addressed to Estlin, the description is not of one touched by atheism, but of one who is more tolerant than Coleridge thinks he ought to be.

On one subject we are habitually silent; we found our data dissimilar, and never renewed the subject. It is his practice and almost his nature to convey all the truth he knows without any attack on what he supposes falsehood, if that falsehood be interwoven with virtues or happiness. He loves and venerates

[1] J. St Loe Strachey, *The Adventure of Living*.

Christ and Christianity. I wish he did more, but it were wrong indeed if an incoincidence with one of our wishes altered our respect and affection to a man of whom we are, as it were, instructed by one great Master to say that not being against us he is for us.

"I wish he did more"—that is, believed exactly about Christ and Christianity as Coleridge, the Unitarian writing to a Unitarian minister, did. Coleridge's complaint is not, as M. Legouis interprets him, that Wordsworth has broken with all religious creeds,[1] but that their data are dissimilar, so that it is difficult for them to find a basis of argument, and that, although Wordsworth loves and venerates Christ and Christianity, he refuses to attack "what he supposes falsehood, if that falsehood be interwoven with virtues or happiness"—in other words, to join the Unitarians in their attacks on priestcraft and ecclesiastical error, that is, on the Church of England in particular. The gospel saying might have been applied to him by his brother Christopher with considerably more justification than by Coleridge.

A last touch of irony lies in Coleridge's later disqualification of himself as, at that date, any true judge of Christianity. "In no proper sense of the word can I call Unitarians and Socinians believers in Christ; at least, not in the only Christ of whom I have read or know anything."[2] "I should deal insincerely with you, if I said that I thought Unitarianism was Christianity. No; as I believe and have faith in the doctrine, it is not the truth in Jesus Christ; but God forbid that I should doubt that you, and many other Unitarians, as you call yourselves, are, in a practical sense, very good Christians. We do not win Heaven by logic."[3]

[1] *Early Life*, p. 470.
[2] *Table Talk*, April 13, 1830.
[3] *Ibid.* April 4, 1832.

It was Wordsworth's recognition of that last truth which made his data so dissimilar from those of the young Coleridge that they could not argue. The report of a later disagreement, in 1803, when Coleridge was using his argumentative powers in favour of one orthodox line of reasoning which Wordsworth always disliked, brings out that point. Coleridge complains (*Anima Poetae*, October 26, 1803) of a "most unpleasant dispute" with an unexpected pair of allies—Wordsworth and Hazlitt: "they spoke so irreverently, so malignantly of the Divine Wisdom that it overset me". The sequel shows that the dispute was not on the "Divine Wisdom" in any mystical sense, but on the "argument from design", Coleridge, as we should hardly have anticipated, taking the Paleyan side, and Wordsworth speaking perhaps too vehemently against it:

But *thou*, dearest Wordsworth—and what if Ray, Durham,[1] Paley, have carried the observation of the aptitude of things too far, too habitually into pedantry? O how many worse pedantries! how few so harmless, with so much efficient good! Dear William, pardon pedantry in others, and avoid it in yourself, instead of scoffing and reviling at pedantry in good men and a good cause and *becoming* a pedant yourself in a bad cause—even by that very act becoming one. . . . O dearest William! would Ray or Durham have spoken of God as you spoke of Nature?

[1] John Ray (1627–1705), naturalist: his *Wisdom of God manifested in the Works of the Creation* (1691) was used by Paley. Ray's unfinished work on insects and his philosophical letters were published by William Derham (1657–1735)—not, as here, Durham—whose own Boyle Lectures of 1711–12, published in 1713 as *Physico-Theology, or a Demonstration of the Being and Attributes of God from his Works of Creation*, were also used and occasionally definitely referred to by Paley. Derham's *Astro-Theology* (1715) continues the same argument.

It is difficult not to suspect *esprit d'escalier* here, and it reads very oddly after Coleridge's earlier complaint, in the letter to Estlin, that Wordsworth would not attack what he supposed falsehood, if that falsehood were interwoven with virtues or happiness. At a much later date, in 1814–15,[1] Wordsworth was protesting against Paleyism as vigorously as on this occasion, if with more measure. Is it possible that Coleridge was mistaken in 1798, that Wordsworth refrained from attacking certain things because, unlike Coleridge at that date, he did not suppose them to be falsehoods? The question is not an idle or over-ingenious one: there is a real danger that we may be led into serious misunderstanding of Wordsworth by the hasty assumption that Coleridge invariably saw correctly into his mental and spiritual condition and his processes of thought.

V

The problem of Wordsworth's religious beliefs is sometimes confused with that of his attitude towards ecclesiastical organization, even, in its simplest form, the question whether he went to church or not. The solution is by no means as simple as that question would imply: men do not always go to church because they agree with everything that is said there, nor stay away because they do not agree. Wordsworth was attending church in 1793 and the following years, when he was in strong disagreement with the implications or explicit declarations of the "State prayers"—

[1] Cf. pp. 247–8 *supra*. And it is worth while to add that Coleridge's often quoted letter to Alsop (August 8, 1820) shows him making exactly the same mistake about Wordsworth's thought as Wordsworth protests against in this letter to Mrs Clarkson.

It was a grief,
Grief call it not, 'twas anything but that,
A conflict of sensations without name,
Of which he only who may love the sight
Of a Village Steeple as I do can judge
When in the Congregation, bending all
To their great Father, prayers were offer'd up,
Or praises for our Country's Victories,
And 'mid the simple worshippers, perchance,
I only, like an uninvited Guest
Whom no one own'd sate silent, shall I add,
Fed on the day of Vengeance yet to come?[1]

It would not be out of place to inquire why Wordsworth, if certain theories of his spiritual allegiance at that time are correct, was in church at all, to be offended also by prayers so full of political error. On the other hand, in 1812, when he was entirely in accord with a congregation praying for victory, he was an irregular attendant, at least in his own parish church. We know that from his own confession, recorded in a passage of Crabb Robinson's diary (May 31, 1812) which is usually quoted incompletely and incorrectly:

> Wordsworth spoke in defence of Church Establishment, and on the usual grounds: said he would shed his blood for it. He declared himself not virtuous enough for a clergyman: confessed he knew not when he had been in a church at home. "All our ministers are such vile creatures", and he allowed us to laugh at this droll concession from a staunch advocate for the Establishment.

Wordsworth, it will be observed, makes an important qualification to his confession: it was when he was at home that he seldom went to church. From 1748 to 1806 the Rev.

[1] *Prelude*, x, 264–75 (1805), 288–99 (1850).

John Craik, who was appointed Rector of Grasmere in 1743, had been mentally incapable of performing his duties, and the succession of curates who filled those years were unsatisfactory characters.[1] The scandal was one of those which have given a bad name to that period in the history of the English Church. In spite of knowing that the unworthiness of the Minister hinders not the effect of the Sacrament, Wordsworth preferred as a rule to stay away from church—though he commended the attendance of the country people and pointed out its significance in a note on the *Epistle to Sir George Beaumont*.

> As a pastor, their curate did little or nothing for them; but what could more strikingly set forth the efficacy of the Church of England, through its Ordinances and Liturgy, than that, in spite of the unworthiness of the minister, his church was regularly attended; and though there was not much appearance in his flock of what might be called animated piety, intoxication was rare, and dissolute morals unknown?

The last part of the sentence is to be interpreted with Wordsworthian liberality: Harriet Martineau would probably have detected enough "sensual vice" to shock her.

Wordsworth himself may have been more tolerant of his spiritual pastors than he always admitted, if we are to include him in Dorothy Wordsworth's declaration to Mrs Clarkson (February 17, 1807): "We are become regular churchgoers, that is, we take it by turns, two at a time, and always two every Sunday when the weather will permit". But it must be allowed that the household could have provided a rota, even

[1] Cf. Armitt, *The Church of Grasmere*, pp. 168–70. Of one of them, Rowlandson, Wordsworth gives some account in a note to the *Epistle to Sir George Beaumont*.

with the omission of the master. At Coleorton the case was different: Wordsworth's letter to Beaumont of November 10, 1806, shows him attending church there as a matter of course, and except for the subject of the sermon, which was on the Gnostics, an unlikely choice at a later date, his description of the service would fit a good many village services at the present day.

We were pleased with the singing; and I have often heard a far worse parson—I mean as to reading. His sermon was, to be sure, as village sermons often are, very injudicious.... I don't know that I ever heard in a country pulpit a sermon that had any special bearing on the condition of the majority of the audience. I was sorry to see at Coleorton few middle-aged men, or even women: the congregation consisted almost entirely of old persons, particularly old men, and boys and girls.

The Rector appointed after Craik's death, Thomas Jackson, was not an absentee, and the later curates were of a better type, especially William Johnson. He was an exceptional man,[1] and his close connection with Wordsworth may have had more influence than we can trace with certainty. His stay at Grasmere was short, since his interest in education attracted the notice of Dr Bell, who met him at Wordsworth's house, and he was enticed away by Bell to take an important part in the reform of popular education. It is he who is mentioned in a letter from Dorothy Wordsworth to Mrs Clarkson (May 12, 1811), a year before Wordsworth made

[1] See *D.N.B.* and Armitt, *op. cit.* pp. 171–2. Miss Armitt identifies this William Johnson with William Johnston, the friend and biographer of Quillinan, quoted on pp. 51–2 *supra*; but the identification seems to be mistaken.

his confession of non-attendance at church: "We are become regular church-goers (we take it in turn!) for the sake of the children; and indeed Mr Johnson, our present curate, appears to be so much in earnest, and is so unassuming and amiable a man, that I think we should often go, even if we had not the children, who seem to make it a duty to us". Wordsworth himself, unless he exaggerated his sins of omission, is not included in this "we", but whether because of the ministrations of Mr Johnson or for some other reason, he did become within the next few years a regular church-goer, at home as well as when he was away. Wilberforce heard this from Southey a few years later: Southey was "always at church. Wordsworth too at Grasmere, not so it is said formerly".[1] Thenceforward he seems to have been able to endure a succession of dull preachers who drove Crabb Robinson on his visits almost to despair, and were not valued above their merits by the Wordsworth family themselves. It was not until R. P. Graves came to Ambleside that the local pulpits provided much intellectual food.

All this deals with externals, and is significant in only one respect—that Wordsworth came to see more value in externals than he had at one time seen. The letter to John Wilson,[2] with its mystical view of the spiritual condition of idiots, gives far more insight into Wordsworth's beliefs in the first decade of the century than can be given by any proof that he did or did not go to church regularly. But there is really something to be concluded from the fact that, after some years of greater or less irregularity, he brought himself to attend

[1] *Diary*, October 4, 1818, quoted in *Life*, IV, 395.

[2] *Letters*, III, 435–43; *Memoirs*, I, 192–200; Grosart, II, 208–214.

services and sermons of no remarkable interest,[1] and that in his last years, as Crabb Robinson and Aubrey de Vere both bear witness, he took family prayers, or listened to his wife's reading of them, with obvious devotion.[2] The conclusion most frequently put forward at present, that Wordsworth's increasing attachment to the outward forms of religion was one symptom of a decay in his poetical, spiritual and intellectual powers, tells us rather more about the critics who favour it than about Wordsworth: that they cannot conceive how a man can develop as he did, religiously as well as

[1] "Sometimes there was a battle between his reverence for Nature and his reverence for other things. The friend already alluded to was once remarking on his varying expressions of countenance. 'That rough old face is capable of high and real beauty; I have seen in it an expression quite of heavenly peace and contemplative delight, as the May breeze came over him from the woods while he was slowly walking out of church on a Sunday morning, and when he had half emerged from the shadow.' A flippant person present inquired, 'Did you ever chance, Miss F., to observe that heavenly expression on his countenance, as he was walking into church, on a fine May morning?' A laugh was the reply" (Aubrey de Vere, Grosart, III, 499).

[2] E.g. Aubrey de Vere, *Recollections*, p. 125; Crabb Robinson, *Diary*, December 26, 1844—"I heard Wordsworth last night read prayers from Thornton's collection. He read with remarkable effect and beauty. He told me this anecdote. The Duke of Wellington, being on a visit, was told by his host that he had family prayers in the morning. Would he attend? 'With great pleasure', said the Duke. The gentleman read out of this book. '*What! you use fancy prayers?*' He never came down again. He expected the Church prayers, which Wordsworth uses in the morning". Cf. also Gladstone's *Diary* (in Morley's *Life*) for June 8, 1836: "Wordsworth came in to breakfast the other day before his time. I asked him to excuse me while I had my servant to prayers; but he expressed a *hearty* wish to be present".

politically, unless his powers of mind have decayed. But the unfortunate truth is that men of great powers do refuse to accept or retain the opinions which we think they ought to hold, and their refusal is no more a sign of decay in them than, let us hope, our refusal to conform with them is a sign of blindness or decay in us. We can no more dispose of a man by saying that he became a fervent Anglican or a Tory than we can by saying that he became a Humanist, in the modern American sense, or a Communist. The labels give us some indication of the turn of his mind, and possibly of its contents, but not of its powers, its growth or decay. This ought to be obvious, but in Wordsworthian criticism more than in any other kind it is frequently forgotten. Whether Wordsworth's poetical powers did, to any real extent, decay, is a question which will be considered in the next chapter: for the moment it is enough to point out that an illegitimate transition is sometimes made from his religion or his politics to his poetry. There is no need to apologize or lament for his having been a fairly cheerful Anglican rather than an Agnostic with a drooping condescension towards undogmatic Christianity, and a dislike of Christian dogma equalled only by his vagueness about it.

There is not the same objection to the other conclusion, drawn, for example, by Professor de Selincourt, that Wordsworth's passionate grief at the death of his brother John turned him towards the Christian faith in the form in which it was familiar to him. There can be no doubt that John Wordsworth's death made him anxious to believe whole-heartedly and intellectually in individual immortality and the survival of personality; as he wrote to Sir George Beaumont (March 12, 1805):

Why have we a choice, and a will, and a notion of justice and injustice, enabling us to be moral agents? Why have we sympathies that make the best of us so afraid of inflicting pain and sorrow, which yet we see dealt about so lavishly by the supreme Governor? Why should our notions of right towards each other, and to all sentient beings within our influence, differ so widely from what appears to be His notion and rule, if everything were to end here?

Would it not be blasphemy to say that, upon the supposition of the thinking principle being destroyed by death, however inferior we may be to the great Cause and Ruler of things, we have more of love in our nature than He has? The thought is monstrous; and yet how to get rid of it, except upon the supposition of another and a better world, I do not see. As to my departed brother, who leads our minds at present to these reflections, he walked all his life pure among many impure....So good must be better; so high must be destined to be higher.

There is no doubt here about the will to believe, and no one reading the *Ecclesiastical Sonnets* of fifteen years later would be likely to doubt that Wordsworth was by that time, if not earlier, a loyal and convinced Anglican. But it does not follow that he was free from intellectual troubles and questionings. It was several years later, in 1824, that he addressed to his wife the poem *O dearer far*: a poem which means nothing at all if it does not mean that he envied not only her unhesitating belief in a matter which might be looked upon as an open question—the belief that we shall recognize in the next life those whom we have loved—but her whole religious attitude.

O dearer far than light and life are dear,
  Full oft our human foresight I deplore;
Trembling, through my unworthiness, with fear
  That friends, by death disjoined, may meet no more!

Misgivings, hard to vanquish or control,
  Mix with the day, and cross the hour of rest;
While all the future, for thy purer soul,
  With "sober certainties" of love is blest.

That sigh of thine, not meant for human ear,
  Tells that these words thy humbleness offend;
Yet bear me up—else faltering in the rear
  Of a steep march: support me to the end.

Peace settles where the intellect is meek,
  And Love is dutiful in thought and deed;
Through Thee communion with that Love I seek:
  The faith Heaven strengthens where *he* moulds
    the Creed.

"*He*" is Love, not Heaven: the stanza, and indeed the whole poem, contradicts Dean Inge's earlier view that the human affections did not play much part in Wordsworth's spiritual progress.[1]

Nor was this intellectual uncertainty about the future life his only trouble. Crabb Robinson records a conversation in the same year (April 19, 1824) between himself, Wordsworth and Edward Irving, in which Wordsworth stated that the great difficulty which had always pressed upon his mind in religion was the inability to reconcile the Divine prescience with accountability in man. Twenty years later again Wordsworth uttered an emphatic negative on one point which would at once have satisfied most of his contemporaries that he was unorthodox, if he could be called a Christian at all—he declared, in strong terms, his disbelief in eternal punishment.[2]

[1] *Christian Mysticism*, pp. 316–17; modified in *Studies of English Mystics*, pp. 194–5.

[2] Crabb Robinson, *Diary*, January 5, 1843. The conversation was with Faber, who did not attempt to defend the doctrine. Wordsworth's arguments were therefore probably more orthodox, in another sense, than Crabb Robinson supposed.

The stress laid by nearly all preachers at this date upon the doctrine of eternal punishment was in part, like the Evangelical stress upon human depravity, due to their sense of the strength of the Divine love which had found a remedy, but it had been made far too heavy, and it is not surprising that it sometimes led to a revulsion against the whole of the Christian faith of which, in a crude and unmerciful form, the doctrine was taken to be almost the essential core. Thomas Cooper explains his own difficulties over the question:[1]

> I could not preach eternal punishment to poor starving stockingers. But when the belief in eternal punishment is given up, the eternal demerit of sin has faded from the preacher's conscience; and then what consistency can he see in the doctrine of Christ's atonement? Whenever I looked inward...I found that I had ceased to be orthodox in my belief.

It might be held that Cooper was more truly Christian in the compassion which prevented him from preaching eternal punishment to poor starving stockingers than in the "orthodoxy" which he afterwards recovered: a different approach to Christianity might have benefited both him and his hearers. And if orthodoxy consists equally in a complete absence of doubts and a stressing of human depravity and the doctrine of eternal punishment, Wordsworth was not and never became orthodox. But faith does not consist in unwavering intellectual certainty, and Wordsworth was in good company in preferring to stress another interpretation of Christianity than that which was most vocal in his time.

It has already been pointed out that Wordsworth was unaffected as a young man by Evangelicalism, and never learnt its language. It was Evangelical theology which emphasized

[1] *Life*, p. 260.

particularly the extreme sinfulness and degradation of man and the Atonement through the death of Christ; and that Wordsworth, even when writing on religious themes, should have very little to say about either, nothing about Hell, and on the contrary a great deal to say about the Divine in man, shocked many religious people. Sometimes their distress was uttered in a form of grave and gentle expostulation which compels respect, as in James Montgomery's review of *The Excursion*.[1]

Every system of ethics which insists not on the extinction of sin in the human soul, by the only means through which sin can be extinguished, and everlasting righteousness substituted, is radically defective; and by whatever subtlety of reasoning, or force of language it may be sustained or recommended, it is a snare to him who receives it as sufficient, because, excellent and unexceptionable as it may be, so far as it goes, it falls short of the extremity of a *sinner's* case, and "*all have sinned*". We do not mean to infer, that Mr Wordsworth excludes from his system the salvation of man, as revealed in the Scriptures, but it is evident that he has not made "Jesus Christ the chief corner-stone" of it: otherwise, throughout this admirable poem, he would not so seldom, or, rather, so slightly, have alluded to "redemption in His blood". The pastor of "the church among the mountains" indeed, touches delightfully on the Christian's hopes on each side of the grave; but this is only in character, and *his* sentiments are *not* vitally connected with the system of *natural religion*, if we may call it so,[2] which is developed in

[1] *Eclectic Review*, January 1815.

[2] Montgomery evidently distinguishes, as many of Wordsworth's religious critics did not, and as others have not done, between his "natural religion" and what Dean Inge calls "the lifeless spectral creed which bore this name in the eighteenth century" (*Personal Idealism and Mysticism*, p. 82). It would even

this poem. The sentiments of the Author, when he speaks in his own person, and of the Wanderer, who is his oracle, *are* connected with it; yet in the fourth book, where a misanthrope and sceptic is to be reclaimed, when there was not only an opportunity, but a necessity for believers in the Gospel to glorify its truths, by sending them home with conviction to the conscience of a sinner, they are rather tacitly admitted, than either avowed or urged; while the soul's own energy to restore itself to moral sanity, by meliorating intercourse with the visible creation, is set forth in strains of the most fervid eloquence, and the theme adorned with the most enchanting illustrations. Now *the Wanderer*

> "had early learned
> To reverence the Volume which displays
> The mystery, the life which cannot die":

and *the Author*, in the exordium of the sixth book, sufficiently proclaims his orthodoxy by a votive panegyric on the Church of England. If then salvation can be obtained only through faith in the sacrifice of Christ, according to that "Volume" which the Wanderer reverenced, and according to the doctrines of that "Church" which the Author acknowledges, how came the terrors of the Lord, and the consolations of His Spirit to make no part even of that discourse which these two zealous preachers of righteousness held with the unbeliever, at the time when his heart might be supposed most accessible to their influence,—when the arrow of Death had just passed *him* by, and slain at his feet one of the four beings, who were the whole human race to him in his little world of solitude? This is not a captious inquiry: we are sure that Mr Wordsworth must have thought much on the subject; we would hope he thinks rightly.

seem that he recognized it for what it was, a faith "based on belief in Divine immanence" (*ibid.*): his complaint is not that it is unchristian, but that it does not express the whole of Christianity.

And again, on the subject of life after death, especially the fate of the wicked:

On other subjects we are willing to pay to Mr Wordsworth, the homage due to his exalted genius, and on this we are anxious to have an opportunity of listening to him with equal deference. But once for all, we must avow our conviction, that "the moral system" of any man professing Christianity, which does not include, as its immortal principle, "redemption through the blood of Christ", is inconsistent with the Author's own creed.

Sometimes this Evangelical disapproval took a grotesquely amusing form, as in that Mr Mulock whom the Wordsworths and Crabb Robinson met in Switzerland, and who found Byron a far more edifying poet than Wordsworth.

His conversation began with me by saying that he considered all Mr Wordsworth's religious poetry as *Atheism*—whose school of poetry he had been "castigating". On my remonstrating on this harsh position, he burst out into a furious ultra-calvinistic rant that all religion was founded on a recognition of the fall of man—that all declamations about God as recognised in the beauties and wonders of nature were mystical nonsense. In perfect consistency with his contempt for Wordsworth he avowed the highest admiration of Lord Byron, a greater poet than Shakespeare: he saw in his works the profoundest views of the depravity of human nature—not, indeed, spiritual views, but though not spiritually minded Lord Byron has developed the human heart, and the intense truth of all his poetry is its great excellence. I admitted that Lord Byron's works do exhibit a most depraved and corrupt heart, but observed that he shares this merit with Voltaire, Lord Rochester, and all the obscene and profligate writers of Italy and France. Mr Mulock did not feel the observation.[1]

[1] Crabb Robinson, *Diary*, September 20, 1820. Cf. Byron to John Murray, March 1, 1820.

Crabb Robinson charitably supposed that Mulock was mad, but his was merely an exaggeration of an opinion held also by a man whose intellect Crabb Robinson respected, his friend Cargill, who once[1]

spoke out on the subject of Wordsworth's religion in a way difficult or rather impossible to gainsay in conformity with his [i.e. Cargill's] religious views, and he said much that deserves to be recollected. He said, "I consider Wordsworth's *Excursion* as anti-Christian". I remarked, "If you had said it falls short of Christianity, I should have understood you, but how *anti*-Christian I cannot comprehend". "Oh, yes, I think it quite contrary to Christianity. Wordsworth represents *faith* as meritorious even without any reference to the *object* of faith—and I hold such faith to be utterly worthless, as much so as the moral virtues. It is only faith in the *Redeemer as the Redeemer* that constitutes the Christian feeling. Everything else is opposed to that."... Southey, he thinks, and I think so too, makes religion a mere party matter—a man may have even family prayer out of conformity only. I asked Cargill whether *faith* had its seat in the understanding or affections. "In the will," he replied, "in the understanding, affections, in the whole man!" He at once admitted that the want of a *clear head* did not spoil a man's faith—if he believed all he could, it was enough.

There is this much of truth in the objections, that, as the Fourth Book of *The Excursion* shows particularly, Wordsworth saw the Spirit of the Lord working in the minds and hearts of men outside the Christian revelation, and that, like many of the greatest saints and theologians, he turned instinctively to that doctrine which sees in the Incarnation rather than in the Crucifixion alone the essence of the Atonement. "The Incarnation, which covers the whole life of Christ in the days

[1] Crabb Robinson, *Diary*, April 20, 1836.

of His flesh, is itself the Atonement", Dean Inge writes of Westcott's "Johannine" theology,[1] and it is noteworthy that the thinkers of the Tractarian revival generally laid the emphasis in the same place; as Professor Clement Webb has expressed it:[2]

> It was an essential feature of the Oxford Movement that it made the Incarnation rather than the Atonement the central dogma of Christianity. This is a feature in which the later stages of the Anglo-Catholic movement have remained true to type....It will at once be obvious that there is a real affinity between this subordination of the Atonement to the Incarnation in Tractarian as contrasted with Evangelical theology, and the emphasis of the former on obedience to the law given to conscience as the root of religion....This more concrete view...as it refused to isolate the Atonement from the general process of the Incarnation, so it refused to isolate the Incarnation itself from the general moral education of the human race. Accordingly, the deepest thinkers among the Tractarians took up the same general position against the "ultra-Protestants" of their day as Hooker had taken up against the Puritans of his, recognizing a certain sacredness in the traditions and customs of "natural religion" which forbade their absolute rejection on the ground that they were not specifically Christian, so long as they were capable of finding a place within the organic life of the Church without injury to its Christian character. There can be no question that in their respective attitudes to natural religion and piety we have here a real historical differentiation between what we may call the Catholic and Protestant tendencies in theology, and one in which the specifically Anglican tradition is, on the whole, Catholic rather than Protestant. The extravagances of the Ritschlian school in denying the kinship of Christian with natural theology...are the exaggeration of a Protestant

[1] *Platonic Tradition in English Religious Thought*, p. 102.

[2] *Religious Thought in the Oxford Movement*, pp. 59–61.

tendency. It must be admitted, on the other side, that the greater readiness of Catholic theology to recognize the element which the Christian religious system, as being a religious system, has in common with others which are not Christian, places it in greater danger of subordinating those quite characteristically Christian values which distinguish the Gospel from every kind of "law", and upon which it has been the historical mission of Protestantism to insist.

Wordsworth may have incurred that danger, but it must always remain a debatable question whether he did, and there is no doubt possible that because he took the Catholic view he was definitely misunderstood, and sometimes misrepresented, by the dominant religious criticism of his day. It was in keeping with the whole trend of his thought that he should find in the Fourth Gospel, rather than in the popular forensic interpretation of the Pauline doctrine of justification by faith, his deepest religious satisfaction:[1]

> Theologians may puzzle their heads about dogmas as they will, the religion of gratitude cannot mislead us. Of that we are sure, and gratitude is the handmaid to hope, and hope the harbinger of faith. I look abroad upon Nature, I think of the best part of our species, I lean upon my friends, and I meditate upon the Scriptures, especially the Gospel of St John, and my creed rises up of itself, with the ease of an exhalation, yet a fabric of adamant.

A faith of that kind would not dwell unduly upon the terrors of the Lord and the pains of the wicked after death: it would trust, with Julian of Norwich, to the Love of God: "I shall save my word in all things, and I shall make all things well", but "how it shall be done there is no creature beneath Christ that knoweth it, nor shall know it till it is done".[2]

[1] To Sir George Beaumont, May 28, 1825.
[2] *Revelations of Divine Love*, ch. XXXII.

There is something of the joyful freshness of a recent spiritual experience in the letter to Sir George Beaumont which has just been quoted, all the more remarkable because it follows after only a few months' interval the poem to Mary Wordsworth, *O dearer far*. It is as if Wordsworth's constant sense of the Divine in nature and man had fused with the Christian doctrine of the Eternal Word and the Eternal Love in a sudden passionate heat which destroyed dogmatic intellectual doubts. Whether he would have been so likely to have the experience, if he had not held on desperately, as the poem shows him doing, without emotional and intellectual certainty, is a question which we might consider with profit. And whether it was the climax of self-deception is one which does not deserve an answer.

It is of course possible that this was not the first experience of the kind, just as it is probable that it was not the last.[1] A touching personal confession gives us much later insight into Wordsworth's heart and spirit. In 1838 he had told his friend John Peace that his "favourite text" was a verse in the *Epistle to the Ephesians* (v, 20): "Giving thanks always for all things unto God and the Father in the name of our Lord

[1] And there may have been later recurrences of doubt. But there is no need to insist, as some have done, upon a "pagan" interpretation of the lines in the *Extempore Effusion*:

How swift has brother followed brother
From sunlight to the sunless land!

There was, however, certainly enough remembrance of his own struggles to make him speak kindly of that *Rhymed Plea for Tolerance* which betrays his friend Kenyon's struggles. "These verses—the author does not venture to call them poetry", wrote Kenyon: Wordsworth's retort, preserved by Crabb Robinson, was, "They are not poetry, but they are something as good".

Jesus Christ". After Dora's death Peace reminded him of it, and he replied,[1]

Many thanks to you for referring to the text in Scripture which I quoted to you so long ago. "Thy kingdom come. Thy will be done." He who does not find support and consolation there, will find it nowhere. God grant that it may be continued to me and mine, and to all sufferers!

The reminder and Wordsworth's reply would suggest a fundamental spiritual serenity in the last twenty years of his life, in spite of superficial rufflings and the one great storm which was then sweeping over him. For the Epistle itself is, with the possible exception of *Philippians*, the most joyful of all the Pauline epistles, and it reaches its height in that verse in which Wordsworth did, as his friend had hoped, find consolation.

The same thought lay behind words which Mrs Davy recorded a few years earlier[2]—

He expressed also his entire want of confidence (from experience, he said) of highly-wrought religious expression in youth—

thereby differing from most of the Evangelicals.

The safest training for the mind in religion he considered to be a contemplating of the character and personal history of Christ. "Work it", he said, "into your thoughts, into your imagination, make it a real presence in the mind." I was rejoiced to hear this plain, loving confession of a Christian faith from Wordsworth. I never heard one more earnest, more as if it came out of a devoutly believing heart.

[1] *Memoirs*, II, 436 and note.

[2] January 22, 1844. Not in Mrs Fletcher's *Autobiography*, which contains most of these recollections, but printed in the *Memoirs*, II, 441–2, and by Grosart, III, 440.

It was partly the reverence and reticence of devotion, reinforcing his natural reticence, and partly a sense of the danger of slipping unconsciously into heresy, which restrained Wordsworth from introducing many definitely Christian references and allusions into even his later poems. He told Aubrey de Vere[1] that "on such matters he ever wrote with great diffidence, remembering that if there were many subjects too low for song, there were some too high". That reverence and reticence, even the shrinking from the frequent use of holy names, is as characteristic of a certain type of Anglican as the abstention from the utterance of the Ineffable Name is of Jews. Wordsworth's Christian sentiment is not to be gauged by the number of times a non-Christian can perceive a definite mention of Christ. The freedom with which some Evangelicals were in the habit of referring to the deepest mysteries of the faith led Isaac Williams to write two of the most abused and misrepresented of the *Tracts for the Times*, those *On Reserve in Communicating Religious Knowledge* (1838 and 1840): Wordsworth was in evident sympathy with him on the principle.[2] Thus he wrote to Dean Alford (February 21, 1840):[3]

For my own part, I have been averse to frequent mention of the mysteries of Christian faith; not from a want of a due sense of their momentous nature, but the contrary. I felt it far too

[1] Grosart, III, 491.

[2] There is even evidence that he approved of Tract 80 itself. Crabb Robinson read it with pious horror on September 29, 1839, and noted in his *Diary*, "I fear I have heard Wordsworth speak favourably of this Tract".

[3] Cf. Wordsworth to Alford, February 28, 1844: "I am far too advanced in life to venture upon anything so difficult to do as hymns of devotion".

deeply to venture on handling the subject as familiarly as many scruple not to do. I am far from blaming them, but let them not blame me, nor turn from my companionship on that account....I might err in points of faith, and I should not deem my mistakes less to be deprecated because they were expressed in metre.

It is to be wished that his scruples were more common among writers of what he called "versified religion", as well as among religious poets.

Wordsworth himself made little distinction between the highest poetry and religious poetry, showing in this the same train of thought as in his letter to Wrangham on libraries for working men. He had written thus in 1808:

I should fear that you, like all other clergymen, may confine yourself too exclusively to that concern which you justly deem the most important, but which by being exclusively considered can never be thoroughly understood....My meaning is, that piety and religion will be best understood by him who takes the most comprehensive view of the human mind, and that for the most part they will strengthen with the general strength of the mind and that this is best promoted by a due mixture of direct and indirect nourishment and discipline. For example, *Paradise Lost* and *Robinson Crusoe* might be as serviceable as Law's *Serious Call*, or Melmoth's *Great Importance of a Religious Life*; at least, if the books be all good, they would mutually assist each other.

It is the same large view which appears in a letter to Landor (January 21, 1824), who had been offended by the phrase "second birth" in the first version of *Laodamia*: Wordsworth, though he afterwards changed it, defended it as not to be objected to "merely because the expression has been degraded by Conventiclers", and passed on to a remark in Landor's last letter:

"that you are disgusted with all books that treat of religion". I am afraid it is a bad sign in me, that I have little relish for any other—even in poetry, it is the imaginative only, viz. that which is conversant [with], or turns upon infinity, that powerfully affects me—perhaps I ought to explain—I mean to say, that unless in those passages where things are lost in each other, and limits vanish, and aspirations are raised, I read with something too much like indifference. But all great Poets are in this view powerful Religionists, and therefore, among many literary pleasures lost, I have not yet to lament over that of Verse as departed.

"All great Poets are in this view powerful Religionists": and the same is true of all who think nobly. Much of what is called Wordsworth's Platonism is to be accounted for on the ground of this natural affinity, and much is due to that closer affinity which is recognized as existing between certain elements in Platonism and Christianity.[1] Those who should know most are curiously divided on the question of direct Platonic influence on him: some remarkable coincidences, even of detail, some of which Wordsworth himself realized, are pointed out, for example, by Professor Rader,[2] whereas Dean Inge even doubted at one time what is usually taken for granted, that Wordsworth was a Platonist, by nature if not by direct influence.

The Platonists...regarded natural beauty, including that of the human form, as the chief hierophant of the heavenly mysteries. Plato represents true beauty not as earthly, perishable, and sensuous, but as heavenly, immortal, and spiritual. Dwelling in the nature of God, it imparts grace by

[1] Cf. p. 240 n. *supra*. [2] *Presiding Ideas*, pp. 196–7, 199–200.

emanations and gleams of loveliness to all that is beautiful in this lower world; and it is by communion with this spiritual essence revealing itself in forms of earthly beauty to pure and loving hearts and chaste imaginations, that the mind of man is cleansed and sanctified and spiritualised, and has visions of God and the eternal "world of ideas"....It is not the *beauty* of nature which Wordsworth finds most elevating. Not the sense of beauty, but of eternal and ubiquitous *life*—of an universe animated throughout, and obeying one law—this thought, which is rather Stoical than Platonic, is most prominent in Wordsworth.[1]

And he emphasizes this later in his comments on "see into the life of things", just as he emphasizes the Stoic element in Wordsworth's development of the idea of spiritual law, which, "though it acts uniformly, does not exclude, but expressly includes, the ideas of will and purpose".[2] It is not always easy to distinguish between beauty and life and law, and it would be dangerous to push the Dean's argument too far. After further consideration, indeed, he himself decided to modify it, admitting that "no purer example of the Platonic type can be found anywhere", and that "this consciousness of a single divine life immanent in but transcending all nature, is quite in the line of the Platonic tradition".[3]

Wordsworth's own view of his relation to Platonism is shown unconsciously in the Fenwick note on the two translations from Michael Angelo which were included in the *Memorials of a Tour in Italy*.

However at first these two sonnets from Michael Angelo may seem in their spirit somewhat inconsistent with each other, I have not scrupled to place them side by side as

[1] *Studies of English Mystics*, pp. 176–8. [2] *Ibid.* p. 182.

[3] *The Platonic Tradition in English Religious Thought*, pp. 68–9, 79–80.

characteristic of their great author, and others with whom he lived. I feel, nevertheless, a wish to know at what periods of his life they were respectively composed. The latter, as it expresses, was written in his advanced years, when it was natural that the Platonism that pervades the one should give way to the Christian feeling that inspired the other: between both there is more than poetic affinity.

The transition in Michael Angelo seemed natural to Wordsworth because he himself had gone through something of the same process; there still remained "more than poetic affinity" between the two poems, but to Wordsworth Platonism was not, as it is to many of his critics, a higher form of thought than the Christianity which contains the best of it, as it contains the best of Stoicism.

vi

The Catholicity, in the general as well as the religious sense, of Wordsworth's thought was an offence to the narrower Evangelical orthodoxy of his time, and it has been the cause of bewilderment and confusion to those of a later generation who have not realized the breadth and largeness of the tradition which he inherited, the many strands of Platonism and Stoicism and early and mediaeval Christian religious thought, as well as the specifically Anglican thought, which were familiar to him without conscious learning of them. It may be suspected that his definitely Anglican writings have suffered in the same way as the rest from an inability in their readers to do more than affix labels, usually inadequate, to them. The *Ecclesiastical Sonnets* are ecclesiastical, therefore, necessarily, conventional, narrow, bigoted, and not to be seriously considered for their poetry. Actually, besides the great *Mutability* sonnet and those on King's College Chapel, they contain much good poetry, they show an historical grasp and a statesmanlike vision which are the same as those we admire in the *Sonnets on National Independence and Liberty*, and they are marked by a lofty absence of partisanship which is sufficiently indicated by the fact that, while Crabb Robinson was touched by their fairness to Nonconformists, Hale White and others have been equally struck by their Catholic tone. It is a proof of the carelessness with which they are read that they have never been made the basis of a charge of "Popery" against Wordsworth. The sequence on the Reformation is a surprising thing, especially at that date, but it is hardly what one recent critic has called it, "a tragic example of Wordsworth's downfall"—unless, indeed, it is a proof of declension to be interested in religious debates and to be able to do justice to both sides of a case. Wordsworth did not like Henry VIII, and did not admire his achievements, in spite of any good which might have followed them. Thirty years later, Yarnall tells us,[1] he spoke of Henry

> in terms of the strongest abhorrence. I wish I could recall his exact words; the concluding sentence was, "I loathe his very memory". I alluded to Holbein's portrait of Henry which I had lately seen at Oxford—at the Bodleian Library. "Yes, there he is", he said, "his hand grasping the dagger."

The sonnet, not in this series, on the portrait of Henry in Trinity College Lodge, Cambridge, is not one of admiration, rather one expressing the same appalled sense of brute power as comes out in the vivid phrase of description quoted by Yarnall; and the *Ecclesiastical* series speaks of the "selfish rage" which caused the Dissolution of the Monasteries, and the "reckless mastery" with which the Crown after that uttered its voice.

[1] *Wordsworth and the Coleridges*, pp. 37–8.

There is, even beyond this, the *Apology* for Roman supremacy as "not utterly unworthy to endure", and the specific honouring of "saintly Fisher and unbending More"

unsoftened, undismayed
By aught that mingled with the tragic scene
Of pity or fear; and More's gay genius played
With the inoffensive sword of native wit,
Than the bare axe more luminous and keen.

More noteworthy still is one of the few examples where the worshipper overcomes the ecclesiastical statesman, that sonnet to the Blessed Virgin which has been described to me by a Roman Catholic priest as expounding the true doctrine of the Immaculate Conception thirty years before it was officially promulgated. It would be temerarious to question such authority, but it is only just to add that most Anglicans, even while rejecting the doctrine, would join in Wordsworth's reverent invocation.

Mother! whose virgin bosom was uncrost
With the least shade of thought to sin allied;
Woman! above all women glorified,
Our tainted nature's solitary boast;
Purer than foam on central ocean tost;
Brighter than eastern skies at daybreak strewn
With fancied roses, than the unblemished moon
Before her wane begins on heaven's blue coast;
Thy Image falls to earth. Yet some, I ween,
Not unforgiven the suppliant knee might bend,
As to a visible Power, in which did blend
All that was mixed and reconciled in Thee
Of mother's love with maiden purity,
Of high with low, celestial with terrene![1]

[1] Cf. also the 1837 sonnet *At Albano* and the Fenwick note to it: "This Sonnet is founded on simple fact, and was written to enlarge, if possible, the views of those who can see nothing but evil in the

The group of sonnets to which this belongs, particularly the five which Wordsworth himself said might be looked upon as a single poem in stanzas of sonnet form, shows how far he was from the most vocal religious sentiment of his time. There were fraud and abuses and "trumpery", and he had to write about them, but he was not happy in the task: the lines about "trumpery" he had to borrow from Milton, and in the sonnet on *Monastic Voluptuousness* he was so far from gloating over the subject that, again, he had to borrow the most startling expression in the sonnet. There might be bad monks and nuns, but monks and nuns were to him persons to be revered, not in the sentimental and unreal fashion which alternated in his time with coarse accusations of hypocrisy and imbecility, but with a genuine recognition of the religious vocation and the ideals of both the active and the contemplative religious life. The desecration of the Grande Chartreuse shocked him as much as the sight of apparently self-indulgent monks arriving at Camaldoli did fifty years later.

> Nuns fret not at their convent's narrow room....

> The holy time is quiet as a Nun
> Breathless with adoration....

In the *Ecclesiastical Sonnets*, though he admits that some nuns may have been glad to return to a world which they had not wished to leave, his first thought is one which no great

intercessions countenanced by the Church of Rome. That they are in many respects lamentably pernicious must be acknowledged; but, on the other hand, they who reflect, while they see and observe, cannot but be struck with instances which will prove that it is a great error to condemn in all cases such mediation as purely idolatrous. This remark bears with especial force upon addresses to the Virgin".

English poet before him had felt, or at least expressed, that of those who went compelled, and his last of the old leaving the home and habits of a lifetime.

The sympathy expressed for the nuns turned adrift at the Dissolution is paralleled by the poem written some years later in which Wordsworth rejoices over hearing the cuckoo at Laverna, not least because it is at Laverna and quickens the associations of the place with St Francis of Assisi. Wordsworth's conception of St Francis was far removed from any that had been current, except among Roman Catholics—and it was not common among them—for three hundred years: it is so usual now that we have difficulty in realizing its distance from the usual contemporary idea, formed out of condescending pity, or disgust for dirty and fanatical friars, of whom St Francis was looked upon as the chief. Yet these are Wordsworth's lines:

> Rapt though He were above the power of sense,
> Familiarly, yet out of the cleansed heart
> Of that once sinful Being overflowed
> On sun, moon, stars, the nether elements,
> And every shape of creature they sustain,
> Divine affections; and with beast and bird
> (Stilled from afar—such marvel story tells—
> By casual outbreak of his passionate words,
> And from their own pursuits in field or grove
> Drawn to his side by look or act of love
> Humane, and virtue of his innocent life)
> He wont to hold companionship so free,
> So pure, so fraught with knowledge and delight,
> As to be likened in his Followers' minds
> To that which our first Parents, ere the fall
> From their high state darkened the Earth with fear,
> Held with all Kinds in Eden's blissful bowers.

Then question not that, 'mid the austere Band,
Who breathe the air he breathed, tread where
he trod,
Some true Partakers of his loving spirit
Do still survive.

It is perhaps worth noting, as indicative of one of the differences between Goethe and Wordsworth, that Goethe when he visited Assisi refused to look at anything but the pillars of the Temple of Minerva, while Wordsworth visited the Portiuncula and discovered St Francis. For it was an actual discovery: Wordsworth seems to be the first Englishman—we might say with little exaggeration, the first modern European—to understand St Francis, and he got his understanding not from books but from less than a full day's visit, on May 25, 1837, on the way to Perugia. "He made enquiries for St Francis's biography", Crabb Robinson wrote in his reminiscences of the tour, "as if he would dub him his Leibheiliger." There was nothing he could have read earlier which would have put him on the track. Hallam's scornful reference in his *Middle Ages* (1818) to that "harmless enthusiast, pious and sincere, but hardly of sane mind", would not inspire him to further inquiry, any more than it would give him his evident knowledge of the Canticle of the Sun or of the relations between St Francis and the birds. Stephen's essay, which sways uneasily between the older and the more modern view, dates from ten years later than Wordsworth's lines, and is based on two French books published only a few years before it was written. Faber's translation of Chalippe's *Life*, not made until 1847, did not appear until 1853. There seems to be no reasonable doubt that Wordsworth was original in his discovery, and the incident is a striking comment on the theory that in 1837 or earlier his mind was closed to new impressions.

vii

On December 11, 1824, Wordsworth wrote to Landor:

What would I not give for a few hours' talk with you upon Republics, Kings, and Priests and Priestcraft? This last I abhor; but why spend our time in declaiming against it? Better endeavour to improve priests, whom one cannot, and ought not therefore endeavour to do without. We have far more to dread from those who would endeavour to expel not only organised religion, but all religion, from society, than from those who are slavishly disposed to uphold it; at least I cannot help feeling so.

This gives only one reason for his general approval of the religious revival which is commonly regarded as having begun about ten years later, and which is variously called the Tractarian Movement, the Catholic Revival, the Anglo-Catholic Revival, and the Oxford Movement. Like a good Cambridge man and a good historian, Wordsworth disliked the last name and protested in a letter to Gladstone (March 21, 1844) against "the great and pernicious error of the Movement being called the Oxford Movement, as if it *originated* there; and had sprung up in a moment. But this opinion, which is false in fact, detracts greatly from its dignity, and tends much to narrow and obstruct its range of operation". He recognized the Movement to be what in fact it was, not a new thing, but a revival, springing from principles with which he had been familiar from his childhood: what he did not apparently realize was his own partial responsibility for it. The connection between what we call, for want of a better name, the Romantic Revival and the Tractarian Revival is now a commonplace, and was to some extent recognized even at the time. Some of Borrow's most amusing outbursts are against Scott for encouraging, through his mediaevalism, the spread of Puseyism and Popery. Actually the derivation was much stronger, as others realized and acknowledged, from the sacramental view of nature in Wordsworth, whose poetry Borrow found useful chiefly as a soporific, to the revived sacramentalism which was perhaps the most marked feature of the religious revival. And Newman in his *Apologia* (Pt. v) mentions Wordsworth, Coleridge and Southey together for their teaching on the importance of the community as well as the individual, for their "principles of thought" on society. Wordsworth was, to a degree which he never suspected, helping to fill the channels of the Church from which he had himself drawn life.

Knowing, as he did, that the Movement was not an entirely new thing and had not sprung up in a moment, he was less concerned than some over its development. He regretted the manner of publication of the *Tracts for the Times*, as he told Gladstone in the letter which has already been quoted:

> It was a grievous mistake that these Tracts issued from the same place, and were numbered and at the same time anonymous....The whole proceeding was wrong, and has led to errors, doubts, and uncertainties, shiftings and ambiguities, not to say absolute double-dealing, injurious to readers and perilous to those in whom they originated....There was one snare into which it was impossible that writers so combined should not fall, that of the individual claiming support for his opinion from the body when it suited him so to do, and rejecting it, and resting upon his individuality, when that answered his purpose better.

But he refused to become excited and indignant over the

mistakes which he saw, and it is significant that he gave high praise to Monckton Milnes's pamphlet *One Tract More*, which defended the position of the Tractarians and, in particular, the thesis of *Tract 90*.[1] It is amusing to note Crabb Robinson's endeavours to get a definite condemnation of "the Puseyites" out of the revered poet whose religious and ecclesiastical views alternately attracted and shocked him, and his almost complete failure. He wrote to Thomas Robinson from Rydal (December 29, 1842):

The poet is a *High* Churchman, but luckily does not go all lengths with the Oxford School. He praises the *reformers* (for they assume to be such) for inspiring the age with deeper reverence for antiquity and a more cordial conformity with ritual observances, as well as a warmer piety, but he goes no further....This great question forms our Champ de Mars, which *we* of the liberal party occupy to a sad disadvantage. Last year we had with us an admirable and most excellent man, Dr Arnold, but whom the poet was on doctrinal points forced to oppose, though he was warmly attached to him. Instead of him we have this year a sad fanatic of an opposite character.

The sad fanatic was F. W. Faber, whose defection a few years later gave Wordsworth pain. He considered Faber guilty of disloyalty in "seducing five of his parishioners into the Romish Church", a criticism which raises a delicate point of ethics, but Crabb Robinson speaks for both Wordsworth and himself in adding (*Diary*, December 19, 1845), "That his act is one of pure conscience no one can doubt—his treachery towards the English Church constitutes the sole subject of blame". Faber defended himself on the ground that he was now "convinced that Romanism is the legitimate conclusion of

[1] Aubrey de Vere, *Recollections*, p. 258.

Puseyism",[1] a point on which Crabb Robinson agreed with him but Wordsworth did not. According to Crabb Robinson,[2] Wordsworth had intended to introduce in the 1845 edition of his poems "a note expressing his regret that he had ever uttered a word favourable to Puseyism"—as, helped by Faber, he had done in the *Postscript*—and excused himself for not having carried out the intention on the ground that "he was at last quite tired—a very insufficient reason", Crabb Robinson commented severely, "and I fear he will never do it". Wordsworth never did it, and it may be thought that Crabb Robinson, in his detestation of the Movement, had perhaps exaggerated the intention. If Wordsworth had felt as strongly as his friend believed, he would not have felt too tired to say so. But that, disapproving of some points, as we know he did, he yet did not involve the whole Movement in condemnation, and found the task of apportioning praise and blame at once too delicate and too heavy, that he therefore decided that least harm would be done if he left things as they were, is shown by his last words on the subject, addressed to Ellis Yarnall in 1849.[3]

I ventured to remark to Wordsworth that I had observed from a note, in the last-published volume of his poems, that he looked with favour on what is known as the Oxford movement in the English Church, the results of which were everywhere visible. I asked him whether late events had led him to alter his judgement. He replied deliberately that his opinion was unchanged. "I foresaw", said he, "that the movement was for good, and such I conceive it has been beyond all question."

[1] Crabb Robinson, *Diary*, January 1, 1846.
[2] *Ibid.* December 19, 1845.
[3] *Wordsworth and the Coleridges*, p. 42.

This, after the staggering blows of 1845, shows as much steady faith in his Church as his latest political utterances do in his country. Besides this, Wordsworth had never been inclined to take part in religious controversy, least of all within the Church of England: it was only on political grounds that he fought against Roman Catholicism and Nonconformity, and then, as we have seen with regard to Roman Catholics, and as Crabb Robinson noted with regard to Nonconformists, without bitterness and with respect for individual convictions.[1] It would have been strange if he had, when he was well over seventy, set himself to inflame the wounds of the Church of his baptism.

And, apart from all these considerations of loyalty and forbearance, it is easy to see in Wordsworth's spontaneous utterances, those unprovoked by a request for an expression of opinion on a definite issue, that he grew gentler and humbler as he grew older. The fiery defence of Burns, in the *Letter to a*

[1] "I have had a little sparring with the poet on the subject [of the Dissenters' Chapels Bill].... Wordsworth, like most other orthodox, has an unreasonable dislike to Unitarians, but really knows very little about them. I have however told him that I am now a member of the Unitarian Association, and he receives this kindly, for he really has no bitterness about him; and though he has strong Pusey-propensities he by no means approves of the excess to which such ecclesiastical firebrands as Henry of Exeter and Charles James of London are now driving their adherents." Crabb Robinson's epithet for those excellent but very dissimilar bishops suggests that he knew as little about them as Wordsworth did about Unitarians. It is difficult to make sense of what follows in the letter: "He thinks that if there be not some relaxation...a civil war is likely to be excited, and which would break out in Scotland" (Crabb Robinson to Thomas Robinson, December 27, 1844). Had Wordsworth illustrated the dangers of enforcing the rubrics by a reference to the troubles of the seventeenth century?

Friend of Robert Burns, against those who shuddered at Burns's yielding to temptations which they themselves were incapable of feeling, finds a more tender expression in the stanza added in 1839 to the poem *Too frail to keep the lofty vow*, and in Wordsworth's comment on it in a letter to Reed (December 23, 1839):

> Your letters are naturally turned upon the impression which my Poems have made, and the estimation they are held, or likely to be held in, through the vast country to which you belong. I wish I could feel as livelily as you do upon this subject, or even upon the general destiny of those works—pray do not be long surprised at this declaration....I am standing on the brink of that vast ocean I must sail so soon—I must speedily lose sight of the shore and I could not once have conceived how little I now am troubled by the thought of how long or short a time they who remain upon that shore may have sight of me.

Then he quotes what had been the concluding verse of the Burns poem, with the additional verse added "the other day":

> Sweet Mercy! to the gates of Heaven
> This Minstrel lead, his sins forgiven;
> The rueful conflict, the heart riven
> With vain endeavour,
> And memory of Earth's bitter leaven,
> Effaced for ever.
>
> But why to Him confine the prayer,
> When kindred thoughts and yearnings bear
> On the frail heart the purest share
> With all that live?—
> The best of what we do and are,
> Just God, forgive!

And he goes on:

> The more I reflect upon this last exclamation, the more I feel...justified in attaching comparatively small importance to

any literary monument that I may be enabled to leave behind. It is well, however, I am convinced, that men think otherwise in the earlier part of their lives, and why it is so is a point I need not touch upon in writing to you.

There is something here of slackening interest in sublunary matters, something of the shifting view of proportions of old age, but also that humility which is found less ambiguously in a letter addressed in 1844 to an unidentified correspondent:

I feel myself in so many respects unworthy of your love, and too likely to become more so. Worldly-minded I am not.... What I do lament most is that the spirituality of my nature does not expand and rise the nearer I approach the grave, as yours does, and as it fares with my beloved partner. The pleasure which I derive from God's works in his visible creation is not, I think, impaired with me; but reading does not interest me as it used to do, and I feel that I am becoming daily a less instructive companion to others. Excuse this egotism. I feel it necessary to your understanding of what I am, and how little would you gain by habitual intercourse with me, however greatly I might benefit from intercourse with you.

The increasing sense of imperfection is a well-known religious symptom, but not of decline. In Wordsworth it was neither artificially induced nor unhealthily cultivated; his candid simplicity in the matter comes out in his confession of what seemed to him his too brief and insufficient penitence:[1] "I cannot raise myself to this state of feeling. I feel and lament my own unworthiness, but the feeling of penitence is lost in sympathy with the virtues of others, or contemplation of our Saviour's character, so that I seem to remember my own shortcomings no more".

[1] Diary of Aubrey de Vere, March 8, 1842; printed in Mr Wilfrid Ward's *Aubrey de Vere*.

The sense of imperfection and unworthiness takes a slightly different form in that reverence for children, more definitely and more obviously Christian in its origin than his earlier reverence, which is shown, for example, in the Fenwick note on *Tynwald Hill.*

One of my companions was an elderly man who, in a muddy way (for he was tipsy), explained and answered, as far as he could, my enquiries about this place and the ceremonies held here. I found more agreeable company in some little children; one of them, upon my request, recited the Lord's Prayer to me, and I helped her to a clearer understanding of it as well as I could; but I was not at all satisfied with my own part; hers was much better done, and I am persuaded that, like other children, she knew more about it than she was able to express, especially to a stranger.

That little incident, like some others, makes one inclined to receive with caution the accounts which were given to Canon Rawnsley by Wordsworth's neighbours at Grasmere and Rydal. They were mistaken in believing him indifferent to dogs, and we should do him injustice to conclude that all children were frightened of the gaunt old man. Harriet Martineau's vivid picture of him in 1845–6 should not be forgotten: "In the winter he was to be seen in his cloak, his Scotch bonnet, and green goggles, attended perhaps by half a score of cottagers' children—the youngest pulling at his cloak, or holding by his trowsers, while he cut ash switches out of the hedge for them".

Dora's death in 1847 came to her father as a grief so heavy that it almost shattered for ever his hard-won serenity. But early in 1849 Crabb Robinson noted that it had softened to an endurable sadness; and though in the following summer Ellis Yarnall noticed the sadness which underlay his animated manner, and Miss Fenwick spoke of his old age as strong but not happy, there was no despair, and there were moods of positive cheerfulness. Even at the worst his sorrow had found pathetic assuagement in tender and unremitting care for his sister. In April of the next year he himself lay dying—slowly, because of his great physical strength, and with a mind, as Quillinan wrote to Crabb Robinson on the last day of all, "perfectly clear...but tranquil and reserved". His son John had asked several days before whether he would wish to receive the Sacrament. "That is just what I want", he answered, and John administered it to him. His wife, not sure whether his mind was clear enough to take it in, but sure that she ought to let him know his condition, told him, "William, you are going to Dora". He took no notice, but on the next day, when one of his nieces drew the curtains to let light into the room, he asked, as if awakening from a quiet sleep, "Is that Dora?"

viii

There is a relation between Wordsworth's religious progress and his poetry, but it is not the one which is put forward by most of his recent critics. The commonest mistake has perhaps been sufficiently indicated: the failure to recognize that Wordsworth shows one of the most usual developments of the mystic who, brought up with certain religious conceptions, finds within his creed spiritual liberty, room to realize his personality and his faith. The "orthodox" mystic is as common a type as the "unorthodox", and less likely to incur those perils of wilfulness which sometimes bring the "unorthodox" to shipwreck. The objection which is felt by some to acknowledge the strength and the survival of the mystical element in Wordsworth seems to depend partly on a genuine misconception of the mystical attitude, a belief that it implies a vague, blurred and sentimental habit of mind, which is obviously far removed from Wordsworth's definite and unsentimental thought; partly on a failure to understand the successive stages of the mystical life.[1] It seems to be supposed that a mystic has ecstasies or intuitions at frequent intervals from the beginning to the end of his life, and that any cessation of the experiences is evidence of declension in spiritual power and insight. Actually this is very far from the truth: the ecstasies, the intuitions, the "consolations", to use a technical religious term, come at the beginning and may never be repeated.[2] They are sometimes accompanied, and always

[1] Professor Rader tells us (*Presiding Ideas*, p. 196) that at the Cleveland meeting of the Mod. Lang. Ass. 1929–30, "a prominent Wordsworthian scholar spoke with some little scorn of the people who foster the 'myth' that Wordsworth was affected by mysticism". The scorn can be accounted for on either or both of two hypotheses: that the "authority" knew nothing of true mysticism, and that he had no real understanding of Wordsworth.

[2] Cf. Inge, *Christian Mysticism*, p. 313 n.: "There seems to be no reason for holding the gloomy view that spiritual insight necessarily becomes dimmer as we travel further from our cradles, and nearer to our graves. What fails us as we get older is only that kind of vision which is analogous to the 'consolations' often spoken of by monkish mystics as the privilege of beginners". The clearest exposition of Wordsworth's spiritual progress is in *Christian Mysticism*, pp. 305–18. A few sentences may be quoted from it: "Wordsworth was an eminently sane and manly spirit. He found his philosophy of life early, and not only preached but lived it consistently. A Platonist by nature rather than by study, he is thoroughly Greek in his distrust of strong emotions and in his love of all which the Greeks included under σωφροσύνη. ...His cast of faith, intellectual and contemplative rather than fervid, and the solitariness of his thought, forbade him to find much satisfaction in public ceremonial. ...He shows his affinity with the modern spirit in his firm

followed, by severe self-discipline, which continues to the end of life, and is not always rewarded by a return of these consolations or of anything like them.

Now this was Wordsworth's experience. Passing over the premonitory gleams of boyhood, we can recognize his first ecstasy, to use a legitimate though much abused term, on that morning when he knew himself to be, "else sinning greatly, A dedicated spirit". It was in essence, though it would not be so acknowledged by all schools of thought, a religious conversion. Like other first conversions, it was not immediately followed by action, or at least not by the right action: though it is perhaps not wholly fanciful to see in Wordsworth's enthusiasm for liberty in France, which nearly led to his irrevocably throwing in his lot with the Girondins, something analogous to the literal building up of the church of San Damiano by St Francis. Wordsworth did not, however, immediately have a clearer vision and understanding of what was required

grasp of natural *law*.... Wordsworth is careful to inculcate several safeguards for those who would proceed to the contemplative life. First, there must be strenuous aspiration to reach that infinitude which is our being's heart and home.... In the spirit of true Platonism, as contrasted with its later aberrations, Wordsworth will have no blurred outlines.... Then, too, he knows that to imperfect man reason is a crown 'still to be courted, never to be won'.... Again, he bids us seek for real, and not fanciful analogies.... Lastly... and this is perhaps the most important of all, he recognises that the still small voice of God breathes not out of nature alone, nor out of the soul alone, but from the contact of the soul with nature. It is the marriage of the intellect of man to 'this goodly universe, in love and holy passion', which produces these raptures.... The first step on the way that leads to God was the sense of the *boundless*"— and so Dean Inge passes to the development of Wordsworth's idea of the nature of God and with it his knowledge of his own personality.

of him: the misery, anger and disillusion which came from the failure of his earthly faiths and ambitions had to precede his enlightenment. But from about 1795 onwards for several years, a longer period than seems to be usual, the mystical experience was frequently repeated, with deepening significance. As early as about 1802, considerably earlier than his critics would put any decay in his poetic powers, Wordsworth recognized in himself the lessening frequency of the visitations, the gradual dulling of the "celestial light". He ascribed it to advancing age, and characteristically refused to be entirely discouraged; but if we are to reason, as we legitimately may, from the experience of others, he had passed beyond the stage of intuitions. Before the fading of the "celestial light", and continuing to the end, came that self-discipline, that necessary element of asceticism, which appears in all mystics who take their experience seriously[1]—in all mystics, that is to say, but not in those who play with the terminology and some of the sensations, to their destruction. The flashes of vision have shown the soul its need of training that it may attain to higher, unspeakable joys.

The greatest poetical triumphs of Wordsworth's self-discipline—evidence of a higher, not a lower, state than *Tintern Abbey*—are certain passages in *The Excursion*, *The White Doe of Rylstone*, and the *Ode to Duty*: that Duty which is not the mere demand for the tithing of mint and anise and

[1] "Wordsworth is also a true guide in insisting on a severe course of discipline as essential to everyone who aspires to a vision of heavenly wisdom.... This asceticism of the will and intellect, rather than of the body, is characteristic of all Platonism. The Platonist who is not an ascetic is a dilettante, but it is the mind, rather than the flesh, which he subjects to stern discipline" (Inge, *Platonic Tradition in English Religious Thought*, pp. 71–2).

cummin, but the requirement to keep the weightier matters of the law, proceeding from the Eternal Justice which is another side of the Eternal Love. There is a clear kinship of thought between Dante's submission to the Love that moves the sun and the other stars, and the great declaration of the *Ode*—

> Flowers laugh before thee on their beds,
> And fragrance in thy footing treads;
> Thou dost preserve the stars from wrong;
> And the most ancient heavens, through Thee,
> are fresh and strong.

Both here and in *The White Doe of Rylstone* he teaches that deliberate, unwavering and entire submission of the will which is the hardest of all earthly lessons, and which results not, as some have supposed, in discouragement and the dwarfing of the personality, but in its development in directions which are otherwise closed to it.

That Wordsworth's development is shown less in his later poetry than in significant fragments of speech and in the impression made upon others who were spiritually capable of receiving it, is due in part to external causes which are discussed in the next chapter, but in part also to reserve and modesty touching holy things. There are, in his own words, subjects too high for poetry; there are also, in St Paul's, things which it is not lawful to utter. That he was in his latest years, as Graves, the Robys and Ellis Yarnall all saw, a man who lived habitually in the presence of God, comes out not from their testimony alone, but from the words on making the character of Christ "a real presence in the mind" and from the repeated insistence at the end of his life on gratitude, as at the beginning on joy.

He was a better man as he grew older, and his more mature experience made him, what he had hardly been while he was wandering in France, a devout Christian and churchman. I think it is worth remembering that Plato also became in some respects a stricter moralist and a more definitely religious writer, in the last period of his life, as we may see by comparing the *Laws* with the *Republic*. It may be that Wordsworth became what is called a better churchman and a worse poet when in presence of nature he was no longer

> Rapt into still communion which transcends
> The imperfect offices of prayer and praise;

but he makes it plain that the offices of the Church, or at least the fundamental doctrines of the Church, did compensate him for the loss of those early visions.[1]

How far Wordsworth may fairly be said to have been a worse poet in his later years is a question which we have now to consider.

[1] Inge, *Platonic Tradition*, pp. 82–3.

IV

THE UNCONQUERABLE MIND

i

THERE used to be a general impression that Wordsworth wrote a small body of great poetry in his youth, and a large amount of prosy stuff during the remainder of his life. The error would scarcely be deserving of notice now, if it had not in recent years appeared in a slightly different form, and sometimes in unexpected places. Thus Mr Bertrand Russell, ironically meditating on the harm that good men do, considers the sad case of Wordsworth:[1]

> In his youth he sympathized with the French Revolution, went to France, wrote good poetry, and had a natural daughter. At this period he was a "bad" man. Then he became "good", abandoned his daughter, adopted correct principles, and wrote bad poetry.

It is perhaps going too far to say with Professor Ernest Bernbaum,[2] "This is the height of pert falsehood". It is pert, and most of it is false, but it is possible to imagine a summing up of Wordsworth's life which contained even fewer correct statements. It is true that in his youth he sympathized with the French Revolution, that he went to France, and that he had a natural daughter. But unless Mr Bertrand Russell

[1] "The Harm That Good Men Do" (*Harper's Magazine*, October 1926). The writer presently adds, "It is difficult to think of any instance of a poet who was 'good' at the times when he was writing good poetry"—an airy generalization which will not bear looking into, the definition of "good" being in effect "politically cautious, a respectable citizen".

[2] *Guide through the Romantic Movement*, p. 125.

really prefers *An Evening Walk* and *Descriptive Sketches* to the rest of Wordsworth's poetry—and that is a matter of taste rather than of fact—his other assertions cannot be maintained. Wordsworth did not abandon his daughter, and as far as the relation between his poetry and his opinions is concerned, the statement exactly reverses the facts.

The surprising thing is that the division made and the explanation implied by Mr Bertrand Russell—who, after all, may be allowed more inaccuracy of statement than is permissible to a literary historian—is also seriously made by others who should be more careful about dates. The belief that Wordsworth's greatest poetry was inspired to a large extent by his love for Annette Vallon and his enthusiasm for the French Revolution receives almost as little support from dates and facts as the fantastic German romance about his love for "Lucy", of which Knight gives a synopsis in his *Life*. Between 1789 and 1797 Wordsworth wrote hardly anything[1] that is now commonly read: *An Evening Walk*, *Descriptive Sketches* and *The Borderers* all contain a few good lines and passages of promise, but that is the most that can be said for them. By 1797 his love for Annette had died down, he had shaken off his brief attack of Godwinism, he had turned against a militaristic France; and from 1797 for nearly twenty years he produced the largest proportion and in most respects the greatest of his work. We cannot fairly give the credit either to the French Revolution or to Annette. A far more reasonable personal claim might be put forward, after Dorothy Wordsworth's had been satisfied, on behalf of Mary

[1] The only poems which can fairly be excepted are *Guilt and Sorrow* and *Lines left upon a Seat in a Yew-tree*, and the second of these was "composed in part at school at Hawkshead".

Hutchinson, whom he consciously loved with deepening affection from the beginning of the period to the end of his life, and who could and did give him intellectual companionship. Some recent critics have been inexplicably unjust to Mary Hutchinson, who was herself enough of a poet to sympathize with a poet, and who was a woman whose rich nature and qualities of heart and head won the respect and affection of Dorothy and John Wordsworth. Everything we know about her proves William Wordsworth's wisdom—not merely his prudence—in seeking her for his wife. If we are not to divide the credit for Wordsworth's poetic flowering between her and his sister, not forgetting the additional stimulus of Coleridge's friendship, we may fall back on another explanation which is equally probable, that Wordsworth, like a long-enduring tree, was slow in maturing. The chief fact remains, however, that he was twenty-seven before his great period began, and at that age his passion for Annette Vallon and his fiercest revolutionary fervour were both several years behind him. It is all very awkward for the doctrinaire.

Wordsworth's great period begins about 1797, and I would extend it to 1815 at least. Critics deserving of respect have made a division at 1807, and I do not deny that within the eighteen years these first ten are the fullest of creative activity and achievement; but the next eight, containing *The White Doe of Rylstone*, *Laodamia*, some of the noblest of the *Sonnets on National Independence and Liberty*, and an uncertain proportion of *The Excursion*, as well as the tract on the Convention of Cintra and the essays in *The Friend*, cannot be called in any sense years of decay. There is less strictly poetic activity than in the preceding decade, but if it had not been for the fullness of those extraordinary years we could scarcely complain even of comparative slackening. No mortal man could have kept up the pace of the years from 1797 to 1807 for another ten years. Even so, it is only after 1815 that there is a real contrast, and then, in contradiction to popular opinion, it is not a contrast of later bad poetry against earlier good. Wordsworth's production after 1815, unlike that of the years before 1797, contains much that is good, some that is magnificent, and little that is positively bad. The list of good things includes, to name only a few poems in chronological order, *Dion*, the Duddon sonnets, the *King's College Chapel*, *Mutability* and other sonnets from the *Ecclesiastical* series, *Ethereal Minstrel*, *The Triad*, the Abbotsford sonnet, *Why art thou silent?*, the lines on Charles Lamb, the *Extempore Effusion*, the *Daisy* poem of 1844,[1] nearly all the poems of 1846—we could add to it considerably. And to it, if we are to do Wordsworth justice, should also be added his revisions of earlier published or unpublished work, which in many poems, besides being technical improvements, indicate an actual return of the inspiration which first caused the composition of the poem: "the emotion is contemplated till, by a species of reaction, the tranquillity gradually disappears, and an emotion, kindred to that which was before the subject of contemplation, is gradually produced, and does itself actually exist in the mind". The result may be observed, for example, in the change from "A voice more sweet" to "A voice so thrilling" in *The Solitary Reaper*; in *Beggars*, which was an infinitely better poem when Wordsworth had finished with it in 1827 than when he first sent it out in 1807; in the great

[1] W. P. Ker used to delight in this, especially in "the beauty of its star-shaped shadow".

Newton lines in *The Prelude*, which were added in 1837; or in the best version of the cuckoo's "two-fold shout", which was reached only in the edition of 1845.[1]

What is notable, however, is the diminution in quantity. If, as we have hitherto done, we make a division at 1815, two-thirds of Wordsworth's poetry falls into the first section and only one-third into the second. If we make the division at about 1820, we leave only about one-eighth for the last thirty years, as against seven-eighths for the first thirty working years of his life. These are rough calculations, but they are near enough for the purposes of all but statisticians. Has the disproportion any real significance? Was Wordsworth's poetic prime unusually short, and if it was, are the explanations which have been put forward by recent critics valid?

The answer is, in the first place, that there is no law of averages in these matters: poets vary in the age at which they begin to write poetry, in the age at which they mature, in the duration of their poetic prime. Even a brief examination of the lives of some of the English poets of the last three centuries will show the folly of dogmatism or of expecting any poet to conform to a preconceived theory of development and production. Shakespeare's working life is covered, as far as we know, by twenty-five years: in little more than ten he produced his greatest plays, and in the last six years of his life he seems to have written nothing: he may have been revising earlier work, or he may have burnt himself out. Milton was writing badly at fourteen and well at twenty-one, and he covers forty years odd from the *Nativity Ode* to

[1] For other examples cf. especially Hutchinson's edition of the *Poems* of 1807, and Professor de Selincourt's of *The Prelude*. Cf. also Ker (*Form and Style*, p. 227)—"Wordsworth was never careless of the art of verse, though at some times less careful than at others".

Samson Agonistes, with the work very irregularly distributed. Dryden covers about the same period; Pope lisped in numbers, but his prime covers twenty or thirty years, according as the terminus is made the first or the second version of *The Dunciad*. None of the other eighteenth-century poets offers a fair basis of comparison, nor do Wordsworth's contemporaries of the younger generation. Of the elder generation, Coleridge can hardly be reckoned in any table of comparison, but if we put him in we can scarcely stretch his prime beyond half a dozen years, with a few exquisite poems both earlier and later in his life. Scott's romances fall within ten years or little more, and again there are exquisite later fragments. Blake has twenty years from the *Poetical Sketches* to the *Songs of Experience*: what are we to do with the Prophetic Books? Crabbe had a short spring, a long period of apparent bareness, and then a late flowering of about fifteen years. Of the Victorians, Tennyson began young, but his prime might be dated from about 1830 to about 1860, and there are magnificent things to the end; Browning, from *Paracelsus* to *The Ring and the Book*, again may reckon over thirty years for his prime, with occasional glories for the next twenty years odd. Matthew Arnold and William Morris both cover twenty years without any falling off, but after that they both produce slighter though still beautiful things. It is impossible to make any standard of normality out of this: if we content ourselves with arguing that a poet will probably be at his best somewhere between the years of twenty-five and forty-five, we invite the retort that the same might be said of any man and that it is obviously true of Wordsworth. There are also the exceptions; there is, for example, Robert Bridges.

When all this has been said, we are entitled to ask why Wordsworth did not anticipate the achievement of Bridges, complete his "great philosophical poem" and publish it in the last year of a long life. He wrote less in the last thirty-five years of his life than Tennyson or Browning did, but what he wrote will compare with what they wrote in quality, if not in quantity. What is weak in his later work is at least sense; there is nothing comparable with the bombast and crudity, not merely of his earliest poems, but even of some written between 1797 and 1807; there is usually hard thinking, and there is often high poetic beauty. And there does not at first sight appear to be any good reason why he should not have used those powers of hard thinking and poetic skill for the completion of *The Recluse*. It is fashionable at present to assert that he had apostatized from the generous ideals of his youth, that his human sympathies had contracted, and that as a natural consequence his poetic powers decayed. But, as we have seen, he had not apostatized from the generous ideals of his youth, his human sympathies had not contracted, he was, in the phrase of his sonnet to Miss Fenwick, old yet unchilled by age, and he was capable to the end of writing poetry which no one would slight if it had appeared in the volumes of 1807. But, and here we come to the point, the poetry which he wrote was on the small scale, sonnets, longer but not long meditative poems, revisions of earlier work. Was there any reason why he should not have been able to go on with *The Recluse*? And the answer is that there was a conclusive reason which is usually minimized or entirely overlooked.

ii

Wordsworth's biographers all note that he suffered from inflammation of the eyes: what they do not note is that for the last forty years of his life he was living under the threat of blindness, that he was frequently in severe pain, and that for long periods, twice at least for more than a year at a time, he was physically incapable of reading and writing and of continuous poetic composition.[1] It was during intervals of comparative but not complete ease that he wrote his later poems, and any additional exertion, whether of composition or correction, was likely to entail a heavy penalty. The symptoms of trouble, though he did not recognize them for what they were, appeared early. From the age of seventeen at the latest he was from time to time prostrated by violent headaches, which he supposed to be of "nervous" origin, brought on by heat, noise or hard work. The first attack of actual inflammation seems to have been in 1804;[2] after that the evidence is scanty for ten years or so. But before 1816, probably before 1814, there must have been a really serious attack, of which a hint may survive in *The Excursion* (IV, 103–12):

[1] Mr Lane Cooper was the first critic, as far as I know, to realize the significance of Wordsworth's eye-trouble as regards his power of reading, and though he suspected its far-reaching consequences he did not carry his investigations further. But, oddly enough, even he overlooked it when he considered possible reasons why *The Recluse* was not finished (*Wordsworth's Reading*, March and April 1907, *Modern Language Notes*; *A Glance at Wordsworth's Reading* in *Methods and Aims in the Study of Literature*, 1915). The facts had struck me, and I had carried out my own investigations, before I came across his papers.

[2] Wordsworth to Landor, April 20, 1822, and Fenwick note to *A little onward*. Professor de Selincourt points out to me that Dorothy Wordsworth's letter to Mrs Clarkson of January 6, 1805 would date the first attack soon after New Year's Day, 1805, that being the day of the walk in which Wordsworth over-exerted himself; but that an unpublished letter from Dorothy Wordsworth to Lady Beaumont of May 25, 1804 speaks of Wordsworth as troubled with weakness in one of his eyes.

Ah! if the time must come, in which my feet
No more shall stray where Meditation leads,
By flowing stream, through wood or craggy wild,
Loved haunts like these; the unimprisoned Mind
May yet have scope to range among her own,
Her thoughts, her images, her high desires.
If the dear faculty of sight should fail,
Still, it may be allowed me to remember
What visionary powers of eye and soul
In youth were mine....

That this is not a purely fanciful interpretation of the passage is suggested by the poem written in 1816 when it became certain that the dear faculty of sight, for this time at least, would not fail.

"A little onward lend thy guiding hand
To these dark steps, a little further on!"
—What trick of memory to *my* voice hath brought
This mournful iteration? For though Time,
The Conqueror, crowns the Conquered, on this brow
Planting his favourite silver diadem,
Nor he, nor minister of his—intent
To run before him, hath enrolled me yet,
Though not unmenaced, among those who lean
Upon a living staff, with borrowed sight.
—O my Antigone, beloved child![1]
Should that day come—but hark! the birds salute
The cheerful dawn, brightening for me the east;
For me, thy natural Leader, once again
Impatient to conduct thee. ...

Now also shall the page of classic lore,
To these glad eyes from bondage freed, again

[1] In editions published after Dora's death this line was altered to "O my own Dora, my belovèd child!"

Lie open; and the book of Holy Writ,
Again unfolded, passage clear shall yield
To heights more glorious still, and into shades
More awful....

But the recovery which was hailed so joyfully was not final. The Wiffen brothers noted signs of weakness when they visited Wordsworth in 1819,[1] and in 1820 the trouble was acute. Thenceforward we can trace it from year to year, sometimes from month to month, now acute, now slightly better, once or twice departing for a time, but always returning, as it had already returned at intervals for fifteen years.

On July 23, 1820, Wordsworth wrote to Kenyon, "My eyes have lately become so irritable that I am again forced to employ an amanuensis". Kenyon thoughtfully sent him some eye-shades, which were acknowledged in February 1821. The condition of Wordsworth's eyes a little later in the year can be guessed from a letter which he sent on September 3 to Landor, who had sent him his volume of Latin poems:

After waiting several months in the hope that an irritation in my eyes which has disabled me both from reading and writing would abate, I am at last obliged to address you by means of the pen of Mrs Wordsworth....I felt myself much honoured by the present of your book of Latin Poems....It arrived at a time when I had the use of my eyes for reading and with great pleasure did I employ them in the perusal of the dissertation annexed to your Poems which I read several times—but the Poems themselves I have not been able to look into, for I was seized with a fit of composition at that time and deferred the pleasure to which your Poems invited me, till I could give them an undivided attention—but alas the complaint in my eyes, to which I have been occasionally

[1] *The Brothers Wiffen*, p. 33.

subject for several years past, suddenly returned, and I have since suffered from it as already mentioned.

By the following March Dorothy Wordsworth was able to report to Crabb Robinson that at least the inflammation was much abated, in April that the eyes were better, yet almost useless for reading, and on April 20 Wordsworth replied to Landor's anxious inquiries:

Could I have assured you that my eyes were decisively better, I should have written instantly on the receipt of your last most friendly letter—but in fact they were rather worse at that time, and I thought you would infer from my silence that there was no improvement. I am truly sensible of the interest you take in this infirmity of mine, which makes me so dependent on others, abridges my enjoyment by cutting me off from the power of reading, and causes me to lose a great deal of time; and the worst of it is, that from the long standing of the complaint, I cannot encourage a hope of getting rid of it. The first attack was 18 years ago, when I had an inflammation in my eyelids, which by frequent returns has weakened them so much, that they enflame upon slight occasions, and are scarcely ever both well at the same time: this affects the eyes by sympathy, and latterly the eyes themselves have been much annoyed by heat.... A few days ago, being something better in my sight, I read your Sponsalia; it is full of spirit and animation, and is probably of that style of versification which suits the subject—

Wordsworth had apologized for venturing an opinion, not considering himself a competent judge of Latin verse—

yet, if you thought proper you could produce, I think, a richer harmony.... The first book whi[ch I] read, unless it be one in large type, shall be these Poems.

By June, as we know from a letter to Allan Cunningham, he

was still not able to read any books not in large print. He seems to have enjoyed comparative ease during the autumn and winter, but with the spring, as he wrote to Kenyon (May 16, 1823), "Out came my own vernal enemy, inflammation in my eyes; and here I am, still obliged to employ Mrs Wordsworth as my amanuensis". The trouble was acute during May and June, but the tour abroad did him some good, though Mrs Wordsworth noted that his eyes, "being so much disordered, made him shun society, and the same cause crippled us in other respects".

1824 was a good year: in April he was able to read by daylight, though not by candlelight, and Dorothy Wordsworth wrote to Kenyon on November 28, "My brother's eyes have during the summer been mostly in their better way, and are still so—very usable for a short while at a time by daylight, but hardly at all by candle-light; and this, I fear, is the best that we may be allowed ever to expect from them". This state of comparative ease continued through the winter, so that Wordsworth was able to lament (to J. Fletcher, February 25, 1825), that so few new books found their way north at a time when he was able to read them: "We have no book clubs in this neighbourhood, and when I am from home—in spring and summer—my eyes are so apt to be inflamed that I am able to profit little by anything that falls in my way". Like other Englishmen to this day, Wordsworth borrowed rather than bought new books and reviews, either from Southey or from a local book club, such as that which existed for some years at Ambleside;[1] any review which concerned himself was almost

[1] Cf. Wordsworth to Wrangham, November 4, 1807; Dorothy Wordsworth to Crabb Robinson, February 25, 1826; Wordsworth to Crabb Robinson, June 18–24, 1838 (2 passages).

sure to be sent to him, particularly if it were abusive.[1] His apprehensions that eye trouble would prevent him from reading later in this year were not fulfilled: he suffered at Coleorton in the autumn, but soon recovered. His eyes were "in their better way" in February 1826, there was an attack of irritability in April, but on November 16 Dorothy Wordsworth wrote to De Quincey, "My brother's eyes are literally quite well.... He reads aloud to us by candlelight, and uses the pen for himself".

Professor de Selincourt has pointed out to me that this cure—only temporary, as it proved—seems to have been effected by the use of blue stone, that is, copper sulphate, a remedy recommended by Frederic Mansell Reynolds, who visited the Lakes during this summer. On August 26 Sarah Hutchinson told Quillinan that Wordsworth's eyes had been bad since the election, but on September 25 she informed him that they had been "magically cured by the blue stone". Two grateful letters from Wordsworth to Reynolds are preserved in the British Museum.[2] The first, dated October 24, is in a shaky hand, but Wordsworth's own:

> It gives me great pleasure to say, which I do with gratitude, that I have derived great benefit from your remedy. The Blue stone was applied by Mrs W— to my eyes, five or six times; it distressed them not a little for the time; but they have not been any thing like so well for many years as since.

[1] Cf. "I have not seen...any one new thing whatever except abuse of myself and sometimes praise, that persons mostly unknown to me are officious enough to forward." Wordsworth to Crabb Robinson, June 24, 1817.

[2] Add. MS. 27925. The two letters are on ff. 105 and 109, but they have been put in the wrong order.

The other is also in Wordsworth's hand, but much firmer; it is not dated by the writer, but "Feb. 1827" has been written in pencil at the top:

I drop you this Note by a Friend going to London, to thank you once more for the service your application has done my eyes. They have been infinitely better than I ever expected they would be, indeed all but quite well, and perhaps if I had more courage in applying the remedy they would be entirely without inconvenience. I can now read two or three hours by candlelight, a practice I had been obliged to abandon all together previous to the use of your remedy.

I could not deny myself the gratification of once more thanking you, and letting you know this. Be assured that if ever I go to London one of my first calls shall be on you, to repeat my acknowledgements, and for the pleasure of renewing my acquaintance with one to whom I consider myself so much indebted.

The use of blue stone, painful though it was, was less painful than the disease, and it seems to have kept Wordsworth in fair comfort throughout 1827 and perhaps 1828.

But by March 1829 things were as bad as in 1821–2, if not worse. On April 26 Dora held the pen for a letter to Crabb Robinson: for the previous month Wordsworth had been unable to read or write, and had suffered also a third privation, "full as grievous—a necessary cessation from the amusement of composition,—and almost of thought". He was better in May, but still unable to write, and after the visit to Ireland, that is, between September and December, there was a recurrence of the trouble; Hamilton was informed of this. A letter to Lamb of January 10, 1830, shows the sort of difficulty under which Wordsworth laboured. Lamb had sent him Hone's *Table Book* twelve months earlier, and Wordsworth here explains why it has not been properly acknowledged:

I wished to enter a little minutely into notice of the dramatic extracts, and on account of the smallness of the print deferred doing so till longer days would allow one to read without candlelight, which I have long since given up. But alas! when the days lengthened, my eyesight departed; and for many months I could not read three minutes at a time. You will be sorry to hear that this infirmity still hangs about me, and almost cuts me off from reading altogether.

And his sister adds:

His eyes, alas! are very weak, and so will, I fear, remain through life, but with proper care he does not suffer much.

A point of some importance, however, is that in the interval between this and the next attack Wordsworth was able, as he wrote to J. Gardner (July 16, 1830), to "read the smallest print without spectacles", though he had for some time "used the first size". This interval lasted for eighteen months, or perhaps not so long.

At the end of the summer of 1831 his eyes were very painful again. When he and Dora left home for their tour in Scotland, as Dorothy Wordsworth afterwards told Crabb Robinson (December 1, 1831), his eyes "were much inflamed, and had been worse than useless to him for more than a fortnight"; and Lockhart gives a touching picture of the two poets at Abbotsford:

On the 22d [of September]...these two great poets, who had through life loved each other well, and, in spite of very different theories as to art, appreciated each other's genius more justly than inferior spirits ever did either of them, spent the morning together in a visit to Newark....

Sitting that evening in the library, Sir Walter said a good deal about the singularity that Fielding and Smollett had both been driven abroad by declining health, and never returned—which circumstance, though his language was rather cheerful at this time, he had often before alluded to in a darker fashion; and Mr Wordsworth expressed his regret that neither of those great masters of romance appeared to have been surrounded with any due marks of respect in the close of life

—thereby indirectly indicating his satisfaction that those marks of respect were being paid to Scott by the Government itself, if perhaps not contradicting Scott's inference.

I happened to observe that Cervantes, on his last journey to Madrid, met with an incident which seemed to have given him no common satisfaction. Sir Walter did not remember the passage, and desired me to find it out in the life by Pellicer which was at hand, and translate it. I did so, and he listened with lively though pensive interest. Our friend Allan, the historical painter, had also come out that day from Edinburgh, and he lately told me that he remembers nothing he ever saw with so much sad pleasure as the attitudes and aspect of Scott and Wordsworth as the story went on. Mr Wordsworth was at that time, I should notice—though indeed his noble stanzas tell it—in but a feeble state of general health. He was, moreover, suffering so much from some malady in his eyes that he wore a deep green shade over them. Thus he sat between Sir Walter and his daughter: *absit omen*—but it was no wonder that Allan thought as much of Milton as of Cervantes.

The change worked a great improvement in Wordsworth's general health and eyesight alike, though when he returned he was still unable to read by candlelight or use his eyes for long together. An attempt in November to help Mrs Wordsworth to make out some of his "mangled and almost illegible MSS.", which naturally led to corrections and revisions, brought on another attack, of which he informed J. K. Miller (December 17, 1831) while it was still going on, but 1832 seems to have been almost undisturbed.

1833–4, however, was another bad period. The trouble was beginning by May 5, 1833, when Wordsworth was writing to Crabb Robinson with his own hand but confessing to "so much uneasiness in one of my poor eyes that I know not how soon it may be necessary or at least proper to lay down the pen". It was so bad later in the year that Aubrey de Vere, as he wrote to Hamilton (November 1, 1833), was hearing from everyone that Wordsworth was going blind, and some of the papers asserted that he had to remain in a dark room.[1] Wordsworth himself did not on this occasion anticipate that end. Kenyon was told on September 23 that he had been and still was unable to write; there was a relapse in October and November, and reading and writing were still imprudent in December: he dared not, he told Crabb Robinson (December 1), read or write or compose. By mid-January he was able to enjoy visitors again, as Dorothy Wordsworth wrote to Lady

[1] Crabb Robinson told him (November 3, 1833) that Mrs Clarkson and others had been alarmed by a paragraph in the *Literary Gazette*: "It is the only occasion on which they are annoyed by an allusion to and comparison of you with Milton. . . . I hope I have been warranted in denying that there has been any *organical* complaint. . . . I have gone so far as to say that I thought the Tories' coming into office might do as much and more for you than any oculist". Wordsworth (November 15) took the last remark rather too seriously, not hoping much from the Tories in 1833, and dictated on that subject until Mrs Wordsworth struck—"and *I*, M. W., *will not* write another word on this subject"—when he added as an afterthought, "My eye has had another relapse, though nothing like as bad as the former, but I recover from it more slowly".

Beaumont, and in April the eyes were not actively inflamed, but in May his nephew Christopher's pamphlet had to be read to him, and Crabb Robinson was told on July 24 that his eyes were of little service for reading or writing—an inconvenient thing, since he was preparing a new edition of his poems. There was no improvement by November, and Crabb Robinson was called in to help as an amanuensis for the *Postscript* in the following year. On Christmas Eve, 1835, however, Mrs Wordsworth was able to give a cheerful report to Mrs Marshall, and to add, "At this moment he takes the pen literally out of my hand (to alter a word in one of his poems)!" He was not reading by candlelight in the following year, but it seems on the whole to have been a good year.

In the early part of 1837 his wife and daughter were doing most of his writing for him, and the trouble of getting work prepared for press before he went to Italy led to one of those storms which occasionally shook the Mount. Wordsworth's amends were made in what Professor Garrod has justly called the noblest of his letters, written from Salzburg on July 5.

> Dearest Mary, when I have felt how harshly I often demeaned myself to you, my inestimable fellow-labourer...I often pray to God that he would grant us both life, that I may make some amends to you for that and all my unworthiness. But you know into what an irritable state this overstrained labour often put my nerves. My impatience was ungovernable, as I *then* thought, but I now feel that it ought to have been governed. You have forgiven me, I know, as you did then; and perhaps that somehow troubles me the more. I say nothing of this to you, dear Dora, though you also have had some reason to complain.

If Mary Wordsworth did not feel that that letter made up for more than she had ever suffered, she was unlike most other women.

There was an unexpected attack in September 1837, which spoilt the Hereford tour and, as Crabb Robinson noted (September 11), made it impossible for Wordsworth to compose. Even by December he was "not able to pen more than a few lines at a time without injury", and he was distressed by the consequent trouble given to his wife. In the following summer, however, Miss Fenwick reported to Henry Taylor (August 18) that he was working hard: "He can apply himself five, six, or seven hours a day to composition, and yet be able to converse all the evening". The result of this over-activity was that in the autumn he suffered, as he told Hamilton (January 20, 1839), from a

> succession of indispositions, one of which disabled me from either reading or writing, such was the state of my eyes, for upwards of two months

—but he was able to do a little work by December, and 1839 itself began well. In March, indeed, Miss Fenwick told Taylor that he had been working at what we know as *The Prelude* for the past month, "seldom less than six or seven hours in the day, or rather one ought to say the whole day, for it seemed always in his mind—quite a possession"; and she added, "This poetic fit seems to have been attended with less physical disturbance than usual and less irritation, though it has not been without its storms and darker moments". In July, however, there was a severe attack (Wordsworth to Reed, December 23). Again in April and June, 1840, there was uneasiness, but he could write; and the inflammation which Haydon noted in 1842 does not appear to have developed. After that date I have not observed any specific complaint until the summer of 1845, when his eyes were very painful in London, and during the last five years of his life he seems to have enjoyed comparative ease.

iii

This collected evidence, together with portraits of Wordsworth at different ages, was laid before an ophthalmologist, whose conclusions were these.

There are two possible explanations of Wordsworth's eye trouble, and it is also possible that they unite to give the complete explanation. In the first place, a small uncorrected error in focusing, which the oculists of his time would not even recognize, would cause severe headaches, then a disinclination for close work; and then, though it would not necessarily depress visual acuity, it might readily lead sooner or later to chronic inflammation, with painful exacerbation, distorting the eyelids—as is seen in all but the very early portraits.

But the use of blue stone—copper sulphate—in 1826 supports the second explanation, that of a definite infection. Blue stone is used to relieve inflammation of the lids, however induced, but it is in particular included in the regular treatment of trachoma and trachomatous conditions. Now trachoma, brought back by troops returning from Egypt and the East Indies, was prevalent in England in the early nineteenth century; and if Wordsworth's eyes were already weakened by overstrain, they would be more liable to infection. Trachoma would account, more completely than the lesser trouble, for the train of inflammatory attacks and for the appearance of the eyes, especially in the portraits by Nash and Carruthers—it is, in fact, the explanation which those portraits suggest at first sight. The use of blue stone also suggests the presence of inflammation worse than might be expected as a result of overstrain. It may be asked why, since the remedy was so effective in 1826, it was apparently not employed in 1829 or in later attacks, and the most probable answer again points to trachoma: blue stone would not be used if the relapse began, as in trachoma it frequently does, with ulceration of the cornea, not of the eyelids.

Against the theory of trachoma is the fact that, if it were of long standing, trachoma would have been likely to damage the eyes so much that good visual acuity at the age of sixty, when Wordsworth could still manage small print, would be improbable; and Mrs Alaric Watts in 1824 and Carlyle twenty years later could hardly have described his eyes, after several attacks, as "clear". The presence of trachoma cannot be definitely proved. But we can be certain that the condition of Wordsworth's eyes in the second half of his life would prevent him from doing any work which depended on continuous and prolonged concentration, and it is possible that their condition was aggravated by that specific disease.

Further inquiry brought out another point of some interest. Would Wordsworth feel a disinclination for close work before he was conscious of anything definitely wrong in his eyesight? Would there, for example, be any discomfort in reading or writing? The answer was unhesitating: there would be some discomfort in reading, and the strain of attempting to focus correctly for writing would make his hand shake and cause other physical distress. In colloquial language, he would "dither". Now Wordsworth's disinclination for writing showed itself early: he put it down to nervousness, impatience and indolence, and was evidently angry with himself and ashamed of an acute physical distress which, it would appear, was not within his control. Three quotations from letters written not many months before the first definite attack of inflammation will serve to illustrate this. The first, to De Quincey, was written on July 29, 1803:

> You probably would never guess from anything you know of me, that I am the most lazy and impatient Letter-writer in the world. You will perhaps have observed that the first two or three Lines of this sheet are in a tolerably fair, legible hand, and now every Letter, from A to Z, is a complete rout, one upon the heels of the other. Indeed so difficult do I find it to master this ill habit of idleness and impatience, that I have long since ceased to write any Letters but upon business.

The second, to Sir George Beaumont, written on October 14, 1803,[1] is more specific:

> I do not know from what cause it is, but during the last three years I have never had a pen in my hand for five minutes, before my whole frame becomes one bundle of uneasiness; a perspiration starts out all over me, and my chest is oppressed in a manner which I cannot describe. This is a sad weakness; for I am sure, though it is chiefly owing to the state of my body, that by exertion of mind I might in part control it.

The third, to Wrangham, was written early in 1804:

> You do not know what a task it is to me to write a letter; I absolutely loathe the sight of a pen, when I have to use it.

The condition of "dithering" could not be more clearly described than in these letters, especially that to Sir George Beaumont; and some of the letters to Daniel Stuart, written a few years later, after at least one attack of inflammation, illustrate Wordsworth's accusation against his own writing.

[1] Knight omitted this passage in the *Letters* and in his *Life*, but it is printed in the *Memoirs*, I, 262 and in *Memorials of Coleorton*.

They begin in a neat hand, almost as neat as Coleridge's, but in half-a-dozen lines the writing is already larger and more irregular, and in less than a dozen it has become the ugly sprawl and scrawl which is most familiar to us as Wordsworth's script. It is no wonder that, out of kindness to his correspondents as well as himself, he frequently asked his wife or his sister-in-law to "hold the pen" even when his eyes were not actually plaguing him.

It may be that Wordsworth's "occasional fits of hypochondriacal uncomfortableness", as Coleridge called them, were due at least in part to eyestrain. This is speculation, but it is not speculation to argue that Wordsworth was physically incapable of completing his "great philosophical poem". He was struggling against an increasingly heavy handicap for at least ten years before 1815, for at least fifteen according to the letter to Sir George Beaumont quoted above; and he had not abandoned his hopes in 1832—if, indeed, the reference in a letter of Hamilton's of that year[1] is to *The Recluse* and not to *The Prelude*:

As to the *Recluse*, it also, I fear is destined to be a posthumous work; but I heard at Cambridge from a nephew of Wordsworth, who is a fellow of Trinity, and who had spent much of the winter at Rydal Mount, that Wordsworth was so much occupied with it then as to forget his meals and even his politics.

Even Dorothy and Mrs Wordsworth were inclined to blame him for neglecting *The Recluse* for slighter things,[2] and he

[1] To Aubrey de Vere, July 3, 1832. With the sentence quoted compare pp. 327–8 above: the attack brought on by his first efforts did not daunt him.

[2] Cf. Dorothy Wordsworth to Crabb Robinson, December 13, 1824; Mary Wordsworth to the same, September 28, 1836.

himself, with his usual preference for blaming himself rather than circumstances or other people, accused himself to Landor (April 20, 1822): "From want of resolution to take up any thing of length, I have filled up many a moment in writing Sonnets, which if I had never fallen into the practice might easily have been better employed". Perhaps, but not on *The Recluse*.

The comparison with Milton which Allan and others made was natural, but in some respects misleading. Milton's blindness was complete, but it seems to have entailed little or no pain after its completion, and not to have hindered him in any but the obvious way. Wordsworth lived for over forty years in suspense, and for much of that time in pain which was sometimes acute and always incapacitating. Monsieur Legouis, in his *Early Life of William Wordsworth*, has pointed out, in his chapter on Wordsworth's optimism, how little outward cause Wordsworth had for cheerfulness in his youth and early manhood, and how much excuse he would have had if he had taken as black a view of the universe as some of his contemporaries and successors in England and France. The physical odds against him were heavier than Monsieur Legouis stated, and grew heavier still as the years passed. But Wordsworth's fortitude did not fail him, and he was one of those who are mellowed and not embittered by physical suffering and disappointment. Sight and hearing were the two senses which gave him the most exquisite pleasure, and of these sight was the chief, whether he used it for looking out on the world or for reading.[1] Yet the

[1] Something has already been said on the mistaken idea that Wordsworth did not enjoy reading, as long as he was able to enjoy it. Cf. also Mr Lane Cooper's papers, cited on p. 319 n. Here is one

contemplation of its loss produced only that passage in *The Excursion*, that briefly expressed resolution to endure and to remember the joys that were gone; and even partial relief was followed by the grateful outburst of *A little onward.* It is possible that his trouble had something to do with the greater delight which he began to show from about 1812 in the external forms of religion, as in certain elements of Christian belief; it is a recognized phenomenon of spiritual development that it often accompanies or follows physical illness. This too is speculation, but the coincidence of dates is not to be overlooked. What is certain is that Wordsworth had what many would consider cause for bitterness and for the abandonment of effort, and that he neither became embittered nor abandoned effort. His friends were still

> exultations, agonies,
> And love, and man's unconquerable mind.

He had learnt much, since he wrote those lines, of the discouragements and doubts which beset the mind of man, but he had not succumbed to them; and of love, both human and divine, he had learnt more.

late instance. "My eye that has plagued me so long is improving daily, but I wish I had seen Rome, Florence, and the Bay of Naples, as the recurrence of these attacks throws a shade over the future. Mrs W....says I am ungrateful to Providence....Be it known however in my excuse that I have not opened a book for nine weeks—a fine holiday!!!" (to Crabb Robinson, May 18, 1829). Miss Fenwick's remark to Crabb Robinson (January 29, 1845), "The poet hardly deserves a book—he so seldom reads one", expresses the rueful humour of someone who knew both why the poet seldom read, and also that her correspondent frequently acted as an agent to buy books for him. Cf. pp. 100–4 and Appendix B for evidence of the considerable knowledge which he managed to obtain, through those who read to him, of the work of his younger contemporaries.

iv

The suggestions put forward in this study may seem to lead to a dull conclusion, lacking in the obvious drama of the theory of the Lost Leader or even of that other theory, flattering to little men and distressing to the more generous, of the gradual decadence of a great mind and soul. They have, on the other hand, the merit of being consistent with the facts of Wordsworth's life, as far as we know them, with the circumstances of the time, and with the witness both of his own writings and of the men and women who came in contact with him. To the end of his life he struck all who talked with him by the strength of his character and personality; his power and insight as a political thinker, keenly interested in the problems of his own time and the future, did not decay; his deepening attachment to the Church of his baptism, though it might be, to some extent, associated with political considerations, was also religious and did not entail, in any true sense of the words, bigotry or intolerance for those of differing opinions; the decline in the volume of his poetic production was due, not to spiritual or moral causes, but to a heavy physical affliction which, beginning soon after 1800 at the latest, was hampering him well before 1815 and had crippled him by 1820: which we have yet been led to minimize or entirely ignore, partly by his own silent endurance, partly by the failure of his biographers to recognize its importance. The ordinary reader of Wordsworth reads, and rightly, his poetry first, and may never proceed to any intimate knowledge of his life or of the circumstances in which the poetry was produced. Wordsworth would have approved of this, and would not have asked for a lenient judgment of his later work on physical grounds. It is a question, however, not of leniency but of justice: not of excusing what is there, which does not, in any greater proportion than his earlier work, need excuse, but of endeavouring to understand it honestly and of explaining why there is not more of it.

This study was not undertaken as a piece of advocacy: if it may seem to have developed into that, it has been through what has appeared, in the course of reading, to be necessary correction of pardonable or unpardonable misunderstandings: the failure both to recognize any historical events but the French Revolution and the Reform Bill, and to look at them through any other eyes than those of Shelley and Macaulay; the repetition from writer to writer of the same statements, uncorrected by reference to any other evidence or any consideration of their original value; most of all, the illiberalism of the liberal and the orthodoxy of the unorthodox. If one is willing to take the risk of appearing to be arrogant, certain questions relating to Wordsworthian criticism may be asked. An amateur in history and theology has no right to speak with the authority of a specialist; but, as Dr Johnson pointed out that it was not necessary to be a carpenter in order to criticize the making of a table, so an amateur may be allowed to point out that other amateurs have not always made their tables well. And as in carpentry a certain minimum of knowledge of the qualities of timber and tools is necessary, so in literary criticism a certain minimum of historical and theological knowledge, as well as of the works of the author under consideration, is necessary. How many of Wordsworth's critics, then, have taken any trouble to understand either the political circumstances of the years 1815 to 1850 or Wordsworth's own opinions of them? A simple test may be made by observing what they say of his attitude to Italian aspirations and comparing it with the evidence collected here. How many, again, have had any sympathy with—or, since that is perhaps an unfair requirement, have made any attempt to understand—his religious history? It would be invidious to mention the names of the living, but what comprehension, in either of those important respects, did he receive from his two critics in the later nineteenth century who have most affected later criticism—Matthew Arnold and John Morley? Neither had any political sympathy with him; Matthew Arnold gently put aside not merely Wordsworth's religion, but all his deepest thought; and Morley, who recognized his own incompetence to deal with certain elements in Gladstone's life and character, did not appear to see that he was equally incompetent to deal with the same elements in Wordsworth's life and character. It is one of the most striking testimonials to Wordsworth's greatness that he should have compelled the admiration of a man who differed from him so profoundly in religious and political matters, and who firmly declared that no impulse from a vernal wood could ever teach any moral lesson. It is also, perhaps, Wordsworth's misfortune that so many of his admirers have been in the same position, and have felt obliged to preserve their own self-respect by apologizing for or protesting against a large proportion of his work, when they have not taken the simpler courses of ignoring it or misrepresenting it.

In the last resort it will be found that most of the recent critics look upon Wordsworth as, in one sense or another, a lost leader—one of the latest books on him even bears that title; that their views of his personality and his political development are derived from Hazlitt and Shelley; that their views of his religion are based upon a vague conception of a "narrow orthodoxy" to which he is supposed to have weakly conformed; even that the facts of his life are selected and wrested to fit theories of psychology and poetry. One may find excuses for the amateur historians and the amateur theologians who make mistakes in their estimate of Wordsworth because of the difficulty which we all experience in freeing ourselves from the prejudices of early education; but for the amateur psycho-analysts who have recently written so copiously on him it is difficult to find any excuse. A few fixed ideas, a sprinkling of the vocabulary, an ignorance of all the evidence which is not printed in the more accessible biographies and a blindness to a good deal that is there, a plentiful lack of common sense, and an assumption of moral and intellectual infallibility which must provoke, in the undistinguished, thankfulness that they themselves will have to answer only to a more merciful Judge: these seem to be the necessary qualifications. The process is then simple. Wordsworth's wife is known to have been a woman of intelligence and feeling, a critic whom her husband did not find it easy to satisfy, herself the author of the lines on "that inward eye Which is the bliss of solitude"; his marriage is known to have been an equal partnership which began well and wore triumphantly; his household, which contained not merely the husband's devoted sister but the wife's sister, elements which might have brought about domestic catastrophe, is known to have been happy, a community of outspoken people with independent minds; let us therefore represent him as married to the wrong woman, wronging an earlier love and his sister's love by the marriage, stifled by the undiscriminating adulation of a stupid wife, and consequently falling into moral decay.

He recognized his obligations to Annette Vallon and their daughter repeatedly and openly, with no care whether the public knew of their relationship or not: let us therefore show him as deserting Annette and deliberately concealing the whole affair. He never failed a friend, though he suffered much from his friends: let us represent him as cold and unfeeling towards Coleridge. His capacity for passion and youthful indignation, whether public or private, remained with him to the end; he hit out at the opponents of the Ten Hours' Bill when he was well over seventy, a few years later he declared, when he heard of a mean action, that he "could kick such a man across England with his bare foot", he accepted as a duty to the public the office of trespassing on ground wrongfully enclosed, he encouraged a Chartist leader with wise advice, he expressed in public and private his sympathy with the Chartists and his understanding of their case, he voiced the claims of the most miserable of the poor against the State with dangerous eloquence: let us therefore represent him as a reactionary and obscurantist in whom the springs of human pity and feeling had dried up. Even his enemies, who wrested as many of his words and actions as they could to produce an impression of excessive egotism, did not attack his veracity; men who did not like him bore witness to it; to impartial observers he was transparently honest and candid: let us therefore represent him as a hypocrite and self-deceiver. He could never compromise on a question of principle: let us therefore—not taking the trouble to understand his principles—represent two-thirds of his life as an ignoble sacrifice to compromise. Matthew Arnold set the example, which has been far exceeded, of representing him as ignorant of or as deliberately ignoring the harsher sides of

Nature and life: as if the man who pointed out to J. T. Coleridge the tragic stories which may be connected with spots "however beautiful and calm", the man whose own father died of the results of exposure on the mountains, whose brother was drowned at sea, whose own and whose friends' lives held tragedy in many forms, could be ignorant of these things; as if the author of *The Brothers*, of the *Elegiac Stanzas on Peele Castle*, of *Fidelity* and the verses on George and Sarah Green, had ignored the cruelties of Nature, or the author of *The Prelude* and *The Excursion* and the *Postscript* and the Fenwick notes and the letters had ignored, even to his latest writings, the sufferings which man has brought upon man! Have we any right to excuse such pretentious fictions, or to call them criticism?

Wordsworth's chief offence in the eyes of nineteenth-century critics was that he was not a Whig or an orthodox Liberal. To-day a tradition of their condemnation survives, but a far greater offence is that he preached, and did his best to practise, the unfashionable virtues of self-restraint and humility. His insistence upon developing in his own way, his refusal to fit into that conventional theory of the poet which rests partly on the idealized figure of Shelley and partly on Blake's remark, usually misapplied, that all poets are on the Devil's side, ought not to make us conclude that there is something wrong with him, and then to send us searching with unscrupulous ingenuity for the something wrong and its cause. There may be something wrong with our conception of a great poet: there is certainly much that is wrong, because inaccurate or based on misunderstanding, in the popular and even the critical beliefs about Wordsworth. We need such an authoritative study of his later political thought as Dicey made of the earlier, such a study of his religious thought as Dean Inge has made of one strand in it. It may be argued that these are matters apart from his poetry, but in fact they are no more separable from it than the political and religious beliefs of Dante and Milton are separable from their poetry, and in practice the separation cannot be made without the weakening of criticism. And it is perhaps not presumptuous to hope that even here some misconceptions may have been cleared away, some material collected which may help to form a truer conception of a poet whose greatness and magnanimity become more apparent the more carefully his life and work are contemplated.

APPENDIX A

WORDSWORTH'S POETICAL REPUTATION TO 1820

THERE is no need here to do again the work which Dr Elsie Smith has done in collecting and comparing the estimates of Wordsworth up to about 1822, but certain points may be made. De Quincey believed that the fight for the recognition of Wordsworth's greatness was fought and won in the 1820's: actually it was over earlier. The turn of the tide came about 1815.

Almost the only favourable review of the 1807 *Poems* was that which appeared in the *Eclectic Review* of January 1808, and was written by James Montgomery, who was conscious of differing from other critical opinion. He wrote accordingly to his editor, Daniel Parken:[1]

> I am almost sure that you and I differ very widely in our opinions concerning Wordsworth's talents, and perhaps more concerning his performances....The cry is up; and it is the fashion to yelp him down. I belong not to the pack, nor will I wag my tongue or my tail, on any occasion, to please the multitude. I am conscious of no personal partiality to prejudice me in favour of Wordsworth.

Indeed, as we have seen,[2] he had even a grudge against him:

> I am sure the poetry of two men cannot differ much more widely than his does from mine. I hate his baldness and vulgarity of phrase, and I doubt not he equally detests the splendour and foppery of mine; but I feel the pulse of poetry beating through every vein of thought in all his compositions, even in his most pitiful, puerile, and affected pieces.

[1] Holland and Everett's *Life*, II, 183–4. [2] Cf. pp. 95–6 *supra*.

Yet even he wavered now and then in his public confession of faith, so that the loyal Crabb Robinson was indignant at certain passages.[1]

> It would be in vain to attempt to characterize all the contents of these incomparable, and almost incomprehensible volumes. A more rash and injudicious speculation on the weakness or the depravity of the public taste has seldom been made....The public may often be wrong in its first judgements, but it is always right at last; and Mr W. can have no hope in its final decision concerning the greater part of the pieces before us....He says, in the preface to his former volumes, that "each of the poems" contained therein "*has a worthy purpose*". Of the pieces now published he has said nothing: most of them seem to have been written *for* no purpose at all, and certainly *to* no good one.

These sentences come, it must be repeated, from what is on the whole a favourable review, one which emphasizes the writer's admiration for Wordsworth's genius and does not hesitate to praise certain poems in the highest terms. Montgomery admired, for example, *Resolution and Independence*, the sonnet *On the Extinction of the Venetian Republic*, most of the *Ode to Duty*, and parts of the Immortality Ode, in spite of what he considered to be its heterodoxy. And Wordsworth, not unreasonably ignorant of having given personal offence, was pleased by a review which showed some appreciation of his poetry and which was in spirit in striking contrast to

Jeffrey's. In the following year Montgomery also reviewed with enthusiasm the tract on the Convention of Cintra, which, though he did not expect it to have a longer life than other political pamphlets, he declared to contain "more of the spirit and fire of genuine poetry, than we have found in many

[1] Holland and Everett, II, 185–6.

a cream-coloured volume of verse, designed to delight and astonish posterity".[1]

A more common estimate of Wordsworth in those years is to be found in the *Quarterly Review* of December 1811, in a review of Montgomery's own poems—*The West Indies* and *The Wanderer of Switzerland*:

Critics . . . will praise one poet in pure malice to another. Thus it has been made part of Mr Campbell's eulogy, that he does not write like Walter Scott; and of Mr Crabbe's, that he does not write like Wordsworth. Even Mr Wordsworth himself is mentioned with praise when the object is to run down Montgomery.

For concentrated scorn that "even" is hard to beat. It is partly explicable as being a stroke in the long war with the *Edinburgh Review*, which had run down Montgomery in exactly that fashion:[2]

When every day is bringing forth some new work from the pen of Scott, Campbell, Rogers, Baillie, Sotheby, Wordsworth, or Southey, it is natural to feel some disgust at the undistinguishing voracity which can swallow down three editions of songs to convivial societies, and verses to a pillow.

[1] *Eclectic Review*, July 1809.

[2] January 1807. The reviewer was Jeffrey (Cockburn's *Life of Lord Jeffrey*, I, 420), and it would be pleasant to conclude that there was for him a depth below Wordsworth's. But as he reviewed Montgomery in January and Wordsworth in October, we may have to argue that the reading of Wordsworth made him revise his opinion.—It is worth noting that Wordsworth and Montgomery were frequently compared, usually to the advantage of Montgomery. A late example will be found in an article by "Alciphron" in the *Gentleman's Magazine*, May 1828.

The sentence might serve as the text for a dissertation on the value and meaning of contemporary judgments. How many people could now name even one poem by Sotheby, sandwiched here between Joanna Baillie, who survives by little more than a single lyric, and Wordsworth?

In this particular instance the rôles of the *Quarterly* and the *Edinburgh* are reversed: in general the attitude of the *Quarterly* was one of qualified friendliness. In an article of April 1814, on Coleridge's *Remorse*, the reviewer quotes, "Heaven lies about us in our infancy" as part of "a passage which strikingly exemplifies the power of imaginative poetry", though the caution is added that "it does not rest on Scripture foundation, and may seem to be contradicted by the experience of every mother". And in October of the same year the

review of *The Excursion* is as enthusiastic in its admiration as Gifford would allow it to be. The explanation is that it was originally written by Lamb, and though he complained bitterly of its mangling by Gifford,[1] something of his spirit survived. Even in this modified form the article was of importance to Wordsworth's reputation: Hazlitt's outbursts of enthusiasm in *The Examiner*[2] and Montgomery's more qualified praise in the *Eclectic*[3] had probably less influence at the moment upon public opinion than the approval of the *Quarterly*. The *Poems* of 1815 and *The White Doe of Rylstone*, which were reviewed there together,[4] received a more chastened welcome than *The Excursion*. The reviewer was William Rowe Lyall, afterwards Archdeacon of Maidstone

[1] To Wordsworth, ? early January 1815 (Lucas, VI, 452–3), and April 28, 1815.

[2] August 21 and 28 and October 2, 1814.

[3] January 1815. Cf. pp. 280–2 *supra*. [4] In October 1815.

and Dean of Canterbury. There is something of the magisterial pomposity of a certain, almost extinct, type of ecclesiastic in his criticism, yet, like Lamb, he may have been the victim of Gifford. A few sentences will show the tone of the review.

Among those who are really qualified to judge for themselves in matters of taste, we think that one opinion only is entertained respecting the productions of Mr Wordsworth,—that they exhibit a mind richly stored with all the materials from which poetry is formed;—elevation of sentiment—tenderness of heart—the truest sensibility for the beauties of nature—combined with extraordinary fervour of imagination, and a most praiseworthy love of simplicity both in thought and language. It would appear, however, upon a first view of the fact, that he has by no means turned these valuable endowments to their greatest advantage.... With regard to the style in which Mr Wordsworth writes [in the *Preface*], we doubt whether it can be greatly praised. There is indeed a raciness about his language, and an occasional eloquence in his manner, which serve to keep the reader's attention alive. But these advantages are more than counteracted by that same ineffectual straining after something beyond plain good sense, which is so unpleasant in much of his poetry.

The reviewer has indeed, as he presently makes clear, no sympathy with "*emotions which lie too deep for tears even with respect to the meanest flower that blows*"; he thinks the poet ought to "*feel* as other men feel". And after discussing *The White Doe of Rylstone* he concludes:

In this, as in any other line of poetry to which he may dedicate himself, Mr Wordsworth has something to learn and a good deal to unlearn; whether he will endeavour to do either at our suggestion, is, perhaps, more than doubtful; he seems to be *monitoribus asper*, in a degree which is really unreasonable;[1]

[1] For a discussion of this allegation cf. p. 104 *supra*.

however, this is his business; all we can say is, that if he is not now or should not be hereafter, a favourite with the public, he can have nobody to blame but himself.

The voice here is surely the voice of Gifford.

The objection to "that same ineffectual striving after something beyond plain good sense", and feeling emotions which not everyone is capable of feeling, is found in different terms in many places. Jeffrey expressed it repeatedly and with vigour, and as late as May 1828 "Alciphron", writing in the *Gentleman's Magazine*, condemns Wordsworth at once because he "not infrequently sinks to puerilities", and because he "often rises to a sublimated sort of cloudiness, ill according with that positive kind of beauty recognized in our best classical poets". "Alciphron" spoke for a good many others. For the opinion of a literary man of average taste and judgment in 1815 it would not be unfair to cite again Crabb Robinson's account, set down with a touch of mischievous enjoyment, of that conversation in which William Taylor of Norwich showed how unthinkable he considered any comparison between Wordsworth and Southey to the disadvantage of Southey.[1] Taylor was polite and self-controlled, and did not do more than rebuke by implication the presumptuous poet and his indiscreet admirer. The general judgment of Wordsworth before 1814, however, was plainly expressed in such parodies as *The Simpliciad* and *Rejected Addresses* and such reviews as Jeffrey's of the *Poems* of 1807. The change of opinion was caused in many readers by the publications of 1814 and 1815, but it is best illustrated by a book which was not actually affected by all of these—by Leigh Hunt's *Feast of the Poets* in its various forms. The moral is even enhanced by

[1] Cf. p. 57 n. *supra*.

Hunt's frank confession that when he wrote the first version he had no personal knowledge of Wordsworth's poems. A good many of the jeerers were in the same position.

The Feast of the Poets appeared first in *The Reflector* in 1811 and was issued separately in 1812; in considering this version Leigh Hunt's disarming confession should be borne in mind, and it is kinder to him not to quote verbatim some of the worst lines he ever wrote. Apollo, having descended to London, invites the best poets of the day to a feast. Certain candidates are refused admission to the table itself, but are consoled, Crabbe by being sent to the kitchen, where he will be far more comfortable: Spencer, Rogers and Montgomery by being informed that they may come to tea afterwards.[1] The honoured guests are Scott, Campbell and Moore. After they have been welcomed a noise is heard below, but the new-comers prove to be only Bob Southey, Sam Coleridge and Billy Wordsworth. Apollo is pleased to see Southey, but the other two, having given a taste of their folly, are dismissed in a flash of divine wrath, with Peter Pindar and other bad poets. The four who remain sit down to the feast, and, after toasts to dead poets, Southey wishes to propose Landor, and Scott suggests William Stewart Rose, but the claims of both are disallowed. A note is appended to Landor's name, accusing him of being "one of those dealers in eccentric obscurity", and turning by an abrupt transition to an attack on certain poets whose names, though not given, would be guessed by any reader, for having changed their political views for personal profit.

[1] Byron thought this was hard on Rogers. "Why *tea*? You might surely have given him supper, if only a sandwich." (To Leigh Hunt, February 9, 1814.)

All this is not much to the credit of Leigh Hunt, but the version of 1814 begins to show improvement. In the interval he had read Wordsworth for himself, and, as far as Wordsworth's poetical character was concerned, had formed an opinion which would not allow him to reprint the verses without change. The new version appeared some weeks before the publication of *The Excursion*, so that there can be no question of his having made the alterations either under the compulsion of Hazlitt's enthusiasm or for less worthy motives. There is indeed some evidence that he did not himself care greatly for *The Excursion*. On December 8, 1814, Crabb Robinson noted in his diary:

Hunt has been so put out of sorts by Wordsworth's *Excursion* that it makes him uncomfortable to hear it mentioned in company, and his friends therefore avoid the subject out of tenderness to him. Hunt at first ridiculed Wordsworth as a contemptible writer; then he mingled warm praise with [re]proof; and now he dislikes his great poem so much that, probably because he is dissatisfied with his own sentiment and dares not avow it, he is made unwell by hearing it mentioned.

Crabb Robinson did not dislike Leigh Hunt at that time, and would not, even if he had disliked him, have invented such a report. Whether Hunt admired *The Excursion* or not, however, it cannot have affected his second version of *The Feast of the Poets*. The first reference to Wordsworth is much modified, and Apollo's rebuke expresses regret that

the very best promise bred up in the school
Must show himself proudest in playing the fool.

Wordsworth is still refused admission to the feast, but instead of being thrown downstairs retires of his own accord, screened by Apollo in his own mantle of cloud. Coleridge is dismissed with ignominy among the bad poets, and Southey remains, unquestioned, with Campbell, Scott and Moore, as in the earlier version. But though Leigh Hunt was changing his view of Wordsworth as a poet, he still preserved his first view of his political character, and the notes in this version are explicit on both points.

Mr Southey, and even Mr Wordsworth, have both accepted offices under government, of such a nature, as absolutely ties up their independence....

It may be as well however to mention, that though Mr Southey is represented as admitted where Mr Wordsworth is not, it is not meant to insinuate that he is a better poet, but merely that he has not so abused the comparative little that was expected of him. He is no more to be compared with Mr Wordsworth in real genius than the man who thinks once out of a hundred times is with him who thinks the whole hundred; but that he is at the same time a poet, will be no more denied, than that the hundredth part of Mr Wordsworth's genius would make a poet....

In revising my verses, and endeavouring to do justice to Mr Wordsworth, I was anxious, whenever I mentioned him, to show myself sensible of the great powers he possesses, and with what sort of gift he has consented to trifle....

If Mr Wordsworth is at present under a cloud, it is one, we see, of a divinity's wearing; and he may emerge from it, whenever he pleases, with a proportionate lustre....It certainly appears to me that we have had no poet since the days of Spenser and Milton,—so allied in the better part of his genius to those favoured men, not excepting even Collins, who saw further into the sacred places of poetry than any man of the last age. Mr Wordsworth speaks less of the vulgar tongue of the profession than any writer since that period; he always thinks when he speaks, has always words at command, feels deeply, fancies richly, and never descends from that pure and elevated morality, which is the native region of the first order of poetical spirits.... It may be asked me, then, why with such opinions as I entertain of the greatness of Mr Wordsworth's genius, he is treated as he is in the verses before us. I answer, because he abuses that genius so as Milton or Spenser never abused it, and so as to destroy those great ends of poetry, by which it should assist the uses and refresh the spirits of life....

And finally:

He himself, though marked as government property, may walk about his fields uninjured, from the usual simplicity of his life and from very ignorance of what he has undergone; but those who never possessed the real wisdom of his simplicity, will hardly retain the virtue.

It is that view, as of a poet with great gifts who has ruined them by becoming a renegade from the cause of liberty, a pensioner of government, which we meet in Byron, Shelley and Hazlitt, and in recent writers who ought to know better. Leigh Hunt himself abandoned it almost immediately, for personal reasons which, in spite of being personal, were generally valid. In 1815 Wordsworth not merely presented him with his works but called upon him.[1] Obviously no creature of government would have risked showing such courtesy to a man who had just undergone two years of imprisonment for libelling the Prince Regent. Clearly, therefore, if Leigh Hunt were to retain his self-respect, he must make some alteration in his references to Wordsworth's politics. And accordingly, when the verses were republished later in the summer, all political accusations, both direct and indirect, against Wordsworth were omitted, and in their

[1] Cf. pp. 65–6 *supra*, and Blunden, *Leigh Hunt*, p. 90.

place an alteration, sufficient to emphasize the difference from earlier versions, was made in the first note from which a quotation was made above. Southey and Coleridge are condemned, but a footnote expressly exonerates Wordsworth:

> Mr Wordsworth's name was added to these two in the first edition;[1] but it seems that he regards his office as a private favour bestowed by an old friend of his family, and still vindicates his right to think and speak as he pleases.

Having thus maintained his own honesty and Wordsworth's in the notes, Leigh Hunt allows his enthusiasm for Wordsworth's poetry full course in the verses. As before, Apollo rebukes Wordsworth for not always rising to the height of his powers, and screens him in his cloud. But then he relents, deciding

> that he shouldn't well know what to say,
> If he sent, after all, his best poet away.

Wordsworth is therefore recalled, and the song which he sings rouses the other poets to such a pitch of admiration that

> all cried at last, with a passion sublime,
> "This, this is the Prince of the Bards of his Time!"

Apollo himself is moved, and in his graciousness allows Coleridge to enter, whereupon all the bad poets try to get in—

> Exclaiming, "What! Wordsworth, and fellows like these?
> Nay, then, we may all take our seats as we please!"

—but are duly dismissed. In the end there are seven poets at the feast: the original four, Southey however being admitted now under protest and not without insult, with the addition

[1] Actually, in the first and second versions.

of Byron, Wordsworth and Coleridge. No question arises about the entrance of Byron, and Byron, as we have seen,[1] did not agree with Leigh Hunt's final ranking of the poets.

This comedy of revision leaves us with a better opinion of Leigh Hunt. He had made handsome amends, if in very bad verse, for his initial sin of condemning before reading, and afterwards for what had been an honest misapprehension of Wordsworth's political standing. He showed his independence and integrity here much more notably than in any attack upon the government: in that he had a large measure of public sympathy, but here he not only held to his own opinion against Byron's refusal to admire Wordsworth, but defended against nearly all his friends the political honesty of a man for whom he did not greatly care. If there is a little too much gush, even for Leigh Hunt, in the awkward lines which attempt to describe Wordsworth's poetry, the reason may be simply the want of sympathy between the two men.[2]

There is much more evidence to the same effect, that before 1815 Wordsworth had a few enthusiastic admirers and many detractors, and that by 1820 the situation was completely changed. In sheer popularity Byron, Scott, Moore, Campbell, and probably Rogers and Montgomery, all surpassed him, and long after 1815 there were repetitions of the earlier

[1] Cf. p. 55 *supra*.

[2] Truth, if not kindness, makes it necessary to add that when Leigh Hunt had come to think of himself as the arbiter of poetic reputations, he suggested a further change. "I should infallibly (or as far as lay in my power) have deposed the god I helped to set up, and put Coleridge in his stead (I mean in the last edition of the *Feast of the Poets*), but I did not like to hurt his feelings in his old age." (Hunt to J. F., July 9, 1848.) Wordsworth was perhaps not so easily hurt.

attacks. But in 1815 it was already possible to name him in the same breath as Scott and Byron, even if he were set below both of them. Byron's rough quiz, as he himself called it, *The Blues,* was actually written in 1821, but it reflects conditions in certain literary coteries of the time before Byron left England, and there it was already the proper thing to admire Wordsworth. A more amusing passage, which brings out the same point, may be quoted from Jane Austen's unfinished *Sanditon.* Twenty years earlier Marianne Dashwood had gone into raptures over Cowper, but in 1817 Sir Edward Denham shows other preferences.

But while we are on the subject of Poetry, what think you Miss H. of Burns Lines to his Mary?—Oh! there is Pathos to madden one!—If ever there was a Man who *felt,* it was Burns.—Montgomery has all the Fire of Poetry, Wordsworth has the true soul of it—Campbell in his pleasures of Hope has touched the extreme of our Sensations—"Like Angel's visits, few & far between". Can you conceive any thing more subduing, more melting, more fraught with the deep Sublime than that Line?—But Burns—I confess my sence of his Pre-eminence Miss H.—If Scott *has* a fault, it is the want of Passion.—Tender, Elegant, Descriptive—but *Tame.* —The Man who cannot do justice to the attributes of Woman is my contempt.

It may seem surprising, particularly when one considers Sir Edward's taste in novels, that there is no mention of Byron here. But he was not ignorant of Byron: he had merely confused him with Scott, just as, from the adjectives, he may be suspected of confusing Scott with someone else.

"Do you remember, said he, Scott's beautiful Lines on the Sea?—Oh! what a description they convey!"..."What description do you mean? said Charlotte. I remember none at this moment, of the Sea, in either of Scott's Poems." "Do not you indeed?—Nor can I exactly recall the beginning at this moment."

It was, or Sir Edward would not have spoken thus, the right thing by 1817 to admire Wordsworth for having the true soul of Poetry and to lament his political apostasy and his arrogance. Sir Edward followed the literary fashion: the personal questions did not interest him, and have been sufficiently discussed here.

APPENDIX B

WORDSWORTH ON HIS CONTEMPORARIES

THIS collection of comments does not pretend to be complete, but it represents Wordsworth's opinions fairly. For convenience it is divided into three sections: (I) Casual pronouncements upon those whose work was before the public; (II) Some passages of good advice and criticism sent to young writers who asked for them; (III) A few passages which give Wordsworth's opinion, in later life, of himself as a critic. In the first section the passages are arranged as far as possible in chronological order under the names of the authors concerned.

I

MRS BARBAULD

He asserts for instance that Mrs Barbauld has a bad heart; that her writings are absolutely insignificant, her poems are mere trash, and specimens of every fault may be selected from them. He quoted, to satirise, a stanza you and I have certainly admired.

(Crabb Robinson to Thomas Robinson, March 1808.)

[Miss Seward's] verses please me, with all their faults, better than those of Mrs Barbauld, who, with much higher powers of mind, was spoiled as a poetess by being a dissenter, and concerned with a dissenting academy. One of the most pleasing passages in her poetry is the close of the lines upon "Life", written, I believe, when she was not less than eighty years of age.

(Wordsworth to Dyce, May 10, 1830.)

I admire the genius of Mrs Barbauld, and am certain that, had her education been favourable to imaginative influences, no female of her day would have been more likely to sympathise with that image, and to acknowledge the truth of the sentiment.

(Fenwick note to *The Idle Shepherd Boys*, about 1843.)

In the estimation of Wordsworth she was the first of our literary women, and he was not bribed to this judgement by any especial congeniality of feeling, or by concurrence in speculative opinions. I may here relate an anecdote connecting her and Wordsworth, though out of its proper time by many, many years; but it is so good that it ought to be preserved from oblivion. It was after her death that Lucy Aikin published Mrs Barbauld's collected works, of which I gave a copy to Miss Wordsworth. Among the poems is a stanza on Life, written in extreme old age. It had delighted my sister, to whom I repeated it on her death-bed. It was long after I gave these works to Miss Wordsworth that her brother said, "Repeat me that stanza by Mrs Barbauld". I did so. He made me repeat it again. And so he learned it by heart. He was at the time walking in his sitting-room at Rydal with his hands behind him; and I heard him mutter to himself, "I am not in the habit of grudging people their good things, but I wish I had written those lines".

(Crabb Robinson, *Reminiscences, sub ann.* 1805–6; printed by Sadler, I, 226–7.)

BLAKE

At half-past ten joined Wordsworth in Oxford Road, and we then got into the fields, and walked to Hampstead.... I read Wordsworth some of Blake's poems; he was pleased with some of them, and considered Blake as having the elements of poetry a thousand times more than either Byron or Scott.

(Crabb Robinson, *Diary*, May 24, 1812.)

BURNS

When I last wrote I forgot to thank you for those verses you were so kind as to transcribe for me. My brother William was here at the time I got your letter. I told him you had recommended the book to me, he had read it, and admired many of the pieces very much, and promised to get it for me at the book-club, which he did. I was very much pleased with them indeed, the one which you mentioned to me is I think very comical. I mean the Address to a Louse; there is one to a mountain daisy which is very pretty.

(Dorothy Wordsworth to Jane Pollard, December 7, 1787.)

Wordsworth talked very finely on poetry. He praised Burns for his introduction to *Tam O'Shanter*. He had given a poetical apology for drunkenness, by bringing together all the circumstances which can serve to render excusable what is in itself disgusting; thus interesting our feelings, and making us tolerant of what would otherwise be not endurable.... Wordsworth also praised the conclusion of *Death and Dr Hornbook.* Wordsworth compared this with the abrupt prevention of the expected battle between Satan and the Archangel in Milton, but this remark did not bring its own evidence with it. (Crabb Robinson, *Diary*, May 29, 1812.)

Finished Goethe's *Aus meinem Leben: Dichtung und Wahrheit....* The remark Wordsworth made on Burns is here applicable: "The poet writes humanely". (*Ibid.* July 26, 1812.)

The queries you put to me upon the connection between genius and irregularity of conduct may probably induce me to take up the subject again, and yet it scarcely seems necessary. No man can claim indulgence for his transgressions on the score of his sensibilities, but at the expense of his credit for intellectual powers. All men of *first* rate genius have been as distinguished for dignity, beauty, and propriety of moral conduct. But we often find the faculties and qualities of the mind not well balanced; something of prime importance is left short, and hence confusion and disorder. On the one hand it is well that dunces should not arrogate to themselves a pharisaical superiority, because they avoid the vices and faults which they see men of talent fall into. They should not be permitted to believe that they have more understanding merely on that account, but should be taught that they are preserved probably by having less feeling, and being consequently less liable to temptation. On the other hand, the man of genius ought to know that the cause of his vices is, in fact, his deficiencies, and not, as he fondly imagines, his superfluities and superiorities. All men ought to be judged with charity and forbearance after death has put it out of their power to explain the motives of their actions, and especially men of acute sensibility and lively passions. This was the scope of my letter to Mr Gray. Burns has been cruelly used, both dead and alive. The treatment which Butler and others have experienced has been renewed in him. He asked for bread—no, he did not *ask* it, he endured the want of it with silent fortitude—and ye gave him a stone. It is worse than ridiculous to see the people of Dumfries coming forward with their pompous mausoleum, they who persecuted and reviled him with such low-minded malignity. Burns might have said to that town when he was dying, "Ingrata—non possidebis ossa mea!" On this and a thousand other accounts his monument ought to have been placed in or near to Edinburgh; "stately Edinburgh throned on crags". How well would such an edifice have accorded with the pastoral imagery near St Anthony's Well and under Arthur's Seat, while the metropolis of his native country,—to which his writings have done so great honour—with its murmuring sounds, was in distinct hearing!

(Wordsworth to John Scott, June 11, 1816.)

How much I was amused yesterday, by a sudden burst of indignation in Mr Wordsworth which would have enchanted ——. We were sitting on a bank overlooking Rydal Lake, and speaking of Burns. I said, "Mr Wordsworth, do you not think his war ode 'Scots wha hae wi' Wallace bled' has been a good deal overrated? especially by Mr Carlyle, who calls it the noblest lyric in the language?" "I am delighted to hear you ask the question," was his reply, "overrated!—trash!—stuff!—miserable inanity! without a thought—without an image!" etc. etc. etc.—then he recited the piece in a tone of unutterable scorn; and concluded with a *Da Capo* of "wretched stuff!"

(Mrs Hemans, June 25, 1830; Chorley, II, 120.)

Tuesday, the 2d of May [1841], Wordsworth and Miss F. came early to walk about and dine. He was in a very happy kindly mood. We took a walk on the terrace, and he went as usual to his favourite points. On our return he was struck with the berries on the holly tree, and said, "Why should not you and I go and pull some berries from the other side of the tree, which is not seen from the window? and then we can go and plant them in the rocky ground behind the house". We pulled the berries, and set forth with our tool. I made the holes, and the Poet put in the berries. He was as earnest and eager about it, as if it had been a matter of importance; and as he put the seeds in, he every now and then muttered, in his low solemn tone, that beautiful verse from Burns's "Vision":

"And wear thou this, she solemn said,
And bound the holly round my head.
The polished leaves and berries red
Did rustling play;
And like a passing thought she fled
In light away."

He clambered to the highest rocks in the "Tom Intake", and put in the berries in such situations as Nature sometimes does with such true and beautiful effect. He said, "I like to do this for posterity. Some people are selfish enough to say, What has posterity done for me? but the past does much for us".

(Lady Richardson, *Memoirs*, II, 438–9; Grosart, III, 436.)

Cf. also the *Letter to a Friend of Robert Burns* (1816).

BYRON

We talked of Lord Byron. Wordsworth allowed him power, but denied his style to be English. Of his moral qualities we think the same. (Crabb Robinson, *Diary*, May 24, 1812.)

With Lord Byron he seemed to have least patience; for though cordially admitting his lordship's extraordinary power, and his claims as a man of genius, he yet firmly believed that his application of that power was reprehensible, perverted, and vicious.

(R. P. Gillies, *Memoirs of a Literary Veteran*, III, 144, referring to 1814.)

I dined at Collier's with a party assembled to see the poet Wordsworth.... Wordsworth was led to give an opinion of Lord Byron which flattered me by its resemblance to my own. He reproached the Author with the contradiction in the character of the Corsair, etc. (Crabb Robinson, *Diary*, May 28, 1815.)

Byron seems to me deficient in *feeling*....I never read the "English Bards" through. His critical prognostications have, for the most part, proved erroneous....My main endeavour, as to style, has been that my poems should be written in pure intelligible English. Lord Byron has spoken severely of my compositions. However faulty they may be, I do not think that I ever could have prevailed upon myself to print such lines as he has done; for instance,

"I stood at Venice on the Bridge of Sighs,
A palace and a prison on each hand."

Some person ought to write a critical review, analysing Lord Byron's language, in order to guard others against imitating him in these respects. (Bishop Christopher Wordsworth's reminiscences of 1827; *Memoirs*, Knight's *Life*, and Grosart.)

The Spenserian stanza is a fine structure of verse; but it is also almost insurmountably difficult. You have succeeded in the broken and more impassioned movement,—of which Lord Byron has given good instances,—but it is a form of verse ill adapted to conflicting passion; and it is not injustice to say that the stanza is spoiled in Lord Byron's hands; his own strong and ungovernable passions blinded him as to its character. It is equally unfit for narrative. *Circumstances* are difficult to manage in any kind of verse, except the dramatic, where the warmth of the action makes the reader indifferent to those delicacies of phrase and sound upon which so much of the charm of other poetry depends. If you write more in this stanza, leave Lord Byron for Spenser. In him the stanza is seen in its perfection. It is exquisitely harmonious also in Thomson's hands, and fine in Beattie's *Minstrel*; but these two latter poems are merely descriptive and sentimental; and you will observe that Spenser never gives way to violent and conflicting passion, and that his narrative is bare of circumstances, slow in movement, and (for modern relish) too much clogged with description.

(Wordsworth to Catherine Grace Godwin: Knight dates the letter in 1829.)

It occurs to me, that I have not noticed as I ought Wordsworth's answer to the charge brought by Wilson against Wordsworth, that he never quotes other poems than his own. In fact I can testify to the falsehood of the statement. But Wordsworth in addition remarked, "You know how I love and quote not even Shakespeare and Milton, but Cowper, Burns, etc.; as to the modern poets, Byron, Scott, etc., I do not quote them because I do not love them. Byron has great power and genius, but there is something so repugnant to my moral sense that I abhor them. Besides, even as works of mere taste there is this material circumstance—they came too late. My taste was formed, for I was forty-five when they appeared, and we cannot after that age love new things. New impressions are difficult to make. Had I been young, I should have enjoyed much of them, I have no doubt". (Crabb Robinson, *Diary*, January 31, 1836.)

See also pp. 54, 98–9, 101 *supra*.

CAMPBELL

Scott he thinks superior to Campbell. I was for carrying down the descent to Rogers, but Wordsworth would not allow it. Rogers has an effeminate mind, but he has not the bad obscure writing of Campbell. (Crabb Robinson, *Diary*, May 24, 1812.)

Of Campbell, as a poet, he seemed to think very lightly, and blended his name with the nameless productions of other modern writers, whose extravagant fables, and guilty heroes, would be hid in oblivion in the next age, when the glare of novelty was worn off, and men found out that those conceptions were unnatural.

(J. H. Wiffen, 1819, in *The Brothers Wiffen*, p. 38.)

CARLYLE

I am slowly reading Carlyle's *French Revolution*...and provided I take only small doses, and not too frequently, it is not merely agreeable but fascinating....He who will give himself the trouble to learn this language will be rewarded by admirable matter. Wordsworth is intolerant of such innovations and cannot and will not read Carlyle. (Crabb Robinson to Thomas Robinson, January 19, 1839.)

I read with deep interest the 3rd volume of Carlyle, of whom Wordsworth pronounces a harsh judgement. It is not only his style that he condemns, but his *inhumanity*. He says there is a want of due sympathy with mankind—scorn and irony are the feeling throughout. There is too much truth in this, and it is too strongly confirmed by the opinion so strongly expressed by Carlyle at table at Craufurd's, in favour of the continuance of negro slavery by the Americans. (Crabb Robinson, *Diary*, January 26, 1839.)

Many thanks for the *Examiner*; it is well that the Copyright Question should be looked at from different points of view. Carlyle's petition and the extract from Landor's are both characteristic—

Carlyle racy, and may startle certain dull persons into attention to the subject—but the expression has often too much the air of burlesque, for my taste. (Wordsworth to Crabb Robinson, April 10, 1839.)

Our Carlyle and he [i.e. Emerson] appear to be what the French used to call Esprits forts, though the French Idols showed their spirit after a somewhat different Fashion. Our two present Philosophers, who have taken a language which they suppose to be English for their vehicle, are verily "Par nobile Fratrum", and it is a pity that the weakness of our age has not left them exclusively to the appropriate reward, mutual admiration.

(Wordsworth to Reed, August 16, 1841.)

HARTLEY COLERIDGE

Not being able to meet with H. C. immediately on receipt of your letter, I wrote him a note a couple of days after and told him its contents. I have since seen him, and done all I could. And now let me give you, in respect to him, a piece of advice, once for all, viz., that you *never* engage with him for any *unperformed* work, when either time or quantity is of importance. Poor fellow! he has no resolve; in fact, nothing that can be called rational will or command of himself as to what he will do or not do; of course, I mean, setting aside the fundamental obligations of morality....I admire his genius and talents far more than I can find words to express, especially for writing prose, which I am inclined to think (as far as I have seen) is more masterly than his verse. The workmanship of the latter seems to me not infrequently too hasty, has indeed too much the air of an Italian's *improvisatore* production.

(Wordsworth to Moxon, February 24, 1840.)

Give up Germany and come to us....Hartley Coleridge is come much nearer us, and probably you might see as much of him as you liked. Of Genius he has not a little, and talent enough for fifty.

(Wordsworth to Crabb Robinson, June 3, 1840.)

He cannot be relied on for unperformed work that is to be done in a limited time. This is a great pity, for both his genius and talents are admirable. (Wordsworth to Moxon, December 13, 1842.)

S. T. COLERIDGE

He and my beloved sister are the two beings to whom my intellect is most indebted, and they are now proceeding as it were *pari passu* along the path of sickness—I will not say towards the grave, but I trust towards a blessed immortality. It was not my intention to write so seriously; my heart is full and you must excuse it.

(Wordsworth to W. R. Hamilton, June 25, 1832.)

I cannot give way to the expression of my feelings upon this mournful occasion; I have not strength of mind to do so. The last year has thinned off so many of my friends, young and old, and brought with it so much anxiety private and public that it would be no kindness to you were I to yield to the solemn and sad thoughts and remembrances which press upon me. It is nearly forty years since I first became acquainted with him whom we have just lost; and though with the exception of six weeks when we were on the Continent together, along with my daughter, I have seen little of him for the last twenty years, his mind has been habitually present with me, with an accompanying feeling that he was still in the flesh. That frail tie is broken, and I and most of those who are nearest and dearest to me must prepare and endeavour to follow him.

(Wordsworth to H. N. Coleridge, July 29, 1834.)

It was the Sunday evening after the event occurred that my brother and I walked over to the Mount, where we found the poet alone. One of the first things we heard from him was the death of one who had been, he said, his friend for more than thirty years. He then continued to speak of him; called him the most *wonderful* man that he had ever known—wonderful for the originality of his mind, and the power he possessed of throwing out in profusion grand central truths from which might be evolved the most comprehensive systems. Wordsworth, as a poet, regretted that German metaphysics had so much captivated the taste of Coleridge, for he was frequently not intelligible on the subject; whereas, if his energy and his originality had been more exerted in the channel of poetry, an instrument of which he had so perfect a mastery, Wordsworth thought he might have done more permanently to enrich the literature and to influence the thought of the nation, than any man of the age. As it was, however, he said he believed Coleridge's mind to have been a widely fertilising one, and that the seed he had so lavishly sown in his conversational discourses, and the Sibylline leaves (not the poems so called by him) which he had scattered abroad so extensively covered with his annotations, had done much to form the opinions of the best-educated men of the day; although this might be an influence not likely to meet with adequate recognition.

(R. P. Graves to Christopher Wordsworth, 1850–1.)[1]

Nor has the rolling year twice measured,
From sign to sign, its steadfast course,
Since every mortal power of Coleridge
Was frozen at its marvellous source;

The rapt One, of the godlike forehead,
The heaven-eyed creature sleeps in earth.

(*Extempore Effusion*, November 1835.)

[Alsop] is a man without judgement, and therefore appears to be without feeling. His rule is to publish all the truth that he can scrape together about his departed friend, not perceiving the difference between the real truth and what appears to him to be true. The maxim *de mortuis nil nisi verum* was never meant to imply that all truth is to be told, only nothing but what is true.

(Wordsworth to Moxon, January 4, 1836.)

Talking of dear Charles Lamb's very strange habit of quizzing, and of Coleridge's far more equivocal *incorrectnesses* in talk, Wordsworth said he thought much of this was owing to a *school-habit*. Lamb's veracity was unquestionable in all matters of a serious kind; he never uttered an untruth either for profit or through vanity, and certainly never to injure others. Yet he loved a quizzing lie, a

[1] Cf. Graves, *Recollections* (p. 299): "I shall always remember the voice, broken with grief, with which he announced to me the death of his friend—the Wonderful—and related to me the attending circumstances, and how anxious he was to clear, as far as possible, that friend's memory, by assuring me that the origin of the pernicious recourse to opium was due to a frightful internal pain, which sometimes caused him, when they walked together in Somersetshire, to throw himself down and writhe like a worm upon the ground".

fiction that amused him like a good joke, or an exercise of wit. There was in Coleridge a sort of dreaminess, which would not let him see things as they were. He would talk about his own feelings and recollections and intentions in a way that deceived others, but he was first deceived himself. "I am sure", said Wordsworth, "that he never formed a plan or knew what was to be the end of *Christabel*, and that he merely deceived himself when he thought, as he says, that he had had the idea quite clear in his mind."

(Crabb Robinson, *Diary*, February 1, 1836.)

I wish to write to Mr Gillman, whose book, I am sorry to say, is full of all kinds of mistakes. Coleridge is a subject which no biographer ought to touch beyond what he himself was eyewitness of.

(Wordsworth to Daniel Stuart, May 17, 1838.)

Poor dear Coleridge—from a hundred causes, many of them unhappy ones—was not to be trusted in his account either of particular occurrences or the general tenor of his engagements and occupations. ...I do not mean to impeach poor Coleridge's veraciousness, far from it, but his credibility. He deceived himself in a hundred ways, relating things according to the humour of the moment, as his spirits went up or down, or as they furnished employment for his fancy or for his theories.

(Wordsworth to unidentified correspondent, June 9, 1838.)

I have been much annoyed by a serious charge of Plagiarism brought against Coleridge in the last number of *Blackwood*. I procured the number for the purpose of reading it. With the part concerning the imputation of the thefts from Schelling, having never read a word of German metaphysics, thank Heaven! though I doubt not they are good diet for some tastes, I feel no disposition to meddle. But when in further disparagement of the object of his remarks he asserts that C. was indebted "to Germans for the brightest gems of his poetic crown", I feel myself competent to say a few words upon that subject. The critic names Schiller and Stolberg as, among others, strong instances in support of his assertion. And what are the passages adduced? Two Hexameter verses, and a hexameter and pentameter, word for word from Schiller, and passed off by Coleridge as his own. If it be true, this was excessive folly on Coleridge's part, but it is beyond measure absurd to talk of this paltry stuff as the Magazinist has ventured to do. So far from the things being gems in his crown, they would be much honoured by calling them farthings in his Pocket....But having admitted that it was silly, if not worse, in my Friend to claim what was not his own, I feel free to affirm that Coleridge had carefully studied and successfully practised English Hexameters before he knew a word of German. And I am astonished that he did not give specimens of his own, with which he had taken, in Hexameters, I know, far more pains than anything of the sort is worth. These are the sole proofs of his robberies of Schiller, but if he had stolen ten times as freely, I could have added in explanation, and partly in exculpation, that he gave to Schiller fifty times more than he took, without thinking worth while to let the world know what he had done. C. translated the second part of *Wallenstein* under my roof at Grasmere from MSS.—about that time I saw the passages of the Astronomical Times and the ancient Mythology, which, as treated in Coleridge's professed translation, were infinitely superior. As to the passage from Stolberg, it was begun, as I know, as a translation, and amplified. Coleridge took incredible pains with the execution, and has greatly excelled the original; but why he did not in this case also speak the plain truth, I am quite at a loss to conceive....I used to beg he would take the trouble of noting his obligations, but half his time was passed in dreams, so that such hints were thrown away. I should not have thought it worth while to write so much, had not the unfairness with which the Blackwoodite treats the *Poet* C. in this point led me to suspect that as a metaphysician he has been used somewhat in the same manner.

(Wordsworth to Crabb Robinson, March 10, 1840.)

He said that the liveliest and truest image he could give of Coleridge's talk was "that of a majestic river, the sound or sight of whose course you caught at intervals, which was sometimes concealed by forests, sometimes lost in sand, then came flashing out broad and distinct, then again took a turn which your eye could not follow, yet you knew and felt that it was the same river: so", he said, "there was always a train, a stream, in Coleridge's discourse, always a connection between its parts in his own mind, though one not always perceptible to the minds of others".

(Mrs Davy, July 11, 1844; *Memoirs*, II, 443; Grosart, III, 441.)

It is not enough for a poet to possess power of mind, he must also have knowledge of the heart, and this can only be gained by time and tranquil leisure. No *great* poem has been written by a young man, or by an unhappy one. It was dear Coleridge's constant infelicity that prevented him from being the poet that Nature had given him the power to be. He had always too much personal and domestic discontent to paint the sorrows of mankind. He could not—

"afford to suffer
With those whom he saw suffer...."

...Not being able to dwell on natural woes, he took to the supernatural; and hence his *Ancient Mariner* and *Christabel*, in which he shows great poetical power; but these have not the hold on the heart which Nature gives, and will never be popular poems, like those of Goldsmith or Burns.

(Recorded by Barron Field in his MS. *Memoirs*, between 1836 and 1840.)

Coleridge, as Wordsworth once expressed it to me, had been "in blossom" only for four years—from 1796 to 1800. The plant was perennial, but the flowers were few.

(*Autobiography of Sir Henry Taylor*, I, 188. The second sentence may be Taylor's expansion of the thought.)

Wordsworth once said to me that Coleridge's twenty-sixth year was his "annus mirabilis", and that if he had not then suffered himself to be drawn aside from poetry he must have proved the chief poet of modern times. (*Recollections of Aubrey de Vere*, p. 42.)

"BARRY CORNWALL" (B. W. PROCTER)

I have read Cornwall's tragedy, and think of it pretty much as you seem to do. The feelings are cleverly touched in it; but the situations for exhibiting them are produced not only by sacrifice of the respectability of the persons concerned, but with great, and I should have thought unnecessary, violation of probability and common sense. But it does appear to me in the present late age of the world a most difficult task to construct a good tragedy free from stale and mean contrivances and animated by new and suitable characters, so that I am inclined to judge Cornwall gently, and sincerely rejoice in his success. As to poetry, I am sick of it—it overruns the Country in all the shapes of the plagues of Egypt—

(Then follows the passage quoted on p. 100 *supra*. Wordsworth to Crabb Robinson, March 13, 1821.)

CRABBE

I am happy to find that we coincide in opinion about Crabbe's verses; for poetry in no sense can they be called.... The sum of all is, that nineteen out of twenty of Crabbe's pictures are mere matters of fact; with which the Muses have just about as much to do as they have with a collection of medical reports, or of law cases.

(Wordsworth to Rogers, September 29, 1808.)

He also blamed Crabbe for his unpoetical mode of considering human nature and society. (Crabb Robinson, *Diary*, May 28, 1815.)

Of Crabbe, he spoke in terms of almost unmingled praise, conceiving that his works would be turned to, with curiosity and pleasure, when the rapid march of improvement, in another century, had altered the manners, and situation, of the peasantry of England.

(J. H. Wiffen, 1819, in *The Brothers Wiffen*, p. 38.)

My Uncle Southey and my father had an equally high opinion of [Jane Austen's] merits, but Mr Wordsworth used to say that though he admitted that her novels were an admirable copy of life, he could not be interested in productions of that kind; unless the truth of nature were presented to him clarified, as it were, by the pervading light of imagination, it had scarce any attractions in his eyes; and for this reason he took little pleasure in the writings of Crabbe.

(Sara Coleridge to Miss E. Trevenen, August 1834.)

Wordsworth considers him a dull man in conversation. He said he did not either give information, nor did he enliven any subject by discussion. He spoke highly of his writings as admirable specimens of the kind, but he does not like the misanthropic vein which runs through them. He was surprised to hear from my mother that Crabbe's prose style was so stiff and artificial in his letters. He said that generally good writers of verse wrote good prose, especially good letters. "Cowper's letters are everything that letters can be, and many of Burns's are marvellous."

(Lady Richardson, 1840, in *Autobiography of Mrs Fletcher*, 1st edition, p. 216.)

The way in which the incident was treated, and the spiritualising of the character, might furnish hints for contrasting the imaginative influences, which I have endeavoured to throw over common life, with Crabbe's matter-of-fact style of handling subjects of the same kind. This is not spoken to his disparagement, far from it; but to direct the attention of thoughtful readers into whose hands these notes may fall, to a comparison that may enlarge the circle of their sensibilities, and tend to produce in them a catholic judgement.

(Fenwick note to *Lucy Gray*, about 1843.)

ALLAN CUNNINGHAM

I have not yet been able to make myself acquainted with more than a few of the first scenes of your drama, one of your ballads, and the songs. . . . The songs appear to me full as good as those of Burns, with the exception of a *very* few of his best; and *The Mermaid* is wild, tender, and full of spirit. The little I have seen of the play I liked, especially the speeches of the spirits, and that of Macgee, page 7. I hope, in a little time, to be acquainted with the rest of the volume. (Wordsworth to Cunningham, June 12, 1822.)

KENELM DIGBY

A dinner party at Mr Quillinan's. . . . An American lady, who, as Wordsworth says, is anxious to see great people and talk herself. . . . Wordsworth made honourable mention of Digby's *Broad Stone of Honour*. (Crabb Robinson, *Diary*, May 28, 1828.)

The subject of the following poem is from the "Orlandus" of the author's friend, Kenelm Henry Digby: and the liberty is taken of inscribing it to him as an acknowledgment, however unworthy, of pleasure and instruction derived from his numerous and valuable writings, illustrative of the piety and chivalry of the olden time.

(Note to *The Armenian Lady's Love*, 1830.)

GEORGE DYER

. . . *The Life of Robert Robinson*, which I have heard Wordsworth mention as one of the best works of biography in the language.

(Crabb Robinson, *Reminiscences*, *sub ann.* 1799;
printed by Sadler, I, 62.)

EBENEZER ELLIOTT

Wordsworth speaks highly of the author of *Corn Law Rhymes*. He says, "None of us have better than he has in his best, though there is a deal of stuff arising from his hatred of subsisting things. Like Byron, Shelley, etc., he looks on all things with an evil eye". This arises naturally enough in the mind of a very poor man who thinks the world has not treated him well. But Wordsworth says, though a very poor man, he has had the means of sending his son to college, who did not succeed there—hence perhaps his hatred of universities. The great merit of Elliott, says Wordsworth, is his industry: he has laboured intensely, and, like the Glastonbury thorn, has flowered in winter—his latter writings are the best.... "Elliott has a fine eye for Nature, he is a very extraordinary man."

(Crabb Robinson, *Diary*, January 29, 1836.)

GOETHE

I have tried to read Goethe. I never could succeed. Mr —— [probably Crabb Robinson] refers me to his *Iphigenia*, but I there recognise none of the dignified simplicity, none of the health and vigour which the heroes and heroines of antiquity possess in the writings of Homer. The lines of Lucretius describing the immolation of Iphigenia are worth the whole of Goethe's long poem. Again, there is a profligacy, an inhuman sensuality, in his works which is utterly revolting. I am not intimately acquainted with them generally. But I take up my ground on the first canto of *Wilhelm Meister*; and, as the attorney-general of human nature, I there indict him for wantonly outraging the sympathies of humanity. Theologians tell us of the degraded nature of man; and they tell us what is true. Yet man is essentially a moral agent, and there is that immortal and inextinguishable yearning for something pure and spiritual which will plead against these poetical sensualists as long as man remains what he is. (Bishop Christopher Wordsworth's reminiscences of 1827, *Memoirs*, II, 478.)

Wordsworth made some striking remarks on Goethe in a walk on the terrace yesterday. He thinks that the German poet is greatly overrated, both in this country and his own. He said, "He does not seem to me to be a great poet in either of the classes of poets. At the head of the first class I would place Homer and Shakespeare, whose universal minds are able to reach every variety of thought and feeling without bringing their own individuality before the reader. They infuse, they breathe life into every object they approach, but you never find *themselves*. At the head of the second class, those whom you can trace individually in all they write, I would place Spenser and Milton. In all that Spenser writes you can trace the gentle affectionate spirit of the man; in all that Milton writes you find the exalted sustained being that he was. Now in what Goethe writes, who aims to be of the first class, the *universal*, you find the man himself, the artificial man, where he should not be found; so that I consider him a very artificial writer, aiming to be universal, and yet constantly exposing his individuality, which his character was not of a kind to dignify. He had not sufficiently clear moral perceptions to make him anything but an artificial writer".

(Lady Richardson, August 26, 1841; Grosart, III, 435–6.)

Of Goethe Wordsworth spoke with his usual bitterness, and I cannot deny that his objection is well founded: that is, an extreme defect of religious sentiment—perhaps I should say, moral sense; and this suffices, says Wordsworth, to prove that he could be only a second-rate man. Wordsworth however does not deny that he is a great artist, but he adds this, in which I do not agree.... [Then follows a passage compressing the argument of the conversation with Lady Richardson.]...Goethe's *Tasso* and his *Iphigenia* Wordsworth declares to be flat and insipid, but then he knows them only in translations. He has formerly said the same of *Hermann and Dorothea*. He expressed disgust at the *Bride of Corinth*.

(Crabb Robinson, *Diary*, January 1, 1843.)

Goethe was amusing himself with fine fancies when his country was invaded; how unlike Milton, who only asked himself whether he could best serve his country as a soldier or a statesman, and decided that he could fight no better than others, but he might govern them better. Schiller had far more heart and ardour than Goethe, and would not, like him, have professed indifference to Theology and Politics, which are the two deepest things in man—indeed, all a man is worth, involving duty to God and to man.

(Caroline Fox, *Memories of Old Friends*, October 6, 1844.)

HAZLITT

There is another acquaintance of mine also recently gone—a person for whom I never had any love, but with whom I had for a short time a good deal of intimacy—I mean Hazlitt, whose death you may have seen announced in the papers. He was a man of extraordinary acuteness, but perverse as Lord Byron himself, whose *Life* by Galt I have been skimming.

(Wordsworth to W. R. Hamilton, September 26, 1830.)

(Brief comments on Hazlitt's "monstrous" statements about his attitude to Shakespeare, Dryden and Pope were written by Wordsworth in Barron Field's MS. *Memoirs of the Life and Poetry of William Wordsworth*, and printed by Knight, *Letters*, III, pp. 121–2. Cf. p. 75 n. *supra*, and also Payne Collier's notes of Wordsworth's praise of earlier poets (Preface to Coleridge's *Seven Lectures on Shakespeare and Milton*, p. lii): "Though [Dryden] was not a great poet, in the sense of invention and imagination, his thoughts were not infrequently new and noble, and his language, in point of strength, fulness, and idiomatic freedom, incomparable....Dryden was the finest writer of couplets...yet Pope was a more finished and polished versifier than Dryden....Wordsworth seemed to be endeavouring to direct my taste towards the best models in our language".)

MRS HEMANS

I avail myself gladly of the opportunity of Mr Graves's return to acknowledge the honour you have done me in prefixing my name to your volume of beautiful poems, and to thank you for the copy you have sent me with your own autograph. Where there is so much to admire, it is difficult to select; and therefore I shall content myself with naming only two or three pieces....I cannot conclude without thanking you for your sonnet upon a place so dear to me as Grasmere; it is worthy of the subject.

(Wordsworth to Mrs Hemans, September 1834.)

JAMES HOGG

I thank you for *The Queen's Wake*....It does Mr Hogg great credit. Of the tales, I liked best, much the best, *The Witch of Fife*, the former part of *Kilmenie*, and the *Abbot Mackinnon*. Mr Hogg himself, I remember, seemed most partial to *Mary Scott*, though he thought it too long. For my own part, though I always deem the opinion of an able writer upon his own works entitled to consideration, I cannot agree with Mr Hogg in this preference....The intermediate parts of *The Queen's Wake* are done with much spirit, but the style here, also, is often disfigured with false finery, and in too many places it recalls Mr Scott to one's mind. Mr Hogg has too much genius to require that support, however respectable in itself.

(Wordsworth to R. P. Gillies, November 23, 1814.)

Mr Hogg's *Badlew* (I suppose it to be his) I could not get through. There are two pretty passages—the flight of the deer, and the falling of the child from the rock of Stirling, though both are a little *outré*. But the story is coarsely conceived, and, in my judgement, as coarsely executed; the style barbarous, and the versification harsh and uncouth. Mr Hogg is too illiterate to write in any measure or style that does not savour of balladism. This is much to be regretted, for he is possessed of no ordinary power.

(The same to the same, December 22, 1814.)

MARIA JANE JEWSBURY

The opinion she entertained of her own performances...was modest and humble, and, indeed, far below their merits; as is often the case with those who are making trial of their powers, with a hope to discover what they are best fitted for. In one quality, viz., quickness in the motions of her mind, she had, within the range of the Author's acquaintance, no equal. (Note to *Liberty*.)

KEATS

See pp. 77–8, 100–2 *supra*.

LAMB

Charles Lamb, my friend, writes prose exquisitely.

(Wordsworth to John Scott, March 11, 1816.)

Charles Lamb's verses are always delightful, like everything he writes, for he both feels and thinks.

(Wordsworth to Moxon, January 14, 1834.)

And Lamb, the frolic and the gentle,
Has vanished from his lonely hearth.

(*Extempore Effusion*, November 1835.)

Not seldom did those tasks
Tease, and the thought of time so spent depress,
His spirit, but the recompense was high;
Firm Independence, Bounty's rightful sire;
Affections, warm as sunshine, free as air;
And when the precious hours of leisure came,
Knowledge and wisdom, gained from converse sweet
With books, or while he ranged the crowded streets
With a keen eye, and overflowing heart:
So genius triumphed over seeming wrong,
And poured out truth in works by thoughtful love
Inspired—works potent over smiles and tears.
And as round mountain-tops the lightning plays,
Thus innocently sported, breaking forth
As from a cloud of some grave sympathy,
Humour and wild instinctive wit, and all
The vivid flashes of his spoken words....
And if too often, self-reproached, he felt
That innocence belongs not to our kind,
A power that never ceased to abide in him,
Charity, 'mid the multitude of sins
That she can cover, left not his exposed
To an unforgiving judgement from just Heaven.
O, he was good, if e'er a good Man lived!...

(*Written after the Death of Charles Lamb*, November 1835.)

LANDOR

He spoke with respect of Landor's power. The tragedy which he is now publishing has very fine touches, he says.

(Crabb Robinson, *Diary*, May 13, 1812.)

It is high time I should thank you for the honourable mention you have made of me. It could not but be grateful to me to be praised by a Poet who has written verses of which I would rather have been the Author than of any produced in our time—what I now write to you I have frequently said to many.

(Wordsworth to Landor, September 3, 1821.)

The first book whi[ch I] read, unless it be one in large type, shall be these Poems. I must express a wish however that you would gratify us by writing in English—there are noble and stirring things in all that you have written in your native tongue, and that is enough for me.... I expect your book with impatience, and shall at all times be glad to hear from you.

(The same to the same, April 20, 1822.)

See also pp. 91–3 *supra*.

LONGFELLOW

Emerson says that Wordsworth spoke highly of Longfellow, and regretted his *name*. (Crabb Robinson, *Diary*, June 17, 1848.)

RICHARD MONCKTON MILNES (LORD HOUGHTON)

I have read also some part of Mr Milnes's[1] book, the dedication of which is, for its length, perhaps one of the most admirable specimens of that class of composition to be found in the whole compass of English literature. Of the poems also I can say, though I have but yet read a few of them, that they added another to the proofs that much poetical genius is stirring among the youth of this country.

(Wordsworth to Moxon, January 14, 1834.)

JAMES MONTGOMERY

I can assure you with truth that from the time I first read your *Wanderer of Switzerland*, with the little pieces annexed, I have felt a lively interest in your destiny as a poet; and though much out of the way of new books, I have become acquainted with your works, and with increasing pleasure, as they successively appeared. It might be presumptuous in me were I to attempt to define what I

[1] Knight's "Milner" is an obvious misprint. The reference is to the *Memorials of a Tour in Greece* of Monckton Milnes, who had travelled in Greece with the younger Christopher Wordsworth. The *Memorials* were nominally published in 1834, but may have appeared at the end of 1833.—It was evidently Milnes about whom Wordsworth made one of his not infrequent but infrequently recorded jokes. It was reported to him that Milnes was going as Chaucer to a Court ball to which Wordsworth, to the amused delight of himself and his household, had also been invited. "What," said Wordsworth, "M. go as Chaucer! Then it only remains for me to go as M.!"—Milnes being as small and dapper as Wordsworth was gaunt and untidy.

hope belongs to us in common; but I cannot deny myself the satisfaction of expressing a firm belief that neither morality nor religion can have suffered from our writings; and with respect to *yours* I know that both have been greatly benefited by them. Without convictions of this kind all the rest must, in the latter days of an author's life, appear to him worse than vanity.

(Wordsworth to J. Montgomery, November 30, 1836.)

See also pp. 95–6 *supra*.

ROBERT MONTGOMERY

See pp. 103–4 *supra*.

MOORE

T. Moore has great natural genius; but he is too lavish of brilliant ornament. His poems smell of the perfumer's and milliner's shops. He is not content with a ring and a bracelet, but he must have rings in the ears, rings on the nose—rings everywhere.

(Bishop Christopher Wordsworth's reminiscences of 1827, *Memoirs*, II, 473.)

ROGERS

Of Rogers, of course, he speaks with great contempt.

(Crabb Robinson to Thomas Robinson, March 1808.)

Rogers has an effeminate mind, but he has not the bad obscure writing of Campbell. (Crabb Robinson, *Diary*, May 24, 1812.)

I have to thank you for a Present of your volume of poems, received some time since, through the hands of Southey. I have read it with great pleasure. The Columbus is what you intended. It has many bright and striking passages, and Poems, upon this plan, please better on a second Perusal than the first. . . . Farewell. I shall be happy to see you here at all times, for your company is a treat.

(Wordsworth to Rogers, May 5, 1814.)

Rogers read me his poem when I was in town about twelve months ago; but I have heard nothing of it since. It contained some very pleasing passages, but the title [*Human Life*] is much too grandiloquent for the performance, and the plan appeared to me faulty. (Wordsworth to Wrangham, February 19, 1819.)

I detected you in a small collection of poems entitled *Italy* which we all read with much pleasure....Some parts of the *Venice* are particularly fine. I had no fault to find, except too strong a leaning to the pithy and concise, and to some peculiarities of versification which occur perhaps too often.

(Wordsworth to Rogers, September 16, 1822.)

Yesterday I received your most valuable present of three copies of your beautiful book, which I assure you will be nowhere more prized than in this house....I cannot forbear adding that as several of the poems are among my oldest and dearest acquaintances in the literature of our day, such an elegant edition of them, with their illustrations, must to me be peculiarly acceptable.

(The same to the same, January 14, 1834.)

RUSKIN

It seems an abrupt transition, but the next subject I find on my notes is Mr Ruskin's *Modern Painters*. Ruskin he thought a brilliant writer, but there was too much praise of Turner in his book, to the disparagement of others; he had hardly a word for any one else.

(Ellis Yarnall to Reed, September 1850, referring to August 18, 1849. This part of Yarnall's letter is not given by Grosart, or in the *Memoirs*, and was not included by Yarnall in *Wordsworth and the Coleridges*, but it is quoted by Knight in his *Life*, cf. p. 49 n. *supra*.)

See also p. 38 *supra*.

SCOTT

He partly read and partly recited, sometimes in an enthusiastic style of chant, the first four cantos of the *Lay of the Last Minstrel*; and the novelty of the manners, the clear picturesque descriptions, and the easy glowing energy of much of the verse, greatly delighted me.

(Wordsworth on his first meeting with Scott, September 17, 1803, in conversation with Lockhart, 1836; given in Lockhart's *Life*, II, 160–1.)

We have at last received your poem....High as our expectations were, I have the pleasure to say that the poem has surpassed them much. We think you have completely attained your object. The book is throughout interesting and entertaining, and the picture of manners as lively as possible. (Wordsworth to Scott, March 7, 1805.)

The books of yours which you offer me I may get from Longman if you will give him orders to that effect; but in fact I must tell you that I do not deserve your kindness; for the second copy of the *Minstrel* I gave away. It was a beautiful book; but when I wished for another copy it was of a pocket size. Any poetry which I like I wish for in that size; to which no doubt yours will one day descend, and then, in spite of the acknowledgement which I have just made, I shall be impudent enough to become a beggar again.

(Wordsworth to Scott, November 10, 1806.)

Thank you for *Marmion*, which I have read with lively pleasure. I think your end has been attained; that it is not in every respect the end which I should wish you to propose to yourself, you will be well aware from what you know of my notions of composition, both as to matter and manner.... With respect to your poem, I can say that in the circle of my acquaintance it seems as well liked as the *Lay*—though I have heard that in the world it is not so. Had the poem been much better than the *Lay*, it could scarcely have satisfied the public, which at best has too much of the monster, the moral monster, in its corporation. (Wordsworth to Scott, August 4, 1808.)

Do not imagine that my principles lead me to condemn Scott's method of pleasing the public, or that I have not a very high respect for his various talents and extensive attainments.

(Wordsworth to R. P. Gillies, December 22, 1814.)

You mentioned *Guy Mannering* in your last. I have read it. I cannot say that I was disappointed, for there is very considerable talent displayed in the performance, and much of that sort of knowledge with which the author's mind is so richly stored. But the adventures I think not well chosen, or invented, and they are still worse put together; and the characters, with the exception of Meg Merrilies, excite little interest.... But these novels are likely to be much overrated on their first appearance, and will afterwards be as much underrated. *Waverley* heightened my opinion of Scott's talents very considerably, and if *Mannering* has not added much, it has not taken much away.

(The same to the same. Dated in *Memoirs of a Literary Veteran* April 25, 1815, but Knight may be right in thinking the month should be March, v. *Letters*, II, 57.)

A trouble, not of clouds, or weeping rain,
Nor of the setting sun's pathetic light
Engendered, hangs o'er Eildon's triple height:
Spirits of Power, assembled there, complain
For kindred Power departing from their sight;
While Tweed, best pleased in chanting a blithe strain,
Saddens his voice again, and yet again.
Lift up your hearts, ye Mourners! for the might
Of the whole world's good wishes with him goes;
Blessings and prayers in nobler retinue
Than sceptred king or laurelled conqueror knows,
Follow this wondrous Potentate. Be true,
Ye winds of ocean, and the midland sea,
Wafting your Charge to soft Parthenope!

(September, 1831.)

You will naturally wish to hear something of Sir Walter Scott, and particularly of his health. I found him a good deal changed within the last three or four years, in consequence of some shocks of the apoplectic kind; but his friends say that he is very much better, and the last accounts, up to the time of his going on board, were still more favourable. He himself thinks his age much against him, but he has only completed his 60th year. But a friend of mine was here the other day, who has rallied, and is himself again, after a much severer shock, and at an age several years more advanced. So that I trust the world and his friends may be hopeful, with good reason, that the life and faculties of this man, who has during the last six and twenty years diffused more innocent pleasure than ever fell to the lot of any human being to do in his own lifetime, may be spared. Voltaire, no doubt, was full as extensively known, and filled a larger space probably in the eye of Europe; for he was a great theatrical writer, which Scott has not proved himself to be, and miscellaneous to that degree, that there was something for all classes of readers: but the pleasure afforded by his writings, with the exception of some of his tragedies and minor poems, was not pure, and in this Scott is greatly his superior.

(Wordsworth to W. R. Hamilton, October 27, 1831.)

Mr Wordsworth, in his best manner, with earnest thoughts given out in noble diction, gave his reasons for thinking that as a poet Scott would not live. "I don't like", he said, "to say all this, or to take to pieces some of the best reputed passages of Scott's verse, especially in presence of my wife, because she thinks me too fastidious; but as a poet Scott *cannot* live, for he has never in verse written anything addressed to the immortal part of man. In making amusing stories in verse, he will be superseded by some newer versifier; what he writes in the way of natural description is merely rhyming nonsense." As a prose writer, Mr Wordsworth admitted that Scott had touched a higher vein, because there he had really dealt with feeling and passion. As historical novels, professing to give the manners of a past time, he did not attach much value to those works of Scott's so called, because he held that to be an attempt in which success was impossible.

(Mrs Davy, July 11, 1844; not printed in *Autobiography of Mrs Fletcher*, but in *Memoirs*, II, 444–5; Grosart, III, 442–3; Knight's *Life*, III, 445.)

See also pp. 60–1, 326–7 *supra*.

SHELLEY

Shelley's exquisite and characteristic poem [*The Skylark*] was greatly admired by the older poet, though for the most part he considered that Shelley's works were too remote from the humanities. (A. de Vere, *Essays, chiefly on Poetry*, I, 201.)

Wordsworth had said [to Maurice in 1836] that Shelley's poem on the Lark was full of imagination, but that it did not show the same observation of nature as his (Wordsworth's) own poem on the same bird did. (Sir E. Strachey in *Life of F. D. Maurice*, I, 199.)

See also pp. 38, 100–1, 374 *supra*.

SOUTHEY

You were right about Southey; he is certainly a coxcomb, and has proved it completely by the preface to his *Joan of Arc*, an epic poem which he has just published. This preface is indeed a very conceited performance, and the poem, though in some passages of first-rate excellence, is on the whole of very inferior execution.

(Wordsworth to Mathews, March 21, 1796.)

I had the pleasure of seeing both Coleridge and Southey at Keswick last Sunday. Southey, whom I never saw much of before, I liked much better than I expected; he is very pleasant in his manner, and a man of great reading in old books, poetry, chronicles, memoirs, and particularly Spanish and Portuguese.

(Wordsworth to Scott, October 16, 1803.)

We have read *Madoc*, and been highly pleased with it. It abounds in beautiful pictures and descriptions, happily introduced, and there is an animation diffused through the whole story; though it cannot, perhaps, be said that any of the characters interest you much, except, perhaps, young Llewellyn.... The poem fails in the highest gifts of the poet's mind, imagination in the true sense of the word, and knowledge of human nature and the human heart. There is nothing that shows the hand of the great master; but the beauties in description are innumerable.

(Wordsworth to Sir George Beaumont, June 3, 1805.)

Wordsworth talked at his ease, having confidence in his audience. ...He spoke of Kirke White. Both he and R. [i.e. Rough] agreed in considering him as a man of more talents than genius, and that the great correctness of his early writings was a symptom unpromising as to his future works. He would probably have been rather a man of great learning than a great poet. "He would not have been more than a Southey", said R. "And that would have been nothing, after all", said Wordsworth, "—when speaking of the highest excellence", he added. He however spoke afterwards of the "genius" of Southey. (Crabb Robinson, *Diary*, May 13, 1812.)

Wordsworth when alone, speaking of Southey, said, "He is one of the cleverest men that is now living". At the same time he justly denied him ideality in his works. "He never enquires", says Wordsworth, "on what idea his poem is to be wrought; what feeling or passion is to be excited; but he determines on a subject, and then reads a great deal, and combines and connects industriously, but he does not give anything which impresses the mind strongly and is recollected in solitude." (*Ibid.* May 24, 1812.)

I need scarcely say that Mr Southey ranks very highly in my opinion, as a prose writer. His style is eminently clear, lively, and unencumbered, and his information unbounded; and there is a moral ardour about his compositions which nobly distinguishes them from the trading and factious authorship of the present day.

(Wordsworth to G. H. Gordon, May 14, 1829.)

We talked of Southey. Wordsworth spoke of him with great feeling and affection. He said, "It is painful to see how completely dead Southey is become to all but books. When he comes here, he seems restless—as if from a sense of duty—and out of his element. He is obliging and amiable, but indifferent to everything. I therefore hardly see him for years together". Now all this I had observed on the journey; Rogers noticed it as a subject of reproach, Wordsworth only of sorrow. Dr Arnold said afterwards, "What you said of Mr Southey *alarmed* me. I could not help saying to myself, 'Am I in danger of becoming like him? Shall I ever lose my interest in things, and retain an interest only in books?'" "If I must", said Wordsworth, "lose my interest in one of them, I would rather give up books than men. Indeed I am compelled in a great measure by my eyes to give up reading." Yet with all this, Southey was an affectionate husband, and is a fond father.

(Crabb Robinson, *Diary*, January 18, 1839.)

See also p. 92 *supra*.

TENNYSON

See pp. 32–5 and 101–2 *supra*.

II

Your tragedies I have read with much pleasure; they are in language, versification, and general propriety—both as to sentiment, character, and conduct of story—*very much* above mediocrity; so that I think everyone that reads must approve in no ordinary degree. Nevertheless I am not surprised at their not having attracted so much attention as they deserve. First, because they have no false beauties, or spurious interest; and next (and for being thus sincere I make no apology), the passions, especially in the former, are not wrought upon with so daring a hand as is desirable in dramatic composition.

(In other words, they are undramatic, and Wordsworth proceeds, carefully and kindly, to show what is wrong. Wordsworth to J. Fletcher, April 6, 1825.)

You will have no pain to suffer from my sincerity. With a safe conscience I can assure you that, in my judgement, your verses are animated with true poetic spirit, as they are evidently the product of strong feeling....Now for the *per contra*. You will not, I am sure, be hurt, when I tell you that the workmanship (what else could be expected from so young a writer?) is not what it ought to be; even in those two affecting stanzas it is not perfect.... The logical faculty has infinitely more to do with poetry than the young and inexperienced, whether writer or critic, ever dreams of.... Let me now come to your sister's verses.... They are surprisingly vigorous for a female pen, but occasionally too rugged, and especially for such a subject; they have also the same faults in expression as your own, but not, I think, in quite an equal degree. Much is to be hoped from feelings so strong, and a mind thus disposed.

(Wordsworth to W. R. Hamilton, September 24, 1827.)

And now for the short piece that "contains the thoughts of your whole life". Having prepared you for the conclusion that neither my own opinion, nor that of anyone else, is worth much as to deciding the point for which this document is given as evidence, I have no scruple in telling you honestly that I do not comprehend those Lines; but, coming from one able to write the Letter I have just received, I do not think the worse of them on that account. Were anyone to show an acorn to a Native of the Orcades who had never seen a shrub higher than his knee, and by way of giving him a notion or image of the Oak should tell him that its "latitude of boughs" lies close folded in that "auburn nut", the Orcadian would stare, and feel that his Imagination was somewhat unreasonably taxed. So is it with me in respect to this germ. I do not deny that the "forest's Monarch with his army shade" may be lurking there in embryo, but neither can I undertake to affirm it. Therefore let your mind, which is surely of a high order, be its own oracle.... The true standard of poetry is high as the Soul of Man has gone, or can go; how far my own falls below that, no one can have such pathetic conviction as my poor Self.

(Wordsworth to Edwin Hill Handley, October 4, 1830.)

See also pp. 102–4 *supra*.

III

I am not a critic, and set little value upon the art. The preface which I wrote long ago to my own poems I was persuaded to write by the urgent entreaties of a friend, and heartily regret I ever had anything to do with it; though I do not reckon the principles then advanced erroneous.

(Wordsworth to J. A. Heraud, November 23, 1830.)

In 1837 Sir William Rowan Hamilton applied to Wordsworth for advice as to useful work which might be done by the Royal Irish Academy. Wordsworth replied (December 21, 1837) first on the general question of the usefulness of patronising youthful genius, of which he was very sceptical, and then on a more particular question:

As to "better canons of criticism, and general improvement of scholars", I really, speaking without affectation, am so little of a critic or scholar, that it would be presumptuous in me to *write* upon the subject to you. If we were together, and you should honour me by asking my opinion upon particular points, that would be a very different thing, and I might have something to say, not wholly without value. But where could I begin with so comprehensive an argument, and how could I put, within the compass of a letter, my thoughts, such as they may be, into anything like order? It is somewhat mortifying to me to disappoint you....I have been applied to, to give lectures upon Poetry in a public institution in London, but I was conscious that I was neither competent to the office, nor the public prepared to receive what I should have felt it my duty to say, however imperfectly.

Hamilton later made it clear that what he really wished was to publish, through the Academy, any critical papers by Wordsworth, but Wordsworth (January 14, 1838) refused: he had nothing handy, and dared not promise anything:

Though prevailed upon by Mr Coleridge to write the first *Preface* to my Poems, which tempted, or rather forced me to add a *Supplement* to it, and induced by my friendship for him to write the *Essay upon Epitaphs* now appended to *The Excursion*, but first composed for *The Friend*, I have never felt inclined to write criticism, though I have *talked*, and am daily talking a good deal. If I were several years younger, out of friendship to you mainly, I would sit down to the task of giving a body to my notions upon the essentials of Poetry—a subject which could not be properly treated without adverting to the other branches of Fine Art; but at present with so much before me that I could wish to do in verse, and the melancholy fact brought daily more and more home to my conviction, that intellectual labour, by its action on the brain and nervous system, is injurious to the bodily powers, and especially to my eyesight, I should only be deceiving myself and misleading you, were I to encourage a hope that, much as I could wish to be your fellow-labourer, however humbly, I shall ever become so.

See also pp. 99–100 *supra*.

APPENDIX C

THE SETTLEMENT ON CAROLINE BAUDOUIN

(NOTE. The greater part of what follows, including the quotations from Crabb Robinson's MS. *Diary* for 1834–5, has already appeared in the *Times Literary Supplement* for April 3, 1930.)

WHEN Caroline Wordsworth became Madame Baudouin in February 1816 no fixed dowry was given to her, possibly because at that time Wordsworth was unable to lay his hands easily on any large sum. But in the *Times Literary Supplement* of September 5, 1929, Mr J. R. M. MacGillivray proved, from a passage in a letter to Daniel Stuart (April 7, 1817), that £30 was sent to her at that date; and in a letter of April 17, 1930, Mr Gordon Wordsworth showed that this was probably the third annual payment which had been made, the first having perhaps been sent in 1815 in anticipation of the marriage, which had originally been arranged for that year. However that may be, the annual allowance of £30—a considerable sum in those days, when £20 was regarded as an ample dress allowance—was continued until the beginning of 1835, when Wordsworth made a final settlement upon his daughter of £400. The evidence which proves this statement is contained in a series of entries in the unpublished portions of Crabb Robinson's *Diary*, which escaped the notice both of Professor Harper and of M. Emile Legouis.

[Dec.] 11th [1834]....I also wrote a letter to Wordsworth on the subject of the £400 he wishes to settle on Madame Baudouin, on which I have been speaking with Sharp, Jaffray, etc.

Monday, 22nd....I was occupied to-day about writing a

letter at Mr Wordsworth's desire to M. Baudouin—see Correspondence—in which I succeeded with Prandi's help better than I expected, I rewriting his draft of a letter with great alterations.

Tuesday, [Jan.] 6th [1835]....A call from Mr Jaffray, who offered his services in the buying of a bill to be sent to Paris. I have received a letter from Baudouin assenting to Wordsworth's proposal, on which I wrote to Wordsworth to-day proposing to him to send to Baudouin in the usual way the £30, and leaving him to determine whether I should send to Baudouin a bill for £400, or send this money to Messrs André and Cottier with directions to lay out the same in the purchase of rentes for Mrs Baudouin....

10th....I had a letter from Mrs Wordsworth to-day, in which she wished me to pay £30 to the house of Minet and Feetor for Mr Baudouin. I went to Mastermann's where £430 were left for me, and there I was directed to a house in Copthall Buildings....I learned there that the house was in the habit of transmitting their annual payment to Paris, and I therefore left the £30 there.

Sunday, 11th....I read the Sunday papers, and also wrote a letter to Wordsworth, giving him an account of what I did on Saturday.

Tuesday, 27th....I called on Jaffray to request him to buy me a bill for £400, which Wordsworth has desired me to appropriate, but he was neither at home nor at Lloyd's. However, I gave him the £400 in the evening. I received £430 at Mastermann's by Wordsworth's order....

Wednesday, 28th. I called on Jaffray, who I found had made no use of the £400 I had left with him to buy a French bill....

31st....Jaffray brought me a bill for F.10,130, being at 25, 32½, for £400. This I sent to André [and] Cottier, with directions to invest it in French stock for Madame Baudouin. I also wrote to M. Baudouin, informing him what I had done....

[Feb.] 5th....A letter from André and Cottier, requiring that Mr Jaffray should declare the bill was on my account which I sent for Madame Baudouin. On this account I had to get a letter from him, which I sent to Paris....

[April] 13th....I had Prandi with me....He assisted me in drawing up in French a letter to M. Baudouin, which I shall forward to-day (14th). Wordsworth wrote to me last week, informing me that the £400 are still lying in the hands of Messrs André et Cottier, and authorising Mr Baudouin to receive the capital sum, instead of purchasing in the French Funds. This I have stated to him, and I at the same time remonstrated with him on his not having taken up the money. This letter I wrote at night at the Athenaeum, and I wrote a letter to Messrs André et Cottier, including the like authority to pay. It is quite clear to me that the Baudouins are trying to extort money without any good feeling or excuse whatever....

Tuesday, 14th....Sent away letters to Baudouin and André et Cottier....

Wednesday, 15....I went to Mrs Hoare's, where were Mr and Mrs Wordsworth. I was invited to breakfast, and I had a very agreeable morning there. Wordsworth approved of the letter I had written to Mr Baudouin....

22nd....Fetched my Mass article from the Antiquarian Society—pleased with it on reading it over again. But more pleased by receiving a letter from André and Cottier which will give great pleasure to Wordsworth. It includes a receipt under the hand of Baudouin and his wife for the money in lieu of the annuity. This will be a great relief to Wordsworth's spirits. (I have since (23rd) received a letter of complaint from Mr Baudouin which I shall not probably worry Wordsworth by communicating.) I wrote to Wordsworth by to-day's post.—I fear that the more serious causes of distress in his own family [Dorothy and Dora Wordsworth were both very ill] will not permit him to derive much pleasure from the termination of this troublesome business....

[May] 4th....I wrote to Wordsworth in answer to a kind letter from him expressing strongly his pleasure that I had brought the French business to a happy conclusion....

Wordsworth's "kind letter" may safely be identified with No. 152 (I, 271–3) in Professor Edith Morley's edition of the *Correspondence of Henry Crabb Robinson with the Wordsworth Circle*. That Wordsworth did not consider any but financial relations as being concluded is shown by his repeated visits to the Baudouins during his stay in Paris on his way to Italy in 1837 (see Crabb Robinson's unprinted *Diary* for March 22, 25, 26), and by his thoughtful procuring for them of rosaries blessed by the Pope (see Nos. 208 and 215 in the *Correspondence*, I, pp. 358–9, 369). If this friendliness was later checked, the fault was not Wordsworth's.

Caroline had received between £500 and £600 from her father since her marriage, and the settlement of 1835 brought the sum to approximately £1000—a large amount to a man of Wordsworth's financial standing and obligations to his other children. The agreement must modify our interpretation of the facts adduced by M. Legouis in his article *Quelques mots encore sur la fille française de Wordsworth* in the *Revue Anglo-Américaine* (October 1923, pp. 66–73). In 1842, when Wordsworth had resigned his Distributorship, but before he received a pension, Baudouin, entirely ignoring the conditions of the settlement, applied to him for more money. Crabb Robinson's *Diary* again shows what happened.

[Aug.] 8th....I received on my return from the North [which was on August 4th] a letter from Baudouin, complaining of the conduct of Mr Wordsworth in not answering his letter. I put it into Quillinan's hands, to have the benefit of his counsel....

Tuesday 9th....A chat with Quillinan about Baudouin's letter—he has since sent me a very sensible letter in French of which I shall make use whenever I answer the letter. Of course I shall not take any notice of the letter here....

Tuesday 16th....Wrote...to Jaffray, enclosing a draft of a letter to Baudouin.

Jaffray's reply is given in the *Correspondence*, No. 304 (I, 467), and a further extract from Crabb Robinson's *Diary* gives us the end of the business:

19th. I went early into the City after hearing from Jaffray, who sent me a corrected copy of my letter to Baudouin, which I altered again and sent next day, so writing that Baudouin may not be tempted to write again—I giving Baudouin to understand that Wordsworth had not the means of doing anything further, and that his means had been reduced. This I sent on Saturday....

In the light of this knowledge of the amount which the Baudouins had already received, and of the definite agreement of 1835, Crabb Robinson's indignation and subsequent suspicions of Baudouin—who immediately after Wordsworth's death threatened "to come here to look after his *interests* if necessary" (*Diary*, August 29, 1850)—must seem less unreasonable than they did to M. Legouis in 1923. There was no question, as he then suggested, of "chantage": one cannot very easily blackmail a man who has taken no pains to conceal his actions; the trouble was sheer breach of faith, and an attempt to extract more money which could only have been supplied at the expense of Wordsworth's other children. More particularly it should be remembered that Dora Wordsworth's marriage in 1841 was made financially possible only by an allowance from her father.

The reason why the settlement was made in 1835 is not, I think, far to seek. Wordsworth was nearly sixty-five, and there was also a strong probability that his office would soon be abolished. He came to London in February on business connected with his possible retirement on a pension, and was at the same time in frequent consultation with Crabb Robinson and Courtenay about his will. (See the unprinted *Diary* for March 2, 4, 19, 20.) It may have seemed to him likely that he would not long be able to continue Caroline's annual allowance, or to provide for her with any certainty in his will, and he therefore made the proposal of a settlement which would secure her from grave loss. The whole transaction is as characteristic in its large acceptance of responsibility as the legally unnecessary consent to the marriage of Anne Caroline Wordsworth twenty years earlier.

BIBLIOGRAPHY

BOOKS, ARTICLES and MSS.
to which reference has been made in the preceding pages, excluding Appendix B.

"ALCIPHRON." "Some Speculations on Literary Pleasures." (*Gentleman's Magazine*, May 1828.)

ALSOP, THOMAS. *Letters, Conversations and Recollections of S. T. Coleridge*. 1836.

ARMITT, MARY L. *The Church of Grasmere*. 1912.

ARNOLD, MATTHEW. "Wordsworth." (Preface to *Selections*, 1879; reprinted in *Essays in Criticism*, Second Series.)

AUSTEN, JANE. *Sanditon*. (Written in 1817; published in 1925.)

BAGEHOT, WALTER. *Biographical Studies*. 1881.

BALLEINE, G. R. *A History of the Evangelical Party*. 1906. New edition, 1911.

BEATTY, ARTHUR. *William Wordsworth: his Doctrine and Art*. 1922.

BERNBAUM, ERNEST. *Guide through the Romantic Movement*. 1931.

BLAKE, WILLIAM. *Works*.

BLUNDEN, EDMUND. *Leigh Hunt*. 1930.

BROWNING, ELIZABETH BARRETT. *Letters to her Sister*, 1846–1859; ed. Leonard Huxley. 1929.

— *Poetical Works*.

BROWNING, ROBERT. *Poetical Works*.

BURNS, ROBERT. *Poetical Works*.

BYRON, GEORGE GORDON, LORD. *Letters and Journals*, ed. R. Prothero. 1898–1901.

— *Poetical Works*.

CAMPBELL, J. DYKES. *Samuel Taylor Coleridge*. 1894.

CARLYLE, THOMAS. *Reminiscences*. 1881.

— *The French Revolution*. 1837, 1839.

CHAUCER, GEOFFREY. *Poetical Works*.

CHORLEY, H. F. *Memorials of Mrs Hemans*. 1836.

COBBAN, ALFRED. *Edmund Burke and the Revolt against the Eighteenth Century*. 1929.

COBBETT, WILLIAM. *Political Register*, July 13, 1833.

COCKBURN, LORD. *Life of Lord Jeffrey*. 1852.

COLE, WILLIAM. *The Blecheley Diary.* 1932.
— *The Paris Journal.* 1932.
COLERIDGE, SAMUEL TAYLOR. *Anima Poetae*, ed. E. H. Coleridge. 1895.
— *Letters*, ed. E. H. Coleridge. 1895.
— *Seven Lectures on Shakespeare and Milton*, ed. J. Payne Collier. 1856.
— *Table Talk*, ed. H. N. Coleridge. 1835.
— *Unpublished Letters to the Rev. J. P. Estlin*, communicated by Henry A. Bright. (*Miscellanies of the Philobiblion Society*, vol. xv, 1877–84.)
— *Unpublished Letters*, ed. Earl Leslie Griggs. 1932.
COLERIDGE, SARA. *Memoir and Letters of Sara Coleridge*, ed. by her Daughter. 1873.
COLLIER, JOHN PAYNE: *see* COLERIDGE.
COOPER, LANE. *Methods and Aims in the Study of Literature.* 1915.
— "Wordsworth's Reading." (*Modern Language Notes*, March and April, 1907.)
COOPER, THOMAS. *The Life of Thomas Cooper, written by himself.* 1872.
CROSS, F. L. "Anglo-Catholicism and the Incarnation." (*Hibbert Journal*, April 1932.)
DE MORGAN, AUGUSTUS. *A Budget of Paradoxes.* 1872.
DE QUINCEY, THOMAS. *Reminiscences of the English Lakes and the Lake Poets.* 1834 etc.
DE SELINCOURT, ERNEST: *see* WORDSWORTH, WILLIAM.
DE VERE, AUBREY. *Essays, chiefly on Poetry.* 1887.
— *Recollections.* 1897.
— "Recollections of Wordsworth." (Grosart, III.)
— *See also* WARD.
DEWEY, ORVILLE. *The Old World and the New.* 1836.
DICEY, A. V. *The Statesmanship of Wordsworth.* 1917.
DIX, JOHN (afterwards Ross). *Pen and Ink Sketches.* 1846.
DOCKRAY, BENJAMIN. *Egeria*, Pts. I and II. 1832 or 1833.
— *Remarks on Catholic Emancipation.* 1829.
DOWDEN, E.: *see* TAYLOR, SIR HENRY.
ELLIOT, HUGH S. R.: *see* MILL.
FABER, F. W. *The Life of St Francis of Assisi.* (Translated from Chalippe about 1847, published in *The Saints and Servants of God*, vols. I and II, 1853–4.)

FAUSSET, HUGH I'ANSON. *The Lost Leader*. 1933.

FLETCHER, MRS, of Edinburgh. *Autobiography*. Privately printed, 1874; 2nd ed. 1875. (The notes of Lady Richardson and Mrs Davy are utilised here and also in the *Memoirs* of 1851, in Grosart's edition of the *Prose Works* and in Knight's *Life*.)

FOX, CAROLINE. *Memories of Old Friends*. Revised edition, 1883.

GARROD, H. W. *Wordsworth*. Second and enlarged edition, 1927.

Gentleman's Magazine. Review of *Memoirs of William Wordsworth*, August 1851.

GIFFORD, WILLIAM, and LAMB, CHARLES. Review of *The Excursion*. (*Quarterly Review*, October 1814.)

GILLIES, R. P. *Memoirs of a Literary Veteran*. 1851.

GRATTAN, T. C. *Beaten Paths and Those who trod Them*. 1862.

GRAVES, R. P. *Life of William Rowan Hamilton*. 1878–91.

— "Recollections of Wordsworth and the Lake Country." (Printed in *Afternoon Lectures*, 1869.)

GREVILLE, CHARLES. *The Greville Memoirs*. 1874–87.

GRIERSON, H. J. C.: *see* SCOTT.

GROSART, ALEXANDER B.: *see* WORDSWORTH, WILLIAM.

HALÉVY, E. *Histoire du peuple anglais au xixe siècle*. 1912, etc.

HALLAM, HENRY. *View of the State of Europe during the Middle Ages*. 1818.

HARPER, GEORGE MCLEAN. *William Wordsworth*. 1916. Revised and abridged edition, 1929. (Quotations have been made, unless it is otherwise stated, from the 1929 edition, on the assumption that this gives Professor Harper's mature opinion.)

— *Spirit of Delight*. 1928.

— *Wordsworth's French Daughter*. 1921.

HAYDON, BENJAMIN ROBERT. *Life of B. R. Haydon from his Autobiography and Memoirs*, edited and compiled by Tom Taylor. 1855. (Several recent editions.)

HAZLITT, WILLIAM. Review of *The Excursion*. (*Examiner*, August 21, 28, October 2, 1814.)

— Article on the revival of *Comus*. (*Examiner*, June 11, 1815.)

— *Lectures on the English Poets*. 1818.

— *My First Acquaintance with Poets*. 1817–23.

— *The Spirit of the Age*. 1825.

HERFORD, C. H. *Wordsworth*. 1930.

HILL, R. H. *Toryism and the People, 1832–46*. 1929.

HOLLAND, J., and EVERETT, J. *Memoirs of the Life and Writings of James Montgomery*. 1854–6.

HOWE, P. P. *Life of William Hazlitt*. 1922.

HOWITT, MARY. *Mary Howitt, an Autobiography*, edited by Margaret Howitt. 1889.

HUNT, J. H. LEIGH. *Autobiography*. 1850. Revised edition, 1859–60.

— *Correspondence*, edited by his eldest son. 1862.

— "The Feast of the Poets." (*The Reflector*, 1811; separately, 1812; revised 1814, 1815, in *Poetical Works*, 1819, and later.)

HUTCHINSON, T.: *see* WORDSWORTH, WILLIAM.

HUXLEY, ALDOUS. "Wordsworth in the Tropics." (*Life and Letters*, October 1928; reprinted in *Do What You Will*, 1929.)

HUXLEY, LEONARD: *see* BROWNING, ELIZABETH BARRETT.

INGE, W. R. *Christian Mysticism*. 1899.

— *Personal Idealism and Mysticism*. 1907.

— *Studies of English Mystics*. 1906.

— *The Platonic Tradition in English Religious Thought*. 1926.

JEFFREY, FRANCIS. Review of Montgomery's *The Wanderer of Switzerland and other Poems*. (*Edinburgh Review*, January 1807.)

JOHNSTON, WILLIAM: *see* QUILLINAN.

JULIAN OF NORWICH. *Revelations of Divine Love*. (First printed, 1901.)

KEATS, JOHN. *Letters*, ed. M. Buxton Forman. 1931.

— *Poetical Works*.

KENYON, JOHN. *Rhymed Plea for Tolerance*. 1833; second edition, revised, 1839.

KER, W. P. *Form and Style in Poetry*, ed. R. W. Chambers. 1928. (The reference on p. 315 n. rests on an oral memory of a course of lectures delivered in 1913–14 but not yet published.)

KNIGHT, WILLIAM. *Life of William Wordsworth*. 1889.

— (Ed.) *Letters of the Wordsworth Family*. 1907.

— (Ed.) *Memorials of Coleorton*. 1887.

— (Ed.) *Wordsworthiana*. Papers read to the Wordsworth Society. 1889.

LAMB, CHARLES. *Works*, ed. E. V. Lucas. 1903–5.

— *See also* GIFFORD.

LANDOR, WALTER SAVAGE. *Gebir*. 1798.

— *Idyllia Heroica*. 1820.

— "Imaginary Conversation between Southey and Porson." (*Blackwood's Magazine*, December 1842.)
— *Satire against Satirists*. 1836.
LEGOUIS, EMILE. *The Early Life of William Wordsworth*, translated by J. W. Matthews. Second edition, 1921.
— "Quelques mots encore sur la fille française de Wordsworth." (*Revue Anglo-Américaine*, October 1923.)
— *Wordsworth and Annette Vallon*. 1922.
LIBERTY, STEPHEN. *Religion in Wordsworth*. 1923.
LOCKHART, J. G. *Life of Sir Walter Scott*. Second edition, 1839.
LOFFT, CAPEL. *Ernest*. 1839.
LUCAS, E. V.: *see* LAMB.
LYALL, W. ROWE. Review of *Poems* and *The White Doe of Rylstone*. (*Quarterly Review*, October 1815.)
MACAULAY, THOMAS BABINGTON, LORD. *Essay on Robert Montgomery*. 1830.
MACGILLIVRAY, J. R. "Wordsworth's French Daughter." (*Times Literary Supplement*, September 5, 1929.)
— "Wordsworth in France." (*Ibid*. June 12, 1930.)
MARTINEAU, HARRIET. *Autobiography*. 1877.
MAURICE, FREDERICK. *Life of Frederick Denison Maurice*. 1884.
MILL, JOHN STUART. *Letters*, ed. Hugh S. R. Elliot. 1910.
MILNES, MONCKTON (Lord Houghton). *One Tract More*. 1841.
MILTON, JOHN. *Poetical Works*.
MITFORD, MARY RUSSELL. *Life, related in a selection from her Letters*, ed. by A. G. L'Estrange and H. Chorley. 1869–72.
— *Correspondence with Charles Boner and John Ruskin*, ed. Elizabeth Lee. 1914.
MONTGOMERY, JAMES. *Poetical Works*.
— Review of *Poems* of 1807. (*Eclectic Review*, January 1808.)
— Review of *Convention of Cintra*. (*Eclectic Review*, July 1809.)
— Review of *The Excursion*. (*Eclectic Review*, January 1815.)
MONTGOMERY, ROBERT. *Poetical Works*.
MOORE, THOMAS. *Memoir, Journal and Correspondence*, ed. Lord John Russell. 1853–6.
MORLEY, EDITH J.: *see* ROBINSON, H. CRABB.
MORLEY, JOHN, LORD. *Essay on Wordsworth*. (First printed in 1889, as introduction to an edition of the *Poetical Works*.)
— *Life of William Ewart Gladstone*. 1903.

MUIRHEAD, J. P. "A Day with Wordsworth." (Letters written in 1841, printed in *Blackwood's Magazine*, June 1927.)

MUNK, ELIAS. *William Wordsworth. Ein Beitrag zur Erforschung seiner religiösen Entwicklung*. (Germanische Studien, 52.) 1927.

NEWMAN, JOHN HENRY, CARDINAL. *Apologia pro Vita Sua*. 1864. (Several recent editions.)

— *Remarks on Certain Passages in the Thirty Nine Articles*. (Tract 90 in *Tracts for the Times*.) 1841.

PARTINGTON, WILFRED. (Ed.) *The Private Letter-Books of Sir Walter Scott*. 1930.

— (Ed.) *Sir Walter's Post-Bag*. 1932.

PROTHERO, R. *Life and Correspondence of Arthur Penrhyn Stanley*. 1893.

Quarterly Review. Review of Coleridge's *Remorse*, April 1814.

— *See also* GIFFORD and LYALL.

QUILLINAN, EDWARD. "Imaginary Conversation between Mr Walter Savage Landor and the Editor of *Blackwood's Magazine*." (*Blackwood's Magazine*, April 1843.)

— *Poems*, with a Memoir by William Johnston. 1853.

RADER, MELVIN M. *Presiding Ideas in Wordsworth's Poetry*. (*University of Washington Publications in Language and Literature*, vol. VIII, November 1931.)

RAWNSLEY, H. D. "Reminiscences of Wordsworth among the Peasantry of Westmoreland." (*Wordsworthiana*: *see* KNIGHT.)

READ, HERBERT. *Wordsworth*. 1930.

ROBINSON, H. CRABB. *Blake, Coleridge, Wordsworth, Lamb, etc., being selections from the Remains of Henry Crabb Robinson*, ed. Edith J. Morley. 1922.

— *Correspondence of Henry Crabb Robinson with the Wordsworth Circle*, ed. Edith J. Morley. 1927.

— *Diary, Reminiscences, and Correspondence*, ed. Thomas Sadler. 1869. (Many of the passages from the *Diary* quoted in this study have never been printed before, Sadler having been restrained sometimes by prudence and sometimes by considerations of space: there were, for example, obvious reasons why he should in 1869 have suppressed the name of Miss Barrett in the passage quoted on p. 102 *supra*. Whether printed before by Sadler or Professor Edith Morley, or not, all quotations here have been checked by the MS. *Diary*. The differences from Sadler's text are sometimes interesting.)

ROBY, J. *Legendary and Poetical Remains.* 1854.
RUSSELL, BERTRAND. "The Harm That Good Men Do." (*Harper's Magazine*, October 1926.)
RUSSELL, LORD JOHN: *see* MOORE.
SADLEIR, M. T. H. *Bulwer, a Panorama. Edward and Rosina.* 1931.
SADLER, T.: *see* ROBINSON.
SCOTT, SIR WALTER. *Letters* (Centenary Edition), ed. H. J. C. Grierson and others. Vols. I and II, 1932.
— *Poetical Works.*
— *Waverley Novels.*
SHAKESPEARE, WILLIAM. *Works.*
SHELLEY, PERCY BYSSHE. *Poetical Works.*
SMITH, ELSIE. *An Estimate of William Wordsworth by his Contemporaries, 1793–1822.* 1932.
SMITH, NOWELL C.: *see* WORDSWORTH, WILLIAM.
SOUTHEY, ROBERT. *Poetical Works.*
— *Life and Correspondence*, ed. Cuthbert Southey. 1849–50.
— *Selections from the Letters...*, ed. J. W. Warter. 1856.
SPENSER, EDMUND. *Poetical Works.*
STANLEY, A. P. *Life of Thomas Arnold.* 1844. (The passage quoted on p. 130 occurs only in later editions.)
STEPHEN, SIR JAMES. "St Francis of Assisi." (*Edinburgh Review*, July 1847; reprinted in *Essays in Ecclesiastical Biography*, 1849.)
STRACHEY, J. ST LOE. *The Adventure of Living.* 1922.
TAYLOR, SIR HENRY. *Autobiography.* 1885.
— *Correspondence*, ed. E. Dowden. 1888.
TAYLOR, JEREMY. *Holy Living.* (Several recent editions.)
TAYLOR, UNA. *Guests and Memories.* 1924.
TENNYSON, ALFRED, LORD. *Poetical Works.*
THOMAS, GEORGE. *A Tenement in Soho.* 1932.
WARD, WILFRID. *Aubrey de Vere.* 1904.
WARTER, J. W.: *see* SOUTHEY.
WATTS, MRS ALARIC. *Alaric Watts.* 1884.
WEBB, CLEMENT C. J. *Religious Thought in the Oxford Movement.* 1928.
WHITE, W. HALE. *An Examination of the Charge of Apostasy against Wordsworth.* 1898.
WIFFEN, J. H. *The Brothers Wiffen: Memoirs.* 1880.
WILBERFORCE, R. I. and S. *Life of William Wilberforce.* 1838.

WILLIAMS, ISAAC. *On Reserve in Communicating Religious Knowledge.* (Tracts 80 and 87 of *Tracts for the Times*, 1838 and 1840.)

WILLIAMSON, G. C. *John Russell, R.A.* 1894.

WORDSWORTH, BISHOP CHARLES. *Shakespeare and the Bible.* 1880.

WORDSWORTH, BISHOP CHRISTOPHER. *Memoirs of William Wordsworth.* 1851.

WORDSWORTH, CANON CHRISTOPHER. *Social Life in English Universities in the Eighteenth Century.* 1874.

WORDSWORTH, DOROTHY. "Letters to Mrs Clarkson." (British Museum, Add. MS. 36997.)

— *See also* KNIGHT and ROBINSON.

WORDSWORTH, GORDON G. "Wordsworth's French Daughter." (*Times Literary Supplement*, April 17, 1930.)

WORDSWORTH, WILLIAM. *Poetical Works*, ed. T. Hutchinson. (Oxford.) 1910.

— *Poetical Works*, ed. Knight. (Eversley edition.) 1896.

— *Poetical Works*, ed. Nowell Smith. 1908.

— *Poems of 1807*, ed. T. Hutchinson. 1897.

— *The Prelude*, ed. E. de Selincourt. 1926.

— *Prose Works*, ed. Grosart. 1876.

— *Prose Works*, ed. Knight. (Eversley edition.) 1896.

— *Wordsworth and Reed. The Poet's Correspondence with his American Editor: 1836–1850*, ed. Leslie Nathan Broughton. 1933.

— "Letter to H. N. Coleridge." (British Museum, Add. MS. 34225.)

— "Letters to W. S. Landor." (Dyce Collection, Victoria and Albert Museum.)

— "Letters to Frederick Reynolds." (British Museum, Add. MS. 27925.)

— "Letters to Daniel Stuart." (British Museum, Add. MS. 34046.)

— *See also* ARNOLD, KNIGHT, MORLEY and ROBINSON.

YARNALL, ELLIS. *Wordsworth and the Coleridges.* 1899.

YOUNG, JULIAN CHARLES. *Memoir of Charles Mayne Young.* 1871.

The Book of Common Prayer.
The Dictionary of National Biography. (D.N.B.)
The Oxford English Dictionary. (O.E.D.)
Tracts for the Times. 1833–41.

INDEX

CAMBRIDGE: PRINTED BY W. LEWIS, M.A., AT THE UNIVERSITY PRESS